*C. A. Ronning*

# China in Crisis VOLUME 1

# China in Crisis VOLUME 1

# China's Heritage and the Communist Political System

Book Two

Edited by Ping-ti Ho and Tang Tsou
*With a Foreword by Charles U. Daly*

SBN: 226-34520-3 (clothbound) ; 226-34523-8 (paperbound)
Library of Congress Catalog Card Number 68-20981

The University of Chicago Press, Chicago 60637
*The University of Chicago Press, Ltd., London*

# Contents

BOOK ONE

v

# Tables and Figures

## *Tables*

## *Figures*

John W. Lewis

**7**

# Leader, Commissar, and Bureaucrat: The Chinese Political System in the Last Days of the Revolution

## *The Relationship of Leader and Commissar*

As Chairman of the Chinese Communist Party after early January, 1935, Mao Tse-tung secured the loyalty of guerrilla fighters in the field as their champion and leader.[1] He symbolized for them the future attainment of vaguely understood revolutionary goals, and his name was invoked to justify their sacrifice in pursuit of those goals.

As a social force, guerrilla communism in China lacked well-integrated institutions above the local level until late in the Anti-Japanese War when, after the rectification campaign of the early forties, the various groups were brought together in a more coordinated and centralized system. Fractionalized in a society suffering from bombardment and enemy occupation, the guerrillas typically conducted operations as expendable pawns in the cause of "liberation."[2] Seeking meaning and

---

[1] In the preparation of this paper, I have profited from reading Mehmet Beqiraj, *Peasantry in Revolution* (Ithaca: Center for International Studies, Cornell University, 1966), pp. 103–7, 115–17; Carl J. Friedrich, *Revolution: Nomos VIII* (New York: Atherton Press, 1966); Chalmers A. Johnson, *Revolutionary Change* (Boston: Little, Brown, 1966); James H. Meisel, *Counterrevolution: How Revolutions Die* (New York: Atherton Press, 1966), esp. chap. 1; Lawrence Stone, "Theories of Revolution," *World Politics*, 18 (January, 1966): 159–76; and Marc J. Swartz, Victor W. Turner, and Arthur Tuden (eds.), *Political Anthropology* (Chicago: Aldine, 1966), pp. 191–220. I also wish to thank Douglas Ashford, Gerry Bowman, Norman Nathan, Myron Rush, and Arthur Wolf for their comments and suggestions on an earlier draft of this paper.

[2] For typical historical novels about these bands, see Chih Hsia, *The Railway Guerrillas* (Peking: Foreign Languages Press, 1966); Wang Huo, *Chieh Chen-*

purpose in their predicament, the members of the guerrilla bands appear to have invested an exceptional faith in their distant leader. Their strong belief in "Chairman Mao" helped bolster their otherwise cheerless relations with one another and produce an *esprit de corps* that sustained their seemingly unpromising fight against the Japanese and hostile Chinese troops. The guerrilla forces were usually manned by a majority of non-kinsmen who frequently appropriated kinship terminology in conducting their affairs. Some, if not most, group members, hoping to emulate and please their distant leader as his chosen sons, reciprocated Mao's "compassionate love" for them by acting as brotherly comrades rather than strangers to one another.

By contrast, the local political commissars and guerrilla chieftains on the spot could not indulge in such emotionalism but were obliged to dispense discipline and enforce group solidarity as a matter of survival.[3] While the leader far away was assumed to care for each fighter and became an object of reverence for him, the political commissar within the guerrilla network had to institutionalize "a centralized totalitarian frame of mind, unity of thinking."[4] Behind Japanese lines in the guerrilla zones the senior political commissar was probably Liu Shao-ch'i.

As in other revolutions, so too in the Chinese, the political commissar was responsible for unifying disparate groups of guerrillas within the wider system of action. He was "the deputy of the distant charismatic leader . . . [and had] full authority to devise operations, to dictate the rules for action, and to control the attitudes of all fighters."[5] His mission was the incitement of the guerrillas to fight. Mao, the leader, symbolized understanding and compassion; the commissar embodied power. This apparent complementarity of roles did not imply their reciprocity: "The fact that compassion determines the state of being of the members of the very small guerrilla unit while aggressiveness struc-

---

*kuo: Guerrilla Hero* (Peking: Foreign Languages Press, 1961); and Liang Hsing, *Liu Hu-lan: Story of a Girl Revolutionary* (Peking: Foreign Languages Press, 1953). For collections of guerrilla stories, see, for example, *Hung-ch'i p'iao-p'iao* [The Red Flag Flutters], 16 vols. (Peking: Chung-kuo ch'ing-nien ch'u-pan she, 1957–1959), and *Hsing-huo liao-yüan* [A Single Spark Will Start a Prairie Fire] (Hong Kong: San-lien shu-tien, 1960).

[3] Cf. Beqiraj, *Peasantry in Revolution*, pp. 105–6. He notes: ". . . the tasks are devised by the distant, compassionate, all-knowing leader, and transmitted by the political commissar. The power of the political commissar is far greater than that of the flagholder [the leader], partly because his power is not softened by compassion."

[4] *Ibid.*, p. 105.                    [5] *Ibid.*, p. 115.

tures the total power system makes evident that compassion serves power but not vice versa."[6]

In the operating units the political commissar had more real power but less status than the leader.[7] To Mao—at least from his present perspective—his image as the benevolent, caring "father" probably seemed decisive to the overall success of guerrilla operations, and his military writings also underscored his estimation that a Communist political victory depended on such successes. Mao seems to have understood that a direct connection existed between his own dominant status and the revolutionary character of Chinese society. What this paper will attempt to show is that Mao did not similarly grasp the pivotal importance of the political commissar and in the end has turned on the commissars while restoring revolutionary chaos in an effort to preserve his own charismatic role. The main theme will examine what happened in 1966 as Mao and Lin Piao attempted to prevent their revolution from dying.

## Mao and Liu on the Revolutionary Party

Most earlier studies of the Chinese political system have assumed, perhaps correctly for the time, that the writings of Mao and Liu Shao-ch'i, though emphasizing divergent aspects of leadership doctrine, were complementary and thus could be legitimately discussed as an organic whole. Where Mao emphasized theory and practice, especially among the general populace, the writings of Liu gave prominence to operation and Communist organization. Both were concerned with the proper attitudes and training of the vanguard, though Mao was principally attracted to the general mass context, while Liu gave relatively greater stress to the elite and the disciplined conduct of party life.[8] Since Mao had also served in the post of political commissar before

[6] *Ibid.*, p. 116.

[7] In the traditional scheme of things, this separation of status and power was common. See Lewis, "The Study of Chinese Political Culture," *World Politics*, 18 (April, 1966): 508.

[8] Liu's writings in this regard are found in: *How To Be a Good Communist* [July, 1939] (Peking: Foreign Languages Press, n.d.); *On Inner-Party Struggle* [July, 1941] (Peking: Foreign Languages Press, n.d.); and *On the Party* [May, 1945] (Peking: Foreign Languages Press, 1950). That the Communists themselves considered the writings of Mao and Liu as an integral whole earlier is suggested by the joint appearance of their writings in the rectification documents of 1942–44. These are found in Boyd Compton (trans.), *Mao's China: Party Reform Documents, 1942–44* (Seattle: University of Washington Press, 1952).

1935, and Liu could properly be considered a party leader, the differences between the two seemed trivial.[9] Whatever dissimilarities existed could be treated as essentially personal ones and were presumably well camouflaged behind the regime's image-making propaganda. In retrospect, however, important "contradictions" may be discerned in the Mao-Liu approaches to the Chinese political system. Such differences may be highlighted by a brief re-examination of the concept of conflict or struggle.[10]

In the Yenan years, conflict dominated the whole society. The fight was a free-for-all in which Mao and his lieutenants devised and applied an endless variety of principles for waging a popular rebellion. At that time, the relatively primitive socioeconomic conditions in the base areas probably played a crucial part in making those principles relevant and successful.[11] Mao, however, was drawn to the process of the struggle itself, according it a significance far higher than any other characteristics of the Yenan-type social environment. Mao held that the violence then disrupting the societal base provided an advantage to the Communists and that the destructive phase was a necessary prelude for the party to impose its will on the Chinese peasants and workers. He commented in 1939:

> It is my opinion that as far as we are concerned, it is a bad thing if a person, a party, an army, or a school is not opposed by the enemy, for it can only mean that that person, party, army, or school is in the camp of the enemy. It is a good thing for us to be opposed by the enemy, for this shows that we have drawn a line of distinction between us and the enemy. It is even better if the enemy opposes us vigorously, and describes us as an awful mess and good for nothing for this shows not only that we have drawn a line of distinction between us and the enemy, but also that we have accomplished something in work.[12]

[9] Mao's writings as a commissar are found in his *Selected Works* (Peking: Foreign Languages Press, 1961–65), vol. 1.

[10] I have dealt with this concept on a preliminary basis in *Leadership in Communist China* (Ithaca: Cornell University Press, 1963), pp. 47–60; and "Revolutionary Struggle and the Second Generation in Communist China," *China Quarterly*, no. 21 (January–March, 1965), pp. 126–47.

[11] A tentative treatment of this subject may be found in Lewis, "The Study of Chinese Political Culture."

[12] "It Is a Good Thing and Not a Bad Thing to Be Opposed by the Enemy," in *Mao Tse-tung chu-tso hsüan-tu* [Selected Readings from Mao Tse-tung's

The party would lead the society by maintaining close ties with the otherwise disoriented people and by giving them alternative structures wherein they could reconstitute their lives.[13] Not wishing his cadres to become overly bureaucratized themselves, Mao was essentially interested in having them "serve the people" without personal career ambitions.[14] The doctrinal formulation for this line of operation is found in Mao's discussion of the "mass line."[15]

Despite the future-oriented view associated with Mao in the Anti-Japanese War, his political commissars performed their mission of fashioning a strong party-army apparatus wherein only limited forms of struggle were tolerated. Mao welcomed such inner-party conflict as follows:

> Opposition and struggle between ideas of different kinds constantly occur within the Party; this is a reflection within the Party of contradictions between classes and between the new and the old in society. If there were no contradictions in the Party and no ideological struggles to resolve them, the Party's life would come to an end.[16]

But, Mao added later, that in dealing with past mistakes, the Party should " 'learn from past mistakes to avoid future ones and cure the sickness to save the patient,' and achieve 'clarity in ideology and unity among comrades' . . . [as] a model of the correct attitude" for over-

Works], A, 1 (Peking: Jen-min ch'u-pan she, 1964), pp. 150–52. A collection of commentaries on this article is found in *Hsüeh-hsi Mao chu-hsi ti chu-tso "Pei ti-jen fan-tui shih hao-shih erh pu-shih huai-shih"* [Study Chairman Mao's Work, "It Is a Good Thing and Not a Bad Thing to Be Opposed by the Enemy"] (Hong Kong: San-lien shu-tien, 1964).

13 See Mao, "Get Organized!" *Selected Works*, vol. 3, pp. 153–61. In this article Mao warned that Communist structures should not isolate the cadres from the masses (*ibid.*, p. 159). For Mao's earlier treatment of the same subject see his section entitled "Get Organized" in his "Hunan Report," *Selected Works*, vol. 1, pp. 24–25.

14 "Serve the People," *Selected Works*, vol. 3, pp. 227–28. This has become one of the major documents in the study of Mao's thought.

15 "Some Questions concerning Methods of Leadership" [June 1, 1943], *Selected Works*, vol. 3, pp. 117–22. Liu, of course, also endorsed the mass line. See especially his *On the Party*, pp. 44–66. For a discussion of the mass line, see Lewis, *Leadership in Communist China*, chap. 3.

16 *Selected Works*, vol. 1, p. 317.

coming errors within the party.[17] Mao described "error" as an essentially personal phenomenon—though one reflecting broader "class contradictions." Error could be eradicated if the non-deviant members of the group would "give full play to inner-Party democracy, develop criticism and self-criticism, proceed with the work of patient persuasion and education, make a concrete analysis of errors and their dangers and explain their historical and ideological roots as well as the means of correcting them."[18] The result of this purifying process would be the creation of pliant party members who would bend to the leadership's will in unison.

Liu Shao-chi's perspective did not fully coincide with that of Mao, although later, of course, every effort was made to connect his line of analysis with the Chairman's.[19] Where Mao primarily discussed the results for the individual "patient," Liu perceived the importance of the integrative effects of a continuing process of struggle on the group. He quoted Stalin to the effect that inner-party struggle strengthened the group[20] and declared that unity must be enforced on matters of principle—that is, questions of goals—and of methods to be used in ob-

[17] "Appendix: Resolution on Certain Questions in the History of Our Party" [April 20, 1945], *Selected Works,* vol. 3, p. 218. This same idea was prominent in the rectification campaign (cf. *ibid.,* p. 164). Mao in April, 1945, accused the "factionalists" of confusing the suppression of counterrevolutionaries with the struggle against incorrect ideas held by old comrades. He recommended that those who had fallen victim to false charges be exonerated and their "memory shall be held in honour by all comrades" (*ibid.,* p. 210). Liu concurred that mistakes and shortcomings constituted a curable illness (*On Inner-Party Struggle,* p. 25), but held that "the aim of inner-Party struggle is to educate the Party and the comrades who have committed mistakes" (*ibid.,* p. 28).

[18] "Appendix," p. 218.

[19] In his major writings before the 1942–44 rectification movement, Liu made no mention of Mao Tse-tung. In revising Liu's *How To Be a Good Communist* for republication in 1962, several passages were changed to bring Liu's thought on practice into conformity with Mao's and to give greater credit to Mao throughout. The added and revised passages are in Liu, *How To Be a Good Communist,* rev. ed. (Peking: Foreign Languages Press, 1964), pp. 7, 21–22, 32, 33, 46, 88. In his first major address in the course of the rectification movement, "Liquidate the Menshevist Ideology within the Party" (included as appendix in *On Inner-Party Struggle*) Liu made his first gestures in praise of Mao. These reached even greater proportions in his discussion of the "Thought of Mao Tse-tung" at the Seventh Party Congress; see *On the Party.* Liu is now accused of failing to accord a proper role to Mao in his earlier writings as well as his works up to 1962.

[20] *On Inner Party Struggle,* pp. 5, 59–70.

taining the goals of the group.[21] Compromise and concession would be encouraged on "questions of purely practical character,"[22] but on ideology and principle absolute unanimity was required.[23] Presumably it was Liu's task in underground travels throughout occupied China and as the political commissar of the New Fourth Army[24] to eliminate dissident elements, making certain that a solid unity prevailed.[25] Debates that contributed to party solidarity thus were the only ones approved and encouraged; these were to be conducted on a routine basis. In summing up and reviewing work, the group would "first deal with 'the case' and then with 'the person.'"[26] This would give the party flexibility by allowing its members and cadres the daily opportunity to weigh relevant courses of action and pertinent points of view.[27] Other forms of intra-party conflict were disallowed, and Liu especially disapproved of divisive or factional elements.[28] Forms of struggle within the prescribed limits, on the other hand, were ritualized in the party and army. Liu said:

> All in all, inner-Party struggle is fundamentally a form of struggle and controversy over ideology and principles. Inside the Party everything must submit to reason, everything must be reasoned

[21] Ibid., p. 17. Lewis Coser generalizes Liu's essential point here when he notes: "Conflicts arising within the same consensual framework are likely to have a very different impact upon the relationship than those which put the basic consensus in question. . . . Insofar as conflict is the resolution of tension between antagonists it has stabilizing functions and becomes an integrating component of the leadership" (The Functions of Social Conflict [New York: Free Press, 1956], pp. 73, 80).

[22] On Inner-Party Struggle, pp. 60–62.

[23] Ibid., pp. 17, 30, 49, 50.

[24] For Liu's role after the New Fourth Army incident, see Chalmers A. Johnson, Peasant Nationalism and Communist Power (Stanford: Stanford University Press, 1962), pp. 140–49. Howard Boorman, in "Liu Shao-ch'i: A Political Profile," China Quarterly, no. 10 (April–June, 1962), pp. 8–9, describes Liu's known activities in the underground in the Yenan years.

[25] For typical stories of Liu's travels, see Lewis, Major Doctrines of Communist China (New York: Norton, 1964), pp. 70–71; and Chih Hsia, The Railway Guerrillas, chap. 27.

[26] On Inner-Party Struggle, p. 63.

[27] Liu developed this theme further in On the Party, pp. 147–53.

[28] On the attitude toward factions in these years, see Lewis, Chinese Communist Party Leadership and the Succession to Mao Tse-tung (Washington, D.C.: Department of State, 1964), pp. 3–16.

out and everything must have some reason for it, otherwise it will not do. We can do anything without difficulty if we have reasoned it out.[29]

In practice, coercion, backing up "reason," ensured proper struggle and rigorous unity.[30]

As understood by Mao (and Lenin and Marx, among others, before him), the organization of the Communist elite system gained its special character and points of reference from its close relationship with the general populace under conditions of stress. Mao as the charismatic figure in Yenan stipulated the absolute need for compassion in the elite system and face-to-face leadership over the people. These constituted for him the essential conditions for success of the Communist movement. Mao analyzed elite cohesion from a perspective different from that of Liu and the political cadres and gave special importance to recruiting leaders suitable for work among the populace.[31] To this end, he demanded that the party's cadre apparatus be kept administratively simple though of high quality.[32]

By tying leadership to the rapidly changing environment under wartime conditions, both Mao and Liu presumed that political structures would operate on a conditional and transitory basis.[33] Their assigned roles again helped produce different points in emphasis. Mao stipulated that change was necessary but required the continuation of a

[29] On Inner-Party Struggle, p. 70.

[30] Ibid., p. 60. Liu stated: "All Party organizations, within appropriate limits, have full right to draw organisational conclusions in regard to any Party member who persists in his errors. The application of Party disciplinary measures and the adoption of organisational measures are entirely necessary under certain circumstances. Such measures, however, cannot be used casually or indiscriminately."

[31] "Some Questions concerning Methods of Leadership," Selected Works, vol. 3, pp. 117–22.

[32] Mao's quotations in the book used by the Red Guards are revealing in this regard for they deal only with those aspects of his writings that stress the service, non-bureaucratic attributes of the cadre role. See Mao chu-hsi yü-lu [Sayings of Chairman Mao] (Shanghai: Chung-kuo shu-chü, 1966), chap. 29. For a discussion of Mao's views on cadres, see Lewis, Leadership in Communist China, pp. 185–95. Liu's public statements on cadres came after 1944 and parallel those of Mao; see, for example, On the Party, pp. 107–31.

[33] See, for example, Liu, On the Party, p. 5; and Mao, "Some Questions concerning Methods of Leadership," Selected Works, vol. 3, pp. 117–22.

revolutionary environment.[34] Continuation seemed assured since the class nature of individuals would outlive classes themselves. A revolutionary environment produced by class contradictions would thus last into the Communist era and the decisive role of the leader would remain untarnished. Liu, by contrast, regarded social change as necessitating a commensurate transformation of leadership and the eventual elimination of class-type contradictions. He said:

> During the period of socialist transformation in the future and the period when socialism is passing into Communism, the proletariat will continuously change society and the substance of mankind, and at the same time, its own substance and characteristics. In Communist society class distinctions between men will die out and so will the class characteristics of men. Then the common character of mankind, namely common human nature, will be formed.[35]

During the period of warfare, this evident disparity between the views of Mao and Liu on leadership endured, gaining practical significance, as will be seen, in the alternating policies on recruitment and elite organization.

A potential for factionalism was thus always quite real. Characteristically, Mao opposed factionalism but also regarded strong bureaucratic structures with suspicion, considering them as potentially inhibiting the cadre's successful operations and creating a wall between the populace and himself. Predisposed toward decentralization and flexibility, Mao granted the political commissars under Liu wide discretionary powers in their spheres of influence (although there was realistically no alternative to this in the guerrilla operations). This authority, in turn, enabled them to form strong, autocratically-run units. Decentralization ended with them. The commissars, moreover, were undoubtedly jealous of their prerogatives and, as indicated by the discussion of relevant deviations at the time, must have frequently turned their power to their own or their local unit's advantage.[36] The trick was to channel that power toward centrally-determined purposes without breaking the solidarity of the local units and sapping their fighting will.

[34] See "Report on the Second Plenary Session . . . ," *Selected Works*, vol. 4, pp. 361–74. For a discussion, see Lewis, "Revolutionary Struggle."

[35] "The Class Character of Man," trans. as appendix to *How To Be a Good Communist* (1953), p. 115.

[36] See Liu, *On the Party*, pp. 107–31.

The historical significance of the 1942–44 "rectification campaign" was that it did just that. It turned the potentially dangerous disparity between these views of the leader and the commissars into a source of strength.[37]

In order to achieve greater co-ordination of the military-political operations, the Central Committee began to advocate the creation of a new kind of organization (though one, as always, labeled "democratic centralism"). Liu at this time mentioned Mao for the first time, giving him high praise, and Mao set forth the details of a new leadership line. According to this line, higher-level organizations would develop from and be responsive to local party activities, while village cadres would become more responsive to general directives and centralized controls. In this way, the stage was being set—perhaps unconsciously—for the large, co-ordinated operations against the Chinese Nationalist armies after 1947.

Despite the importance of this compromise in the rectification campaign, it seems probable in retrospect that viewpoints were temporarily adjusted rather than fundamentally altered. In the continuing struggle with the Kuomintang (KMT), the system which rested on basically incongruent points of view worked with extraordinary success. That success masked the unresolved differences in outlook. These differences apparently endured, but were never seriously confronted in the open until the problem of training the second generation in the lessons of the revolution became an acute one.[38]

## Two Political Systems and the Rise of the Bureaucrat

Mao's political system, as outlined above, was not so much a revolutionary one as a type of local-traditional or even primitive political system. Evans-Pritchard's work on the Nuer, for example, describes a society in which social homogeneity and the absence of political centralism could be shown to be associated with a special kind of political and legal order.[39] Decisions would be made within the context of ritualized

[37] The party reform documents on which this paragraph is based are cited above, in note 8.

[38] It is of course virtually impossible to date the earliest signs of open disagreement in this regard. The views of Kao Kang, for example, may have reflected this problem since Kao essentially favored organizational measures to sustain the revolution and control the party in a period of modernization. See Lewis, "Revolutionary Struggle," pp. 129–33.

[39] E. E. Evans-Pritchard, *The Nuer: A Description of the Modes of Liveli-*

norms that could not themselves be changed. The ritual leader of the Nuer tribes played a religious function and received unchallenged devotion from his tribesmen. Retaliation ("tit-for-tat struggle") in a state of primitive warfare dominated tribal affairs. As summarized by Roger Masters, "retaliation and the threat of violence serve to unite social groups and maintain legal or moral criteria of right and wrong."[40] In decentralized primitive systems such as this, a preference for self-help characterized the group's outlook. In China's "ordered anarchy," Mao as leader played a magical or charismatic role rather than one of concrete decision-making.

Mao derived his model of the political system from his understanding of peasant villages. His available collections of "village investigations" in the Kiangsi Soviet show that Mao returned to the traditional Chinese villages in a quest for insights into the proper functioning of leadership as well as for information on how to control and mobilize the peasants themselves.[41] Mao's later discussions of ideal conflict ("contradictions") constituted a perceptive abstraction of traditional conflict management within local institutions. It is not by accident that the kind of primitive system described in the previous paragraph closely parallels the one that existed in many Chinese villages.

Uniquely suited to the wartime environment, Mao's political system was singularly inappropriate for ruling a country moving toward

---

hood and Political Institutions of a Nilotic People (Oxford: Oxford University Press, 1940), esp. chaps. 4 and 5. Maurice Freedman contrasts this type of system with the Chinese lineage in his Chinese Lineage and Society: Fukien and Kwangtung (London: Athlone Press, 1966), p. 38. Mao's opposition to lineage is discussed in ibid., pp. 179–80; and Freedman, Lineage Organization in Southeast China (London: Athlone Press, 1965), p. 111.

40 Roger Masters, "World Politics as a Primitive Political System," World Politics, 16 (July, 1964): 607. Cf. Coser, The Functions of Social Conflict, pp. 87–95. Mao in Yenan said: "From the special characteristics of war arise special organizations, a special series of methods and a special process. . . . Hence war experiences are of a special kind. All participants in war must free themselves from ordinary habits and accustom themselves to war before they can win victory" (Selected Works [New York: International Publishers, 1954], vol. 2, p. 203).

41 See Mao Tse-tung, Nung-ts'un tiao-ch'a [Village Investigations] (Shanghai: Hsin-Hua shu-tien, 1949), and Nung-min yün-tung yü nung-ts'un tiao-ch'a [The Peasant Movement and Village Investigations] (Hong Kong: Hsin-min-chu ch'u-pan she, 1949). For an examination of the populist strain in early Chinese Marxism, see Maurice Meisner, Li Ta-chao and the Origins of Chinese Marxism (Cambridge: Harvard University Press, 1966).

modernization.[42] Even though Mao recognized that the requirements for leadership would change after the seizure of power, he rejected the notion that the essential attributes of his system would also need to change. Nevertheless, after the takeover in 1949 (and more especially after the Korean War), it was virtually inevitable that Mao's previous charismatic role would lose its centrality. To the extent that his status had depended on the revolutionary conditions within China, relief from such conditions came to place Mao's position in doubt—and it was doubt which could do the most damage. The modernization of China would also contribute to this erosion by bringing about a "dispersion of charisma," to borrow Edward Shils' phrase.[43] The recipients of Mao's mantle were his party and its cadres. And this was the crucial change that had to occur if China was to become a modern state. As S. N. Eisenstadt (citing Weber) notes: ". . . the creation of new institutional structures depends heavily on the 'push' given by various 'charismatic' groups or personalities, and . . . the routinization of charisma is critical for the crystallization and continuation of new institutional structure."[44] The problem was that Mao, the charismatic personality, was not inclined to "crystallize" and continue a new institutional structure.

As the leader, Mao insisted instead that his potential heirs acquire those intangible qualities found in his revolutionary role rather than those of the political commissar or the newly emerging scientific-technical generation.[45] Not regarding the party bureaucracy as a bulwark of his

---

[42] See Benjamin I. Schwartz, "Modernization and the Maoist Vision—Some Reflections on Chinese Communist Goals," *China Quarterly*, no. 21 (January-March, 1965), pp. 3–19; Lewis, "Revolutionary Struggle"; and Lewis, "Political Aspects of Mobility in China's Urban Development," *American Political Science Review*, 60 (December, 1966): 899–912.

[43] "The Concentration and Dispersion of Charisma," *World Politics*, 11 (October, 1958): 1–19.

[44] *Essays on Comparative Institutions* (New York: Wiley, 1965), p. 55.

[45] See Lewis, "Party Cadres in Communist China," in James S. Coleman (ed.), *Education and Political Development* (Princeton: Princeton University Press, 1965), pp. 423–36. For relevant discussions on the stages of revolution see James C. Davies, "Toward a Theory of Revolution," *American Sociological Review*, 27 (February, 1962): 5–19; Rex D. Hopper, "The Revolutionary Process," *Social Forces*, 23 (March, 1950): 270–79; and Crane Brinton, *The Anatomy of Revolution* (New York: Random House, 1957), p. 18. The loss of charisma in the post-takeover period is of course not unique to China. Fifteen years after Indian independence, Prime Minister Nehru told a news conference: "An atmosphere is growing in India that I found not only dis-

revolution, Mao viewed the Communist organization with suspicion. Later, finding that his revolutionary outlook was not the one shared by the majority of his political cadres or achievement-oriented youth, he restricted his search for successors to young militants, mostly soldiers, irrespective of class background.

The fundamental point of Mao's objection in this respect can be seen with particular clarity from an examination of the changing definition of class and the consequent shift in class analysis. Mao's first words in his *Selected Works* began as follows:

> Who are our enemies? Who are our friends? This is a question of the first importance for the revolution. . . . To distinguish real friends from real enemies, we must make a general analysis of the economic status of various classes in Chinese society and of their respective attitudes towards the revolution.[46]

Having conducted his own social investigations, Mao stipulated that class categories denoted concrete behavior and were not simply convenient labels for abstract analysis.[47] It was his consistent assumption in analyzing social groups that economic class status corresponded to a class member's actual and potential behavior in war and to his attitudes with respect to the revolution and Communist leadership.

In the Yenan years, Mao assigned the principal responsibility for on-the-spot class analysis to his propaganda departments.[48] These de-

---

turbing but suffocating. . . . We are losing our sense of mission. What to do? I don't know" (quoted in I. R. Sinai, *The Challenge of Modernisation* [London: Chatto and Windus, 1964], p. 75).

[46] *Selected Works,* vol. 1, p. 13. At the time Mao wrote this article in March, 1926, he was responsible for organizing peasant groups in advance of the Northern Expedition.

[47] For a discussion of Mao's class analysis, see Lewis, "Political Aspects of Mobility," pp. 906–12. Compare Liu, "The Class Character of Man," p. 110: "The class character of man is determined by his class status. That is to say, if a given group of people have for a long time held the status of a given class, i.e., a given position in social production, and have for a long time produced, lived and struggled in a given manner they will create their particular mode of life, and their particular interests, demands, psychologies, ideas, customs, viewpoints, manners and relations with other groups of people and things, etc."

[48] The Communists still refer to the Propaganda Department's basic "Outline concerning the Propaganda and Agitation Work of the Party" (1941), the full text of which is not available to this writer. Excerpts may be found in Chung-kung chung-yang tsu-chih pu yien-chiu-shih [Communist party, Central Committee, Organization Department, Research Office], *Tang-ti tsu-chih kung-tso wen-ta* [Questions and Answers on the Organizational Work of the Party], 2d ed. (Peking: Jen-min ch'u-pan she, 1965), p. 10.

partments had the task of insuring that timely changes in analysis would be made as classes were transformed in the historical process and that to the extent possible people would be made conscious of their proper place in society according to their class label. Thus the propaganda department had a twofold function: (1) initial class analysis, and (2) education in "class consciousness" through agitation (*ku-tung*) and indoctrination. From its analysis would follow the organization of the society and all leadership structures. The propaganda or political line would always precede and determine the organizational line. Mao in 1945 said:

> whenever an erroneous political line became dominant, an erroneous organizational line inevitably emerged, and the longer the domination of the erroneous political line, the more the harm done by its organizational line. . . . The correctness or incorrectness of any political, military or organizational line has ideological roots—it depends on whether or not the line starts from Marxist-Leninist dialectical materialism and historical materialism and whether or not the line starts from the objective realities of the Chinese revolution and the objective needs of the Chinese people.[49]

This reiterated the theme of a 1941 directive of the Propaganda Department that "propaganda-agitation work and organization work form two organic departments in our party, and they also serve as the two organic components in the work of all other departments. Like two wings of a bird or two wheels of a cart, neither propaganda-agitation work nor organizational work can be dispensed with in the work of our entire party." When class analysis and education had been properly performed by the propaganda units, the organization department could easily accomplish its mission of discipline and control.

By party practice, it was the propaganda line that also set forth the deviations requiring discipline and against which all structures would be judged. With the assumption that objective class analysis was possible and essentially based on economic criteria, the party could assume that deviations both to the "right" and to the "left" would be harmful to the conduct of organizational leadership. Since any deviation constituted a personal failure—because the analysis of groups was always held to be correct—all punishment in the party was handled on an individual basis. Special precautions were taken against punishing "working people" unduly and against holding others guilty by association. Deviations in the more highly regarded classes were seen to be susceptible to

---

[49] *Selected Works*, vol. 3, pp. 208, 210.

minor remedies rather than to major social surgery. Re-analysis of classes at periodic intervals would also help keep organizations from becoming inflexible as the society changed. This would be particularly true in a period of "continuing revolution," which Mao prescribed for the years beyond the takeover in 1949.

At that time, Liu Shao-ch'i took responsibility for the first major analysis of classes, the "Decisions concerning the Differentiation of Class Status in the Countryside" (promulgated June 30, 1950).[50] In discussing these decisions, Liu argued that "the class status of most of the population in the rural areas is clear and can easily be differentiated without much divergence of view. . . . Impatience in determining the class status of these people must be avoided lest errors should be made which lead to their dissatisfaction."[51] Early the following year, the Central Committee announced a related decision to establish a propaganda network that would "build up a direct relationship between the leadership of the party and the masses of the people."[52] In this and other similar decisions the Central Committee sought to augment the strength of the party and increase its popular following. Propagandists would publicize the legitimacy of the party's relationship with the population and help in training and recruiting for its organizations. The building of the party in the midst of various propaganda campaigns became a firmly established principle with Liu Shao-ch'i's famous "eight standards" for party membership as reportedly given in November, 1951.[53] The party members would constitute a new "elite" among the workers and laboring people, and propagandists would play a crucial part in national construction work led by the party and the building of the party itself.[54]

After the landmark events in the winter of 1955/56, this relationship of class analysis, propaganda, party-building, and national construction underwent a fundamental change. The party in this crucial period substantially completed the programs of nationalization of industry and

[50] Text in *The Agrarian Reform Law of the People's Republic of China* (Peking: Foreign Languages Press, 1959), pp. 17–50.

[51] Text in *ibid.*, p. 84.

[52] Text of "Decision on the Establishment throughout the Party of a Propaganda Network for the Masses" (January 1, 1951), in *Hsin-Hua yüeh-pao* [New China Monthly], 3 (January, 1951): 507–9. Quote is from editorial in *Jen-min jih-pao* [People's Daily], January 3, 1951.

[53] For discussion, see Lewis, *Leadership in Communist China*, p. 105.

[54] See the *Jen-min jih-pao* editorial of September 10, 1952, commenting on the buildup of the number of propagandists to over 2,920,000.

collectivization of agriculture and with them erased the economic conditions of the previous class analysis. Though there were many critical ramifications to these developments, the most important for this discussion was the party decision that the groundwork had been laid for national harmony rather than "antagonistic" class struggle.

The leadership's first reaction affected intellectuals. According to Premier Chou En-lai at a meeting on intellectuals in January, 1956, the Communists would rely in national construction "on the energetic labour not only of the working class and the broad masses of the peasants, but also of the intellectuals. In other words we must rely on close co-operation between manual work and brain work, on the fraternal alliance of workers, peasants and intellectuals."[55] Here the emphasis would be on mobilizing a new kind of political-technical elite whose creative powers would be set loose through the implementation of the May, 1956 policy of "let a hundred flowers bloom, let a hundred schools of thought contend."[56] Assuming the existence of a spirit of unity throughout China, the party would join with all advanced elements in China "to promote the common cause." This judgment was reiterated throughout 1956 and was confirmed as doctrine by Mao in February, 1957. He said: "Never has our country been as united as it is today. . . . Led by the working class and the Communist Party, and united as one, our six hundred million people are engaged in the great work of building socialism."[57]

According to Mao's analysis of "non-antagonistic contradictions," classes in China were to be differentiated on a political basis since the economic equality of the people had been substantially realized. "At this stage of building socialism," Mao said, "all classes, strata and social groups which approve, support and work for the cause of socialist construction belong to the category of the people. . . ."[58] Individuals opposed to that cause would constitute the "enemy," whose numbers had undergone a "radical change" since 1956, Mao added, because "the main force of counterrevolution has been rooted out."[59]

At this moment in Communist China's political development, the Chinese polity had shaken loose from its primitive origins. Guided and

[55] *Report on the Question of Intellectuals* (Peking: Foreign Languages Press, 1956), p. 5. For a discussion, see Lewis, "Political Aspects of Mobility."

[56] Lu Ting-yi, *Let Flowers of Many Kinds Blossom, Diverse Schools of Thought Contend* (Peking: Foreign Languages Press, 1957).

[57] *On the Correct Handling of Contradictions among the People* [February 27, 1957, as revised] (Peking: Foreign Languages Press, 1960), p. 7.

[58] *Ibid.*, p. 8.          [59] *Ibid.*, p. 30.

dominated by party structure, that system had made the initial transition to an elite system according priority to the goals of modernization and the requisite recruitment from scientific and technical sectors of the society. The party apparatus was at its zenith, and the term "thought of Mao" was dropped from the 1956 party constitution.[60] Charisma, now routinized, had shifted from Mao to the party, and with Leninism supplanting "the thought of Mao Tse-tung," the Chairman had subsumed his image under the party and lent it his authority.[61]

Thus 1956 was the undisputed year of the Yenan political commissars, notably Liu Shao-ch'i and Teng Hsiao-p'ing. At the time of the reorganization of the Chinese Communist Party (CCP) in September, 1956, the fundamental unity of the People's Republic was assumed. There was no further need for rigorous class analysis, and the party in theory would thereafter adjust to the rising industrial China rather than remain chained to its revolutionary doctrines. The party opened its doors to a vast number of intellectuals and others previously accorded a lesser status and in all ways shifted its emphasis in contrived struggle from the mass base to the political system itself.[62] The old-line commissars were attempting to adjust the Communist organization to the rising numbers of technicians and managerial bureaucrats in the industrializing state. China was firmly directed toward what Mao later called revisionism.

## The Maoist Reaction

This situation lasted for a year. The assumption that the mobilization of the urban elite in accord with modernization would produce a new era of production did not materialize but rather was discredited with the upheaval among intellectuals the following May.[63] Though the details

[60] For texts of two constitutions, see Liu, *On the Party;* and Lewis, *Major Doctrines of Communist China.* For a discussion of the "changing position of ideology," see Franz Schurmann, *Ideology and Organization in Communist China* (Berkeley and Los Angeles: University of California Press, 1966), pp. 21–38.

[61] See Manfred Halpern, *The Politics of Social Change in the Middle East and North Africa* (Princeton: Princeton University Press, 1963), p. 285. Cf. Hans Gerth and C. Wright Mills, *From Max Weber: Essays in Sociology* (New York: Oxford University Press, 1958), pp. 245–52.

[62] See Lewis, "Revolutionary Struggle."

[63] See Theodore H. E. Chen, *Thought Reform of the Chinese Intellectuals* (Hong Kong: Hong Kong University Press, 1960), chaps. 25–28; Roderick MacFarquhar, *Hundred Flowers Campaign and the Chinese Intellectuals* (New York: Praeger, 1960); Dennis Doolin, *Communist China: The Politics of Student Opposition* (Stanford: Hoover Institution, 1964).

of this "Hundred Flowers" period are beyond the scope of this paper, it is clear on balance that Mao judged the emphasis on elite mobilization to have been premature and misguided. As suggested by Professor Oksenberg, he may have received support in this judgment from tradition-minded cadres in the lower-level rural bureaucracy. Following the anti-Rightist campaign of suppression that began in June, 1957, the question was thus reopened whether intellectuals were sufficiently reliable to base major programs on them in the future.[64] Since the intellectuals now dominated the urban apparatus, the only alternative was to base these programs on the "masses" in the countryside.

Still assuming that the 1956 political line and its underlying class analysis were essentially correct, however, the Chinese Communists for the next months became desperately concerned with finding the right kind of organizations to match that line. In general, emphasis shifted back to the mass line and from elite to mass mobilization. The "conservative" goals of the "Hundred Flowers" era for industrializing and modernizing China through a series of general twelve-year plans and more specific five-year plans were revised upward to the level of "great leaps" according to a new line of "socialist construction." Nevertheless the shift was one of degree rather than kind: the Communist leadership still emphasized the industrial growth of China as a matter of organizational priority. By bringing the CCP and peasants together in the communes, party leaders predicted the elimination of flood and drought and "the comparatively stable advance of agricultural production."[65] Despite some signs of debate within the Central Committee between 1956 and 1958, there is no evidence to demonstrate that significant disagreement existed among top members of the Political Bureau with respect to the new national goals.

What the evidence does suggest is that major party and state bureaucrats placed a restrictive interpretation on the means to achieve the goals. Under the slogan "red and expert" advanced first by Liu Shao-ch'i,[66] a balance was retained between elite and mass mobilization. In one sense this slogan merely rationalized the erosion of ideological purity that had occurred in those institutions (party and state) that had been most subject to rapid growth and turnover of personnel in the

[64] See the speech by Teng Hsiao-p'ing, *Report on the Rectification Campaign* [September 23, 1957] (Peking: Foreign Languages Press, 1957), pp. 5–11.

[65] "Resolution on the Establishment of People's Communes in the Rural Areas" (August 29, 1958), *Peking Review,* September 16, 1958, p. 21.

[66] See *Lun yu hung yu chuan* [On Red and Expert] (Peking: Chung-kuo ch'ing-nien ch'u-pan-she, 1958), pp. 3–4.

preceding years of the People's Republic.[67] The expanded range of contacts for the most mobile (the Communists and intellectuals) required an adjustment of Communist norms as well as those of the non-Communist groups. Although the slogan "red and expert" was used to spur the campaign of sending cadres to the lower levels,[68] it was also possible to construe its meaning in such a way as to support the need for the integrity of technical experts. This interpretation may well have been the one adopted by the military under P'eng Te-huai,[69] who continued to build up his power until the showdown at the Central Committee's Eighth Plenum in 1959.[70] And it was this meeting at Lushan that may well have marked the initial rupture between the Maoist conception of the political system and that envisaged by Liu Shao-ch'i. For the first time the unity of the two was explicitly asserted rather than tacitly assumed.

The more immediate issue at the 1959 meeting was the establishment of political objectives as the paramount ones for the military and the putting down of those people such as P'eng Te-huai who expressed opposition to the Great Leap Forward. In the society at large, the leadership attempted to maintain a balanced emphasis on both the instrumentalist party (experts) and the political rituals associated with Mao.[71] As the communes collapsed, however, the party placed a greater stress on organizational systems and control mechanisms which further promoted the theme of leadership solidarity. This was the theme

[67] Lewis, "Political Aspects of Mobility"; and Eisenstadt, *Essays on Comparative Institutions,* pp. 287–303. Eisenstadt notes: "Mobility necessarily entails the intensification of contacts between various kinds of groups which were previously to some extent separated from each other" (p. 289).

[68] For a discussion, see Lewis, *Leadership in Communist China,* pp. 220–32.

[69] Compare Ellis Joffe, *Party and Army* (Cambridge: East Asian Research Center, Harvard University, 1965), pp. 100–106; Ralph L. Powell, *Politico-Military Relationships in Communist China* (Washington, D.C.: U.S. Department of State, 1963), pp. 2–3; and John Gittings, "Military Control and Leadership, 1949–1964," *China Quarterly,* no. 26 (April–June, 1966), pp. 82–101.

[70] With respect to the Lushan meeting, see *Eighth Plenary Session of the Eighth Central Committee of the Communist Party of China* (Peking: Foreign Languages Press, 1959). Many recent discussions allude to the importance of this meeting.

[71] On the occasion of the 40th anniversary of the Chinese Communist Party Liu Shao-ch'i continued the 1956 stress on unity (*Peking Review,* July 7, 1961, p. 10). The following month, on August 10, Chen Yi made a famous speech emphasizing the experts' importance. For a discussion, see Lewis, "Party Cadres in Communist China," pp. 433–35.

trumpeted at the Central Committee's Ninth Plenum in January, 1961, when the party called for a rectification movement "to help cadres enhance their ideological and political level."[72] In this movement a balance was not only retained between elite and mass mobilization, but—to the extent that the elite received concessions—greater leeway was given to its technical and scientific members. Within the general population in 1961 some effort was made to increase the appreciation of peasants and workers for class labels and for the proper behavior and attitudes associated with those labels. Yet the principal characteristic of party policies in these years was to allow the peasants to take their own path and rarely to mention the cities.[73]

Major changes with respect to the 1956 assumptions finally occurred at the Central Committee's Tenth Plenum (September 24–27, 1962), which is usually given as the date for the beginning of a movement for socialist education and class struggle. In early 1963 *Jen-min jih-pao* renewed the idea of a "three-in-one" leadership of cadres, experts, and the masses, and henceforth the topic of the class struggle received the highest priority.[74] The themes in class indoctrination were even more clearly revealed in March in the "learn from Lei Feng" campaign which the following year was to be expanded into the "learn from the People's Liberation Army" campaign.[75] In essence the party at the Tenth Plenum began to challenge the assumptions of 1956 on the unity of society—though it was to take an additional two years before the full implications of this were realized.

That realization came in 1964. It began with an effort throughout the government to erect political departments wherein officials would be made more aware of the class aspects of the economic institutions they were attempting to create.[76] Once again leaving aside the many significant details of this period, it is clear that by this year, elements within the party were becoming increasingly conscious that the manipulation of cadre organizations was not having the prescribed effect. And the presumed need to cleanse the cadre ranks seemed particularly important for the preparation of a younger generation to succeed Mao in

[72] Communiqué of the Ninth Plenum, *Peking Review,* January 27, 1961, p. 6.

[73] See Lewis, "The Leadership Doctrine of the Chinese Communist Party" and "The Study of Chinese Political Culture."

[74] *Jen-min jih-pao,* February 11, 1963.

[75] For a discussion see John Gittings, "The 'Learn from the People's Liberation Army' Campaign," *China Quarterly,* no. 18 (April–June, 1964), pp. 153–59.

[76] For details, see *Jen-min jih-pao,* April 4 and June 7, 1964.

the leadership.[77] Although experiments with organizational forms had often been carried out with unusual imagination and flexibility, and even with great risk, from Mao's point of view the organizational effort under the control of the former commissars and urban experts had little to show for the effort by 1964. Where there was restored control and regularity, there was just as often indifference to the party and pursuit of individual or traditional interests at variance with the broad ideological standards. Only in the army was the leadership reasonably successful in establishing both regularized organization and active ideological programs. It was with the experience of these programs in mind that Mao laid forth his blueprint for his successors[78] and for a restoration of the central features of his ideal political system. Essential to this was a reconsideration of class struggle and his own role as leader.

For reasons probably associated with the Vietnam war and perhaps with difficulties in the army,[79] the effort begun in 1964 was abruptly postponed. Some changes were wrought within the Young Communist League and in the field of the literary and performing arts. The main effort, however, was to wait until early 1966. At a secret meeting of the Central Committee in the fall of 1965, Mao reportedly decreed the launching of the "Cultural Revolution," but it was only the army's Lin Piao who responded with any noticeable enthusiasm.[80] A period of almost six months then followed in which many senior leaders, including Mao himself, disappeared from public view.

Whether it was a sickly Mao who returned in early May or simply an angry, revitalized Mao, there can be little doubt that the Chairman had made up his mind to initiate basic changes throughout China and, finally, to smash the very organizations on which the Chinese Communist state had been built. He clearly hoped to recreate the environment of struggle in which successors could be properly trained in the manner of revolutionaries and be made to depend on the authority of

[77] A collection of the relevant documents on this theme is in *Training Successors for the Revolution Is the Party's Strategic Task* (Peking: Foreign Languages Press, 1965).

[78] *On Khrushchov's Phoney Communism and Its Historical Lessons for the World* (Peking: Foreign Languages Press, 1964), pp. 64–71, and *Jen-min jih-pao*, August 3, 1964.

[79] Morton H. Halperin and J. W. Lewis, "New Tensions in Army-Party Relations in China, 1965–1966," *China Quarterly*, no. 26 (April–June, 1966), pp. 58–67. See also Lewis, *Communist China—Crisis and Change* (New York: Foreign Policy Association, 1966).

[80] Lin Piao's "five points" in New China News Agency release, November 26, 1966, in *Survey of China Mainland Press* 3588. Hereafter cited as *SCMP*.

the charismatic leader. The balance now was swinging back to mass mobilization, and step-by-step in the revolution of 1966 the target became the fundamental restructuring of the bureaucratic apparatus. Although this implied a distrust of all structures and organizations that had taken shape in the past 17 years, there is little evidence to suggest that the Yenan commissars at first viewed the selective purging of their ranks (notably the removal of Lo Jui-ch'ing and P'eng Chen) with alarm or knowingly opposed the aims of the Cultural Revolution. They were, however, operating on assumptions that were no longer shared by Mao. The leader was moving to recreate the political system of Yenan as well as to promote its values.

## The Cultural Revolution: The Purge of the Commissars

The Cultural Revolution thus began with Mao's strong stand against the ideology of the commissars and the bureaucratic apparatus they had fashioned. His first moves came in the cultural and educational spheres, always critical barometers of revolutionary pressures in Mao's China. Their radical nature was revealed in the novel formulation of deviations and class analysis. While the creation of formal structure had been the objective of operations, deviations were to be avoided on both the right and left. When training in an environment of unremitting struggle became the aim, however, the party's leaders under Mao revised the line on class analysis and with it the entire rationale for right and left. The Eleventh Plenum directive of August 8, 1966, summed up the conclusions as follows:

> The question of who are our enemies and who are our friends is a question of prime importance in the revolution and a question of prime importance in the great cultural revolution. With respect to left elements, the party's leading cadres should be skillful in discovering them, developing and expanding them as a force, and resolutely relying on them as revolutionaries. . . . All forces should be concentrated to attack the handful of extremely reactionary right elements and counterrevolutionary revisionists, and thoroughly expose and criticize their crimes against the party, against socialism, and against Mao Tse-tung's thought, and to isolate them to the maximum extent. This movement stresses purging the ruling elements within the party that follow the bourgeois line.[81]

[81] Text in *Jen-min jih-pao,* August 9, 1966. For early references to leftism, see *Jen-min jih-pao,* June 3, 1966; *Chieh-fang-chün pao* [Liberation Army

With the emphasis on struggle and revolutionary leftism,[82] especially for the youth, the Maoists began to talk more and more of the need for destruction and destructive activity rather than of construction and rational organization.[83] Everything was to be in flux, particularly in those organizations such as schools[84] and youth groups which provided the training for China's emerging "successors." Though some references were made to "a great leap forward" this was fundamentally different from Liu's discussion of that line in 1958 when the aim was a massive upsurge in construction and party building.[85]

As we have noted, the duty of propaganda departments was to conduct the necessary class analysis basic to the formulation of organizational lines. Thereafter, this branch of the party bureaucracy had the function of overseeing the educational system and mobilizing the population. When it became clear that the class analysis of 1956 was being questioned, it was also only a matter of time before doubts would be raised concerning the Propaganda Department itself and thence spill over into the educational system for which it was responsible. It was because of the fate of class analysis, one could argue, that Chou Yang (deputy director of the Propaganda Department) and those associated with the department were charged as being the leaders of the black gang of "monsters and freaks."[86] The former head of the Peking

---

Daily], October 6, 1966. The latter said that the directive was written under the "personal direction of Chairman Mao." *Chieh-fang-chün pao,* November 11, 1966, stated: ". . . the method of recalling family histories and comparing the sharp contrast between the new and old societies will also permit the raising of the class consciousness of cadres and fighters to a higher level and make them realize even more the significance of Chairman Mao's instructions and carry out every task with better results in accordance with Chairman Mao's instructions."

[82] On revolutionary leftism, see *Jen-min jih-pao,* June 4, 15, 16, and 18, 1966; *Chung-kuo ch'ing-nien pao* [China Youth News], June 23 and July 12, 1966; and *Hung-ch'i,* no. 9, 1966, p. 30.

[83] See, for example, *Hung-ch'i,* no. 8, 1966, p. 9; and *Chieh-fang-chün pao,* May 10, 1966.

[84] The Central Committee on June 13, 1966, issued a directive suspending university examinations and postponing the opening of all universities and many lower schools. For text, see New China News Agency release, June 18, 1966 (*SCMP* 3724). For other important documents, see *Hung-ch'i,* no. 14, 1966; NCNA release, June 19, 1966 (*SCMP* 3724), July 15, 1966 (*SCMP* 3742); *Jen-min jih-pao,* June 18, 1966, July 12 and 13, 1966.

[85] Liu's report is in *Second Session of the Eighth National Congress of the Communist Party of China* (Peking: Foreign Languages Press, 1958).

[86] The first salvo against Chou Yang was launched in *Hung-ch'i,* no. 9, 1966,

municipal propaganda apparatus, for example, was accused of doing "his best to propagate the theory of 'extinction' of class struggle in socialist society."[87] And if they in their role as overseers of the intellectual community were considered protectors of a black gang, then it was only a short step to assume that other members of the gang had been infiltrated into all schools and into the circles of performing and literary arts. As each stage of the Cultural Revolution gave way to the next, Mao and his associates progressively turned on ever larger segments of the bureaucracy. Whereas Liu Shao-ch'i and Teng Hsiao-p'ing were placed in charge of the revolution in the summer of 1966, they subsequently became its chief targets. The evidence available suggests that only then did they begin to think and act as a force in opposition fighting for its existence.

Thus by late 1966, Mao and his allies had turned with full fury on the commissars of the Yenan years and the political system fashioned by them and by the bureaucrats below them. In doing so the Maoists were opposing order and regularization[88] and were attempting to establish a political system designed only to perpetuate itself and the charismatic leader.

Previously, the Communists had succeeded in fusing the Mao-Liu system into what Irving L. Horowitz calls "party charisma":

> What has become apparent, but thus far remains relatively unexamined in the literature of political sociology, is how discipline and charisma, rational authority and personal appeal, are fused in the political party which at the same time is the national party. This party, which embodies both the charismatic leadership responsible for making the national revolution of independence and the bureaucratic directors responsible for guaranteeing the follow-up national revolution of development, in effect transforms the Weberian duality . . . into search for a "higher unity"—into what . . . [may be] called party charisma.[89]

---

pp. 35–44. See also *Current Background,* no. 802 (1966), and Merle Goldman, "The Fall of Chou Yang," *China Quarterly,* no. 27 (July–September, 1966), pp. 132–48.

[87] *Kuang-ming jih-pao,* June 25, 1966. See also *Jen-min jih-pao,* July 7, 1966.

[88] *Hung-ch'i* (editorial), no. 10, 1966, pp. 11–12 states: "The order of revolutionary affairs cannot be pre-arranged in a routine manner, but should be arranged in accordance with the masses' own experience gained in struggle."

[89] Quoted in K. H. Silvert, "Parties and Masses," *Annals of the American Academy of Political and Social Science,* no. 358 (March, 1965), p. 105 (italics in the original have been omitted).

The preservation of party charisma in the Chinese case, however, depended on the leader's perception of the system's goals and revolutionary prospects. In 1956 the favorite slogan of the Chinese Communists had been: "Without the Chinese Communist Party there is no new China."[90] This slogan was in accordance with the interpretation of the mass line which gave the decisive role in the Chinese state to the CCP and its higher echelons. In 1966, this slogan was changed to read: "Without the thought of Mao Tse-tung there is no new China."[91] All senior echelons of the party were criticized for their failure to acknowledge Mao's thought, and those on the revolutionary left, particularly the young students, now were seen as the legitimate protectors of that thought.[92] The assault against those "waving the red flags to oppose the red flag" was in part the result of Mao's conclusion that the Communist bureaucratic system constituted an antithesis to his own and was leading the country to revisionism.

As many writers have remarked, the most serious test of a system such as China's takes place when power must be transferred from one leader to another.[93] At such a time the weakest legitimating principle is the charisma of a past leader.[94] The dilemma of Mao is that he must choose to smash the elements of party and state which can ensure continued legitimacy in order to gamble on the unique kind of legitimacy to which his name had been attached.

In doing this Mao has had to redefine that entire component of the Communist system associated with the political commissars. The implicit rationale of the Cultural Revolution is that the economic transformation of 1956 changed the economic base, but the ideological superstructure did not change accordingly.[95] The approved and relevant ideology will promote the concept of public interest, which can only be introduced after the destruction of the old concepts of "self." Mao, of

[90] Quoted in Lewis, *Leadership in Communist China*, p. 75.

[91] *Hung-ch'i*, no. 8, 1966, p. 5.

[92] *Jen-min jih-pao*, November 10, 1966, stated that workers and peasant masses could not "seek revolutionary ties" in other localities. This privilege had been explicitly given to the Red Guards who were allowed to "exchange revolutionary experiences" in virtually any part of China.

[93] Joseph LaPalombara and Myron Weiner, *Political Parties and Political Development* (Princeton, N.J.: Princeton University Press, 1966), p. 411.

[94] F. W. Riggs, "Bureaucrats and Political Development: A Paradoxical View," in Joseph LaPalombara (ed.), *Bureaucracy and Political Development* (Princeton, N.J.: Princeton University Press, 1962), pp. 161–63.

[95] *Chieh-fang-chün pao*, November 3, 1966.

course, is depicted as the very soul of the public interest, while the commissars and lesser bureaucrats, by Maoist fiat, are made to symbolize selfishness and corruption. Thus is the purge of the commissars justified; and increasing urgency has been attached to this since June, 1966, when the party apparatus under Teng Hsiao-p'ing sent "work teams" to the universities and high schools in an effort to take over and control the Cultural Revolution.[96]

The spirit of urgency thereafter permeated all Maoist policies toward the struggle, particularly in his use of the Red Guards. The aims of the new and more frenetic type of struggle were explicitly opposed to the organizational goals of intra-party struggle advanced nearly three decades earlier by Liu Shao-ch'i. It was thus not surprising that the activities of the Red Guards so clearly fit this description by Liu of "unprincipled" struggle:

> There are still some comrades (in fact, they can no longer be called comrades) who openly rely upon and make use of the forces outside the Party to conduct inner-Party struggle and to blackmail and intimidate the Party. For instance, relying upon their partial achievements, their troops and rifles, their prestige among the masses and their relations with a certain section of the United Front, some people conduct a struggle against the Party and the higher organisations.[97]

Mao was attacking the organization of the party in order to preserve his conception of party and his own prior high status in the polity.[98] Perhaps for the first time in the history of a Communist state a leadership faction had gone outside the party for its main support.

Mao increased the intensity of popularly-felt antagonistic feelings

[96] See reports to this effect in *Hung-ch'i,* no. 10, 1966, p. 11; *Nihon Keizai,* October 18, 1966; Peking Radio, December 4; and *New York Times,* December 18, 1966.

[97] *On Inner-Party Struggle,* pp. 34–35.

[98] Compare the excellent work by Ernst H. Kantorowicz, *The King's Two Bodies* (Princeton, N.J.: Princeton University Press, 1957). Mao's closest associates are Lin Piao, Chou En-lai, Ch'en Po-ta, K'ang Sheng, Li Fu-ch'un, and his wife Chiang Ch'ing. That this is a very unstable group—especially for those members associated with both camps—may be seen by the career of T'ao Chu whose rapid rise was apparently ended in his abrupt downfall in January, 1967. See *New York Times,* January 6 and 7, 1967. On this group's use of the Red Guards to offset the power of the party, see the editorial in *Hung-ch'i,* no. 15, 1966, pp. 14–16.

against party and state officials, labeling them a black gang and a faction worthy only of contempt and destruction. The Maoists have said:

> In the present great cultural revolution the principal contradiction is the antagonistic one between, on the one hand, the broad masses of the workers, peasants, soldiers, revolutionary functionaries and revolutionary intellectuals, and, on the other hand, you, the handful of antiparty and antisocialist representatives of the bourgeoisie. This is a contradiction between revolution and counterrevolution, an irreconcilable contradiction between the enemy and ourselves. As for your counterrevolutionary speeches and actions, we must subject them all to merciless criticism and sound the call for attack.[99]

From the late spring of 1966, the Mao-Lin group emphasized the life-or-death nature of the struggle[100] and later in encouraging the Red Guards set loose the entire student community of urban China against the highly respected core of senior Chinese intellectuals, scientists, and technicians. Even the workers and peasants came under attack, and there were signs that there had been a resurgence of regionalism as local leaders attempted to insulate themselves from the national-level upheaval.[101]

Opposition to order thereby unleashed the social tensions that had been tightly constrained within agreed limits in the past.[102] Acting on his belief that bureaucratic institutions represented barriers between the leader and his followers, Mao made eight appearances in person before 11 million "revolutionary masses," achieving, it was said, a major breakthrough in the mass line.[103] The consequences of the new policy were to encourage youth to destroy the "four olds": old ideas, old culture, old customs, and old habits. From the resultant sharp antagonism, the society was expected to become polarized, leaving no room for

[99] *Hung ch'i,* no. 8, 1966, p. 10.

[100] See, for example, *The Great Socialist Cultural Revolution* (Peking: Foreign Languages Press, 1966), vol. 4, pp. 1, 6, 23, 38.

[101] Most reports of this kind have come from the wall posters in Peking as read and interpreted by Japanese newsmen. See, for example, *Asahi,* November 2, 1966; *Mainichi,* November 5 and 10, 1966. See also *New York Times,* November 24, 1966.

[102] Examples of this may be found in *Chieh-fang-chün pao,* August 1, 1966; and *Hung-ch'i,* no. 10, 1966, pp. 11–12.

[103] Peking Radio, November 27 and 28, 1966; and *Jen-min jih-pao,* November 27, 1966. Mao's appearances were on August 18, August 31, September 15, October 1, October 18, November 3, November 10–11, and November 25–26.

a middle group to exist in peace. The clear model to be avoided was that of the Soviet Union and Yugoslavia. The unity sloganized by the Soviet Communist Party in terms of the state of the whole people and the party of the whole people had made a deep impression on the Chinese.[104] What was produced as a "corrective" to the Soviet unity was a fundamental schism within the Chinese polity.

Presently (February, 1967) Mao's system is in the ascendancy. The primitive aspect of that system has been reasserted with only minor modifications from the revolutionary war. Indeed an editorial in *Hung-ch'i* (Red Flag) on July 1, 1966, made the point that the Great Proletarian Cultural Revolution is like a revolutionary war in which victory goes to the side that can best mobilize the general populace.[105] In the same month *Jen-min jih-pao* argued that in winning the masses the proletarian leadership, meaning Mao, had "won the confidence of the masses, gained the initiative, a right to speak and a right to lead in work and is therefore able to guide the movement successfully."[106] Under these conditions *Hung-ch'i* has added that the revolutionary elements "cherish boundless love for Chairman Mao . . . without reservation."[107]

Geared to combat and unable to adapt and transform itself, Mao's system has adopted the language of violence and retaliation in a system of discipline, obedience, and self-help.[108] Condemned are all "authorities" and those who regard Mao's system as simple or vulgar.[109] In a call

[104] See, for example, the article by Wang Li, Chia I-hsüeh, and Li Hsin, "The Dictatorship of the Proletariat and the Great Cultural Revolution," in *Hung-ch'i*, no. 15, 1966, pp. 17–24.

[105] No. 9, 1966, p. 28. This is symbolized with particular point in the emphasis from late October through November on Red Guards undertaking long marches. See *Jen-min jih-pao*, October 22, 1966.

[106] *Jen-min jih-pao*, July 21, 1966.

[107] No. 9, 1966, p. 34. On November 11, *Chieh-fang-chün pao* repeated the same theme. This has also been interpreted to mean that no one is red by nature and can only be socialized into being red by learning from Mao. See, for example, *Jen-min jih-pao*, October 22, 1966.

[108] In this connection, Gabriel A. Almond and G. Bingham Powell, Jr. note: ". . . primitive political systems . . . have all the capabilities which are to be found in the more elaborate and complicated types of political systems [but] they have relatively little ability to adapt to new and difficult situations" (*Comparative Politics: A Developmental Approach* [Boston: Little, Brown, 1966], p. 221). The most authoritative statement on self-reliance for revolutionaries is Lin Piao, *Long Live the Victory of People's War* [September 3, 1965] (Peking: Foreign Languages Press, 1965), pp. 37–42.

[109] *Kuang-ming jih-pao*, October 4, 1966; and *Chieh-fang-chün pao*, October 6, 1966.

that preceded the emergence of the Red Guards in early June, Peking Radio on June 1 stated: "All revolutionary intellectuals, now is the time to fight!" Similarly the Maoists attack professionalism and an instrumentalist definition of the mass line. According to *Hung-ch'i* on June 8:

> The watershed dividing Marxism-Leninism from revisionism, revolution from counterrevolution, lies between the alternatives of whether one supports or opposes the placing of Mao's thought right in the forefront, whether one supports Mao's thought in command, supports politics in command, or one advocates money-making in command and the placing of professional skill in command.[110]

The purposes of Mao's system are thus to achieve "revolutionization" for the transformation of man and to defeat its alternative, revisionism through "peaceful evolution." All other tasks are secondary.

In contrast to Mao's objectives as just outlined, the national goals associated with Liu Shao-ch'i gave priority to the role of the political apparatus and its adjustment to the requirements for modernization. According to Liu in 1956 a higher Marxist-Leninist understanding by party cadres was necessary for them to "distinguish between correct and wrong opinions, between good and bad leading personnel" and thereby to increase their ability in work.[111] Three years later Liu again emphasized the point that the CCP's tasks required the placing of politics in command.[112] Leadership would be brought to the masses in order to make organization as realistic as possible and to avoid making mistakes in work.[113] Liu consistently stressed the need for a kind of "democratic life" that would strengthen the party's centralism and discipline and create the basis for the party to give proper leadership to all other structures in the Chinese state.[114] Although it is naïve to believe that Liu's

[110] *Hung-ch'i,* no. 8, 1966, p. 2.

[111] "Political Report," *Eighth National Congress of the Communist Party of China* (Peking: Foreign Languages Press, 1956), vol. 1, p. 98.

[112] "Report on the Work of the Central Committee . . . ," *Second Session of the Eighth Party Congress of the Communist Party of China* (Peking: Foreign Languages Press, 1958), pp. 61–66. It is significant that in this report Liu was extremely concerned with counterrevolutionaries and others who broke "law and order" (*ibid.,* p. 23).

[113] "Political Report," p. 103.

[114] Cf. Mao, *On the Correct Handling of Contradictions among the People,* pp. 12–16.

system would have adapted itself without severe strains to an industrialized China, its willingness to compromise in principle with technical and bureaucratic requirements made it a potential instrument for change.

Liu's political system also gave an important place to the state as an instrument for modernization. The "main question of the revolution," Liu had said in 1959, was the seizure of state power. With that power, the Chinese leadership, he concluded, had "kept a firm hand on the essential economic mainsprings of the state, energetically established a powerful socialist state economy and secured its leading position in the entire national economy."[115] It was Liu who delivered the principal report at the First Session of the First National People's Congress (September 15, 1954) on the draft state constitution.[116] In this report, he emphasized the transitional character of the constitution,[117] and noted the steps to be taken by state institutions in bringing about socialist industrialization and socialist transformation.[118] The aim of this transition, he added, could be "achieved by peaceful struggle, through the control of the administrative organs of state, the leadership of the state-owned economy, and supervision by the masses of the workers."[119] Liu stressed the importance of the people's congresses in the political system[120] and expressed confidence that the state apparatus would grow in strength. The party, of course, would be "the core of the leadership in the country"[121] in building up this strong state system.

The fact that this system was based on an assumption of unity of classes has made it a special target for the Red Guards. Typical Red Guards' posters have thus demanded that the constitution of 1954 be revised in order to restore the earlier "proletarian dictatorship."[122] These posters declare that the state must be based on Mao's "unified guidance ideology." The proposed constitutional reforms would elimi-

[115] "The Victory of Marxism-Leninism in China," *Peking Review*, October 1, 1959, p. 8.

[116] "Report on the Draft Constitution of the People's Republic of China," in *Documents of the First Session of the First National People's Congress of the People's Republic of China* (Peking: Foreign Languages Press, 1955), pp. 9–73.

[117] *Ibid.*, pp. 31–41.

[118] For a discussion, see H. A. Steiner, "Constitutionalism in Communist China," *American Political Science Review*, 69 (March, 1955): 1–21.

[119] "Report on the Draft Constitution," p. 37.

[120] *Ibid.*, pp. 42–45.

[121] *Ibid.*, p. 71.     [122] *Tokyo Shimbun*, October 27, 1966.

nate all rights of the bourgeois classes and maintain a "strict distinction between enemy and friend." Other posters in late 1966 have called for the immediate ouster and punishment of Liu as the President of China.[123]

Since October 1, 1966, the Cultural Revolution has been described as a struggle between two roads or the conflict between the proletarian and bourgeois lines. At the time of this writing (February, 1967) these two systems are locked in a stalemate.[124] The small group of leaders around Mao and Lin have explicitly rejected the organizational base from which they could effectively project their own power. Even the bulk of the army remained on the sidelines until early 1967, though its potential involvement always provided, it was assumed, a deterrent to the active mobilization of party cadres in defense of Liu Shao-ch'i and Teng Hsiao-p'ing. The main force arrayed against these two main targets are the "revolutionary masses." *Jen-min jih-pao* on June 24, 1966, said: "The fact that the party can mobilize the masses to uncover them, dismiss such people from office, strip them of their power, and resolutely remove them from our ranks testifies to the strong militancy, the unity, and the consolidation of our party." Perhaps the best recent indication of the present deadlock between the two systems was given in a speech by Chiang Ch'ing (Madame Mao Tse-tung) on November 28, 1966.[125] In this speech Mme Mao made the plea for all forces to rally behind the thought of Mao Tse-tung and added that in referring to the question of minority and majority one could not discuss this independently of class viewpoint. She noted: "It is necessary to see who has grasped the truth of Marxism-Leninism and Mao Tse-tung's thought, who is genuinely carrying out the correct line of Chairman Mao."[126] By

[123] *New York Times,* November 30 and December 15, 1966; Agence France Presse release, November 23, 1966; *Mainichi,* October 17, 1966. The Red Guards reportedly have also picketed government institutions. See Hamburg Radio, October 23, 1966. After this paper was written, the campaign against Liu as the "top party person in authority taking the capitalist road" began in the public media.

[124] See the editorial "Win New Victories" in *Hung-ch'i,* no. 15, 1966, pp. 14–16. Beginning in January, Maoist groups attempted to break the deadlock by resorting to "seizures of power" or the forcible ouster of the previous leadership in cities and provinces.

[125] Peking Radio, December 4, 1966.

[126] The 16-point directive of August 8 stated: "The minority should be defended, because sometimes truth belongs to them" (*Jen-min jih-pao,* August 9, 1966). Some sources have interpreted this to mean that the Maoist group did not command a majority on the Central Committee.

definition Mao and his adherents would always comprise the "majority."

The present Cultural Revolution thus provides the context for an emergent and presumably long-term power struggle in China. In this context neither side has been able to assert its position in purest terms (and in February, 1967, the Maoists were forced to accommodate the bureaucracy in order to save the economy, especially spring planting). To assert its position in purest terms would alienate its potential support and disrupt disastrously the Chinese economy.[127] There have even been signs that the Maoists have offered their conditions for making "peace" with some of their senior opponents.[128] The reasons for this, if true, may have been the mounting costs to economic production which the Maoist press has now declared must never be harmed by the Cultural Revolution. The long-term costs, however, have not been fully calculated as Mao's group has contemplated the even further postponement of the opening of higher schools in 1967.[129]

Meanwhile the purge goes on and the list of those attacked grows longer. Many people previously allowed to remain neutral are now no longer allowed to do so. *Hung ch'i* has praised Lu Hsün who "bitterly hated the 'peacemakers,' those seemingly 'fair' and 'just' people, the 'fence-sitters' who pretended to be 'unbiased' in the battle between the two opposing armies. 'Conciliation' or 'eclecticism' means to 'obliterate

[127] For an editorial on production in the Cultural Revolution, see *Jen-min jih-pao*, November 10, 1966. Cf. the discussion of the "10-point principle urging Red Guards not to obstruct production" in *Mainichi*, December 20, 1966. Perhaps even more significantly the 16-point directive (cited in note 126) gave special protection to "scientists, technicians, and ordinary members of working staffs, as long as they are patriotic, work energetically, are not against the party and socialism and maintain no illicit relations with any foreign country. . . ."

[128] See the article entitled "In Memory of Lu Hsün, Our Forerunner in the Cultural Revolution," *Hung-ch'i*, no. 14, 1966, pp. 4–10. In this article, Mao's adversaries were offered the following terms for their "surrender": they must (1) openly confess to the masses that they have carried out the wrong line; (2) openly reverse their judgments and restore honor to the "revolutionary masses"; (3) support the revolutionary actions of those masses; (4) criticize their own mistakes; (5) undergo mass criticism; and (6) not resist any excessive actions from their critics. See also the editorial "Win New Victories" in *Hung-ch'i*, no. 15, 1966, pp. 14–16, for a slightly different formulation of these terms.

[129] On February 11, a "big character poster" signed jointly by the Central Committee and the State Council announced that all primary schools would re-open after the Chinese New Year (on Monday, February 13) and that all junior middle schools would resume classes on March 1.

the difference between black and white' and to 'act as the paws of the tiger.' "[130] For those already under attack, the party press has declared that it will "show no mercy to the dogs that are already in the water."[131] Since these enemies are believed to be within their own organization, there is every possibility that the struggle will become more intense. As Lewis Coser notes, once conflict has begun within an organization, it will be much fiercer than a struggle between organizations because of the previously close ties of the members and their former great involvement with one another.[132] Given time, alleged deviation within the group casts doubt on the suspect's loyalty, and, as has long been noted, Communist movements are particularly hostile toward those considered to be disloyal or heretical.

This present impasse is neither stable nor predictable and raises again the question of how revolutions die. Mao as the super-revolutionary has found it impossible simply to pass from the scene as a revered figurehead. Viewing the rising strength of the party and state apparatus as a potential for counterrevolution, he has postponed China's march toward industrialization and vowed a fight to the finish with his adversaries. Mounted to create rational institutions for a chaotic China, his original revolutionary drive built up irrational compulsions and emotional commitments of its own, based on a special relationship between Mao and the general populace. In attempting to restore his own charisma, the Communist leader in 1966 had to attack the very rational social institutions that he had set out three decades earlier to establish.

That attempt to revive charisma has brought the leaders and the commissars of the People's Republic of China to a state of near internal war. The rupture of personal and political relationships within the central elite has accentuated again the long-dormant differences of approach to the political system. The differences between the leader and the commissar may well be found in any political system. They are even reminiscent of the points at issue between the Confucianists, who wished to lead by moral persuasion and the emulation of men of merit, and the Legalists, who, skeptical of emulation, put their faith in bureaucracy and legal coercion. Now fundamental as well as extremely personal, the hostility within the leadership will not be easily erased or forgotten. Watching the conflict required to keep the revolution alive, the Chinese people can anticipate many more months of convulsion and domestic upheaval.

[130] *Hung-ch'i,* no. 14, 1966, as reported on Peking Radio, October 31, 1966.
[131] *Ibid.*
[132] Coser, *The Functions of Social Conflict,* pp. 68–72, 111–19.

# Comments by James T. C. Liu

China today is in the throes of a transition crisis of the first magnitude. This crisis involves a great deal more than what is usually entailed in a leadership struggle. There are, as one may gather from fragmentary and often unreliable reports, such features as the dogmatic reliance upon charismatic appeal, the puritan-like, doctrinaire call for unselfish re-dedication to the revolutionary cause, and the frequent resort to direct mass action. In an attempt to penetrate this confusing picture, probably confusing even to most Chinese themselves, Professor Lewis has sharply focused his attention on the relative differences in thought between Mao Tse-tung and Liu Shao-ch'i (of which he gives us an excellent analysis).

As Professor Lewis suggests, polarity seems to exist between the charismatic leader of mass appeal and the chief commissar of the regular party hierarchy. The Maoist line may well be "uniquely suited to the wartime environment" and, one should add, to a deliberately induced atmosphere of great agitation as (it can hardly be overemphasized) the tense international circumstances force China into a nearly wartime preparedness. But, as Professor Lewis asserts in his essentially Weberian analysis, Mao's political system is "singularly inappropriate for . . . modernization"; and China would fare much better under a disciplined elite leadership with the support of organizational solidarity, something closer to what Liu Shao-ch'i advocates and what presumably many other like-minded commissars and their followers wish to see.

Some immediate comments on charisma are in order. First, while few would disagree that its routinization would be eventually necessary for functional continuity or, in other words, stability, it should be noted that Professor Lewis also admits that charismatic appeal can nonetheless give a push to the creation of new institutional structure, and the creation of new institutions is precisely what Mao and his supporters

482

have aimed to do, though they may well fall short of their goal. Second, the power exercised by Mao's wife, Chiang Ch'ing, especially her influence in the army organization, seems to be a rather unusual extension of charisma, but this exercise of political power by a woman is not without some roots in the Chinese heritage. It resembles not so much the numerous cases of formally proclaimed regency on the part of an empress dowager as it does the few outstanding cases in which the consort played a leading role; for example, the case of Empress Lü in assisting and then acting in the name of her husband, the founder of the Han empire, and the case of Empress Wu, who eventually reigned herself, the only genuine female sovereign in Chinese history. To be exact, it is not in accord with the elite tradition of formal state organization, but it does come from the popular tradition of peasant rebellion. Occasionally, when a peasant rebel leader died or was incapacitated, his wife took over. Still, one should emphasize that even in the popular tradition the wife's acting on behalf of her husband was merely temporary; it was never legitimized or institutionalized for any long period of time, for she simply could not project a father-image in a patriarchal society (what Professor Francis L. K. Hsu more specifically defines as a basically "father-son dominated" society). To put Chiang Ch'ing in a leading role in the Great Proletarian Cultural Revolution is, a student of history would suspect, definitely a sign of Mao's weakness and even desperation.

Before going on to other points, the writer must qualify his comments. Trying to see the present in the light of the past is unfortunately an occupational hazard of historians. This is particularly true in China's present crisis. No matter how decisive the Chinese heritage was in affecting many evolutions in the past, it has been breaking down in the present century and in fact has completely broken into pieces since 1949. No mater how much influence its broken pieces may continue to have, they would not be particularly relevant to the shaping of a revolutionary campaign.

To qualify the comments even further, one may go so far as to suggest that not only is the present crisis without precedent in China but hardly does it have a close historical parallel elsewhere in the world. We know of innumerable cases of power seizure from the top, massive uprising from below, and regional rebellion. But there has rarely been a comparable case of such a great split from top to bottom on a national scale with no particular regional pattern. For example, some similarities to Stalin's purges no doubt exist; yet these are far outweighed by the outstanding features peculiar to the Chinese Cultural Revolution itself: the massive mobilization of the youth all over the country; their struggle against party officials and the common people without necessarily inflicting bodily harm on either; the intensity of the mass media propaganda on the spot; the supportive intervention of the army units, and the release of emotions against targets of the remote as well as the recent past, coupled with the absence of a clear set of new policy directions projecting toward the future.

These qualifications are not meant to deny the usefulness of history. They intend to emphasize that in assessing the relevance of historical parallels, we should resist the temptation of overrating their significance. Instead, we must bear in mind the overriding importance of the present situation itself, and direct our attentions toward long-term trends rather than try to make short-term predictions.

Returning to the recent crisis in China, one may point out that getting rid of the "meritorious officials" often recurs in Chinese history, from the ancient period of the *Spring and Autumn Annals* to the early Ch'ing, when a ruler, particularly a founding emperor, felt politically safe or compelling enough to do so. The remarkable case of the early Sung, in which all generals were smoothly relieved of their military power by the method of compensating them with generous pensions, shows an exceptional maturity in statecraft, but not an exception at all in its objective. In any event, what would probably follow such a purge is a restructuring of the once powerful roles into more restricted ones, with lesser replacements assuming them.

But the present occurrence is in other essential ways very much different from a historical recurrence. Unlike the "meritorious officials" of the past, the present-day commissars are well experienced in controlling and manipulating large-scale organizations. They would resist and counterattack, as it has been reported, by organizational means. China may have thus plunged into not exactly a state of civil war—so long as no large number of troops are engaged in fighting—but what one might call a state of civil or organizational strife. Assuming the Maoist purge of the experienced leaders and the rank-and-file to be successful or partially successful in the short-run, what could come next? Would the Maoists restructure this modern monolithic state with reduced and decentralized roles for the succeeding commissars? Could they effectively meet the exigencies of international insecurity and internal discontent arising from slowed-down industrialization? It seems probable that to some extent a continuing instability would be the immediate outcome.

What would be the long-term prospect of stability? Do the historical parallels of the Ch'in-Han sequence and the Sui-T'ang sequence have any relevance for an attempt to answer this question? In the pattern shared by these two sequences, the first empire was most energetic but paradoxically short-lived, having overexerted itself in destroying the old order, in imposing a new one, and in international conflicts, while the second empire had a much easier task in perpetuating the new order because this new order did not have certain objectionable features, at least insofar as the new ruling class was concerned, and because there was an atmosphere of international peace.

Citing these historical parallels is said to reflect a wishful thinking common among many overseas Chinese such as myself. I should not deny that; but as a historian I beg to draw on some comparable experience in European history as well as to support a proposition for world history in general: A "break-through" revolution with radical innovations may well be followed in the next stage by a revisionist evolution toward moderation and stability. This transition between the two stages is a highly critical turning point and it always involves tremendous difficulties. It is this transition which we are witnessing now. The old leadership becomes divided and some leaders overreact against the trend toward moderation and insist on introducing even more radical innovations over the objections of the rest who see little hope in pushing on further.

Normally, the irreconcilable radicals would lose, because the historical tide would be generally in favor of the transition, and their rearguard actions would not arouse enough support. Yet the present case of China seems different. The radicals are able to mobilize a vast number of Red Guards and score considerable success. Mao's charismatic appeal is only part of the explanation. Perhaps his obsessive and romantic revolutionary mentality is no more than a powerful precipitant. A more basic set of factors centers around the discontent among the youth, a modern phenomenon by no means peculiar to China but fairly common among all developing nations. This discontent develops when the educational advancement of the new generation simply outstrips the career opportunities available to them, when improvements in general entail much hard struggle and yet still lag far behind the upsurge of rising expectations, and particularly when a phase of rapid economic growth is followed by that of slowing down, stagnation, frustration, and even decline, which will bring with it the strong emotional reaction of looking for scapegoats as well as making some radical demands. In other words, it would be too much of an oversimplification to focus our major attention merely on the thought of Mao, on his differences with Liu, on sheer power struggle among the leaders, or even on the political events. To get over this critical transition and to reach for eventual stability, the ruling party, be it the pragmatic revisionists or otherwise, must fulfill one essential condition: they must convince the politically active elements that of all the alternatives considered, the prevailing system is in the long run the best possible one for producing sustained economic growth. This is the fundamental question upon which everything else depends.

In concluding, one may suggest that crucially connected with this fundamental question is the issue of upward social mobility. Pivotal in Chinese history for the achievement of long-term stability, irrespective of short-term crisis, has been the role of the bureaucratic elite. The traditional Chinese historians were fond of observing that the man on horseback may conquer the country, but he cannot continue to govern it in this manner. Hence, the need for such institutions as the civil service, recruitment by recommendation and examination, and the Confucian orientation for the society in general. However, as modern conditions outweigh historical continuity, one must not carry the parallel too far. Today, the party and the government organizations take in many aspiring young men and young women and the armed forces provide another "ladder of success," though not so much for women. But given the explosion or continuing expansion of educational opportunities, the best hope for upward social mobility, in addition to the outlets provided by the civil and the military bureaucracy, ultimately lies in an equally rapid expansion of the economy through industrialization, particularly through making industrial aids available to agriculture. This expanding economy will provide enough positions for the young talents to become members of the managerial elite.

Full employment, after all, is an ultimate goal of orthodox Marxism. In this respect, the Maoists are themselves a kind of deviating revisionists. Full employment is also the carrot that inspires the coming of a revolution. Without this carrot, one wonders how the Maoists, in continuously pressing for greater rededication without offering much relief in the near future, can keep the momentum of their agitation going for very long with their big stick alone.

# Comments by Michel Oksenberg

With the dangerous and tricky advantage of hindsight, Professor Lewis has presented us with a thorough analysis of the doctrinal issues which have shattered the forty-five-year-old union of Mao Tse-tung and Liu Shao-ch'i. Professor Lewis has also drawn widely from the field of political sociology to suggest that whereas the doctrines advocated by Liu Shao-ch'i are generally congruent with the needs of a modernizing, integrated China, the policy pursued by Mao Tse-tung is hopelessly anachronistic. Mao is pictured, in the winter of his years, as a man "restoring revolutionary chaos in an effort to preserve his own charismatic role." Mao, Lewis concludes, is motivated by "irrational compulsions and emotional commitments," which Lewis traces to the relationship Mao enjoyed with the masses in his guerrilla days.

There are several aspects of Lewis' paper which I believe deserve more careful examination. Specifically, the paper rests upon important, yet perhaps challengeable, points concerning (1) the origins of the Mao-Liu split; (2) the intellectual respectability of Mao's thought; (3) the loyalties, aspirations, and values of the former guerrilla "political commissars" and their underlings; (4) the process of policy formulation in China; and (5) the political implications of China's demographic trends and economic change. In the five sections of these comments, I briefly raise questions about these aspects of the paper which seem to merit further study.[1] Without such further study, I conclude, I am not persuaded that the strategy adopted by Mao and his associates is *more* unsuited to China's needs than the strategy Lewis attributes to Liu. Nor am I persuaded that the origins of the Mao-Liu split can best be traced to their different guerrilla experiences.

[1] [This paper was prepared in January, 1967, for the Conference. In the first point of his comments, Professor Oksenberg arrives independently at a conclusion similar to that of Professor Schwartz in his paper, "China and the West in the 'Thought of Mao Tse-tung,' " pp. 365–79, this volume.—EDITOR.]

## The Origins of the Mao-Liu Rift

I have some reservations about Lewis' description of the origins of the Mao-Liu rift. While Lewis traces this split to Yenan, I suggest that the split, at one and the same time, is more the reflection of a deep-seated conflict in the Communist ideology dating back to the founding of the party and more the product of events in the 1960's.

Professor Lewis ascribes the rift between Mao and Liu, in large part, to their different experiences and responsibilities during the Chinese Communist Party's (CCP) guerrilla days. Lewis believes that, as the leader who coordinated the activities of the guerrilla units spread over China, Mao became sensitive to the importance of his role as inspirer and unifier of the movement; his position caused him to have an exaggerated view of the capabilities generated by a proper rapport between the leader and the masses. Liu Shao-ch'i and other political commissars working at the middle echelons of the bureaucracy acquired a somewhat different perspective of the dynamics of a guerrilla movement. These commissars, working directly with the masses, became more sensitive to the limitations of the masses and became more aware of the importance of effective organization and discipline. Lewis concludes that, unlike the commissars, Mao remained exceedingly distrustful of bureaucracy and that Mao never grasped the pivotal importance of the middle-echelon political commissars.

This analysis is exceedingly interesting and deserves further research in the documents of the Yenan period. Certainly it is reasonable to believe that different responsibilities produced different values and perspectives. But we must guard against exaggerating the differences between Mao and Liu in the pre-1966 period. If we draw their differences too starkly, we will not be able to understand why they co-operated for so long a period of time.

Rather than ascribing the Mao-Liu rift to their different guerrilla experiences, I prefer to say that their separation reflects conflicting elements within the ideology of the CCP which predate the Yenan period. Since its inception, the CCP has harbored two strands of thought which are diametrically opposed in their explanations of the relationship between human will and man's material environment.[2] One of these strands can perhaps be called "Scientific Marxism" and can be traced to the legacy of one of the founders of the CCP, Ch'en Tu-hsiu. This strand of thought stresses that the building of a socialist society depends

[2] See Benjamin Schwartz, *Chinese Communism and the Rise of Mao* (Cambridge, Mass.: Harvard University Press, 1951), pp. 7–28. Stuart Schram, *The Political Thought of Mao Tse-tung* (New York: Praeger, 1963), pp. 15–21.

ultimately upon the technological and productive capacity of society. The Scientific Marxists believe that the "superstructure" of society, that is, its government, politics, and social relations, reflects the material basis of society. To change the superstructure, there must initially be a change in the base.

Another strand of thought which has had an enduring impact upon the CCP is "voluntarism." This intellectual tradition emphasizes that human will, when properly organized, can overcome all obstacles and achieve all goals. This strand of thought, with its infinite faith in the people, should perhaps be linked to another of the founders of the CCP, Li Ta-chao. For the voluntarists, old customs, habits, and beliefs are what prevent mankind from realizing its potential. Transformation of a human's beliefs, a liberation of the human mind from the myths and superstitions which shackle it, will enable man to transform his material environment.

These two conflicting beliefs have coexisted in the Chinese Communist movement for forty-five years. In fact, so deeply embedded are these divergent beliefs that most leaders of the CCP appear to embrace them both. Many of the policy debates since the founding of the People's Republic have been waged in terms of this conflict between Scientific Marxism (with its priority upon the improvement of technology and the means of production) and voluntarism (with its priority upon the destruction of old institutions and the instilling of new attitudes). In the early 1950's, for example, vigorous debate was waged between those who believed that the collectivization of agriculture was appropriate only after Chinese agriculture was mechanized, and those who believed that a collectivized agriculture was a prerequisite for increased production and the mechanization of agriculture. In military affairs, there has been a sharp and continuing debate over the relative importance of sophisticated weaponry and the morale of the army in warfare.

The Mao-Liu split can be seen as another manifestation of the underlying tension between the Scientific Marxist and voluntarist positions. Mao, taking the voluntarist position in this instance, apparently believed that the Cultural Revolution would provide a powerful motive force for increasing production. Liu and others apparently adopted the Scientific Marxist stance, and counterposed the Cultural Revolution against the development of production.[3] Available evidence indicates

[3] Item 14 of the "Sixteen Point Decision on the Cultural Revolution" stated: "Any idea of counterposing the great cultural revolution against the development of production is incorrect," in "Decision of the Central Committee of

that some of Mao's opponents, consistent with Scientific Marxism, felt that China's economic conditions in 1965–66 did not provide a suitable basis for launching an effort of the sort Mao envisioned. The differences which separated Mao and Liu in 1966, then, reflect very profound discrepancies within the Chinese Communist ideology. When policy debate is pursued in terms of Scientific Marxism vs. voluntarism, differences become particularly visible. Compromise and mutual adjustment become more difficult, and polarization occurs. This is what seems to have occurred in the fall of 1966. This by no means implies, however, that Liu had always been the Scientific Marxist and Mao the voluntarist. On the contrary, if one examines the history of the CCP, one finds Mao appearing to emphasize Scientific Marxism on some occasions, and voluntarism on other occasions. The same can be said for Liu; he was, after all, one of the most enthusiastic spokesman for the voluntarist Great Leap Forward.

Rather than attributing the Mao-Liu rift to their guerrilla experiences, then, I am attracted to the following hypothesis. The developments leading to the Mao-Liu split began in the 1950's. The available evidence suggests that the different positions which Mao and Liu advocated were related to their divergent power interests and the different lessons which each had derived from the Hundred Flowers, the Great Leap and its aftermath.[4] An important reason for Mao and Liu's inability to reconcile their differences, however, lies neither with developments in the 1950's, nor with the Yenan period, but with the origins of the CCP. For, in 1966, Mao and Liu found themselves on opposite sides of the irreconilable controversy between Scientific Marxism-voluntarism. The seeds of discord planted in the ideology had yielded their fruit.

## Mao in Different Perspectives

Mao is thus the product of diverse and conflicting intellectual traditions, and his beliefs reflect the many diverse experiences which have had an enduring impact upon him. One's perspective of Mao is inevitably colored by the emphasis which one places upon the various ideas and experiences which shaped him. This brings us to a second

the Chinese Communist Party Concerning the Great Proletarian Cultural Revolution" (*Peking Review*, August 12, 1966, p. 6–10). See also Meng Kuei and Hsiao Lin, "A Critique of Sun Yeh-fang's Reactionary Political Stand and Economic Program," *Hung-ch'i* [Red Flag], no. 10 (August 10, 1966), pp. 26–38.

[4] Particularly interesting in this regard is "Self-criticisms of Liu Shao-ch'i and His Wife," *Tokyo Mainichi,* January 18, 1966.

aspect of the Lewis paper that merits further attention. Lewis stresses that the leadership doctrines distilled from Mao's Kiangsi and Yenan guerrilla experiences form a dominant strand in the fabric of his beliefs. Further, Lewis likens the political system based on these doctrines to a "primitive" or even tribal system, which is "singularly inappropriate for ruling a country moving toward modernization." In this section I suggest that emphasis upon another important strand in Mao's background, his early attraction to anarchism, places him in a somewhat different, more respectable perspective.[5] Rather than the advocate of a "primitive" political system, he is in the mainstream of one influential modern intellectual current.

Seen in its best light, Mao's case is based upon the belief that the concentration of authority tends to perpetuate itself, that centralization tends to be coercive and evil, and that the best hope for the development of a just society rests in the persuasion of men by rational argument and in their participation in public affairs. When viewed in this context, the doctrinal differences separating Mao and Liu in 1966 are, in many ways, the differences which have divided revolutionary movements at least since 1776. Not surprisingly, one easily finds parallels to the Mao-Liu split in those countries where the anarchist tradition had considerable influence—Russia, Spain, and France.

Looking at Russian history, Isaiah Berlin sees two centuries of conflict between libertarians and federalists on the one hand and the Jacobins and centralizers on the other. Bakunin denounced the Marxist demand for the dictatorship of the proletariat as something that would merely transfer power from one set of oppressors to another. The Populists of the eighties and nineties remained vigilant against all those whom they suspected of conspiring—whether they realized it or not—to destroy individual spontaneity and freedom. "In due course," Berlin states, "Lenin himself, while he never abandoned the central Marxist doctrine, expressed his bitter disappointment with these very consequences of it which his opponents had predicted—bureaucracy and the arbitrary despotism of the party officials; and Trotsky accused Stalin of the same crime."[6]

The issues separating Mao and Liu also find their echo in the disputes between the anarchists and Communists during the Spanish Civil War. The anarchists advocated a militia system and demanded the suppres-

[5] Robert Scalapino and George Yu, *The Chinese Anarchist Movement* (Berkeley: Center for Chinese Studies, 1961).

[6] "Introduction" *Roots of Revolution,* by Franco Venturi (New York: Grosset's University Library edition, 1966), p. xvii.

sion of salute, equal pay for all in the army, newspapers at the front, and soldier councils. The Communists, forging an alliance with staff officers of a liberal Republican persuasion, stressed discipline, professionalism, and unity.[7] One also sees a parallel to the Mao-Liu debate in France of the pre-1871 period, when "two main lines of thought emerged: on the one hand, the idea that the Republic One and Indivisible should be led by a revolutionary Paris; on the other, that a federation of autonomous local units, usually called "communes," should be established and that Paris would merely be the largest of them and act as their guide."[8]

Mao's concern also seems similar to the one which preoccupied Jefferson in his oft-quoted remark, "The tree of liberty must be refreshed, from time to time, with the blood of patriots and tyrants. It is its natural manure." As Hannah Arendt so strongly emphasizes, Jefferson continually addressed himself to the problem of preserving the revolutionary spirit once the revolution had come to an end. Jefferson, Arendt observes, was acutely aware of the inconsistency in the values and behavior of revolutionaries. In Arendt's terms, revolutionaries cherish the opportunity to participate in "the potentialities of action and the proud privilege of being beginners of something altogether new."[9] But often these revolutionaries erect centralized power structures which deny similar opportunities to their successors. Such was the case with Robespierre and Stalin. Mao harbored the fear that many in the CCP apparatus were similarly willing to build a bureaucratic apparatus which deprived the masses of the opportunity to participate in the affairs of state.

Of all intellectual traditions, it is the anarchists who have "consistently pointed out the dangers of making the wrong kind of revolution, and their warnings over the last hundred years that Marxism would lead to dictatorship and to the replacement of the old tyrannies by a new one have proved all too right."[10] Possibly sensitized to this problem by his early attraction to anarchism, Mao may have initiated the Cultural Revolution, in part, to cope with the problem of the

[7] Hugh Thomas, *The Spanish Civil War* (New York: Harper Colophon ed., 1963), p. 364.

[8] Frank Jellinek, *The Paris Commune* (New York: Grosset's University Library edition, 1965), p. 12.

[9] *On Revolution* (New York: Viking Press Compass Books, 1965), p. 235.

[10] James Joll, *The Anarchists* (New York: Grosset's University Library edition, 1966), p. 278.

effective participation in public affairs by the Chinese people in the post-revolutionary period. On one other occasion, in his initiation of the "Hundred Flowers" campaign, Mao has displayed his awareness of the dimensions of this issue.[11] At that time, as in 1966, he sought to involve the people, in a limited way, in the criticism and direction of public policy. Several aspects of the Cultural Revolution suggest that Mao and his associates are still searching for institutional forms that will involve the population in the affairs of state, forms that are not totally controlled from above. The *ta-tzu-pao* ("big character posters") and the appearance of "revolutionary rebel organizations" in factories and schools are indicative of that search. And it is the forms of popular participation in the Paris Commune which attract Mao and his associates today.[12]

I do not wish to imply that reference to his anarchist heritage provides an adequate explanation or justification for the Mao of the mid-1960's. The complexity of power struggle, bureaucratic politics, and policy debate precludes simple explanations. But, I do suggest that the doctrinal conflict between Mao and Liu is open to at least a twofold interpretation. As Professor Lewis argues, it may be viewed as a conflict between bureaucracy and institutionalized authority on the one hand and revolution and personal charisma on the other. Seen in this light, Mao's policy fosters disorder and retards industrialization; Mao appears to be irrational, destructive, thirsting for even more power and glory.

But Mao's policy may also be seen as an effort to secure the commitment particularly of the younger generation to the building of a more just society, a commitment that arises from participation in the revolutionary act of defying authority. Mao would rather delay China's industrialization than have its industrialization serve the purposes of an entrenched bureaucratic elite. In this respect, Mao continues to be true to his revolutionary heritage. At the same time, Mao shares with many the belief that bureaucracy and industrialization do not necessarily lead to an improved quality of life. To the extent that Mao's desire is to insure that industrialization serves the interests of his society, he is dealing with the central intellectual problem of our age. Seen in this light,

[11] Interestingly, when the "Hundred Flowers" campaign came to an end, non-Communist Chinese suggested that Mao had been forced to agree to the reversal under pressure from less "liberal" party officials led by Liu Shao-ch'i. See Roderick MacFarquhar, *The Hundred Flowers* (London: Atlantic Books, 1960), p. 13.

[12] Cheng Chih-szu, "The Great Lessons of the Paris Commune," *Peking Review*, April 8, 1966, and April 15, 1966.

Mao cannot be discussed in terms of "success" or "failure." To call his system "primitive" is to do him injustice, for in many ways we are reduced to value judgments. And we can be sure that the faith in voluntarism, egalitarianism, and permanent revolution which captured a long line of revolutionaries before Mao, and which have gripped Mao in his life, will continue to attract political figures who come after him.

## The "Political Commissars" and Their Underlings

Thus far, I have suggested that the differences between Mao and Liu possibly were less stark than Lewis describes, and that Mao is less removed from the intellectual currents of our time than Lewis implies. This section compares the coalition around Mao with the Liu-Teng led organizations, and suggests that the Maoists may be more modern and the former commissars and their organizations less flexible and pragmatic than Lewis suggests.

Indeed, this is the aspect of the Lewis paper which troubles me most. I find it difficult to embrace a theme which presents Liu Shao ch'i, Teng Hsiao-p'ing, P'eng Chen, Lu Ting-yi, Chou Yang, and Lo Jui-ch'ing—the victims of the purge—as paragons of virtue, the defenders of China's industrialization effort. A list of the major spokesmen for China's costly Great Leap certainly would include these men, for example. On the other hand, many of those generally identified as being among the more pragmatic, flexible leaders of China can not easily be labeled former "political commissars": Chou En-lai, Ch'en Yi, Li Hsien-nien, Ch'en Yün, and Nieh Jung-chen. These people now appear to form part of the Mao coalition.

Nonetheless, Professor Lewis argues strongly that the political commissars of the CCP's Yenan guerrilla days have proven to be particularly educable men. Within limits, he believes, by 1956 the former political commissars had begun to adjust the organizations under their command to the needs of an industrializing nation. One way of assessing the "modernity" and "educability" of Liu Shao-ch'i, Teng Hsiao-p'ing, and the other former commissars is to evaluate the organizations they built, and compare these organizations with those which Mao has protected during the Cultural Revolution. Specifically, one wants to know how the organizations under the former commissars have responded to China's industrialization. One also should inquire into the values of the lower-level cadres that staffed the organizations of the former commissars. What evidence is there that the interests of these lower-level cadres converged with the demands of modernization? And one wants to know more about the sources of Mao's support.

It is possible, for example, that the coalition around Mao includes the nation's younger scientists and technicians. In this regard, it is interesting to note that one of the most active Red Guard organizations comes from the Peking Aeronautical Institute, while the politically oriented Peking Peoples' University does not seem to have played a major role in the Red Guard movement. Moreover, it must be recognized that the Cultural Revolution has not attacked *all* bureaucratic organizations in China. Up to late 1966, in fact, the purge largely exempted the military and the economic apparatus. Only a few ministries are known to have suffered heavily. The groups under attack included intellectuals in the social sciences, arts, and humanities whose association with the CCP extended to the pre-1949 era. More important, also coming under attack were full-time party workers, particularly at the provincial and municipal level—the party secretaries, organization and propaganda officials, and personnel working with mass organizations. These are the party underlings whom one associates with Liu Shao-ch'i, Teng Hsiao-p'ing, and Lu Ting-yi. What do we know about these lower-level officials? What are their values? How have they reacted to the rise of the new generation of trained youth? Did they welcome this generation into their ranks? Or, did their tenacious grip upon choice cadre jobs both retard the industrialization effort and foster generational conflict? To what extent were the excesses of the Great Leap Forward the product of their scorn for the role of the technician?

At this stage, can it be safely assumed that the values and attitudes of the cadres in Liu's and Teng's organizations are more suited to industrialization than the values of Mao's Red Guards? I am not sure that this can be assumed. One might also legitimately hypothesize that many —if not most—rank-and-file lower-level cadres have been and would continue to be impediments to China's modernization effort. Indeed, this is the picture I have of many county-level party cadres: they are still affected by old traditions of regionalism, familialism, and other particularist loyalties, concerned with status and seniority, distrustful of youthful technicians, and marked by a proclivity for bureaucratic practice.

These lower-level cadres may be so thoroughly entrenched that they will be able either to resist Mao's effort to dislodge them or to bring the regime down with them. But this possibility does not exclude two others. First, if Mao did not attempt to remove the former commissars and their underlings from the scene, it is possible that China's modernization effort would stall, choked by a particularist party apparatus in the same way that the Ch'ing bureaucracy retarded the industrialization effort of the 1870's and 1880's.[13] Second, it is possible that if Mao even partially succeeds, historians will record the years 1965–67 in China as a period of high social mobility, when the gains of the revolution were consolidated and when a young elite educated under Communist rule began to shape the nation's modernization effort. If this young elite, steeled in the turmoil fostered by Mao, remains committed to such values as self-sacrifice, national achievement, and individual initiative, the effects of the Cultural Revolution may yet prove to be compatible to the demands of industrialization.

## Mao's Role in Policy Formulation

In the preceding sections, I have accepted Professor Lewis' premise that the attempt to destroy China's bureaucratic apparatus is the product of Mao's conscious design. As Lewis demonstrates, in fact, there is good evidence for this. Perhaps to do injustice to his balanced presentation, however, I am not entirely comfortable with an argument that relies so heavily upon Mao's irrationality and control. We are reduced to the model which each of us has of the process of policy formulation in China.

In my opinion, the evidence does not allow one to point to a single decision, reflecting the blueprint in Mao's mind, which has determined the course of the Cultural Revolution over the past eighteen months. Rather, the Cultural Revolution seems to have passed through several stages, each stage culminating in new decisions and new purges in response to a changed internal and external environment. In the course of the Cultural Revolution, Mao's coalition has changed and narrowed; the options available to him have changed and perhaps narrowed. Mao has tried to change the course of events to accord with his vision of the future, but he has had to compromise his vision to meet unforeseen contingencies.

The model I have of policy formulation in China is one of gradual changes which in unforeseen ways foreclose future options and create new pressures, and of an interaction process between leader and led.[14]

[13] Relevant here are Mary Wright's *The Last Stand of Chinese Conservatism* (Stanford: Stanford University Press, 1957) and Albert Feuerwerker's *China's Early Industrialization* (Cambridge, Mass.: Harvard University Press, 1958).

[14] The model I have in mind is derived from Charles Lindblom, *The Intelligence of Democracy* (Glencoe, Ill.: Free Press, 1966).

What must remain an open question is: (1) the extent to which the reestablishment of Mao's personal charisma is his own conscious design; (2) the extent to which the symbol of Mao is being manipulated by his entourage, independent of his wishes, for their power and policy purposes; and (3) the extent to which the symbol is demanded in some sense by specific sectors of society.

Most likely, in my opinion, is that all three of these elements are involved, to differing degrees at the different stages of the Cultural Revolution. But recognition of this likelihood forces one again to suspend judgment about the anachronism or irrationality of the Cultural Revolution. Rather, one wants to know more about the political environment in which decisions are made in Peking. Are we witnessing the dynamics of uncontrollable, bureaucratic purge politics? If out of control, then we cannot speak of the Cultural Revolution's havoc as entirely due to Mao's design. Moreover, one wonders about pressures and deadlines impinging upon Mao and his inner-court—Lin Piao, Chiang Ch'ing, Ch'en Po-ta, and K'ang Sheng.

All too often, analysts attribute public policies to irrational world views of decision makers because these analysts only dimly perceive the forces producing those decisions. This may well be our problem with the Cultural Revolution. Acknowledging this, one is driven to inquire into the main developments in Chinese society since the mid-1950's and the Great Leap. One then can explore the changes in the demands upon and resources available to the Peking government. To the extent that the Cultural Revolution appears to be a response to these changes, it becomes a more understandable phenomenon and cannot be attributed solely to Mao's irrational initiative.

## The Political System and the Environment

This leads to the final point, one not examined in the Lewis paper. What are the political implications of China's demographic trends and recent social and economic change? More specifically, do aspects of the Cultural Revolution seem to be connected with these changes? Pinning down the answers to these questions is no easy task. It is possible, however, to offer some plausible hypotheses which relate aspects of the Cultural Revolution to some apparently underlying social forces. One aspect of the movement—its turn to youth—might be linked to demographic trends. Another aspect, the campaign's purge of the middle echelons (particularly the provincial level) of the party apparatus, may be related to a possible growth of vested local and departmental interests. A third aspect of the campaign, the increased manipulation of the symbol of Mao Tse-tung, may be related to the rapid expansion of transportation and communication facilities.

The dimensions of the problem of youth are suggested by some rough demographic projections, based on the 1953 census. According to tentative estimates, the number of youth in the bracket between 5 and 24 years of age has jumped from approximately 225 million in 1953 to 255 million in 1958, 300 million in 1963, and will be an estimated 350 million in 1968.[15] This increase places an undeniable burden upon an educational system dedicated to achieving universal literacy and upon the economy for generating new jobs. The Japanese economist Shigeru Ishikawa recently estimated that approximately 8–10 million additional people would enter the job market annually in the coming few years, while at a maximum, the industrial, modernized sector of the economy is generating 1.5 to 2.0 million new jobs annually.[16] Clearly, with the rapidly expanded educational system, many youths will find that the skills which they have acquired will be under-utilized. And this is happening in a society where fifteen years ago, any person who had acquired literacy automatically could expect upward social mobility. The necessity for the rulers to respond to these pressures appears urgent. The Red Guards give the youth an opportunity to engage in at least one aspect of society's activities toward which their education has encouraged them—to participate somehow in political affairs. Perhaps this will serve as a substitute for their demands for better employment. At the same time, Mao and his associates may hope that the educative effect of this campaign upon youth will be to convince the youth of China's poverty. This in turn, they hope, will cause the youth to lower their demands and expectations for good jobs and high wages. To delay China's industrialization effort in order to deal with youth now (rather than meet their demands as adults later) may be wise precaution.

Second, and this point can only be raised in question form, to what extent has departmentalism, regionalism, and localism spread in China in the aftermath of the Leap? Has the central government found it increasingly difficult to exact tax revenue from the provincial or regional organizations? In fact, the problem may be more complicated than that. What has been the total amount of revenue available to the

[15] United Nations, Department of Economic and Social Affairs, *Future Population Estimates by Sex and Age*, Report 4: *The Population of Asia and the Far East*, 1950–1980 (Population Studies, no. 31, ST/SOA/Series A/31; New York, 1959).

[16] "The Chinese Economy: A General Framework for Long-term Projection," *The China Mainland Review*, 2 (September, 1966): 75.

public sector—government on all levels—over the past ten years? Ishikawa raises the possibility that the amount has not increased appreciably since 1958. If so, the competition for available resources among the competing units and levels has intensified. Are there provinces where the economic stagnation is particularly serious, and the inexorable population increase continues all the while? For such provinces, it would seem, maintenance of the same level of payments to the center inevitably would mean a drop in revenue available to provincial officials. Drawing a lesson from Chinese history, regionalism flourishes under such circumstances. And it is quite possible that these were the circumstances in many areas over the past decade. Is it possible, therefore, that as soon as the relatively good crops of 1965 were harvested, the rulers decided that the time had come to deal with incipient localism via a party rectification campaign? And further, is it possible that departmentalism and localism, in fact, have become so strong that Mao is driven to ever more extreme measures to root them out? These are the questions that deserve to be answered, but to the best of my knowledge, the firm budget data are simply not available.

Finally, one notes the improved transportation and communication network. On several occasions since 1960, the mainland press has described the extension of rural broadcasting networks, the increase in autobus and river transportation in rural counties, and the improvements in civil air transport.[17] The ramifications of these changes for China's political system have as yet not truly been felt, but undoubtedly the long-run impact will be profound. In the absence of solid evidence, reasonable hypotheses about the immediate effect of communications development must be derived from the experiences of other industrializing countries. Indeed, the theoretical literature on communications and political development suggests that an expanding communication and transportation network increases both the practicability and the need to utilize the personal symbol of the nation's ruler.[18] This is what Lewis tells us the Cultural Revolution involves—the increased use of Mao as the personified symbol of authority. Nor is this a totally irrational development. First, the better the communications,

[17] "Rural Wired Broadcasting Networks," *China Topics*, 368 (February 15, 1966). Victor D. Lippit, "Development of Transportation in Communist China," *China Quarterly*, no. 27 (July–September, 1966), pp. 101–20. See also Radio Nanchang, December 8, 1966; Radio Nanning, December 8, 1966; Radio Sian, December 6, 1966.

[18] See Lucian W. Pye (ed.), *Communications and Political Development* (Princeton, N.J.: Princeton University Press, 1963).

the easier it may be to bring the symbol of Mao to the village and to bypass the intermediary propaganda apparatus. For example, recent reports describe peasants in different parts of China listening to broadcasts of the mass rallies in Peking during the autumn of 1966; such reports of a peasantry linked directly to Peking were carried less frequently in the local press of the mid-fifties. Second, rapidly expanding transportation systems often destroy existing institutions (marketing systems, kinship loyalties, etc.) more rapidly than new institutions can develop that can perform equivalent functions.[19] Thus, as articles in the Pye volume cited above suggest, an increased probability of the disintegration of society paradoxically may be one of the short-run effects of improved communications. While the new institutions are taking root, resort to the unifying symbol of the ruler—in China's case, Mao—may be an appropriate response.

To summarize, I have tried to raise some questions generated by Professor Lewis' stimulating paper. Two things give me pause. First, the keys which unlock the doors to economic development have yet to be discovered. A country with effective bureaucracies and political parties does not necessarily have the prerequisites for economic growth. Increasingly, American economists are beginning to recognize the role of attitudes in fostering growth, and it is precisely attitudes with which Mao's Cultural Revolution is concerned. Second, since the Cultural Revolution was so unexpected, we find it tempting to attribute our lack of foresight to Mao's irrationality. We had assumed that the irresistible trend in China had been toward gradual industrialization. The fact is, however, that social scientists in this country have not yet published much substantive work on China in the early 1960's. When we finally come to grips with the developments of the 1960–65 period, the Cultural Revolution perhaps will be seen less as an aberration than as a natural outgrowth of the preceding period.

[19] For a thorough statement of this theme, see Samuel P. Huntington, "Political Development and Political Decay," *World Politics,* 17 (April, 1965), pp. 386–430.

C. K. Yang

8

# Cultural Revolution
# and Revisionism

This paper presents some tentative thoughts on the Cultural Revolution. More than a year has elapsed since this historic campaign broke out into the open, and yet, as of this writing (May, 1967), its basic nature remains unclear to the outside world. In early 1967 in the watching post of Hong Kong, one often heard that even Communist functionaries who came out to the colony were vague on the fundamental issues and objectives of the upheaval. There is a woeful shortage of empirical data. A seasoned Chinese journalist with extensive contacts in the colony said in early 1967 that there was only about 20 per cent reliability in the news on the Cultural Revolution coming from mainland China, for such news stemmed mainly from wall posters ("big-character newspapers") put up by Red Guards and various agitation committees more for propaganda than for informing the public. This situation imposes a serious limitation on the reliability of the analysis attempted in this paper. But I will try to confine my analysis within the area of documentary evidence in order to minimize subjective judgment or unfounded imagination.

The Cultural Revolution is an extensive and complex campaign affecting every major phase of the Chinese Communist revolution. An editorial of *Jen-min jih-pao* (People's Daily) on July 17, 1966, identified it as the most significant movement since 1957 (the year of Hundred Flowers and subsequently the anti-rightist campaign). My present comments will be confined mainly to one of its many facets, namely revisionism, although I will also touch upon related aspects to support my argument. My approach is based on my view that revisionism appears to be the central issue of the campaign: Mao charges Liu and his faction with using their administrative authority to effect revisionism, which will inevitably lead to the "restoration of capitalism," while the opposite camp charges Mao with personality cult and impractical policies.

501

All the ramifying and seemingly puzzling features of the movement appear to center on this main issue.

Such a comprehensive issue naturally contains many possible points of significance for the student of revolutionary movements. From the viewpoint of organizational theory, the problem lies mainly in the goal sector of the Chinese Communist society, and structural problems are subordinate to it or stem from it, although the "personality cult" issue can be treated as a problem of leadership pattern in the structural sector.

A puzzling aspect of the Cultural Revolution is the seemingly erratic Red Guards, but their activities can be understood in terms of the goal orientation of the entire Communist movement, for Mao has employed them to force a change of party leadership in order to keep the movement from forsaking the original revolutionary course and thus losing its ideological goal under the pressure of revisionism. In the formal structure of the Chinese Communist society, it is the party's function and prerogative to set the ultimate ideological goals for the state and to formulate policies (immediate and intermediate goals for their implementation). It is also the party's function to exercise control over the population—the organizations and enterprises as well as the government—to assure effective maintenance of the party line leading to the established goals. The last function includes internalization of Communist values, rectification of conduct (*cheng-feng*) by criticism, self-criticism and confessions, police surveillance, and application of social and economic sanctions as integrative and pattern-maintenance measures. Essentially the party's function is the setting of goals and the maintenance of a proper course to assure their achievement.

Interpreted in this light, the campaign's struggle for the control of the party leadership and its policies is a struggle for the determination of the immediate, intermediate, and ultimate goals of the entire Communist revolution. Therefore, the whole turmoil may be viewed as conflict between divergent goals which will affect the ideological destiny of the Chinese nation. Hence the charge by the *Jen-min jih-pao* editorial that, should China follow the revisionist course, she will "change color" [away from red].[1] Goal conflicts have been recurrent in the history of the Chinese Communist movement, though this one may dwarf the preceding ones in terms of the affected levels of leadership, the number of participants, and the magnitude of areas involved.

This fact suggests the hypothesis that goal instability is an inherent characteristic of major revolutionary movements. Revolution is a sud-

[1] *Jen-min jih-pao* [People's Daily], December 10, 1966.

den and drastic process of changing the basic pattern of a social order and involves extensive alteration of its institutional bases. As such, it ventures into uncharted areas of social life where the old institutional base has been shattered or disrupted but where the new institutional guidance is still an unstable experimentation requiring continuous readjustment to reality. In the shifting situations of a revolution, social reality to which the new institutional devices must adjust themselves is fraught with unexpected changes which may force drastic alterations in a revolution's strategy, policies, or even ultimate goals. Hence the many flip-flop turns in the conduct of the revolutionary leadership of both the Soviet Union and China, turns which baffle Western observers who are accustomed to the logic and process of a stable and consistent social order. Goal instability and its concomitant violent conflicts will continue to characterize the process of a major revolution until institutional stabilization is achieved for the new pattern of social order.[2] The case of the Chinese Communist revolution, through the Cultural Revolution, serves to test this theme on the nature and process of major revolutions.

## Historical Setting of the Policy Conflict

A summary of the historical setting of policy conflict between the two contending factions in the party may facilitate the analysis of the Cultural Revolution as a struggle of goals. An intellectual who left Communist China in 1965 and who had observed the early phase of the campaign pointed out the following sequence of relevant developments, which can easily be documented:

Until 1955, the party leadership seems to have been quite unified, and any policy difference that may have developed among them does not seem serious or to have assumed the form of open struggle. But fissures began to appear in the party unity after that year. At the conclusion of the socialist transformation of industry and commerce (turning business firms into nationalized organizations, public-private joint enterprises or co-operatives) in 1955 and 1956, Liu Shao-ch'i made the public statement that henceforth there would be no more violent and stormy campaigns but only mild and gentle reforms. After he visited Moscow in 1956, he publicly praised the momentous decision of de-

---

[2] A new institution may be considered fully stabilized when it can transmit its main values and structural features for the fourth generation when most individuals no longer have physical contact with the founding generation but receive their notion of the institution through established internalized guidance.

Stalinization by the Communist Party of the Soviet Union. Both of these actions, we now know, were at odds with Mao's stand.

In 1957 Liu toured ten provinces of the Southwest and Central-South regions, and when he reached Canton, he suggested to the local party leadership as a topic of discussion the comparison between the "contract system" of employment and compulsory assignment of employees to organization units. His talk was tape-recorded and later played back to different organizations. After Mao was forced to relinquish the post of Chairman of the People's Republic and administrative leadership, Liu assumed power in 1959, and employment in production units was generally changed to the form of contractual commitment. Because of this, the people felt a gradual relaxation of party political pressure and control.

Following this change came the reopening of free rural markets in 1961 and the restoration of private plots to the peasants under the collectives. In the cities, cash compensations were given for small tools and production capital goods which had been forcibly taken in 1958 into urban co-operatives. These measures, together with increased remuneration for jobs and material benefits after the Great Leap, go under the Maoist label of "economism" or, more accurately, "economic incentivism," a focal point of heated contest in the Cultural Revolution, as we now know by hindsight.

In September of 1962, the Tenth Plenary Session of the Central Committee of the Eighth Congress of the party was held to decide on the proper policy regarding the paralyzing economic crisis after the Great Leap. In the spring of 1963 came the reorganization of the State Council and Chou En-lai, as its head, conducted a self-criticism on behalf of the State Council personnel, admitting that the economic difficulties in the past few years were caused by the Council's wrong methods of operation as well as by extraordinary and protracted natural calamities. Chou at the time seemed to share at least partly the views of the Liu faction in criticizing the Great Leap and its associated measures.

These political actions were taken in the midst of a rising anti-Mao trend in the cultural fields from philosophy to art, especially after 1961. The Chou Yang and Teng T'o clique in the Ministries of Culture and Propaganda fired broadsides at Mao's policies and generated, in the early 1960's, movements for restoration of traditional culture, importing knowledge from the West, and developing democratic freedom of individual expressions in art even if these measures contradicted party dogmas.

This series of political and cultural moves was finally labeled by Mao as revisionism designed for undermining the Communist cause and for restoring capitalism, thus effecting a goal substitution in the Communist revolution. Mao's counterattack seemed to begin in 1963 with the nation-wide socialist education movement which tried to reaffirm Mao's policy of "three red flags"—the general line in socialist reconstruction (large quantity, speed, high quality, economy), people's communes, and the Great Leap Forward. In 1964 came the campaign against Yang Hsien-chen's philosophy of "combining two into one" as a heretical view opposed to the theory of class struggle. In November, 1965, an attack was launched against historian Wu Han for his writings which criticized the party's authoritarian rule by historical analogy. From this point on, the Maoist counterattack developed steadily until the struggle of goals and policies erupted into open conflict, with the emergence of the Red Guards as a ramrod to dislodge the anti-Mao opposition from party power. The Cultural Revolution became an official action when it was sanctioned by a resolution adopted by the Eleventh Plenary Session of the Central Committee of the Eighth Party Congress on August 8, 1966.

### Goal Orientation, the Name "Cultural Revolution," and the Involvement of the Cultural Field

I stated at the beginning that the central issue of the campaign is revisionism or the scaling down of the idealistic goal of communism. As the campaign unfolded, its immediate aims shifted from purging "reactionary" intellectuals to "seizing power" (*to-ch'üan*) through the destruction of the entrenched, anti-Mao party leadership. It has become a power struggle: "In the final analysis, this is a fight for leadership power between the proletariat class and the capitalist class," declared an editorial of *Jen-min jih-pao*.[3] How does this justify the name, the Great Proletarian Cultural Revolution, when the object of the campaign is power, not culture, and the immediate target of struggle for the freewheeling Red Guards has become party leaders and not the "cultural circle"?

The term is justified because revisionism was systematically expressed in the cultural fields from philosophy and economics to literature and art, and the revisionist thoughts were transmitted to the population by "unregenerated" intellectuals through the media of schools, publication and popular arts (literature, drama, motion pictures, music, dance,

---

[3] *Jen-min jih-pao,* July 17, 1966.

painting), thus creating a popular revisionist movement drifting toward the "restoration of capitalism." As in traditional China, the function of setting goals and formulating policies for society and the state in Communist China still rests with the educated elite. Revisionism did not originate with peasants and workers; they follow the lead of the intellectuals. Thus, revisionist ideas and "schemes," an intellectual product, must be eliminated from the minds of the carriers (intellectuals and party leaders) through the process of "struggle" and reform, and the carriers themselves must be removed from power in the party and government. Thus, the Cultural Revolution started as a purge in the cultural field, and spread to the high party leadership which was accused of lending support to the cultural revisionists. This, in fact, has been the pattern of development of the movement.

The composition of the Red Guards furnishes another link of the term "Cultural Revolution" to the power struggle. Red Guards are mostly students, especially high-school students. In a country where student movements spearheaded major revolutionary upheavals from the New Culture Movement and the May Fourth Movement on down, the use of students once again as a means to dislodge a political leadership group follows a set pattern in modern Chinese history, with the intellectual elites retaining, then as now, the leadership of initiating political action. It is a struggle of intellectuals (Red Guard students) against intellectuals (teachers, cultural workers, and officials). The Western world may not consider students intellectuals, but they are low-ranking intellectuals in the eyes of workers and peasants who until recently had high rates of illiteracy in Chinese society.

Why do the Maoists use students, especially high-school students, as Red Guards, instead of young workers and peasants? Young workers and peasants may have minds as imaginative, plastic, and adventurous as those of young students, but their minds are relatively confined to the restricted niche of a job and the limited activities of manipulating tools, whereas the young minds of students interact with concepts and ideals about the greater society, unrestrained by the concrete world of jobs and tools. The ranging imagination of the young students, when oriented toward social values and political problems, induces an inclination or susceptibility for social causes and political adventures. It was the young intellectuals who broke the crust of nineteenth-century Chinese conservatism, led the Republican revolution, conducted the many cultural and youth movements which helped to shatter the old social and political order, and risked death to join the Communist party to vanquish a traditional world and lead it on to the road of revolutionary idealism. Now, to combat or remove an entrenched leadership in the powerful Communist party, young students appear readily as a history-proven tool to the professional revolutionaries who know from a lifetime of agitation work that these classroom youngsters, more than any other type of youth, can be quickly fired into action for a cause. Thus, the struggle for power which may determine the future character of the country is set in motion from the intellectual sector as before—even though workers and peasants are supposed to be the leading forces in a Communist state.

So far as the substance of culture is concerned, the movement aims at removing revisionist or anti-Mao ideas from cultural media ranging from the educational system to the popular arts. In spite of the puzzling slogan of turning *all* major forms of organizations (factories, government agencies, the army) into schools of the thought of Mao, there is no discernible sign of a new culture being promoted to replace the present one, such as may be suggested by the name Cultural Revolution.

If planners of the Cultural Revolution were motivated by a memory of the potency of student movements in critical periods of modern Chinese history, from the May Fourth Movement, the Northern Expedition to the *Chiu-wang* ("national salvation") Movement on the eve of the Japanese invasion, it is interesting to raise the question whether students can develop into as dynamic a force in the post–Great Leap period as they did during the pre-Communist Republic. Then, the physical presence of imperialism on the home soil acted as a stimulus to nationalism, there was the romantic incentive of serving an untried social and political idealism, and the existence in the social system of such factors as an oppressive traditional social order, a fragmented national body politic, and an ineffective government was conducive to political action. Will students develop sustained political potency in an intra-party power struggle when considerable ideological disillusionment has set in? Chou Yang made an incisive remark along this line:

> Literary writers in the 1930's had fervent revolutionary enthusiasm, for they had a very clear notion as to who were the enemies they must oppose, but in the present period of socialist revolution, there is no similarly clear idea as to who are the enemies they should oppose.[4]

In theoretical terms, what is the intrinsic nature of students (especially high-school students who lack the higher level of sophistication

[4] *Ibid.*, July 15, 1966.

of college students) as a collective dynamic force in social movements, and what are the environmental or system conditions necessary for its development and effectiveness? The Cultural Revolution may provide data to answer this question.

### Personality Factor in the Campaign Target of "Seizing Power"

Is this foundation-shaking turmoil solely and purely a contest over goals of the Communist revolution—revisionism versus unsullied Marxist-Leninist-Maoist communism? We can gain some insight into this problem by analyzing the campaign's main battle cry: "Seize power!"[5]

The campaign target of "seizing power" implies two objectives as presented in the campaign literature: to eliminate revisionism, and to eliminate the leadership which generates or upholds revisionism. Each of these two interrelated factors has a separate significance which may or may not be a part of the goal orientation of the movement. Is the demand for elimination of the anti-Maoist leadership motivated solely by the need for abolishing revisionism and protecting the idealistic goal of the Communist movement? In addition to honest conflict of goals and their concomitant policies, there is operating, in my view, Mao's egoistic drive for complete dominance of his own personality and views. Though deeply intertwined with ideological matters, Mao's implacable insistence on complete personal dominance has a separate significance for the authoritarian character of the leadership structure of the Communist organizational system. It cannot be entirely subsumed under the struggle for ideological purity of the Communist cause.

There is indeed sweetness and light in the guideline for handling internal conflicts among the "people" during the Cultural Revolution as "formulated personally by Chairman Mao":

> In debates, we must adopt the use of factual evidence and reasoning, and we must convince the opposite side by reason. It is not permissible to force a dissenting minority to yield through duress. We must protect the minority, for sometimes truth lies in the

[5] If we define authority as institutionalized power, what the Maoists try to "seize" may not be power but formally constituted authority. But a fully institutionalized authority system includes internalized values and a stabilized pattern of leadership role succession as necessary components. The system of formal authority in Communist China has not attained either, and thus, in reality, it is still power and not authority that is the focus of contention.

minority's hands. Even if the minority opinion is erroneous, we should permit them to state their grounds, and permit them to retain their own opinion.[6]

We cannot detect a trace of megalomania and authoritarianism in these and similar lines attributed to Mao by Communist publications. But thin and often unpredictable is the dividing line between "people" and "people's enemy," enemy for whom purgatory instead of gentle treatment of difference in opinion will apply. It is necessary to look at the bloody split within the Red Guards to see the difficulty of distinguishing "people" from enemy.

But even in treating members of the "people," it is difficult to determine whether Mao's style of leadership would consistently follow this reasonable democratic line in treating differences of opinion and policy. In his occasional interviews in Hong Kong, defector Chang Kuo-t'ao recalled frequent scenes of violent outbursts of swearing and cursing in Mao's dealing with his close associates over differences of opinion.

More indicative of the non-goal factor in the Cultural Revolution are the innumerable symbols of "personality cult" which fill the air. To the men on the street in Communist China, so far as we can infer from the Communist press, the entire Cultural Revolution appears as a struggle between Mao and the anti-Mao forces. It is the personality of Mao and not the campaign issue which first meets the eye and strikes the consciousness. Mao's likenesses in pictures and sculpture and the adulation of Mao in the lyrics of popular tunes ("Chairman Mao is our Sun," "Chairman Mao is dearer than Papa and Mama")[7] are ubiquitous. The entire cause of Chinese Communism is so identified with the personality of Mao that any expression or action against it summarily and automatically becomes a crime and the object of "struggle." "Mao Tse-tung and his thought are invincible magic of the Revolution, whosoever against it becomes our enemy," thus goes the lyric of a song.[8] Yet the Communist leader Teng Hsiao-p'ing has stated: "Personality cult is a social phenomenon with a long history, and it may well appear in certain forms in our party and our society; our duty is to firmly oppose glorification of the individual as decided by our central policy."[9]

To the anti-Maoists, the Mao symbol is an oppressive force encompassing all the wrong thoughts and actions. The opposition did not

[6] *Hung-ch'i* [Red Flag] (editorial), no. 12 (September 17, 1966).

[7] Song sheets brought to Hong Kong by travelers and printed in *Hua-nan wan-pao* [South China Evening Post], September 15, 1966.

[8] *Ibid.*          [9] *Ming pao* (Hong Kong), January 3, 1967.

raise any open anti-Mao symbol, but the anti-Mao campaign is nevertheless real and total in character. An indicative case is that of Chou Yang, vice-minister of propaganda in charge of literature and publications. *Jen-min jih-pao* charged him with severely restricting publication of Mao's writings despite pressing popular demand. He not only limited the printing of Mao's *Selected Works* but also reduced the display of Mao's books at the Hsin-Hua Book Stores (the largest official outlet of publications).[10] At the Theatrical Workers discussion group at Ch'angch'un, Chou criticized, as repetitious and monotonous, writings which spread and praised Mao's ideas: "What I hear day in and day out is either Chairman Mao or his thoughts."[11] After the purge of Chou Yang from the post controlling publications, the first Maoist act was the forceful reassertion of the Mao image by printing an avalanche of Mao's writings in all forms for popular consumption.

When so much campaign action is involved with a personality symbol, either pro-Mao or anti-Mao, ego vindication becomes a dominant motivation of the Cultural Revolution alongside policy conflicts which have implications for goal alteration of the Communist movement.

### Red Guards as a Transient Measure

Whatever its relative importance as a factor in the drastic split in the Communist party leadership, Mao's personality symbol helps to generate fervor for the Cultural Revolution which aims at the immediate objective of "seizing power" in order to reorient party policies toward the idealistic goal of Communism. The means of "seizing power" are the anarchistic, violent, and puzzling Red Guards.

The Red Guards episode cannot be adequately analyzed for the moment due to insufficient data, but all available signs in the Communist press and from escapees' accounts in Hong Kong point to the probability that this is a transient measure for capturing control of the party leadership and government machinery. It is unlikely that the unstable Guards are the forerunners of a decentralized and anarchistic type of political order. Their transient character is suggested by the disappearance of the Red Guards in the early stage of the Communist revolution after they had discharged their power-struggle function. Mao's call for all people in the country, including the Guard members, to learn from the model of the People's Liberation Army (PLA)[12] ar-

[10] *Jen-min jih-pao*, July 15, 1966.

[11] *Kuang-ming jih-pao*, August 7, 1966.

[12] Decision of the Eleventh Plenary Session of the Central Committee of the Eighth Party Congress, *Jen-min jih-pao*, August 13, 1966.

gues against the likelihood of using the chaotic youth groups as the base for building a permanent anarchistic system, for the army represents a rigidly hierarchical system of organization which stands unaffected by the abolition of certain outward symbols of rank (for example, insignia) among the officers.

The likelihood that the anarchistic Red Guards are a transient means of "seizing power" but not the spearhead of a decentralized pattern of political organization for the country[13] is also indicated by the restriction of attacks to cultural workers and to party leaders of units above the county level who hold significant decision-making power. Repeated orders have been issued to preserve the structural integrity and to protect the administrative officials of government organizations which execute policies set by the party leadership. A special object of protection consists of production organizations. Chou En-lai ordered out-of-bounds for the Red Guards all factories, economic enterprises, and production units from the county level on down, including rural communes.[14] A Chinese journalist in Hong Kong was told in early 1967 by

[13] The assumption can only be tentative due to insufficiency of adequate data. It is as yet not possible to determine even now whether the rural communes were designed for facilitating effective centralized control (it would be easier to control some 40,000 to 70,000 communes—the number varying according to periods—than some 1,250,000 agricultural production co-operatives), or whether they were products of Mao's philosophy to build a basic comprehensive unit of local life large enough to have the manpower and financial resources needed for modern economic development with a significant degree of self-sufficiency (including modern agriculture and small and medium industries to meet mainly local needs), yet small enough to enable the population to maintain group contact and to effectively participate in the local political process with a modified democratic structure ("democratic centralism") so that local initiative of the individual and small groups would not be stifled under an intensively centralized hierarchical system. If the latter is true, the report of transforming cities like Shanghai into huge communes (like the Paris commune) would be a significant subject for serious study, for then if the policy is adopted, all of China would become a conglomeration of urban and rural communes. each of which would be a relatively autonomous and comprehensive unit of local life encompassing economic production and consumption (distribution), political power, and military defense. Such units would be quite free to develop their local initiative without being subjected to the rigid control of the central power. Another fact of possible relevance is the decentralization of control over industrial enterprises after the Great Leap, but it is not entirely clear whether this is Mao's decision or that of his opposition, for some of the officials known to be connected with the measure are now objects of purge in the Cultural Revolution for opposing the Great Leap.

[14] *Jen-min jih-pao*, September 15, 1966.

one of his Communist contacts that the Cultural Revolution confined its attack to policy-makers in the party and in the government, but left alone executive and technical personnel so as to avoid disrupting the administrative system of the country. Thus, the Red Guards' function is to effect a change of policy-makers in the party and government, but not to alter the pattern of, or to substitute themselves for, the existing system of political organization.[15]

There may be certain non-transient aspects to the Red Guards. In recent years Mao and his aging associates talked of training successors for the Communist revolution.[16] With the party leadership structure under revisionist control, Mao perhaps would not look to it as the proper source of supply of successors who would continue to lead the revolution toward the original idealistic goal. This suggests the possibility that Mao may use the Red Guards as a training ground for the unspoiled youth from whom successors for the revolution's leadership may eventually arise. Hence the name "the Long March units" (*ch'ang-cheng tui*) for many Red Guard groups walking long distances from their home territories to Peking or other cities in simulation of the historic Long March, and many other measures designed to revive the spartan Yenan spirit among the young. All these may be relevant to the purpose of the Cultural Revolution: to check revisionism and to reassert the ideological goal of communism. In this light, the Red Guards may have long-term significance for the political leadership and ideological destination of the country in addition to their immediate function as a tool to help Mao recapture political power.

### Revisionism in the Party Leadership

It has been stated above that turning the rampaging Red Guards on the policy-making leaders is an act which aims at eliminating revisionism, not at destroying the party or government organizations. This is based

[15] This is again a tentative assumption, supported by a cursory survey of the Communist press and by unsystematic verbal information from Chinese travelers from the mainland into Hong Kong. Further research is needed to substantiate the assumption, such as a comprehensive statistical survey of all those who were purged in the campaign in terms of policy-making role (how many were policy-makers and how many technical or administrative personnel), or a detailed study of critical cases of party or government agencies to find out the extent to which the policy-making and the executive personnel has been affected.

[16] See the reiteration of this need in the decision of the Eleventh Plenary Session of the Central Committee of the Eighth Party Congress, *Jen-min jih-pao*, August 13, 1966.

on the Maoist charge that the leaders in power are revisionists. Thus declared the Communist theoretical journal, *Hung-ch'i* (Red Flag):

> When the capitalist class wants to capture political power, they must work through the extremely small number of leaders in power who follow the capitalist ideological line, these leaders are counter-revolutionary revisionists. . . . Wherever they succeed in usurping the power of leadership, what they practice is capitalist dictatorship. They use their usurped power to protect capitalistic rightists and to suppress proletarian leftists. If they are not deposed . . . they will one day arise to usurp the leadership power of our whole party and state, and change the color of our country. Concentrate all our might to attack a tiny minority of capitalistic rightists, to attack the faction of party leaders who follow the capitalistic line, this is the main direction of our struggle.[17]

If *Hung-ch'i*'s charge is couched in generalized terms, the Communist press abounds with specific accusations to uphold the point. The Ministry of Propaganda is one of the organizations where the "revisionists" or "capitalistic rightists" gained control of leadership, and Chou Yang, the vice-minister in charge of literature and publications, was identified as the ringleader and singled out for "struggle." The press and the group meetings throughout the country poured venom on this aging, seasoned leader of the Communist party. Thus charged a "big-character poster":

> Chou Yang . . . Lin Mo-han and others formed a clique, utilized their authority to attack and expel the proletarian revolutionary group, to put in their own trusted lieutenants, to monopolize many agencies of literary work, and to practice their counter-revolutionary black line. . . . Chou Yang placed Hsia Yen, T'ien Han, Yang Han-sheng, Shao Ch'üan-lin and other black-line literary big names of the 1930's in leading posts in the Ministry of Culture and in various member organizations of the United Literary Association. . . . This is a group of typical representatives of the capitalist class. . . . In 1959 in Shanghai, Yuan Wen-ch'u was criticized for serious political error. But Chou Yang and Lin Mo-han put him together with Hsia Yen and Ch'en Huang-mei to gain control of the Association of Motion Picture Workers, so that they could promote and execute Chou Yang's revisionist policy in literary work, and commit anti-party, anti-socialist and anti-Mao Tse-tung criminal activities in the motion picture field.[18]

[17] *Hung-ch'i* (editorial), no. 12 (September 17, 1966).

[18] *Jen-min jih-pao*, August 4, 1966.

Another accusation charged Chou Yang with using his authority as vice-minister of propaganda in 1962 in Ch'angch'un

> to change the leadership of the Ch'angch'un Motion Picture Company, expel the revolutionary leftists, and put in Lin Shen and other agents of the capitalist class to gain dictatorial control in the company. From then on, [many motion pictures] peddling capitalist and revisionist thoughts were made in succession under the leadership of the Lin Shen group, and these pictures poisoned the mind of the entire country.[19]

While we have concrete accounts of accusations against the leadership of cultural organizations, we lack similar accounts on the party organization involving highly placed leaders. But the instances involving the cultural field have indicated the basic nature of the Cultural Revolution in its struggle against the revisionist leadership which is accused of betraying the ideological goal of communism.

## Issues of Revisionism

A central problem of the Cultural Revolution is the content of revisionism and the way in which it threatens the basic Communist goal. Some knowledge of this problem can be gained by analyzing the outstanding issues which constitute the general charge of revisionism. We will list a few selected issues from the limited available data to indicate the nature of the problem. The issues are intricately interrelated and cannot be treated as completely separate entities.

### Subjectivism and Reality

The most persistent charge against the revisionists is the generalized and all-inclusive crime of anti-Maoism. While a large number of issues are subsumed under this accusation, one with general significance is the dissident's characterization of Mao's thoughts and policies as a product of subjectivism in disregard of reality. This general line of opposition against Mao seems to have developed in the wake of the fiasco of the Great Leap. After 1958, especially in the years of 1961 and 1962, the charge of subjectivism was openly expressed in the Communist literature by cultural as well as political leaders.

A party theoretician, Hsiao Shu, wrote in *Hung-ch'i:* "It is incorrect just to follow one's own desire in deciding on or enacting a certain task without considering the necessary physical conditions, or to undertake a certain task now while such a task only holds certain possibility in the

[19] *Kuang-ming jih-pao,* August 7, 1966.

future."[20] Sun Yeh-fang, former director of the Economic Research Institute in the Chinese Academy of Sciences, laid down a long series of written and verbal charges against Mao's policies, especially concerning the communes and the Great Leap. Such grandiose schemes, in Sun's views, were impractical subjective thoughts, for they did not have the support of needed production capacity and modern techniques, they disregarded the economic law of value or the principle of gaining maximum results at minimum costs, and they ignored cost accounting. Sun proposed, among many other measures, the emphasis on profit as a criterion in socialist economic administration: "In the state's relation to enterprises, it is necessary to control only the value criterion (profit criterion), all other things can be left alone to the initiative of the enterprises, allowing them to act under the law of value to turn out products of low prices and high quality."[21] Urging the use of incentives to stimulate individual efforts in production, he wrote: "The use of materialistic incentives yielded some good results when Khrushchev proposed it in 1953 for the development of agriculture."[22]

This tenet, in the Maoist view, promotes individualism in opposition to collectivism, and it allows the law of value and free market to take control of the operation of the economy in opposition to socialistic planning. If successfully carried out, these steps would lead straight to the restoration of capitalism. The same revisionist charge is laid against Ch'en Yün, former leader in Communist finance, who expressed similar criticism against the communes. Ch'en supported the restoration of private plots, advocated the peasants' retention of a portion of the produce above the assigned quota, and proposed the extension of the production quota contract system down to the peasant household (as farming unit), even by dividing the land down to the unit of the household.[23] Party leader Teng Hsiao-p'ing also proposed restoration of individual farming to replace collectivism. These measures of individualistic incentives, according to the Maoists, would basically alter the system of collective, socialist economy.

[20] Hsiao Shu, "Objective Conditions and Subjective Effort," *Hung-ch'i*, no. 8 (April, 1961).

[21] Kung Wen-sheng, "Sun Yeh-fang's Theories Are Revisionist Nonsense," *Jen-min jih-pao*, August 8, 1966. This summarizes Sun's views expressed from 1958 to 1963.

[22] *Ibid.*

[23] An anonymous article, "Ch'en Yün as Spearhead for Restoration of Capitalism" in *Ts'ai-mou hung-ch'i* [Red Flag Journal of Finance and Trade], February 23, 1967; reprinted in *Ming pao* (Hong Kong), April 17, 1967.

## Political Primacy vs. Diversification of Interests and Objective Reality

A dominant concept in Mao's thought is *cheng-chih kua-shuai,* supremacy of politics, or political primacy. Theoretically, it demands that political considerations take precedent over any other considerations in the formulation of policies or in the guidance of action. But in practice, it became the concept of complete dominance of politics to the exclusion of other considerations in many aspects of life in Communist China. To the Maoists, this serves to keep the population keyed up for socialist reconstruction, for continued class struggles at home and anti-imperialist struggles abroad.

But to the revisionists, political primacy often becomes impractical, irrelevant, or unnecessary to realistic situations, and as such it offers obstacles to the intelligent development of the socialist order. Chou Yang, for instance, opposed applying the notion of political primacy to publication policy. He said: "Politics will lose its meaning if we keep talking about politics at every breath." Hence he limited publication of manuscripts dealing with class struggle and other political subjects. Under his influence, the themes of motion pictures disregarded Mao's policy of making art serve politics exclusively. He insisted: "Motion pictures should be entertaining and wholesome; it is not necessary that they must have strong political character." The lighthearted, entertaining pictures made under his influence did not touch the subjects of class struggle or the socialist revolution.[24]

For Hsia Yen, former vice-minister of culture in charge of motion pictures, political primacy resulted in sterility and monotony: "Our present motion pictures contain nothing but 'canons of revolution' and 'ways of war.' We will never produce new products by following this line." He therefore proposed to "depart from the canons and rebel against the ways," to achieve new creations and diversity of subject matters, and to stress the line against war so that "the world can bask in the sunlight of peace" and "infants can slumber in the cradles, and mothers and wives may no longer live in nightmares." Lin Mo-han, an important member of Chou Yang's group, expressed the same feeling: "Motion pictures are either about war or tear-shedding. This greatly depresses the people's spirit."[25] Party leader Teng Hsiao-p'ing took a

[24] *Jen-min jih-pao,* July 15, 1966.

[25] "Thoroughly Expose the Anti-Party Crimes of Hsia Yen, the 'Old Man' of Motion Pictures," *Jen-min jih-pao,* November 10, 1966.

similar stand: "Motion pictures show only troops and fighting. . . . This is not permitted to be shown, and that is not permitted to be shown."[26]

In the field of economic development, Sun Yeh-fang charged that the party line of political primacy caused the Great Leap disaster, for "political primacy was used to replace objective economic laws, and political reasoning was substituted for economic reasoning."[27] The line of political primacy, if indiscriminately applied, violates objective reality.

To the Maoists, this rebellion against the concept of political primacy is tantamount to surrendering the Communist cause, for it dampens the masses' political enthusiasm and dedication and depresses the spartan spirit of the revolution. To diversify the subject matters of the motion pictures and to provide non-political "lighthearted entertainment" is to "popularize capitalist thought and style of life" and to restore capitalism. To give up the line of class struggle and war is to turn one's back on Mao's teachings that revolutions everywhere rely on armed struggle for success, and that the promotion of peace serves only to divert the Chinese revolution on to the road of peaceful transformation toward revisionism. The charge of the lack of economic realism in the political primacy concept is viewed as an attempt to install the line of supremacy of capitalistic politics. To alter the line of political primacy is nothing less than to abandon the idealistic goal of the Communist revolution.

## Redness or Expertise

The argument of "redness or expertise" which has been raging in Communist China for some years is a corollary to the issue of political primacy, and it is related to the problem of goal orientation of the Communist cause. The issue began to take shape in the 1950's with the argument on the primacy of technological modernization of the Communist army versus the importance of political dedication of the troops. The insistence on technological primacy was among the five crimes for which old Chu Teh was attacked by the Red Guards.[28] Implicit in this accusation was Chu Teh's view of the superiority of expertise over redness in the development of the Communist army.

[26] *Hung-ch'i chan-pao* [Red Flag Battle Bulletin]; reprinted in *Ming pao* (Hong Kong), January 3, 1967.

[27] See note 21.

[28] "Grave Crimes of Chu Teh, the Great Warlord and the Great Ambitious Politician," *Chan pao* [Battle Bulletin], no. 6 (February 24, 1967); reprinted in *Ming pao* (Hong Kong), April 26, 1967.

Following the economic failure of the Great Leap, a widespread charge against the Maoists was their imposition of a subjective plan on the country, their ignorance of technical knowledge of economics, and finally the meddling of party political officers in technical operations of economic enterprises. The Maoist rebuttal was that, if the party political officers were pulled out of the enterprises and the "experts" were left alone to their technical jobs, the latter would revert to pre-Communist corruption, inefficiency, and disorganization. On the surface and in their formal statements, both sides grant importance to redness as well as expertise in the development of the socialist society, but in actuality, the issue was one of dominance by one or the other of the two sets of leaders, the political officers or the experts.

This is clearly indicated in the accusation against Chou Yang, the vice-minister of propaganda. In the Maoist account, Chou Yang opposed party leadership of literary work and regarded this as "administrative interference" with what should be experts' tasks. He suggested "joint leadership" to replace complete dominance by party political officers: "In reconstruction work, the mass line has to be combined with the scientific and technical personnel; such a mass line should be guided by scientists." Chou was accused of opposing thought reform for literary workers, of following the capitalistic line of "expertise without redness," and of stating to a meeting of engineers and technicians in Port Arthur and Dairen: "Staff ranks should be determined by technical knowledge and skill alone without any other qualifications." To the Maoists, this is in opposition to the requirement of political qualification in the employment of staff members and is a rejection of the supremacy of proletarian political power. This would lead the young intellectuals to refuse thought reform and to boycott Chairman Mao's writings. Chou's proposition of "joint leadership" under the guidance of scientists is regarded as an attempt to use "reactionary capitalistic experts' leadership" to capture the power of the party and to establish "hegemony" by the capitalistic class.

> Proletarian literature and art is a part of the entire revolutionary enterprise. It is the wheels and screws in the revolutionary machinery. It must be placed under the party's absolute leadership in order for it to serve the interests of the workers, peasants and soldiers, and to serve the interest of proletarian politics.[29]

[29] Kung Wei-tung, "What Poison Did Chou Yang Spread in the Northeast?" *Kuang-ming jih-pao*, August 7, 1966.

The elevation of the experts to a controlling position, free from interference by party political officers, is regarded as a policy leading to dominance by bourgeois intellectuals, the destruction of the party's political leadership and the eventual restoration of capitalism. It is interesting to speculate whether this threat of "expert dictatorship" has any relation to Mao's order for workers, peasants, and soldiers to learn each other's trades, which is an attempt to reduce the importance of experts by minimizing specialization, at least on the operatives' level.[30]

## Liberalization of Party Control

At stake in the "redness or expertise" issue is the control of the country by the Communist party or by the bourgeois experts, and this would determine the nature of the future social order. Hence, a corollary of the "redness or expertise" issue is the question of liberalization of party control.

In the Cultural Revolution, this question is reflected in the attack on the literary work of Chou Yang. Chou expressed dissatisfaction with the "narrowing of the road" of literary creation [by being restricted to the party line] and wanted to "widen the road and the vision." He proposed that authors ought to write on the spontaneous democratic revolutionary struggles during the 109 years between 1840 and 1949, struggles which were waged all without the Communist party leadership. In painting, Chou opposed Mao's restriction of subject matter to "workers, peasants and soldiers," and he initiated in the Central Art Academy a studio system in which the opinions of experts and authorities completely prevailed, with the Communist party leadership thoroughly excluded. "This put into practice what the rightists failed to realize, namely, administration of schools by professors." He further suggested that the Association of Artists should be an independent organization in which the Communist party ought to form only a part of the leadership and non-party members ought to constitute more than half of the leaders.[31]

Lo Jui-ch'ing, former chief of staff of the Liberation Army, took the same stand as early as 1958 when he stated: "Counter-revolutionaries have become very few in number. The main function of our basic political power is no longer class struggle but economic and cultural recon-

[30] Decision of the Eleventh Plenary Session of the Central Committee of the Eighth Party Congress, *Jen-min jih-pao*, August 13, 1966.

[31] See note 27, and *Jen-min jih-pao*, July 15, 1966.

struction." To him, party dictatorship was gradually becoming unnecessary, for class struggle was becoming a matter of the past.[32]

But in the Maoist view, if the party yielded its controlling power it would depart from the Communist ideological goal and would lead the country down the road of revisionism.

## Promotion of Traditional Culture and Revisionism

Another prominent target for the Cultural Revolution is the promotion of traditional culture under the leadership of Chou Yang, Hsia Yen, and Teng T'o, who held power in the propaganda and cultural ministries. They proposed to reaffirm the traditional "moral heritage" as support for the social order. They published a large volume of reprints of traditional literature including classics, philosophy, history, prose, poetry, and drama. Traditional paintings like those of Ch'i Pai-shih were printed in large numbers for the popular market. In the field of the theater, the group was accused of popularizing feudal and capitalistic art, and of following the policy of coexistence of traditional plays, revised historical plays, and modern (socialistic) drama.[33] Under this influence, traditional plays accounted for 38 per cent of all motion pictures produced in 1962. In the same year, the Ministry of Culture produced more than sixty traditional stage plays, all singing the praise of emperors, mandarins, and "talents and beauties."[34] On the other hand, production of modern drama reflecting the revolutionary struggle of the workers, peasants, and soldiers faced obstruction and attack.

The promotion of traditional culture, which reached its height in the early 1960's, is a complex movement of multiple significance, but it is clear that it tends to "revise" the general line of revolutionary development as defined by Mao. In the Tenth Plenary Session of the Central Committee of the Eighth Party Congress, Mao reiterated his warning, "Don't ever forget class struggle."[35] But a major intention of reviving traditional culture is to unify the people through the appeal of common historical sentiments and nationalistic pride, thereby mitigating class conflicts and enhancing internal peace. The use of traditional cul-

[32] *Chan pao,* January 30, 1967; reprinted in *Ming pao* (Hong Kong), May 19, 1967.

[33] "Chou Yang Trying to Wreck the Great Cultural Revolution," in the "big-character poster" of the Central Propaganda Department; reprinted in *Jenmin jih-pao,* August 4, 1966.

[34] "Big-character poster" of the Ministry of Culture; reprinted in *Hsing-tao jih-pao* (Hong Kong), August 3, 1966.

[35] See note 29.

ture as a unifying influence to nullify class struggle came in the same general period as the new theme of unity in philosophy against the Marxian concept of class contradiction, in an intellectual attempt to negate the basic justification for class struggle.[36]

The promotion of traditional culture, in the Maoist view, also has the effect of diluting the revolutionary spirit and crowding out revolutionary content from literature and art. To be true to the revolutionary party line, culture must have only a single purpose: the reflection of the struggle of the workers, peasants, and soldiers for the socialist revolution and socialist construction. Any digression from this policy will weaken the masses' dedication to the revolution, and the concurrent production of traditional, revised historical, and modern plays has this diluting effect. This is perhaps what lies behind Mao's statement in 1964: "For the past 15 years the literary leaders basically failed to follow the party policy; they became mandarins; they did not make contact with the workers, peasants and soldiers, or describe the socialist revolution and reconstruction. In the recent several years, they even deteriorated to the brink of revisionism."[37] In making this charge, Mao was perhaps not forgetting that the publication of his own collected works was severely restricted while traditional literature was pouring out from the printing press—revolutionary content was being crowded out of literature and art by the promotion of traditional culture and diversification of interests!

All this is one phase of another long-standing issue—"whom does literature serve?" The diversification of contents forms a part of Chou Yang's slogan, "literature for the whole people" (ch'üan-min wen-i). Besides serving the cause of the proletarian revolution, literature (and culture as a whole) should serve the interests of all classes including technical personnel and should provide them with non-political entertainment and moral elevation. But from the Maoist view, literature and art have a very definite class nature; they are a part of either proletarian culture or the capitalistic culture; if they do not serve the proletarian cause, they will serve the interests of the capitalistic class and thus help the restoration of the capitalistic social order.

[36] See, for example, Yang Hsien-chen's theory of "combining two into one," (which postulates that a unifying relationship exists between two opposing aspects of any phenomenon), in "New Polemics on the Philosophical Front," *Hung-ch'i*, no. 16 (August 31, 1964); Chou Ku-ch'eng's theory that there is an undifferentiated state of matter where there is no contradiction, in Ju-hsin, "Critique of the Philosophical Foundation of Chou Ku-ch'eng's View of Art," *Hung-ch'i*, no. 15 (August 15, 1964).

[37] See note 31.

## Conclusion

A cursory survey of available data indicates that the Cultural Revolution represents the culmination of a long series of outstanding issues between Mao's lines and the opposition. These issues become focused on the central problem of revisionism, which would change the course of development and the final goal of the Communist revolution. The dramatic action of the Red Guards and their furious accusations are a part of the Maoist effort to dislodge a "handful of revisionists" from power in the party and the government so as to restore the ideological goal orientation of the Communist revolution and the correct policies as conceived in Mao's thought. The issue of Mao's "personality cult" is undoubtedly a central one in the Cultural Revolution, but it is inextricably woven into the substantive issues of his thought on the goal and policies of the Communist revolution, so that personality cult and opposition to revisionism merge into a single issue in actuality, even if the two are conceptually separable.

By mid-1967, the craze for Mao Tse-tung has swept the entire country. Giant portraits of Mao glare down on the throngs at every street intersection, and songs praising him swell above the hubbub at every public gathering. The personality cult is nowhere more evident. But the copies of Mao's writings in every hand and Mao's quotations on every lip emphasize his insistent demand that the people, particularly the young generation, abide by his "canons and ways," that they keep the revolution's goal forever in view, and that they stamp out revisionist thoughts and style of living.

Occasional return of pre-Communist comforts—even luxuries—especially among the Communist leadership, seems to worry Mao who regards it as a detraction from the spartan spirit and dedication needed to carry the revolution to its fruition. This is shown in the wall poster attacking the "August First School" for the high-ranking cadres' children in Peking. The appointments in the school are described as lavish and the students' life as corrupt. The youngsters wear fine woolens, eat luxury foods, and walk around with cigarettes in their mouths. In addition to the aristocratic living furnished free by the school, each student gets from 20 to 25 yuan for monthly spending, a sharp contrast to the total monthly earnings of a farmer, for example, which is about 12 yuan. "This is an ideal hotbed for nurturing the seedlings of capitalism. . . . How can such youngsters ever learn the lesson of hardship and thrift needed by the revolution?"[38] Such a view explains the occasional de-

[38] *High School Cultural Revolution Bulletin*, February 10, 1967; reprinted in *Ming pao* (Hong Kong), April 20, 1967.

struction of what are regarded as luxury articles in stores and in private homes by the rampaging Red Guards.

Available evidence, some of which has been presented above, gives a rather convincing ring to the major charges that the "revisionists" did tend to divert the course of the Communist revolution from its purely proletarian character, and did revise the ideological goal of a classless society by catering to the interests of different classes, especially the intellectual and technical groups. The idealism of a planned society is threatened by the revisionist call for less party control, greater individual initiative and freedom, profit criteria, materialistic incentives, and recognition of the laws of value and prices so fundamental to the capitalistic economy. These revisionist propositions and activities are involved in the issues in the cultural fields, where the basic arguments and accusations were set forth in the early stage of the Cultural Revolution.

There seems little doubt that revisionism is the genuine central issue of this convulsive campaign which began with a purge in the cultural circles and swept on to involve the highest political leaders in a fierce power struggle, especially after the alleged "February Revolt" plot to overthrow Mao by force.[39] What remains uncertain is the magnitude of the revisionist faction—whether they are only "a handful" of leaders in power as stated by the Maoists, or are very extensive in number at all levels of Chinese Communist society, from the pinnacle of party and government power down to the ranks of peasants and workers. The revisionists' numerical weight and their strategic distribution (geographical, economic, and political) will be important determinants of the final outcome of the current struggle. We know little about these factors, but research in this direction will have major predictive value.

Available information, limited in quantity and inadequate in quality, seems to indicate that Mao has considerable control in the party central organization in Peking, but the relative strength of the two contesting factions seems indecisive for the moment in the middle and lower echelons of the party leadership as well as among the "masses," especially in the provinces. An additional point here is that we have not dealt with the question of the practicality and realistic nature of Mao's ideological vision and his single-minded unrelenting drive for its realization. An analysis of this phase of the problem may throw light on the

[39] *Chan pao*, January 30, 1967; reprinted in *Ming pao* (Hong Kong), May 19, 1967. This accused Lo Jui-ch'ing, former chief of staff of the People's Liberation Army, of participating in the "February Revolt" plot as well as following a "capitalistic military line" stressing his personal gain and adventurism.

possible tendency of the "masses" and the middle and lower echelons of party leadership toward the struggle against revisionism, for they may well find in revisionism a practical solution to their problems on the operational level.

The central issue of goal revision—what kind of society is to be built in China now and in the foreseeable future—in the Cultural Revolution tends to support the assumption that goal instability is an inherent characteristic of major revolutions which must face the vicissitudes of unforeseeable developments brought on by bold and imaginative plans involving the destiny of a whole society being put into experimental operation. The constant need for adjustment to the reality of rapidly shifting circumstances seems to make goal alteration inevitable, at least so far as immediate and intermediate goals are expressed in policies for the present and the foreseeable future, even if the ultimate ideological goal stands unchanged. An intriguing question here is whether the conflicts generated by goal instability would become so disruptive that they may cause the whole revolutionary movement to fail—to be overcome by an antagonistic force of a different ideology. Insofar as the case of the Cultural Revolution is concerned, present evidence does not show serious disintegration of the Communist regime, for the government administrative organization seems to have remained intact, and the disorganized party apparatus could be re-stabilized by putting Maoist elements into all ranks of party leadership. But this question poses a complex theoretical and empirical problem for which our present state of knowledge offers no reliable answer.

Franz Schurmann

# 9

# The Attack of the
# Cultural Revolution on
# Ideology and Organization

## Introduction

I had been asked to write this paper on the subject of "organization and social control." A year earlier, this task would not have posed great difficulties, but the eruption of the Great Proletarian Cultural Revolution has made doubtful what seemed clear only a short time before. The Red Guards, who embody the spirit of the Cultural Revolution, seem to be the antithesis of everything the Chinese taught about organization: flying squads of excited students who head out from some base point to force big and little party cadres to *chien-t'ao* ("confess") before the masses; once the party committee has crumbled before their attacks, they dissolve back into their schools.[1] As a result, organization is left weakened and social control is put in jeopardy. The Russians have been saying—loudly and voluminously—that the Red Guards are destroying the Chinese Communist Party and that loyal workers and peasants have been resisting. In Hong Kong, people shrug their shoulders and say *fa-feng* ("crazy"). A common question abroad is—Why is Mao throwing

[1] The Red Guards appear to have begun as student groups in the great universities of Peking formed to denounce party cadres of those universities who were in league with P'eng Chen, head of the Peking City party organization. Though as many as a million student Red Guards existed by August, it was not until August 18, after the Eleventh Plenum (where opposition to Mao was voiced) that a great demonstration on T'ien-an-men Square made them into a national movement. Though the Russians have carefully refrained from calling them Red Guards (either using the Chinese term *hung-wei-ping* or *krasnaia okhrana*), the Chinese apparently did not intend patterning them after the Red worker guards of the Russian Revolution. The later are called *ch'ih-wei-tui* in Chinese histories of the Russian Revolution, and clearly refer to workers groups. In Shanghai, worker Red Guards (both loyal to Mao and opposed to him) appeared who called themselves *ch'ih-wei-tui*. See *Jen-min jih-pao* [Peoples Daily], January 9, 1967.

it all away? After all, six years of careful rebuilding of the economy and the growing threat of the Vietnam war had given the Chinese government widespread support from its people within the country and from millions of Chinese abroad. Many Americans, impressed by the Chinese Communists' extraordinarily powerful structure of organization and their sophisticated methods of social control, wondered whether China was not committing political suicide for some obscure reason.

All of us think in certain categories, and we tend to analyze events according to those categories. The danger in this is that these operational categories can subtly turn into ideology, that is, a systematic set of ideas for explaining any and all phenomena which jells into a fixed outlook. The corrective to this is to examine one's premises critically. So I would suggest that we begin our analysis of the Cultural Revolution by examining the ideas "organization" and "social control."

In a larger sense, every people is a victim of its own ideology until reason and consciousness show that the gap between ideology and reality is too great to be ignored any longer. Thus it took us as Americans a long time to realize that, far from still being a nation of Jeffersonian individualists, we are organization men. We have built the most highly organized society in human history, and recently have come to understand that organization has a power of its own, regardless of the will of the men who direct it and who work in it. Our organizations take the form of large-scale corporate, administrative, and military structures. Though each relates to different sectors of our national life (economic, political, and international), the forms of organization are becoming increasingly alike, as Morris Janowitz points out in his studies of the American military.[2] Organization has become large-scale because of the nature of our economy: a highly integrated and increasingly centralized system of planning, production, and exchange which mobilizes factors of production on a world-wide scale. And as our administrative and military systems have taken on the characteristics of the economy, so they too have generated similar forms of organization. As a result, we have changed our traditional suspicion of organization into an attitude of fascination—we begin to see in organization a set of tools by which ambitious goals can be obtained, much as we earlier regarded the power of machines.[3]

[2] *The Professional Soldier* (Glencoe, Ill.: Free Press Paperback, 1960), pp. 21–36.

[3] This curious fascination for the manipulative power of organization can be found in much contemporary writing on the subject. See Douglas Pike, *Viet Cong* (Cambridge: M.I.T. Press, 1966).

Thus, as we examine the Great Proletarian Cultural Revolution, we must take into account our attitudes toward "organization," for "organization" is what appears to have suffered most at the hands of the Red Guards. Philip Selznick defines organization as "an *expendable tool*, a rational instrument to do a job." But his description of the spirit of organization is more appealing: "a certain bareness, a lean, no-nonsense system of consciously co-ordinated activities."[4] In its most primitive form, organization is a working body of men all of whom work together in a division of labor to acquire or produce some particular object or goal. In its more complex forms, the objects and goals multiply so that it often is no longer clear what the original objectives were. But no matter how complex organization becomes, it must always remain goal-minded. This is so, I would suggest, because of the nature of modern societies, which are condemned to expand or face the danger of contraction, without ever finding that equilibrium which classical economists and modern sociologists see as the essence of economic and social systems respectively.[5] If constant expansion then too is the driving force of organization, its concrete expression is the striving for objectives (objects and goals). Organization is our collective human tool by which we try to achieve the ambitious and complex objectives of contemporary life.

Unlike machines, the component elements of organization are human, and so not subject to the scientific laws of matter (human beings too may be subject to scientific laws of behavior, but we are far from having "discovered" them). Thus the masters of organization must face the problem of "compliance," to use Amitai Etzioni's term—that is, how do you get men to do what you want them to do over long periods of time?[6] In earlier periods of our modern organizational history, coercion

[4] *Leadership in Administration* (Evanston, Ill.: Row, Peterson, 1957), p. 5.

[5] Much of contemporary sociology assumes that all social systems tend toward integration, hence stabilization. That may be true, but it seems to me equally valid to assume the opposite, namely, that modern social systems undergo constant change, of which one form is expansion and contraction. Selznick, in his dichotomy of "organization" and "institution," has posed the two alternatives. If society is "institution," then indeed the tendency toward integration would appear to be there. But if society is still essentially "organization," then I suggest that it is change and not integration which still marks us. It has been said that the Chinese Communists have changed the basic values of their society from "harmony" to "struggle." They have merely realized what I believe to be a fact of all modern and modernizing societies.

[6] *A Comparative Analysis of Complex Organizations* (New York: Free Press of Glencoe, 1961), pp. xi ff.

was the usual way of eliciting compliance. Since man had to eat, wages, particularly in a context of a plentiful labor supply, were sufficient to get him to comply. Now things have become more complicated, and more sophisticated methods of eliciting compliance have to be used. This takes us to the second term in the subject of this paper: *social control*. As sociologists generally use the term today, social control refers not only to external mechanisms for keeping people in line with the requisites of society, but to internal psychological mechanisms which lead to self-discipline, so that the individual of his own accord avoids wrong and does right.[7] Social control thus is a product of socialization: internalization of values within the family, inculcation of public values and norms through education, and finally adjustment to the work situation. Social control and, in a broader sense, socialization serve to bring about compliant individuals. Socialization is accomplished through a long process of training and education by which the individual comes to accept the authority of certain values and norms.

Perhaps the most important contribution of sociology to the subject of organization has been the study of bureaucracy and bureaucratization. Bureaucratization has been generally seen as a process of organizational institutionalization marked by the acceptance of legitimate authority on the part of all those in the organizational structure.[8] Workers thus no longer regard their administrative superiors just as holders of coercive power over them, but see them as men who hold to values and norms which they themselves believe in. The conceptual distinction between *power* and *authority* is important here. Power is the capacity of a man (or an organization) to elicit compliance from individuals to achieve his (or its) particular goals. Authority, on the other hand, is the generalized status of an individual (or an organization) which makes it possible to elicit compliance from individuals whether there are objectives to be attained or not. Power means that I can make others obey me. Authority means that others respect me and will regard seriously

[7] Talcott Parsons sees social control as deviance-combatting mechanisms within the personality of the individual which go hand in hand with the mechanisms of socialization. But social control and socialization both have the same purpose: to elicit compliance from the individual to the requisites of society. See *The Social System* (Glencoe, Ill.: Free Press, 1951), pp. 206–7.

[8] Note Reinhard Bendix's formulation of bureaucracy: " 'Bureaucracy' refers to the universal tendency of men who are employed in hierarchical organizations to obey directives and to identify their own interests and ideas with the organization and with all those persons in it who share this identification" (*Work and Authority in Industry* [New York: John Wiley and Sons, 1956], p. xx).

my words and actions. Power is a matter of the moment.[9] It vanishes when the elements which make up the moment are no longer present. Thus the power of a captain over his soldiers vanishes the moment he is

[9] While the distinction between power and authority has been widely recognized in sociology, I like Robert Nisbet's formulation: "Power, I conceive as something external and based upon force. Authority, on the other hand, is rooted in the statuses, functions, and allegiances which are the components of any association. Authority is indeed indistinguishable from organization, and perhaps the chief means by which organization, and a sense of organization, becomes a part of human personality. Authority, like power, is a form of constraint, but, unlike power, it is based ultimately upon the consent of those under it; that is, it is conditional. Power arises only when authority breaks down" (*Community and Power* [New York: Galaxy, 1962], p. xii).

Two points of disagreement need to be made, however. First, I see power as the chief instrument by which organization secures compliance from its members. Organization is an hierarchical structure of roles, into each of which power and constraints are built. A private will obey a sergeant first and foremost because of the power invested in the sergeant's role. However, organizations, to survive, all strive to generate authority, that is, generalized status and respect. Thus organization hopes that the private will obey the sergeant not just because of the latter's power, but because he is a leader, a man of experience, a man worthy of respect. It is here that the shared values of sergeant and private create a bond of authority and compliance. Such values, I would suggest, come either from a traditional ethos or a new ideology. Bendix's study of work and authority in industry argues that the traditional values of Protestant Christianity helped managers establish their authority in the early phases of British and American industrialization. In Russia and China, ideology has been used for this same purpose. The second point of disagreement relates to the last sentence in Nisbet's formulation. I do agree with his implication that power and authority act against each other (he would say, in effect, that if the sergeant cannot get what he wants by persuasion, he will use the power of command). However, I feel that power is always present in an organizational situation. Power is the surest means of reaching a goal, whereas authority is more indirect, more time-consuming. Power and authority constitute an ever-shifting dialectic which goes through organization. Too much power means that the organization becomes a structure of naked coercion. Too much authority means that the organization will settle down to sluggish routine, excellent in its human relations but poor in its goal achievement.

Bendix, I believe, sees the institutionalization of legitimate authority as the process whereby social structures achieve stability. I agree with this, but I also believe that the goal-oriented character of modern society (the expansion-contraction dynamics) is so strong that forces will always arise to prevent such institutionalization from going too far. The form that this takes is an erosion of statuses, which are the concrete expression of the institutionalization of legitimate authority. When this happens, the status elites (Weber's *Stände*) either fall or turn into a true power elite, ruling by power and constraint and shorn of authority. I would suggest that even the United States of America is no stranger to this process.

released from the army, but the authority of an educated professional accompanies him wherever he goes. His authority derives from the values of knowledge, wisdom, and skill which all in society accept. Since it is authority with its values and not power with its coercion which creates our sociological form of social control, current theses on bureaucratization imply a conception of society with significant elements of stabilization built into it.

Whatever success socialization and social control have in establishing authority and stabilizing social behavior, organization remains a power structure concerned primarily with the achievement of objectives. Since power is necessarily coercive, even when exercised in a benign manner, the fact that social control is there to assist organization to make its members more compliant to the demands of the organization appears to have given society a major additional option to do away with the disruptive effects arising from the exercise of power. One of the consequences, however, of the growth of authority within the contexts of power-oriented organization is the formation of elites—an increasingly recognizable body of men who, by virtue of their talents and achievements, are accepted as leaders in society, regardless of the particular organizational positions they occupy. Elites are the collective body of men who exercise power and enjoy authority in society.[10]

I think it is fair to say that American academics today are no longer antagonistic to the Soviet Union. The days of Stalinist terror have passed, and Russia appears to have entered a period of *embourgeoisement*. It remains a highly organized country, but humanization has set in. Khrushchev's denunciation of Stalin was accompanied by calls for a

---

[10] This is the key theoretical thesis of this paper. On my conception of elites see *Ideology and Organization in Communist China* (Berkeley: University of California Press, 1966), pp. 1–8. I see the concept of elite as particularly related to the organizational character of modern societies. A true elite has power in some sector of organization (managers, officials, officers, etc.) but also has acquired the authority of status (e.g., respect gained by intellectual and professional education). The spread of organization in contemporary society has vastly increased the volume of public power open to men who desire to wield it. But we must also accept the Weberian argument that all such concrete groups of men (here, the holders of power in organizational sectors) will tend to become "status groups." The essential element in this transformation is "ideas," that is, values, norms, and beliefs which exercise authority over men. Men want not only power and wealth, but also prestige. The traditional Chinese gentry was an ideal example of a true elite. Though there are few examples of true elites in the contemporary world, every human society is affected by the processes of elite formation.

return to "socialist legality," that is the law of rules, a phenomenon essential to the Weberian argument on the formation of a just, legitimate, and routinized society.[11] Russia has its elite, a rather numerous one, namely the Communist Party.[12] Perhaps they constitute a "new class," or they are just the most talented sons and daughters of Soviet society. In any case, they are the people who exercise power in organization and enjoy the authority of status in Russia. They are essentially the products of Soviet education, not just the technical universities, but the party schools which have turned out leaders and administrators like Brezhnev and Kosygin.[13] Since people tend to judge others by their own realities, it is not surprising that the Russians are horrified and angered by what the Chinese are doing to their Communist party. The Russians regard themselves as a successful society, and feel that, in one way or another, all other socialist countries must tread the same path—taking the time factor into consideration. Thus the Chinese appear to be destroying the instrumentalities they developed over the years to become a socialist country as successful as the Soviet Union—they are weakening organization, they are wrecking the schools, the major instrumentality of socialization and social control, and they are grinding their emerging elites into the dust. For the Russians, it is madness or a repetition in China of the terror they once experienced under Stalin.

The reactions of the overseas Chinese are somewhat similar. Confucian elitism remains strong among them, but Western organizational and scientific-technological thinking is equally strong. They are in

[11] Though Weber sees "law" as rooted in the values of Western civilization, and "rules" as derivative from law, his discussion of bureaucracy lays great stress on the importance of rules. In the Soviet Union, legality or the binding effect of rules has grown greatly in recent years, even though the value basis of Soviet ideology is basically anti-legal, as is that of Communist China. Thus it may be that both the rule of law and the law of rules will lead to the same thing: societal integration and stabilization. Cf. Reinhard Bendix, *Max Weber, An Intellectual Portrait* (Garden City, N.Y.: Doubleday Anchor, 1962), pp. 423–24.

[12] See Alex Inkeles and Raymond Bauer, *The Soviet Citizen* (Cambridge, Mass.: Harvard University Press, 1959), p. 323.

[13] Inkeles and Bauer found that social origin played an important role in occupational advancement in the Soviet Union, namely, that children of high-status parents tended to get ahead faster than the children of low-status parents. Fragmentary evidence indicates that this may also be true in China (children of bourgeois parents still are disproportionate to those of worker-peasant parents—a reason for the upheaval in enrollment policies now going on). However, aside from social origin, education appears to be the major determinant of mobility (*ibid.*, p. 85).

favor of China becoming a great nation in the Western sense, but also consider it correct that men of authority and status should once again arise to become the elite leaders of the society. Thus many of them looked with favor on the developments of the last six years: the economy was carefully rebuilt from the shambles of the Great Leap Forward, technical education was again stressed, a more easygoing atmosphere prevailed in the country, and men of achievement were gradually coming to the fore again. Every Chinese of learning remembers the Ch'in and the Han dynasties. The Ch'in gave a fragmented China organizational unity, and the Han gave it authority and stability. While many had hoped that a new Liu Pang would arise to supplant the rulers of China, many others were content that the same transition might take place under the red flag. The Cultural Revolution came as a blow to those hopes. The fantasies which go through their minds, often tied in with historical analogies, are of more cultural than social scientific interest, and are best left unsaid here. *Fa-feng* seems a general reaction—except among many of the young.

American academics, I believe, have always had a certain admiration for the Chinese Communists. After all, the Communists won a war against great odds, rebuilt and unified a sprawling country which had sunk about as far as a great country could, organized the people into an efficient work force, and socialized them with values which once had been predominant in America itself (hard work, discipline, striving for achievement, love of science and technology, and personal virtue). There was fascination for the techniques of thought control, horror at the blue ants, and fear that a new Communist expansionism had come into being. For some China became distantly alien, for others it became the enemy, and for others again it was still basically, despite the ideology, a practical country. Nevertheless, the admiration remained, and for the social scientist, it was because of the Communists' achievement in the areas of organization and social control. It was felt that China, after going through its growing pains, would eventually go the way of the Soviet Union, that is, toward *embourgeoisement.*

## Organization and Social Control in Traditional China

The Chinese now maintain that the Cultural Revolution is combatting, "old, bourgeois, and revisionist thoughts" still left within the society. These three adjectives refer to the three great historical legacies of China: its traditional "feudal" past, its modern Western "semi-colonial" influences, and the heritage of emulation of the Soviet Union.

Each of these three legacies relates to different sectors of Chinese society: the "feudal" to the villages, the "semi-colonial" to the cities, and the "revisionist" to the organized structure of state power (party, government, army). Thus, in examining the effect of the Cultural Revolution on organization and social control, let us look briefly at the forms they took in traditional China.

If we think of organization as goal-oriented structures of power in contrast to institutions (in Selznick's sense), then traditional China (pre-1850) was essentially a land of institutions. Even though clans, associations, and guilds had goal-oriented aspects, over time they turned into institutions bound together more by common values (religion, kinship, occupation) than by common goals. In the realm of state power, however, the elements of organization become more pronounced. But even here, one must admit that the traditional state administrative bureaucracy, despite its elaborate tables of organization, was more of an elite club than a cold, grim organization. Its members ruled more through authority than through power.

Organization existed essentially in only one sector of society—the military. The armies, benefiting from centuries of warfare, were well-organized bodies of men concerned with two main tasks: (1) the securing of China's frontiers (in a defensive or offensive fashion), and (2) the maintenance of domestic stability. The borderland armies were professional, bolstered by convict labor, whereas the garrison troops were often citizen-soldiers, reinforced by varieties of local militias (such as the *pao-chia*). Military and civilian structures were clearly delineated, not just for reasons of Confucian philosophy but because of the fundamentally different orientations of both. The armies were supposed to be prepared for emergencies, such as attack from abroad or an unexpected internal rebellion. The civilian structures, however, were almost entirely oriented to keeping society in an equilibrium. The government made two basic demands on its people: that they keep quiet (the military's task was to assure that) and that they pay whatever quota of taxes was expected of them (the major task of the administrative bureaucracy). Beyond that, the government did not care what the people did (the prevalence of customary law in the administration of justice reflected the government's unconcern with society except in matters directly affecting its interests).[14]

Despite its long tradition of bureaucracy, there were numerically few government officials in traditional China. Nevertheless, the magistrate

[14] On the interests of the state in traditional China, see my *Ideology and Organization in Communist China*, pp. 405–8.

in the local county *yamen* was a man of immense prestige and power. He symbolized the state to the local population and had at his disposal the military and civilian power of the government to enforce his decisions. Thus it is not surprising that each magistracy became a local center of political power. Surrounding the magistrate was a corps of local politicians (*hsü-li*) who had knowledge, connections, and entrenched power like American ward bosses. They were informed on the sociopolitical nature of the county and were indispensable to the magistrate who, according to the principles of Chinese statecraft, had to come from a different region. In addition to the local politicians, the magistrate had close relationships with the local elites, who, by virtue of their official educational attainments, enjoyed the same status as the magistrate. They could enter into personal contacts with him and so had unique access to power to gain decisions favorable to their interests. If there were no uprisings in the county and no wave of complaints (as expressed in law suits), and the correct quota of taxes was remitted upward each year, the magistrate was accounted successful and could await a promotion upward in the bureaucratic hierarchy.[15]

The guiding principle of rule was that authority exercised by stable local elites was the chief instrument of eliciting compliance from the people. Organized power, largely in military and police forms, functioned as a latent option only to be used if all other means of eliciting compliance had failed. Authority had been built up over the centuries through the inculcation of the Confucianist ethos, which at elite levels was imparted through formal education, and at popular levels was imparted through a religious cult (Confucian temples served the poor, and Confucian values were also transmitted through ancestor worship and even by Buddhism and Taoism).[16] The educated man was a symbol of veneration. Whether an aspiring man created his power through wealth or had special access to bureaucratic position, in the long run he sought to give solid foundation to his authority and that of his offspring through education. A man who combined the wealth of land, the power of bureaucratic position, and the authority and prestige of education had it made. In collective form, he created the foundations for *local* elites on whose existence the stability of the dynasty rested. A monarch could feel secure to undertake new policies of serious national

---

[15] See T'ung-tsu Ch'ü, *Local Government in China under the Ch'ing* (Cambridge, Mass.: Harvard University Press, 1962), chaps. 2, 3, and 10.

[16] See C. K. Yang, *Religion in Chinese Society* (Berkeley: University of California Press, 1961), pp. 164–5.

consequences if he felt that these local elites guaranteed the security of his society.

The long-term effect of this tradition of rule was the gradual weakening of the organizational character of the empire. The armies became increasingly subject to civilian influences and the bureaucracy turned into an elite club. The process of weakening was not perceptible until the Taiping Rebellion of one hundred years ago, when revolutionary armies destroyed the enfeebled troops of the monarchy. To re-establish their rule, the Manchus had no choice but to turn to the entrenched, traditional local elites. The elites realized their organizational weakness and turned from authoritarian social control back to power-oriented organization. Naturally, the first expression of this new trend was the organization of new-type armies. Toward the end of the nineteenth century, some of the local elites began to adopt Western organizational methods and forms (as in Chang Chih-tung's development of industry). When the Republic collapsed shortly after its establishment, local (provincial) elites in conjunction with new military forces (warlords) began to organize de facto autonomous areas within the country. Perhaps the most successful was Shansi under Yen Hsi-shan, who even applied Communist organizational methods.

But the pendulum had swung too far to the other extreme. The warlord territories were structures of naked power and, to make it worse, inefficient and ineffective. The charisma of local authority had all but vanished in the eyes of the people. With their prestige gone, the local elites ruled through power and wealth. Attempts to rekindle Confucianism, as in Chiang Kai-shek's New Life Movement, failed. Communist revolutionary ideology had already spread far and wide in China by the mid-1930's and was sowing the seeds of new values, and so of a new authority. Chiang Kai-shek realized that in a country torn by decay and revolution only concentrated organized power could suppress revolt and reunite the country. Thus, not unnaturally, he fashioned a powerful military weapon. Nevertheless, while his armies remained efficient for a while, his government came under the control of traditional and new elites. In the countryside, the gentry moved back into positions of local bureaucratic power, and in the cities the emerging urban bourgeoisie put its grip on the instruments of state power. In time, the armies as well became infected with China's inherent tendencies toward elitism and degenerated from fighting weapons into sluggish bodies of conscripts ruled by vested interests. Chiang's mistake, of course, was that he thought he could create a new dynasty in the traditional manner: pacify the country and re-establish bureaucratic rule with whatever elites were available, and *then* tackle whatever developmental problems had to be faced. His failures, however, were not due to mistakes, as his supporters maintain (for example, the "bad luck" of the Sian Incident), but to the fact that China had changed in a drastic manner.

### Organization and Social Control in Communist China

Over one hundred years ago, Georg Wilhelm Friedrich Hegel gave his sociology to the world. He saw human society consisting of three interrelated parts: the state, civil society, and the family. As did many other thinkers of the Enlightenment, Hegel saw the state as the carrier of the idea of freedom (the greatest achievement of the West), but freedom would only be realized in civil society.[17] Karl Marx's sociology saw a somewhat different trinity: the state, civil society, and the individual (the family was subsumed into civil society). Freedom would be realized through the state, but to achieve it civil society had to be destroyed (in time, Marx saw the emerging economic system of capitalist Europe as the true foundation of civil society). As early as 1843 he wrote:

> Political emancipation means in effect the *dissolution* of the old society on which the state, the ruling power alienated from the people, rests. The political revolution is the revolution of civil society. What was the character of the old society? One word characterizes it: *Feudality.*[18]

It has been the Communist parties of the world which have carried this revolutionary hostility to civil society to the farthest parts of the globe. Moreover, the farther east one goes, where civil society is increasingly "feudal" (that is, traditional), the assault on civil society has been most intense. In rural China it took the form of a revolutionary terror against the ancient gentry class of China, and a revolutionary liberation of the peasant from the past. Curiously, when the Communists triumphed in China in 1949, the onslaught against the emerging bourgeoisie was far less thorough (a "national bourgeoisie" may even now remain in China). What was left in rural China after the revolution was a new state power facing an immense population of peasants, still living as families yet themselves with an emerging indi-

---

[17] On the role of the state in the spread of the idea of freedom, see Nisbet, *Community and Power,* pp. 106–8.

[18] "Zur Judenfrage," *Marx-Engels Gesamt Ausgabe* (Berlin, 1964) 1:367.

vidualistic consciousness. Post-revolutionary rural China was somewhere between Hegel's and Marx's conceptions of society.[19]

Once civil society had been destroyed, the state had to replace it. Marx saw the state as organized power, and believed that the post-revolutionary state would adopt the most advanced forms of capitalist organization to realize its new proletarian goals. And so it is not surprising that in the early years of the Soviet Union, the new rulers of that country assiduously studied the secrets of the centralized, efficient, organized power of the Ford Motor Company. The Chinese Communists closely followed the Soviet example, and created a Soviet-style administrative structure to govern the country. As in the Soviet Union, the basis of the structure of organized state power was the nationalized economy. The business of the state bureaucracy in China is business!

However, as is clear from the persistent trend toward decentralization, a revolutionized Chinese society could not be totally organized through modern state power alone. It was relatively easy to nationalize and then operate industry and business (bureaucratic capitalism and the tight linkages of the emerging bourgeoisie with government before 1949 already had created bases for a centrally directed modern economy). But organizing China's rural areas was a very different matter. Since even the Russians have been unable to transform their collectivized villages into modern state farms, it is even more unlikely that the Chinese would be able to achieve this. Thus, after a decade and a half of rural reorganization, China's villages remain at a low level of collectivization.

What modern organized state power could not do, the Chinese Communist Party (CCP) was called on to do. After a brief period of proletarianization after 1949, the party not only once again began to recruit peasants, but became the dominant organization in China's rural areas. The new leaders of local society were CCP members: poor peasants, new rural intellectuals, demobilized veterans, and, then, *hsia-fang*'ed ("downward transferred") urbanites. The party grouped these people together, trained and indoctrinated them, and functioned as the link between the distant state and the local society in which they operated. Thus the party arose as a positional equivalent to the old local gentry which had been destroyed during the revolutionary land reform, that is

[19] The discussion in this section is presented *in extenso* in my book, in my article "Chinese Society" for the new edition of the *Encyclopedia of the Social Sciences*, and in my article "China's Power Structure" in *Diplomat Magazine*, vol. 17, no. 196 (September, 1966), pp. 89–95.

to say, it assumed the position once held by the gentry but with new functions dictated by the new polity.

Despite its unity and power, the party is not a technical organization, in the manner of a corporate structure or an administrative bureacracy. The party, as such, has no particular goals. It serves as a transmitter of policies made at higher echelons and then its members work to implement them in some formal organizational situation other than the party: factory, farm, school, military unit, and so on. It is the unified and disciplined body of China's new leaders—its new elites, if you will. But precisely because of its non-technical character, it requires authority even more than it does power (power is imbedded in the commands coming from the organizations of state power), and this necessitates the elaboration of methods of socialization and social control.

We need not go into detail on the importance of ideology, thought reform, education in the training and performance of party members. The party member probably spends more time "studying" than he does in the actual performance of work tasks. The masses are supposed to look for guidance to the party member, and so this means that they fully accept the values from which his authority flows and, conversely, that he has fully internalized those values. How deeply the new values (I supposed now symbolized by the thought of Mao Tse-tung) have gone into the masses and the leaders cannot be known, but that elites generate authority is a fact, and that education, whether technical or political, is a major instrument for producing elites is also a fact, particularly in the poor countries.

From what we can gather, China's state bureaucracy is a modern administrative structure, often inefficient like most bureaucracies but still performing in terms of its technical requirements. Foreigners who have had dealings with Chinese state agencies are impressed with their modern business-like outlook. Contracts once signed are scrupulously observed. The modern sector of China's economy appears to be well handled by the state bureaucracy. The party, on the other hand, is not an administrative bureaucracy. It is hierarchically organized and certainly subject to centralized policy controls, like a bureaucracy. But the purpose of party membership is not to produce organizational expertise but to make men into committed leaders who can command men in a variety of concrete problems to be resolved.

In addition to government and party, the army today plays a major role in Chinese society. Unlike the classic functions of the army (external defense and internal peace-keeping), the People's Liberation Army (PLA) operates in close contact with the masses. I do not think one can appreciate the role of the army in Chinese society unless one keeps in mind a basic fact about the social environment in China today. The leaders of China see their nation in a state of war: foreign aggressors, notably America and Russia, are preparing to destroy China and, when they get the chance, will do so. Whether this paranoia has a base in reality or not is a matter of dispute. I think it does, but others do not. Nevertheless, the paranoia exists.[20] Russia went through its period of fear of "capitalist encirclement" (after all, Germany finally did attack Russia), and now China is in a comparable period. I do not think that paranoia was there in the mid-1950's, nor was it there during the Great Leap Forward. It clearly is the product of the Sino-Soviet split, which, in Chinese eyes, assumed serious form with the Camp David meeting of Eisenhower and Khrushchev—it was then that the "Holy Alliance" was born. In North Vietnam, women and children fire at American planes— acts of an entire population fighting in a war. In effect, the same happens in China, except that the bullets do not yet have targets. As the danger of war grows, so the army enters more and more into the life of the society.

The trinity of government, party, and army ruling over expanding modern cities and over villages which, albeit still poor, have performed creditably during the last six years appears as a most remarkable achievement, considering the size and backwardness of China. China has modern organization, but it also has an effective system of social control. There has been relatively little resistance, in particular after the great crisis. Moreover, people work hard and efficiently. China has made great technical progress and has pulled itself up by the bootstraps after the trauma of the Russian withdrawal of aid and the natural disasters of the late 1950's. Every foreign observer has reported the good behavior of the Chinese people. So we again ask the question we did at the beginning: Why is Mao throwing it all away? Or is he?

## The Great Proletarian Cultural Revolution

Before we consider the impact of the Cultural Revolution on organization and social control, let us sketch out the broad lines of Chinese society today. Sociologically, China can be described as a society consisting of two great divisions, cities and villages, over which a trinity

---

[20] As Morton Halperin and John W. Lewis note, "the Army and the Party agree that an American invasion is likely . . ." ("New Tensions in the Army-Party Relations in China, 1965–1966," *China Quarterly*, no. 26 [April–June, 1966], p. 61).

of party, government, and army rule (a conception of state power now officially expressed by the Chinese). The Chinese Communists always had difficulties fitting their own practical class analysis of Chinese society into standard Marxist categories, but today, at a time when they are not too concerned with the doctrines of pure theory, they distinguish five major socioeconomic sectors: industry (workers), agriculture (peasants), business (bourgeois), schools (students), army (soldiers)— *kung-nung-shang-hsüeh-ping*.[21]

Power, wealth, and prestige appear to be universal determinants of social stratification, that is, a division of a social community into a range of superiors and inferiors. In traditional China, power arising from bureaucratic position, wealth arising from ownership of land, and prestige arising from education gave a man absolute elite status. If he had wealth, he or his descendants would aspire to supplement it with power and prestige, and so with the other determinants of status. That tendencies toward social stratification remain in the People's Republic is admitted every time the Communists speak of "class war." To become a cadre means to acquire power (the instruments of leadership) and so to set oneself above others who do not have it. With its powerful organizational structures, Communist China generates large amounts of power which, by and large, are seized by the cadres. The search for wealth does not appear to be so pronounced as in the Soviet Union. Moreover, wealth, particularly in the cities, is a sure path to gaining pariah status. The millionaire capitalists not only constitute a pariah stratum, but this may represent the only instance in world social history where rich people have social statuses earlier held by actors, prostitutes, and gypsies. In the rural areas, the situation may be different, in view of the persistent recurrence of "rich peasants," although, given the intensity of the Socialist Education Campaign during the last years, it is not likely that the rich peasants, such as they are, constitute a politically effective force. Prestige gained through education appears to be as important a status-determining factor as it is in the Soviet Union. China has a large and rapidly growing corps of educated people, though the "half-work half-study" campaigns of recent times, not to mention the upheaval in the educational system brought about by the Cultural

---

21 *Hung-ch'i* [Red Flag], no. 12, 1966, p. 12, states this conception of Chinese society. It speaks of the three "branches" (*pu-men;* see *Ideology and Organization,* p. 89): party, government, army; and five "sectors" (*chieh*): industry, agriculture, business, schools, and army. This may be said to be the current Chinese conception of their state and society.

Revolution, testify to the determination of China's leaders not to allow a new literati stratum to develop in China.

Despite the undeniable forces of social stratification at work in China, I do not think that the existence of a new or old *bürgerliche Gesellschaft* constitutes a major problem in China today. Many anthropologists disagree and feel that revolution is never so thorough that it can uproot a society with millennia of development behind it. The test, I believe, at least for China, is the relative strength of the kinship system. Josef Schumpeter argues that classes are essentially aggregates of families, and this strain of argumentation can be found even in C. Wright Mills. Kinship is an organizing principle for the perpetuation of authority. If it should turn out that the "rich peasants" of a certain county are related and actively pursue the achievement of kinship ties (through intermarriage), and if it should be that the party functionaries of a province are similarly related, then familism, that most ancient of China's sociational principles, still remains a strong force and China has indeed not changed that much. We obviously do not know. Yet, to my knowledge, cliquism based on kinship has not been raised by the Communists as a target for revolutionary action, at least not since the early 1950's, nor has it been raised now during the Cultural Revolution.

The Communists now speak of the need to continue the "class war" during the Cultural Revolution, yet the open struggle between real segments of the population, in my opinion, ended sometime in the 1950's. During the revolutionary land reform of 1946–49, peasants killed gentry. During the *san-fan* and *wu-fan* campaigns of 1951–52, bourgeois were liquidated. During the collectivization of 1955–56, rich peasants were "struggled against." And during the anti-rightist campaign of 1957–58, the intellectuals were bitterly attacked. These were real acts of class destruction, comparable to what happened in the French and Russian revolutions. True, the Socialist Education Campaign of the early 1960's lashed out again and again against feudal and capitalist elements of the peasantry, but the thrust was more educationl than liquidational. The enemy seemed to exist more in the minds of people than in social actuality, and so "thought" had to be transformed. The same is true now in the Cultural Revolution, at least as far as the general population is concerned.

The Cultural Revolution may turn out to be the greatest purge China has experienced since the triumph of Communism—one we all hope will not produce the bloodshed of the Russian purges of the mid-1930's. This is not a simple educational campaign but a real struggle where some win and others lose. But despite the talk, the thrust of the revolution is not against a segment of the population, as it was in the past, but essentially against one of the structures of the trinity of organized power, namely the CCP.

The Russian press has taken the position that the "Maotsetung'ists" are destroying the CCP, and to a large extent that position is shared by other Asian Communist parties (notably those of Japan and North Korea). As of the writing of this paper, one after another of the Old Bolsheviks of the CCP is coming under attack. The purge has gone much deeper than the top level; provincial and local party organizations have felt the onslaught of the Red Guards. In city after city, party secretaries have been paraded around the streets with dunce caps on their heads. Teen-age students have taken the lead in attacking men of long records of service to the cause. Though in the early weeks of the Red Guard movement old men and Hong Kong types were beaten up, it is clear by now that the real thrust is against the party bosses, high and low. Army men and government officials have also been attacked, but as influential members of the party, not as military professionals or bureaucrats. Professionals who for years have been known mainly as such (Li Hsien-nien and Li Fu-ch'un in the economic field or Liu Po-ch'eng and Su Yü in the military field) have not been prominent targets of attack. Those who are attacked are men like Liu Shao-ch'i, Teng Hsiao-p'ing, Lo Jui-ch'ing, P'eng Chen, P'eng Te-huai, Lu Ting-i, and others—men of ideology and of policy convictions who enjoyed major power and influence at the top policy-making levels of the country. Obviously something was terribly wrong with the party.

Perhaps we might here reflect on the words chosen to designate this vast purge: "Great Proletarian Cultural Revolution." "Great" conjures up the Great Leap Forward—what it signifies is a campaign of nation-wide proportions going into the deepest fabric of society. "Proletarian" implies anti-bourgeois and so means that the targets are mainly those of the city and not of the country (in fact, the Red Guard movement has been almost entirely an urban phenomenon). "Culture" means ideology and so the basic values which guide human behavior. "Revolution" is the most awesome sounding word of all, for it connotes a change of such magnitude that what follows must be radically different. Not since the land reform had the Chinese Communists used the word "revolution" to designate a domestic campaign. What appears to emerge from this is a movement determined to transform the very nature of the CCP. If this is so, then the Russians may be right in their attacks.

What was so wrong with the party that it had to suffer such an onslaught? To try and answer this question, we must briefly review the history of the party over the last years. The party has always been the organization of leaders—shock brigade foremen, commune cadres, squadron captains, and so on. What did they lead? They led organized units of people in the many campaigns to transform society. In 1958 they had their greatest chance. The Great Leap Forward was the product of millions of small leaps carried out throughout the country by enthusiastic party cadres. I have argued that the communes themselves were essentially local products, though obviously deriving from a general policy decision made in Peking. When the Great Leap Forward ended late in 1960, a rectification campaign began to purge the party of adventurists who had been responsible for the excesses of the Great Leap Forward. (A similar purge took place in 1950 when thousands of peasant heroes of the civil war and of land reform were dismissed from the party, largely on grounds of too low an educational level.) The year 1960 marked the beginning of a period when China was without an ideology. No one in Peking knew what to do except use any and all means to pull China out of the morass. Domestically, China entered its pragmatic phase. For a while there were debates on correct ways of doing things, but all the solutions offered were practical. Then even the debates ceased and pragmatism took over. To the present, China is without a practical ideology as to what to do with its economy and society to achieve the progress needed. The achievements in such eminently practical fields as nuclear engineering and synthetic chemistry indicate that pragmatism has paid off handsomely. China's nuclear devices may indeed be the product of the thought of Mao Tse-tung, but Mao has never indulged in the Lysenko-type idiocies with which Stalin dabbled.

On July 1, 1961, it was announced that China had 17,000,000 party members. The party may have grown since then, but even if not, the number remains immense. It may be an exaggeration to say so, but in effect, these 17,000,000 party members had nothing to do, except what they had to do otherwise in their practical roles (for example, as factory directors).

To compensate for this, China's leaders decided to launch a campaign of ideological indoctrination designed to preserve the party member's leadership role in the realm of ideology, even if practically there wasn't much for him to do. The turning point was the summer of 1962, when Liu Shao'chi's writings on how to be a good communist were widely republicized. In September, 1962, the Central Committee held its Tenth Plenary Meeting, proclaiming policies eventually leading up to the Socialist Education Movement (aimed at China's rural areas) and launching a struggle against "modern revisionism" (directed against the Soviet Union). The decisions of the Tenth Plenum had two practical consequences. At home, millions of cadres were sent to the rural areas to help uplift the peasantry. Abroad, Chinese armies attacked India and the CCP launched a powerful drive to organize an anti-Soviet and anti-American international movement. Both of these ideological moves, however, had their peculiar practical counterparts. In the rural areas, Peking adopted a program of technical development of agriculture, investing heavily in some areas and relying on material incentives in others. Abroad, the ideological foreign policy was accompanied by an ambitious drive to develop foreign trade ties with a whole array of nations, primarily bourgeois as it turned out.[22]

The ideological campaign, both at home and abroad, gained in intensity. Party cadres spent more and more time "studying" the works of Mao, attacking Khrushchev, preaching the virtues of the PLA, presenting films and dramas to the people. The haranguing went on and on. As the conditions of life improved markedly, and the pounding tones of the haranguing did not let up, a certain apathy began to come over the population. Demonstration after demonstration against imperialism turned them eventually into holidays which people welcomed as time off from work. Chinese have a remarkable capacity to adjust to all conditions of life, and so the ideological campaign too, in time, became subject to the corrosive forces of routinization.

Under these conditions, something did happen to the party. For one thing, I would suggest that the ancient tendencies of elitism, localism, and authoritarianism reappeared. Since party membership was the main road to success and access was presumably narrowed by the slowdown in recruitment after the Great Leap Forward, the average party member undoubtedly cherished his special status more than ever. Without his party membership, he was nothing. In films made during the early 1960's, the party secretary was often portrayed in the manner of fatherly local magistrates of earlier years. That is more or less what he was. He had the power, prestige, and authority to arrange deals for

[22] The communiqué of the Tenth Plenum (*Jen-min jih-pao,* September 29, 1962) did not announce the socialist education movement but once again expressed concern that the capitalistic elements were reappearing in the villages (after a year and a half of discreet toleration of these phenomena). The communiqué also attacked revisionism, and warned against revisionistic tendencies within the party. It is significant that three new men were elected to the party Secretariat: Lu Ting-i, K'ang Sheng, and Lo Jui-ch'ing (the first and the third have been victims of the Cultural Revolution).

people. The party, in fact, often became the clearing house for making economic contracts; in law, it played Solomonic roles of adjudicating disputes—hardly a leadership role if we remember the glorious fighting history of the party. There is evidence that local party machines began to grow up again, after the big shifts in local party personnel of 1957–58. As several Western scholars have noted, mobility was slow and promotion difficult. Little local cliques began to form once again, by no means disloyal to Peking but, in typical bureaucratic fashion, concerned with the maximization of their own interests. And, of course, with the ideological campaign, the authority of the party grew and grew. Expertise may have been tolerated on practical grounds, but "redness" was shrilly proclaimed the one and only source of the right to rule and lead. The same thing happened to the Communist Party of the Soviet Union in the late 1920's and early 1930's. When Stalin struck at the party in 1935, it was a powerful commanding organization, with the same tendencies toward elitism, localism, and authoritarianism which now exist within the CCP. After the trauma of collectivization, it, too, was interested in restabilizing the country.

But the other two segments of the trinity of power also underwent development during these last six years. After the bureaucratic dismantling of 1957–58, the state administrative bureaucracy had slowly rebuilt itself. Our best evidence for this comes from the dealings foreign businessmen have with Chinese state agencies. Port operations are handled efficiently, negotiations are carried out competently, and deliveries are made promptly. Unless the state bureaucracy were guided by practical principles, such performance would hardly be possible. The poor performance record of many developing countries in business relations with outside interests can usually be attributed to administrative bungling caused by overstaffed bureaucracies who do not know what they are doing. The comprehensive planning and engineering needed to produce nuclear weapons requires efficient administrative operations. The preparations for the Third Five Year Plan also indicate that Peking felt that, administratively, it was in a position once again to implement central planning (for all practical purposes, there was no planning during the immediate post-disaster years).

The developments in the army are the most obscure but also the most significant for what gave rise to the Great Proletarian Cultural Revolution. The army played a key role in holding the country together during the crisis years. Late in 1960 the doctrines of Lin Piao became the official ideology of the armed forces. In 1961, an intensive "Communist education" campaign was launched among the soldiers.

Subsequently, the army emerged increasingly as a model for society to follow (for example, "emulate the PLA campaign"). Soldiers began to assume administrative positions within the state bureaucracy (for example, in the so-called general political departments within the branches of economic administration). The guerrilla spirit became stronger and stronger, and in the summer of 1965 it was announced that all ranks were to be abolished. Early in 1966, command was partially decentralized and linkages established between provincial party committees and garrison units.[23] At the same time, there can be no doubt that despite the attacks on professionalism, the technical capabilities of the Chinese armed forces underwent intensive development.

Looking at these three segments of the trinity of state power, one cannot but have the feeling that the role of the party was becoming increasingly unclear. The state administrative bureaucracy planned and operated the economy and seems to have acquitted itself well. The army was doing its best to provide for China's defense and certainly must be credited with having developed a deterrent force of major magnitude. Both must be regarded as superb organizations, and superb instances of organization, not just because of a de facto acceptance of technical and practical ways of doing things, but because they have real tasks to perform.[24] Organizations need goals—without goals they start to wither and dry up. The party, on the other hand, was turning into the country's *lao-shih*, schoolmaster. Thus it would appear that, despite its unified structure, its concerns were less and less those of organization and more and more those of social control. And, in the process, it was turning into an elite club of authoritarians.[25]

If the party was indeed turning into the schoolmaster of the nation, then its functions were becoming more and more similar to those of universities, schools, theaters, newspapers—the organizational sectors which have been the prime source of attack of the Cultural Revolution.

[23] See Hsiao Hua's speech, January 25, 1966, in *Jen-min jih-pao*.

[24] Whether the army is "red" or "expert" in spirit has nothing to do with its organizational as opposed to institutional character. Judging from their hostility to the party elite, what the Mao-Lin group would fear in the army is not an emphasis on modern weapons (the timing of China's nuclear and missile experiments to coincide with critical periods of the Cultural Revolution appears to me as a message telling the world that China does not propose to fight with sticks and stones) but the generation of a professional officer corps. The abolition of ranks announced by Ho Lung in August, 1965, climaxed a campaign to level status differences within the military.

[25] One of the epithets now applied to the opponents of Mao Tse-tung is *tang-ch'üan-p'ai* ("authoritarian clique").

If we disregard for the moment the high political issues involved in the Cultural Revolution, then obviously something was profoundly wrong with the way the party was performing its tasks of imparting ideology, the chief instrument of social control.

To try and get at what was wrong with the party's ideological role, let us see how it was performed until the advent of the Cultural Revolution. Despite the unprecedented use of mass media by the Chinese Communists, oral transmission and personal (or group) persuasion still played the leading part in the process of imparting ideology to people. Since everyone in China is a member of one or more organizational units, everyone has to attend "study" sessions several times each week. These study sessions are concerned with "political" problems which range from macroscopic problems of foreign affairs to problems of immediate concern to the members of the group. Crucial to these study sessions are the cadre leader and the documents (*wen-chien*), which everyone is expected to have read in preparation for the discussion. The leader is invariably a party member who has been briefed by higher echelons on the esoteric meaning of the documents or who knows what particular policy line is being propounded. The documents may consist of articles from *Jen-min jih-pao*, reports on work performance of the organizational unit in question, or personal documents of the members (self-criticisms, autobiographies, and so on). During the session the leader expounds the real meaning of the documents, and the group members, by voicing their "opinions," indicate to what extent they have grasped what is being told them. Discussions are often heated, inasmuch as contrary opinions are welcomed so that the "backward" person can be convinced as to what is right. Since there are millions of such organizational units throughout the country, there presumably was no lack of ideological work to be performed by the party. In his capacity as leader of the study group, the party cadre acquired a unique form of authority: he became the main link between the masses and the leaders in distant Peking. Without the oral transmission of ideology by the party cadre, the true messages of the mass media would not get through to the masses.

The Cultural Revolution has been a revolt against the "professors"—in the universities, other schools, newspapers, radio, films, and in the party. They have been accused of old, bourgeois, and revisionist thoughts; as noted above, these three adjectives symbolize the three great social enemies of Chinese Communism—gentry feudalism, Western capitalism, and Soviet revisionism. During the avalanche of denunciations, hundreds of writings from purged individuals have been dredged up to show how, under the subtle cover of teaching the thought of Mao Tse-tung, they really imparted values of the enemies of Chinese Communism. For the outside observer, it is hard to see how Wu Han's or Chien Po-tsan's treatment of history could have had a subversive effect on the minds of the masses. For one thing, these tales hardly served as the major documents for "study" sessions, and for another, such poison as there was in them was too subtle to have had a direct effect on their readers. However, there is one thread which goes through all the literary works denounced—a veiled criticism of the supreme leader. This is illustrated by the attack on Chou Yang. Chou Yang has been accused of hostility to China's greatest writer Lu Hsün (the analogy to Mao Tse-tung is obvious). When the League of Left-Wing Writers was disbanded in 1936, Chou Yang, ever faithful to the new party line, organized a writers' group propounding what was called "National Defense Literature" (*Kuo-fang wen-hsüeh*). Since a war of resistance against Japan based on a new popular front had become the dominant party line, Chou Yang argued that it should be expressed by writers committing themselves fully to the cause. Opposed to Chou Yang was the more nationalist Hu Feng (bitterly attacked in 1955 by none other than Chou Yang himself), who maintained that Chinese writers must remain faithful to the masses and describe their sufferings. Strongly influenced by the Proletarian Cultural Movement in Japan, this group adopted this name for itself. Lu Hsün clearly moved to the Hu Feng group, which forced Chou Yang, in the mid-1950's, to explain away Lu Hsün's apparent defection from the CCP—a series of historical reinterpretations for which Chou Yang has now been bitterly criticized. The message, however, is obvious. When forced to make a choice between the party and the great man (Lu Hsün = Mao Tse-tung), Chou Yang made the wrong choice.[26]

Anyone who has interviewed Chinese from the mainland cannot help noting how they constantly speak of the "party" in the sense of a reified source of authority. Since the whole thrust of the Cultural Revolution has been to pound the thought of Mao Tse-tung into the minds and hearts of the Chinese people, it becomes clear that the party dare not

[26] On Chou Yang's nefarious agitation against Lu Hsün, see *Hung-ch'i*, no. 9, 1966, pp. 35–37. Chou Yang has now been accused of following the Wang Ming rightist and capitulationist line. What is curious is that Chou Yang's "National Defense Literature" is now branded as the enemy of Lu Hsün's "Mass Literature of the National Revolutionary Struggle." However, the latter literary current was led by Hu Feng, who was bitterly attacked and apparently even legally convicted of counter-revolutionary crimes in 1955. His chief accuser then was Chou Yang.

aspire to be that same ultimate source of authority. The party must function as an instrument, as an organization, just as do the army and the state bureaucracy, but it is not the creator of the core values of the Chinese people. Chou Yang's mistake was not that he obeyed party decisions when he should not have (not a case of the classic Communist majority-minority split where, as Liu Shao-ch'i has repeatedly emphasized, the minority should stick to its opinions while faithfully carrying out the decisions of the majority) but that he tried to elevate party policy to the level of supreme value. In any society, it is the arts and not the sciences which proclaim values to the world. (If we relegate theology to the arts and not the sciences, as do modern philosophers, then the value-transmitting functions of the arts become even more clear.) Thus what the Cultural Revolution is about is not so much that the party was poisoning the minds of the people with anti-revolutionary thoughts, but that it was becoming the collective body of final authority in China. It was the party which determined the ideology and not the reverse.

We must now ask ourselves what really has been the ideology which the party propagated to the Chinese people. Ideology and organization are interdependent. Over time, an organization generates a certain set of ideas with which it is stuck, whether it likes it or not. Since ideology, in turn, plays an important role in holding the organization together, the leaders cannot arbitrarily change that ideology, except at grave risk to the organization. A single man can change his ideas as Lu Hsün (and Mao Tse-tung) have done, but an organization finds this far more difficult. We Americans might simply reflect on the ideological shackles which our own foreign policy has created and how difficult it is to change them. We have huge bureaucracies that have become so involved with those ideologies that a radical change would have major organizational consequences. The accumulated ideology of the CCP is what in China is called Marxism-Leninism, of which the thought of Mao Tse-tung is a derivative.

Until early 1966, the publishing houses of Peking turned out millions of pamphlets on the classics of Marxism-Leninism. When the Sino-Soviet dispute erupted publicly in 1960, Peking began to republish crucial works of Lenin, not only in Chinese, but also in Russian, English, and many other languages. Since then, other classics of Marx, Engels, Lenin, and Stalin have been reprinted, including such works as Marx and Engels on the Paris Commune, a theme strongly in line with Mao's thinking on the communes in China. The open letters to the Soviet Communist Party were written in finest Marxist-Leninist style. The economic debates were all written from the point of view of Marxist economics. Anyone who reads the Chinese press now cannot but help noticing a change in its style and content. *Jen-min jih-pao*, despite its effusive praise of Mao, has become lively, non-jargonistic, and quite free from Marxist doctrine. The stories printed on the back pages are written in down-to-earth, colloquial Chinese. The critiques of "the demons and monsters" are filled with references to Mao and only occasionally to Marx, Engels, and Lenin.

Clearly the Cultural Revolution constitutes a break with ideological currents prevalent till then, and apparently bound up with certain conceptions of Marxism-Leninism. Despite the voluminous material that has come out of China on the Cultural Revolution (official newspapers, foreign dispatches, Red Guard newspapers, reports of visitors, etc.), we still are not certain about the ideological differences between the "Maoists" and the "Liu-ists." Were there basic disagreements about the economy? Were the former in favor of social mobilization, and the latter in favor of material incentives? This line of thought has been fairly popular among American observers but does not appear very convincing to me. One forgets too easily that the first encroachments against the "small freedoms" of the peasants (granted in the aftermath of the 1960 crisis) were made after the Tenth Plenum where Liu Shao-ch'i played a decisive role. Moreover, some of the most prominent advocates of material incentives have either not been criticized at all or lightly (for example, Ch'en Yün). The political survival of Ch'en Yi, who several years ago told students it was all right for them to be mainly experts, suggests that differences over economic ideology may not be as neat as is suggested in America. The notion of setting up Paris Commune–type political structures appears to be clearly Maoist, and here we may have a real ideological difference. But the Paris Commune was not just an idle experiment in setting up a just political order but rather the instrument of an insurrectionary working class defending itself against an approaching foreign enemy. The Paris Commune takes a prominent place in the writings of Marx and Engels; yet the classic texts of Communism are rarely cited in China today. The thought of Mao Tse-tung is today far more important than the works of Marx, Engels, Lenin, and Stalin.

A change apparent to those of us who have been regularly reading *Jen-min jih-pao* over the last years is the marked reduction in foreign news.[27] Articles on revolutionary movements still appear, but since the

27 The amount of foreign news which appeared on page 1 of *Jen-min jih-pao*, space normally reserved for reports on policy and operations, between 1962 and 1966, is staggering. Since May, 1966, however, with the exception of the

August 18, 1966, demonstrations, Peking has experienced few, if any, of those great outpourings of people protesting the actions of imperialism; the greatest of the demonstrations on foreign matters have been those directed against the Russians (and to a lesser extent the Yugoslavs and the French). While there is no blatant nationalism such as one saw in Russia in the late 1930's, there also is none of the "proletarian internationalism" which was so prominent in Chinese newspapers throughout the first half of the 1960's. The Red Guards seem to be primarily concerned with sickness in their own country.

Every act performed by the Red Guards has had the effect of discrediting authority. During the land reform (1946–49)—that is, its revolutionary phase—landlords were publicly humiliated to discredit them as a class in the eyes of the peasants. Today the students are doing the same even to the highest figures of authority. The discreditation has gone right to the top, to Liu Shao-ch'i and his wife, who have been forced to engage in debasing self-criticism. This revolution against authority has deep roots in China. Among the peasants it began in the Taiping Rebellion. Among the students it began during World War I with the Chinese renaissance and found its most violent expression in the May Fourth Movement, whose main targets were the old bureaucrats who had betrayed China to the Japanese. Anyone who knows how Chinese revere teachers (including foreigners) realizes the emotional trauma the placing of a dunce cap on a teacher's head must produce in the student. For decades now, elite upon elite has been dragged into the mire of discreditation. We have already listed those elites within the population as a whole who underwent the onslaught through the 1950's (since then, intellectuals, for example, have been again and again forced to put their hands into the mud to work with the people). Today the new elite of the party is sharing their fate. And with them go their ideas.

Are the Russians correct that the leaders of China today are destroying the organization that holds China together? I think not. So far there

___

first twenty-two days of July, the main items on page 1 have been eulogies of the thought of Mao Tse-tung. The bitter attacks on the Soviet Union, which go far beyond the days of the polemic, stop just short of announcing a capitalist restoration in the Soviet Union. Note, in particular, the accounts of Chinese students who have returned from the Soviet Union, for example, the account of the almost total corruption of the Soviet system which appeared in *Jen-min jih-pao*, November 15, 1966. The Chinese attacks on the Soviet Union closely resemble the Trotskyite criticisms of the new bureaucratic despotism of the Soviet Union heard in the late 1930's.

have been no great purges within the state bureaucracy. What is happening in the army is obscure, but so far nothing like the Soviet purges of one-third of the officer corps of the Red Army appears to have taken place. (Individual generals like P'eng Te-huai and Lo Jui-ch'ing have been severely criticized but mainly in their role as top policy makers.) Thus the two great organizations of China have remained unaffected by the Cultural Revolution, at least as far as their operations are concerned. But the party has been severely struck. The Communist Youth League, the organizational helpmate of the party, has been (temporarily?) dissolved. Party committees throughout China have been overturned. As of the writing of this paper, the American press is filled with stories of clashes between workers and Red Guards, indicating that the onslaught against the party is meeting stiff resistance. By the time this paper is finished and distributed, many things may have changed in China—or they may not. One has to wait and see. Meanwhile, in the manner of academics, we must hold to our more abstract concerns of "organization and social control." If the party had indeed been becoming less and less of an "organization" and more and more an elite club, then what it is now ordered to surrender is its grip on the instruments of social control. Others are now to come to the fore to educate the youth of China.

## Consequences of the Cultural Revolution

It seems presumptuous to end this paper with a section on the consequences of the Cultural Revolution when (at the time of writing, January 9, 1967) the real turmoil appears just to have begun. I have written this paper on the assumption that the political system prevailing in China, no matter how great the turbulence through which it is going, will persist well into the future. But now I see great headlines in the newspapers predicting an imminent civil war, a downfall of Mao Tse-tung, and even a possible end to Communism in China. Perhaps the situation is as serious as it has been made out in the papers. Perhaps also the endemic wish for China's "collapse" has broken out again in the American mass media. We shall have to wait and see what the future brings.

One event in the history of Communism to which the present Cultural Revolution has some similarities is the great purges which Stalin carried out against his opponents in the mid-1930's. By the end of the purges in 1938, Stalin had succeeded in sweeping away virtually the entire Soviet political elite: party secretaries, the officer corps, officials of the state bureaucracy, and finally, even the secret police, the instrument of the terror.[28] Despite the volumes of writing on the subject and the new evidence released in the Soviet Union during the de-Stalinization campaign, the reasons for the purge still remain obscure. Scholars still seem to have no other answer than "madness" or the criminal mentality of Stalin. Certainly the killing and jailing of these unfortunate men ranks as a crime against humanity and could be explained in no other terms than the insanity of despotic power. Yet the purge must be separated from the killings. And the present Cultural Revolution in China, which we all hope will never approach the stage of terror, indicates that a general sweeping out of the men of power and authority, at a point in the development of a Communist system, may arise from some inherent organizational logic. Both in the Russia of the mid-1930's and now in China, the brunt of the attack was against the party. In the 1920's and the early 1930's, the Soviets had eliminated their class enemies in the population: bourgeois, czarist intellectuals, counter-revolutionaries, and finally the kulaks. China, too, had more or less disposed of its class enemies by the late 1950's. By the early 1930's in Russia and by the early 1960's in China, there no longer were major segments of the population in serious opposition to the new regimes—the old elites had been eliminated. The onslaught against the party was the last and greatest of the Soviet purges. (Stalin contemplated a new purge in the early 1950's, but it was not carried out because of his death.) China now is experiencing its own party purge, and so comparison of these two great purges may aid our analysis of the Cultural Revolution in China.

One of the themes that has emerged most prominently in the Cultural Revolution is indicated by the Red Guard slogan "Defend Chairman Mao." Recently, some posters have described Mao's dissatisfaction at having been deposed from the chairmanship of the Republic in December, 1958. Mao had been in seclusion during the six months preceding the volcanic outburst of May, 1966. Certainly, Mao's dramatic public reappearance late in July (swimming the Yangtze) and the pilgrimages of the Red Guards from all over the country to view him in the flesh on T'ien-an-men Square indicate that every attempt is being made to convince the masses that Mao is firmly in control of the country, that he is indeed the "helmsman." There is little doubt that several times in the past Mao had been "outvoted" in the Politburo and in the Central Committee. For example, his ambitious twelve-year plan for the reorganization of agriculture was tabled in April, 1956, only a few months after it had been announced with great fanfare in a widely publicized

[28] Leonard Schapiro, *The Communist Party of the Soviet Union* (London: Eyre Spottiswoode, 1960), chaps. 22 and 23.

meeting of state. After the Tenth Plenum of September, 1962, Liu Shao-ch'i emerged as Mao's putative successor. Liu is, of course, China's great organization man and presumably exercised direct control over the party. The Red Guards now try to give the impression that Mao had been edged out of power by being "promoted upward" to the status of a living god, more in heaven than on earth.

Here there appear to be some similarities with 1934 in the Soviet Union. The Seventeenth Party Congress of early 1934 was not an unqualified victory for Stalin. Several of his erstwhile enemies had been taken back into the party, and some of the speeches given then indicated themes not entirely in accord with the tone set by Stalin.[29] Stalin had launched the collectivization drive, as Mao launched the Great Leap Forward, but both periods were followed by attempts to slow down the pace. The Second Five Year Plan of the Soviets was, at least in tone, a more moderate economic program than its predecessor. The trauma of collectivization had a severe impact on the party and behind-the-scenes criticisms of Stalin were undoubtedly not rare. Stalin's grip on the apparatus of power was weaker in 1934 than it had been in 1928.

One of the allegations made at the Soviet purge trials was that the defendants were plotting to remove Stalin from power. It is likely that, even if a united anti-Stalin conspiracy did not exist, opposition currents had been growing up to the time of the fateful assassination of Sergei Kirov. "Sectarianism" (that is, factionalism) has always been regarded by Communist parties as a grave danger, and Stalin may have decided that the only way to eradicate that danger once and for all was to tear it out by the roots: sweep away the entire power elite of the Soviet system. From foreign reports and indirect admissions by the Chinese themselves, a comparable threat appears to have been directed against Mao. Just as Stalin swept away all to the left ("Trotzkyists") and to the right ("rightists") of himself, Mao now is attempting to do the same. Moreover, Stalin's purges reached deep down into every sector of organization, creating vacancies which were soon filled by aspiring contenders. The Soviet Communist Party was all but wrecked at the time. But the purges did not stop at the party; they reached out everywhere to the state bureaucracy and the army as well. Perhaps the Chinese Cultural Revolution has not yet ended and the other two segments of the trinity of state power will have their turn. Perhaps psychopathology is still the only explanation for the Soviet purges, as *fa-feng* seems to be

[29] The new Politburo elected at the Seventeenth Party Congress included several men suspected to have been in opposition to Stalin; see *ibid.*, pp. 397–98.

a common overseas Chinese reaction to the Cultural Revolution. What we do know, however, from the Soviet purges is that organization was not wrecked. The great central ministries determinedly advanced the program of rapid heavy industrialization. The schools kept on turning out scientists and technicians. The army certainly acquitted itself well in the battles against the Japanese at Nomonhan in 1939. The slave labor camps with their millions did not frighten the Russian people into passivity. Those who suffered most were the elites of Russia, and it is possible that Stalin benefited from the people's traditional hatred of men in authority. After all, the Party *apparatchik* by the 1930's looked again like the old czarist *chinovnik*. We know enough of "totalitarian democracy" to realize that the masses do support absolute dictators and that the liquidation of intermediate elites is often welcomed by them. Intellectuals, in particular, appear to occupy a very fragile place in society. They have the privilege of speaking up, but they enjoy little love from the masses.

Yet in reflecting on the Soviet purges, it is difficult to believe that it was only a case of two or more factions contending for positions of power. That the purges finally became a wholesale cleansing (*chistka*) of the power structure is clear, but the initial confrontation must have grown out of some fundamental conflict over real issues. Organizations are goal-oriented structures of power, which means that if a particular group of men gain control of organization, they get the power to pursue policies they advocate. Thus in the initial confrontation there must have been some very basic issues over which bitter conflict took place. It is either the limitations of historical scholarship or the sealed secrecy of the power hierarchy which, so far, has not revealed what issues were debated behind the Kremlin walls at that time. However, the purge trials pounded home again and again that the "rightists" and "Trotzkyists" were said to have forged a league to overthrow Stalin and sell out Russia to its foreign enemies, specifically German and Japanese imperialism. There are signs that similar accusations are being made against Mao's former friends. When questioned by Kosaka Zentaro, former Japanese foreign minister, about the purges, Foreign Minister Ch'en Yi replied that China was threatened by new Wang Ching-wei's and Wang K'o-min's ("puppets of the Japanese"). Western observers, who have seen a foreign-policy issue in the purges, have concluded that the label of "revisionist" meant not only one who wanted to stress rational planning and incentives in the Chinese economy but one who favored a return to collaboration with the Soviet Union. But why would the alleged "revisionists" wish to collaborate with the Soviet Union?

The only explanation lies in the area of China's national security, namely, that in the event of an armed American attack, China's best defense still lies with the Soviet nuclear shield. Thus, presumably, the "revisionists" advocated concessions to the Soviet Union in return for its protection.

If we keep in mind the analogy with the Soviet purges, we might focus on the definition of the international situation out of which such "revisionist" tendencies came. Almost every foreign writer who has close contact with the Chinese has reported their absolute conviction that sooner or later America will attack. Some have been even more specific: not only will America unleash its aerial might to destroy China's military-industrial complexes, but chemical and biological weaponry will be employed to lay China waste. It does no good arguing that despite America's massive build-up in eastern Asia and its accelerated chemical warfare program Washington has no intention of using them against China. What counts is what the Chinese believe, which, after all, is the basis of their action. From the public documentation available, there does not appear to have been any disagreement among the top leaders of China as to the eventuality of war with America.

During the 1930's, the Soviets similarly believed profoundly in the expressed intentions of "capitalist encirclement." In 1933, Hitler came to power. In the summer of 1934, with the support of the German army, Hitler destroyed his opposition and launched Germany on the road to rearmament. The Comintern, in that same year, proclaimed a new international situation—the menacing rise of Nazi Germany. As a consequence, it adopted a popular-front policy. Defense of the Soviet Union became the watchword for all Stalinist parties. In the face of this new threat, the Soviet Union sharply changed its foreign policy. Whereas the chief enemy had hitherto been the liberal democratic countries and Social Democratic parties, Moscow now sought alliance with them. And similarly, whereas earlier the Soviet Union had maintained close ties with Germany through a lively trade and through collaboration between the Soviet and German armies (the von Seeckt policy), the enmity became exacerbated, reaching a high point with the conclusion of the Anti-Comintern Pact of 1936.

Before the purges began early in 1935, there must have been sharp debates within the Soviet Union regarding policy toward Germany. Some of those later purged, like Bukharin, had long been bitterly anti-German, and presumably advocated a strong policy to combat Hitler. Others, perhaps located largely in the military (Tukhachevsky), may have still believed that the von Seeckt policy would triumph in the long run and that Germany's aggressive energies would be directed against France. Perhaps, in the atmosphere of growing fear and paranoia, a party-army controversy began to develop (there are indications that the army supported Stalin in his moves against the party leaders).[30]

Since concrete information is lacking, let us see whether we can try and reconstruct the situation in terms of what we know now of bureaucratic politics. The Chinese Communists realized long ago that state bureaucratic power structures tend, when faced with profound issues, to create polarities rather than pluralities of contending interests. This appears to be the case in the United States, where "hawk-dove" polarities are the expression of bureaucratic conflict over military and foreign-policy issues (in contrast to the greater pluralism of conflict over domestic and economic issues). The graver these issues become and the more prolonged the conflict, the more each side tends to jell into a faction, acquiring ever-increasing organizational power to advocate its own interests. The decision-maker finds himself in a difficult position. To decide for one faction may provide, at best, the disorientation of the losing faction (thus depriving the decision-maker of their loyal services), and at worst may unleash a furious counterattack. The simplest modus operandi is to opt for a middle-of-the-road position, or to give a little to one side, and then a little to the other, and so on in unending fashion (so far this seems to be Lyndon B. Johnson's manner of decision-making). It is of interest to note that both Stalin and Mao have had the reputation of being conciliators—perhaps a necessary requisite for a supreme decision-maker in a complex bureaucracy. However, if the "hawk-dove" conflict becomes extreme, then the positions advocated by both sides tend to become increasingly extreme, making compromise more and more difficult, and also conjuring up the possibility that an unequivocal or a clear-cut decision for one or the other may have dangerous and incalculable consequences.

The only other alternative to the supreme decision-maker is to give himself maximal flexibility for ad hoc action by sweeping away all the factions who press in on him. He may be inclined toward one or the other, but he knows that they will always advocate one policy approach, whereas what he wants is to have a free hand to do what he feels correct in terms of his own judgment of the situation. Thus in the Russian situ-

---

[30] Max Beloff notes the increasing concessions made to the army during the years preceding the great purges (see *The Foreign Policy of Soviet Russia*, vol. 1 [London and New York: Oxford University Press, 1947], pp. 178–85). The purge of the army did not begin until 1937, when Stalin had rid himself of his opponents in the party.

ation, some Western observers have argued that Stalin was paving the way for a rapprochement with Germany. That something of the sort was on Stalin's mind is clear from his speech at the Seventeenth Party Congress. But on the other hand, Russia, during the years leading up to Munich, consistently sought to create an anti-Fascist alliance against Germany. That Stalin supported this policy approach as well is undoubtedly true. The truth is probably that Stalin was unwilling to make any firm policy commitment which would bind him. And so to give himself one-man dictatorial control over the situation, he had to strike, not at the roots of the power structure, but at its apexes. Not lacking courage, he decided to make a tabula rasa of all who opposed him. That, I would suggest, is what has happened in China. But one must not forget the atmosphere in which all this has occurred: *patrie en danger!*

In our initial discussion of organization and social control, we pointed out that while organization must remain a structure of power capable of achieving goals, social control, exercised through the authority of elites, serves to gain compliance from the members of the organization. Thus, bureaucratization is an institutional manifestation of the degree to which legitimate authority is accepted within organization, and hence serves as an index of stabilization. One can also argue the reverse, namely to the extent that the environment is defined as potentially stable, bureaucratization will occur, and hence elites exercising legitimate authority will arise. I would say, sociologically, this is what happened in the Soviet Union. Although the process of elite formation began during Stalin's regime, it was only under Khrushchev that national and international peace was accepted as the environment within which the Soviet Union would live in the coming decades. As a result, Soviet elitism flourished. The Chinese damn this phenomenon and fight against it as revisionism.

But the Chinese, neither those now in power nor those purged, have ever accepted this definition of the environment. In fact, the warnings of an imminent war were most shrill during the winter of 1965/66 when Liu Shao-ch'i, P'eng Chen, and Lu Ting-i were still in power. Moreover, campaigns to combat tendencies toward routinization at home had been going on throughout the 1960's. However, we have already pointed out the gap between ideology and practice in China. While the ideology defined the environment as one of continuing struggle, pragmatic reality allowed a process of elite formation centered on the party. Mao has warned several times that unless corrective measures were taken, in the future China would "change color" (that is, cease being red), and revisionism, even fascism, might insidiously triumph. Thus, presumably what Mao means is that, no matter what the ideology says, authoritarian elitism will eventually produce tendencies toward stabilization of the sort which have occurred in the Soviet Union.

But if all the leaders of China feared an eventual war, why then the worry about routinization? If American bombs start falling on China, enemy troops begin to make incursions onto Chinese territory, Chinese soldiers fight in Vietnam, Thailand, or even in the Soviet Far East, it is hard to imagine that the Chinese people would not fight with united determination against the attackers. Some analysts of the Cultural Revolution have argued that Mao unleashed the struggle when he became convinced that the war would not spread to China and therefore concluded that China would benefit from some years of peace and security. In that interim period he was determined to produce those sociopolitical conditions which would guarantee the survival of the New China after his passing from the scene. However, if he made such a determination, it took place at a very peculiar time. The first big blows of the Cultural Revolution fell during the middle of April, 1966, as one can judge from the *Chieh-fang-chün pao* (Liberation Army Daily) editorials which began to appear in *Jen-min jih-pao* (that is, the army striking against the party). The months March and April saw a great intensification of the war in Vietnam. The Buddhist riots erupted in the South, but unlike October, 1963, America gave no indication of welcoming a new government in Saigon and tacitly supported Ky's efforts to suppress the Buddhists. But far more significant was the escalation of the air war over North Vietnam. More bombs were dropped on North Vietnam in March than ever before, and during the first half of April the March tonnage was surpassed. Rail lines leading to China were bombed, and Washington reaffirmed its determination not to allow North Vietnam to use China as a sanctuary, or "rear base area" in the Chinese terminology. Even today North Vietnam formally regards itself as the "rear base area" for the National Liberation Front—and it suffers aerial bombardment. On July 22, 1966, China proclaimed itself the "rear base area" for North Vietnam—interestingly announced by Liu Shao-ch'i in his last public statement. That Mao Tse-tung may not have fully agreed with this position is indicated by the dramatic publicity given his swim down the Yangtze River only a few days later and subsequent Chinese failure to re-emphasize the position taken on July 22. Curiously, Mao swam the Yangtze on July 17, but it was not made public until July 25. Liu Shao-ch'i, in his alleged confession, says that he was in command in Peking "for more than fifty days after June 1"—a time which would extend to July 22, the date when the statement on Vietnam was made. At the very least, one can say that no one in China could have definitely concluded in the spring of 1966 that China need not fear the danger of war crossing its borders.

The question was rather, I would argue, how war should be fought, once it came. I have elsewhere argued that Mao Tse-tung favored his classic strategy of protracted war: not attacking, but digging in, organizing the country, and struggling for an eventual victory in the distant future.[31] Lin Piao, as Mao's designated successor, agreed. But whom did Lin Piao replace as Mao's successor? Liu Shao-ch'i, the man who, since the Tenth Plenum, had been prominently publicized as Mao's closest friend and comrade. If we accept Liu as the real chief of the party, then Mao decided that when war came he wanted the army, not the party, in charge of the country. Clearly he had no fear of the state bureaucracy taking over—bureaucrats have no capacity for war—and so this may explain why the leading state administrators (from Chou En-lai down) have been spared in the Cultural Revolution. I have argued that elements in the top leadership of the party were proposing adventuristic courses of action, and that Mao struck to prevent them from implementing these policies. That Mao has an almost Kutusov-like defensive streak in him is apparent from the whole history of the Chinese Communist movement. In March, 1958, when he was in full command of the Chinese Communist Central Committee (his power emerged decisively in the September-October, 1957, Plenum), he withdraw all Chinese troops from North Korea. In the four years since the Tenth Plenum (September, 1962), Peking had pursued an aggressive ideological foreign policy, generally along the lines of the new Marxist-Leninist ideology. All those purged were leading figures in this foreign policy. Almost without exception, the policy failed—the crowning humiliation being the destruction of the Indonesian Communist Party. Was the party, under the command of Liu, P'eng, and others again proposing another aggressive action, this time in the direction of Vietnam? If so, then once the action started no purge could have erupted in China, for wars unite peoples. An intervention in Vietnam would have confirmed the power position of the party in the manner it was constituted, presumably well into the period after Mao's passing.

If I may be permitted a general observation, I would say that armies are not generally adventuristic and do not want to get involved in wars, but once in, they stick it out to the end. This has been the case with the

---

[31] See my article in the *New York Review of Books,* November 17, 1966.

American armed forces vis-à-vis Vietnam—McNamara's counter-insurgency program was not welcomed by America's military brass, but now the military has become the leading supporter of a war to be fought to final victory. Politicians, on the other hand, tend to be much more adventuristic in the beginning but are also much more prone to compromise when things get tough. The Chinese are fond of citing Khrushchev as their favorite "politician"—he put missiles into Cuba (which the Chinese said they would never have done), but once confronted by the United States he backed down (which the Chinese say was wrong). That the Chinese have also acted in Khrushchevian fashion (for example, Quemoy) is beside the point (every nation has its "politicians"). But Mao detests *cheng-k'o* (politicians) and may have begun to detect in his old comrades such character faults. Suppose China intervened in Vietnam, a war were fought for a few years, and then both sides compromised as happened in Korea? Peace would break out, the country would relax, and the revisionistic tendencies of the party would then appear in full force. And by then Mao might already be out of the picture.

We have suggested an analogy of the Cultural Revolution to the Russian purges. The big difference is that in 1935 Russia was not faced with immediate war, whereas now immediate war cannot be ruled out for China. However, there are indications that Stalin feared a united front against him. After all, he was forced to take a mild position at the Seventeenth Party Congress. Today the leading accusation hurled against the anti-party elements in China is that they "opposed Chairman Mao." Historians like Wu Han and Chien Po-tsan have been bitterly criticized for having covertly criticized Mao in the form of ancient officials berating their emperors. "Defend Mao Tse-tung" has become the chief rallying cry of the Red Guards. If there is substance to these accusations, then some group must have been conspiring to seize absolute power within the country. There is evidence that the Red Army supported Stalin's initial moves against the Old Bolsheviks, and the same appears now to have been the case in China.

In Russia the cult of personality around Stalin arose with the revival of Russian nationalism. It reached its extreme expression during the war against the Germans when Stalin was regarded by almost all Soviet citizens as their personal leader. Now in China the cult of Mao Tse-tung is accompanied by a new nascent nationalism—pride in China and hatred of things foreign (the Russians accuse the Chinese of great-power chauvinism and xenophobia—phenomena they well understand from their own history). Stalin's foreign policy from the time of the purges to the invasion of Russia can be described as a series of efforts to delay attack on the Soviet Union as long as possible. The policy of trying to organize a popular front, of seeking alliances with France and England, and finally the Nazi-Soviet Pact were all aspects of this policy. Stalin, first and foremost, advocated the primacy of Russia's national interests. Stalin was not an expansionist but a man cautious to an extraordinary degree. I suggest that we have in Mao a similar figure. Like Stalin, Mao is reaching toward the cult of personality and a new nationalism as more reliable instruments of ideology than the classic Marxism-Leninism of his Old Bolshevik comrades.

If we see the Cultural Revolution as an attack against the party as a source of authority and against the Old Bolsheviks as a threatening source of power, then the violent attacks against the Soviet Union begin to make sense. The entire ideological thrust of Marxism-Leninism rested on the assumption that Russia, no matter how degenerate, was still a socialist state, one that by virtue of its inherent nature had interests in the long run identical with those of China. The doctrine of a "Holy Alliance" of America and Russia against China could not be espoused in Marxist-Leninist terms, for then Russia, like Yugoslavia, would have reverted to a capitalist stage, annulling the laws of world history. The bitter anti-Soviet internationalism propounded by P'eng Chen, Lu Ting-i, and others foresaw an eventual return of the Soviet Union to the camp of true Marxism-Leninism. In November, 1965, Soong Ching-ling hailed the forty-eighth anniversary of the October Revolution in terms of warmest friendship for the Soviet Union and its people. But in 1966, the Chinese gesture was minimal, as its references to Marxism-Leninism are minimal. What the propagandists of China are now demanding of the people is that the thought of Mao Tse-tung be accepted as the canon of ideological truth, and not what hitherto had been called Marxism-Leninism. However, Marxism-Leninism is not attacked directly (just as Stalin did not attack Bolshevik ideology directly but under the guise of Trotzkyism and Menshevism), though the Soviet Union is. The concrete message is clear—China has nothing to hope for from the Soviet Union and may even have to suffer joint attack by Russia and America on its territory. When Khrushchev appeared to respond positively to Averell Harriman's suggestion that Russia and America collaborate to destroy China's nuclear installations, the Chinese Marxist-Leninists argued this away as the product of a degenerate leadership. Such action could not conform with the true interests of the Soviet Union. Today, the new ideology argues simply that this is but the natural expression of a modern revisionism which has infected all of Soviet society. The attacks on revisionism, however, have the effect of undermining the ideological authority of the CCP, without cutting it off entirely from its Marxist-Leninist past.

We would do well to remember that the present leaders of China, whose Chinese heritage and Communist past both have trained them to think in historical terms, regard America as a reincarnation of German and Japanese imperialism. No amount of intellectual protestation that this is not so will convince the Chinese otherwise. Even policy changes will only be regarded by the Chinese as tactical moves, made under pressure or because temporary accommodation with China would serve American interests somewhere else on the globe. The Chinese are convinced that Americans want to destroy them and that only counterforce will deter them and, if they try, defeat them. Russia they see as a cowardly, frightened nation willing to make any and all concessions to America to avert attack. China must stand alone.

China's development over the last decade and a half is inconceivable without its Communist party—a powerful leadership organization motivated by a Marxist-Leninist ideology. Nationalists are poor organizers and developers, and so most nationalist movements in the developing countries have little to show for their economic efforts—unless they have opted to depend heavily on one of the great power blocs. But nationalism is a powerful unifying force during times of war and crisis, and the personal charisma of a Stalin and a Mao is one of the most intense expressions of modern nationalism. Mao's attack on the party derives from his conviction that a new authoritarian elite would gradually erode the revolutionary fervor of China's people, her youth in particular. My own belief is that Mao sees revolutionary fervor as China's main hope of survival in the face of a threatening war. Stalin did not believe that Germany was going to attack Russia in 1935, and it is not likely that Mao feels that a massive American onslaught against China will begin in 1967. After all, the American build-up in eastern Asia has not yet been completed. However, Mao thinks in terms of long spans of time and has no faith in the ability of men of good will to affect the course of world history. Whether the Vietnam war ends in negotiations or in further escalation will not likely affect Mao's belief in the inevitability of the Sino-American armed confrontation.

Unless we assume he is insane, Mao cannot fail to realize that the Red Guard movement will "affect production," and that the weakening of the party deprives the leadership of its main peacetime instrument for mobilizing the population toward greater economic efforts. During the great crisis of 1960–61, Peking undertook a widespread rectification movement within the party which was not halted until late 1961. In

1962, it reversed itself and began building up the party again. The weakening of the party, in the context of the great economic failures, led to pragmatism as the only method of getting the economy moving again. On the other hand, if China is to enter a permanent state of mobilization in preparation for a large-scale war, then there may be a reason for the anti-organizational and anti-ideological aspects of the Cultural Revolution. In North Vietnam, judging from the reports of Harrison Salisbury and others, the population has been mobilized not just by organizational manipulation from the top, but by a spontaneous involvement of the people in the defense of their country motivated by an intense nationalism and national pride. That mobilization Mao undoubtedly regards as an ideal example of a people's war, an example of "centralism" (organizational leadership, control, and direction) coupled with "democracy" (the spontaneous enthusiasm of the masses). China underwent its six years of bureaucratic centralism during the recent recovery period. Now Mao has decided that it must be balanced with "extensive democracy." Whether this man of grand visions and schematic thinking is right or wrong remains to be seen.

# Comments by Ezra F. Vogel

Just as Professor Schurmann's book, *Ideology and Organization in Communist China* opened up new and uncharted territory, so his present paper is a great stimulus for analyzing the movement now in progress, the Great Proletarian Cultural Revolution. The core of Professor Schurmann's argument is that it was an urgent sense of external danger to the fatherland that led to the Cultural Revolution. I believe this interpretation has considerable merit because it accurately reflects a mood inside China. The Cultural Revolution was launched in the fall of 1965 when American involvement in Vietnam made threat of attack on mainland China more real than ever before and within months after it became clear that China could no longer count on the Soviet nuclear umbrella. The period between the first Chinese nuclear explosion and the development of an effective delivery capacity is one of maximum vulnerability, and the Chinese were acutely sensitive to discussions in America about the possibility of "taking out" Chinese nuclear capacity. The intense mobilization for guerrilla warfare throughout China in mid-1965, to say nothing of the partial evacuation of southern Chinese cities, attests to the sense of crisis. As limited as information is about high-level Chinese thinking in mid-1965, the speeches of Lo Jui-ch'ing and Lin Piao alone make clear that an intense debate was raging about ways to defend against enemy attack.[1]

I believe, however, that two qualifications should be made to Professor Schurmann's main thesis. The first is that the Chinese Communist setbacks in Africa and Southeast Asia have not been as devastating and disappointing to the Chinese as most foreigners have assumed. Chinese and foreigners who have traveled in Communist China beyond the limited foreign diplomatic community reveal that there is a very low level of interest in events in foreign countries. Africa and even Southeast Asia seem much more remote to people in Peking than to people in Washington, and current setbacks seem less final in a country like China with very long historical perspective than in America where yesterday's news looms much larger. The sense of crisis in Peking was thus less affected by what Americans view as "Peking's disastrous foreign failures" than by the fear that the fatherland itself might be attacked.

The second qualification is that the sense of danger to the fatherland was merely a touchstone, an efficient cause, setting off the Cultural Revolution. The disputes revealed in the Cultural Revolution had become serious long before 1965 when the sense of danger became acute, and the Cultural Revolution not only continued but expanded even after the sense of acute danger subsided.

A tacit understanding seems to have been reached in late 1965 between the United States and China which restricted the expansion of the war and removed the danger of involvement. Beginning in late 1965 the evacuation of south Chinese cities was gradually discontinued. In 1966 Foreign Minister Chen Yi told a visiting Japanese leader, Zentaro Kosaka, that he did not believe the United States would attack China. Yet the Cultural Revolution continued to expand.

In tracing the roots of the struggle before 1965, I feel that I should begin with a self-confession, just as low-level functionaries in mainland China must confess errors every time a policy changes to bring their thought and activity into line with the new policy. Although we academicians had been aware of serious problems within the party for some

[1] [For an analysis of this debate, see chapter 2 and chapter 9, vol. 2.— EDITOR.]

years, none of us predicted the nature and severity of the Cultural Revolution. We must now modify our analysis of this period in line with the seriousness of the struggle and subsequent revelations. In defense of China watchers, I might ask how many Americans in 1959 would have predicted the composition of the President's cabinet in 1967 or the content of the latest State of the Union message, and how many today could predict which public figures will be on the ascendancy eight years from now and which major issues will occupy their attention. We have even less information about high-level thinking in China and this forces us China watchers to proceed with modesty, caution, and tentativeness. With this confession, I would like, in the light of what we now know of the seriousness of the recent Cultural Revolution and the revelations it brought, to highlight some of the inner tensions which formed the background of the Cultural Revolution.

Serious internal tensions and struggles have characterized the Chinese Communist Party (CCP) from its very early days. Nevertheless, I believe that from 1945 until 1955, despite the problems of regularizing and disciplining local party groups as the nation was brought under Communist rule, the CCP enjoyed an impressive degree of solidarity.

The year 1956 in many ways represents a watershed in the development of internal dissent. The criticisms of Stalin for his excesses and his cult of personality at the Twentieth Party Congress in early 1956 could not have come at a less opportune time for Chairman Mao. He had resolved the debates about collectivization in mid-1955 with a decision to move rapidly. The excesses of collectivization and the accompanying *Su-fan* Campaign were already disturbing to the Chinese when socialist transformation reached its peak in January, 1956, just before the denunciation of Stalin, and the similarities between Mao and Stalin were not lost on critics within China. Recent official Red Guard newspapers have revealed that Teng Hsiao-p'ing and Liu Shao-ch'i criticized Mao in 1956 for the "cult of personality," forced the convening of the Eighth Party Congress in mid-1956 (the first in eleven years) and led the drafting of a new party constitution which emphasized inner-party democracy.

Mao tried to defend himself by showing that he and the party, unlike Stalin, could accept criticism. He even launched an ill-fated campaign encouraging criticism, but in 1958 he again resolved internal debates in an equally radical manner. By now the failure of the Great Leap Forward is familiar to everyone. But new information coming from the Cultural Revolution and recent Red Guard publications enables us to confirm the intensity of the personal attacks on Mao which resulted from these failures. The painfulness of the growing rift with the Soviet Union later added further fuel for criticisms of Mao.

Criticism was sufficiently severe that by December, 1958, at the Wuhan Plenum Mao gave up his presidency, and in the summer of 1959 at the Lushan Plenum he "fought off a rightist attack."

The Ninth Plenum of January, 1961, opened up new freedoms and also new criticisms. Materials from the official Chinese Communist press make it abundantly clear that there were serious criticisms of Mao and his closest allies, published in such newspapers as the *Peiching wan pao* (Peking Evening News) and the Peking party's theoretical organ, *Ch'ien-hsien* (Front Line). Some of the 1961–62 criticism recently re-published went so far as to suggest that Mao was suffering from amnesia and was not in full possession of his faculties. It is now clear that some leading members of the Politburo had tried to reduce Mao's power and prevent him from exercising active control over internal party and government activities.

The crises created by the Great Leap Forward—the food shortages, the precarious economy, and low morale—made it difficult for Mao to launch a counterattack as early as 1961–62. Mao endured considerable criticism in this period, but by the fall of 1962 as conditions began to take an upswing, Mao undertook a counterattack. Conditions had not yet sufficiently improved to permit launching a full-scale purge, if indeed he then felt it necessary. Beginning at the Tenth Plenum in the fall of 1962 he initiated not a purge but a Socialist Education Campaign, with a content almost identical with that of the Great Proletarian Cultural Revolution. An important component of the series of campaigns which began in the fall of 1962 was the attempt to rehabilitate the image of Chairman Mao. Unable to speak Mandarin without a strong accent and confronted by numerous dialects throughout the country, Mao, as always, made his broad appeal through the written word. The campaigns to study Mao's writings, despite their excesses, undoubtedly helped to enhance his image and to create serious obstacles for would-be critics.

It is quite possible that as the study of Mao's works reached a height in 1963–64 (March, 1964, being the apex), Mao was trying to create a high tide of enthusiasm that would permit some limited purges of his opposition. Indeed, by 1964 Mao was initiating some highly selective purges. His criticism of Yang Hsien-chen, head of the party school in 1964, was in the classic Chinese Communist (and even traditional Chinese) mold of criticizing one figure to warn others. The Yang Hsien-chen case was interpreted in precisely this way by the opposition as well as by Mao. It now appears, however, that Mao was unable to isolate his opponents. This confronted him with the dilemma of living with the opposition or carrying out attacks on a very broad scale.

At the end of 1964 Chou En-lai in a speech to the National People's Congress acknowledged serious debates over the course of the Third Five-Year Plan and detailed some of the serious criticisms within the party. Some comrades favored the extension of private plots and free markets, and urged that small enterprises be responsible for their own profits and losses. Some comrades wanted greater concessions in United Front work; in foreign policy, they wanted "three conciliations and one reduction": conciliation with imperialism, with reactionaries, and modern revisionism, and the reduction of assistance and support to the revolutionary struggles of other peoples. In other words, some opponents within the party were advocating closer relationships with Russia and the United States.

These debates intensified in 1965 partly because the American pressure in Vietnam created the possibility that China might become involved in the conflict with the United States without the Soviet nuclear shield. China had sometimes talked with bravado about not fearing nuclear war, but the talk had come easily because China had assessed the possibility as remote. In 1965 China lacked this luxury, and the intensity of pressure for greater, though limited, co-operation with the Soviet Union is revealed in Lo Jui-ch'ing's speech of the summer of 1965 and by the efforts of Japanese Communist Party members. To return to Professor Schurmann's main theme, the country was in danger. To many party leaders it was the adventurism of Mao in pushing the break with the Soviet Union, in pushing toward hostilities with the United States, and in making inadequate preparations of modern military equipment that put the country in danger. Who could better give reassurance to the people than the leading military hero and leader, Lin Piao? Lin Piao in his famous speech on the anniversary of victory against the Japanese, emphasized the success of guerrilla warfare. In other words, the country was not in such serious danger, for even if invaders came, guerrillas could stand against aggression just as they had won out over the seemingly superior Japanese. In 1961–62 Mao could not launch a strong counterattack for fear of disrupting a precarious economy, and in 1964–65 he could not launch a strong attack on internal enemies for fear of risking internal disorder while there was a serious possibility of foreign conflict in Vietnam. It was thus only in late 1965 when the situation with the United States over Vietnam had eased and war seemed very unlikely that Mao took the initiative in launching a serious attack against his opposition. It was the easing of the Vietnam situation and the decreased likelihood of confrontation that made the launching of the Great Proletarian Cultural Revolution feasible.

The decision to focus the campaign initially on cultural activities was, I think, dictated by at least two considerations. One is that the most vocal and vehement opposition to Mao had come through the cultural and propaganda media. Mao's intellectual critics had used historical analogies and parables but their attack was vicious and their impact, especially on youth, serious. The second consideration is that if Mao wished to push an all-out campaign, he first had to consolidate his control over the mass media. The purges in mid-1966 were almost entirely among party figures in the propaganda-culture-education spheres, thus insuring a responsive mass media if and when the purges were expanded beyond the propaganda-culture-education sphere.

Any upheaval as large as the Cultural Revolution cannot be explained by any simple single cause. Many other factors, some of which have been dealt in other papers, are also involved: the difference between the visionaries and the political commissars, the concern about the hardening of bureaucracy into traditional patterns, and the loss of revolutionary fervor, especially among young people. While these factors provide a background, I do not feel that the current turmoil can be understood apart from the active political maneuvering of the leading figures.

Anyone aware of the turmoil in China over the last century—the costs of disunity and the painfulness of building an organization capable of uniting the country—cannot but share Professor Schurmann's anxieties about the assaults on existing organizations. Never before has Mao had to use an ad hoc organization outside the party to carry on purges within the party. The encouragement to revolutionary alliances modeled after the Paris Commune hardly contributed to organizational regularity. The seriousness of fissures within the party will make it difficult ever to achieve the level of unanimity and responsiveness that the CCP could once command. These internal fissures cannot be sealed over quickly or easily. But the demise of the party, so eagerly discussed by poorly informed American journalists and romantic European leftists, has been exaggerated. Although party committees were frontally assaulted and party members afraid to meet, select party members were given responsible positions in Triple Alliances and Revolutionary Military Committees. Official statements emanating from Peking have stressed that the party will remain the supreme power and that only a small number of people in authority need be attacked. Party members can be required to spend more time studying the thoughts of Mao and to mouth all the current slogans. Some can be replaced. But even a visionary rebel like Mao, who still commands an enormous following, lacks the will and the power to overturn completely the powerful party which he and his opponents created. It is unlikely that the powerful party organization which survived the economic disasters of the Great Leap Forward will be destroyed by teen-agers, wall posters, or its own chairman.

# Notes by Richard H. Solomon:
# Mao's Linking of Foreign Relations with China's Domestic Political Process[1]

U.S. Imperialism sees in China the biggest obstacle in the way of its domination of the world. Its inveterate hatred for the Chinese people, this kind of mad hostility, is itself evidence that the Chinese people are the most revolutionary and most progressive. If things were not this way, U.S. Imperialism would not be opposing us. To be opposed by our enemy is not a bad thing; it adds to our glory.[2]

What is the relationship between China's foreign involvements and her domestic political and economic life? This is one of the more intriguing questions raised by the Cultural Revolution. During the years 1966 and 1967 Communist China initiated conflicts with practically every nation on her borders, and in what seems an almost systematic fashion alienated her few remaining "neutral" or socialist friends through an aggressive diplomacy and subversive intervention in their

---

[1] [Professor Solomon's paper was written for the Second Conference on China sponsored by the University of Chicago Center for Policy Study. It is printed here because it bears on the theme of this collection of papers and is a good supplement to Professor Schurmann's paper.—Editor's note.]

[2] "Observer," in *Jen-min jih-pao* (People's Daily), February 20, 1966.

internal affairs. As Cambodia's Prince Sihanouk observed at a September 1967 press conference: "The change in China's policy toward us and the giving up of the Bandung principles of nonintervention dated from the Cultural Revolution exactly."[3]

The Mao-Lin leadership faction seems to want to take on the entire world, yet paradoxically with policies that appear to work at cross-purposes to each other: attempting to counter the United States in Vietnam through continuing support for a "people's war" while at the same time actively exacerbating China's relations with the Soviet Union; seeking rapid economic progress at home, yet threatening to abolish the wage incentives, rural markets, and private plots, which have been some of the mainstays of the recent recovery from the production failures of the Great Leap Forward. In these brief remarks I would like to explore the twisted logic which evidently lies behind the policies of the Mao-Lin leadership group, for from their perspective this orientation to the world may not *seem* so contradictory or self-defeating. (Whether or not it *is*, in fact, a viable policy position is quite another question!) In particular, foreign relations seem to occupy an important place in Mao's strategy for energizing the Chinese people for the tasks of building a modern nation. And of late, it should be added, dealings with the foreign world seem to be playing an equally vital role in Mao-Lin's efforts to consolidate (or perhaps now just simply to preserve) their power within China.

In the broadest sense the Cultural Revolution now working its way out on the mainland seems to be an attempt by Mao to insure the continued vitality of the Chinese social revolution. And of necessity for the aging leader, this effort has involved the issue of succession.[4] The extraordinary, and I would say totally unexpected, break in discipline of the Long March generation of leaders seems related above all to Mao's uncompromising efforts to see leadership and policy preserved in his own image. From the perspective of hindsight, it appears that Mao has viewed the problem of succession at two levels: first, at the level of immediately maintaining "correct" leadership and policy orientation within the party; and second, in terms of insuring the continued revolutionary enthusiasm and discipline of the younger generation. In

[3] Phnom Penh Radio, September 18, 1967.

[4] Indeed, if we are to believe wall poster reports that Mao was actually voted out of office as State Chairman in 1958, the Cultural Revolution represents an attempt by Mao to *reassert* his leadership. See *New York Times*, January 6, 1967, p. 1.

practice the distinction between these two levels is not always clear, for they are linked in the way the Red Guards have been set against Mao's opponents within the party; yet for analytical purposes I would like to approach these two levels separately, as foreign relations seems to influence each in a somewhat different manner.

Concerning the maintenance of revolutionary élan among China's young people, during 1964 a number of articles appeared in official party publications dealing with the necessity of "cultivating revolutionary successors." The leadership appeared to have grave doubts about the political reliability of Chinese youth. One of the extraordinary things about this concern was the degree to which it was perceived by the party within the context of its foreign relations. In an unusually frank statement which betrays a self-conscious, looking-over-the-shoulder quality, a *Hung-ch'i* (Red Flag) editorial commented:

> Seen in terms of the state of the international and domestic class struggle, the question of cultivating successors [to lead the revolution] has become increasingly urgent and important. Internationally, imperialism headed by the United States has placed its hope of realizing "peaceful evolution" in China on the corruption of our third and fourth generations. *Who can say that this way of thinking of theirs is not without a certain foundation?*[5]

But while the United States was seen as entertaining all too realistic hopes for a corruption of the younger generations' revolutionary will, the "revisionist" policies of the Soviet Union were perceived as a more direct threat:

> . . . if . . . youths who have been influenced or exploited by capitalist or revisionist thinking become successors, then the revolution might not be brought to completion; then socialism might "peacefully evolve" towards capitalism, there might come about a capitalist restoration. Within the world communist movement there is already the lesson of this happening: the modern revisionists are doing their utmost to use bourgeois individualist thinking to corrupt the revolutionary will of the younger generation, causing them to become pampered little gentry who will only know how to seek after personal pleasure, who will only know how to eat, drink, and play. . . .[6]

---

[5] "P'ei-yang chieh-pan-jen shih ko-ming shih-yeh ti ch'ien-nien wan-nien ta-chi" [The Cultivation of Successors Is an Unending Great Task of Revolution], *Hung-ch'i* [Red Flag], no. 14, 1964, p. 34 (italics added).

[6] *Ibid.*, p. 35.

Through the Marxist rhetoric comes the unmistakable terminology of what some have considered to be a bygone era in China: "pampered little gentry who will only know how to . . . eat, drink, and play."

Mao apparently finds himself in much the same position as a traditional *chia-chang*—a clan or family leader—who through struggle and sacrifice has raised up family fortunes only to find, or fear, that his younger, pampered charges are interested only in eating up the fruits of his labors. Indeed, I do not think it would be too much to say that Mao is highly conscious of the continued existence of those social factors, deeply rooted in Chinese tradition, which have contributed to the recurrent historical pattern of political vitalization and expansion, decline, and collapse—the so-called dynastic cycle: the tendency of the political class to be vulnerable to "sugar-coated bullets"; their anxious striving for the security found in bureaucratic entrenchment; and the inclination of those with power to produce overpampered and under-disciplined offspring.[7]

Mao breaks with Chinese tradition, however, in seeking a solution to the problem of maintaining mass revolutionary discipline and commitment within the broader context of doctrinal and political threats from abroad. In the simplest terms his answer might be phrased as, "the need for enemies."[8] Out of his experience born of the protracted struggle for power in a society by tradition politically passive, Mao perceives in the tension of political "contradiction" and conflict the engine of popular mobilization and the motive of change. Enemies, in Mao's view, are crucial to stimulating popular involvement in the tasks of social development, for "changes in society are due chiefly to the development of the . . . contradictions between the old and new."[9] Or

[7] See *Jen-min jih-pao* and *Hung-ch'i* editorial, "Carry the Great Proletarian Revolution through to the End," *Peking Review*, no. 1, January 1, 1967, p. 8. It is notable that Mao has grafted this distinctly Chinese view of historical processes onto Marxism's unilinear concept of social progress. The notion of the possibility of a "restoration of capitalism" seems to me to be particularly Chinese in quality; a distinct "revision" of Marxist theory. Indeed, Mao now claims to have faced up to the problem of "whether or not the proletariat is able to *maintain* political power and prevent a capitalist restoration after it has seized political power" (italics added), whereas the October Revolution only solved the question of the seizure of power.

[8] An early example of Mao's perception of the positive political value of an enemy is his 1939 article, "It is a good thing and not a bad thing to be opposed by the enemy," republished in *Selected Readings from Mao Tse-tung's Works* (Peking: People's Publishing House, 1964).

[9] Mao Tse-tung, "On Contradiction," in *Selected Works of Mao Tse-tung*, vol. 1 (Peking: Foreign Languages Press, 1964), p. 314.

in the rather more forthright language of an authoritative "Observer" writing in the official party paper, *Jen-min jih-pao:*

> The Chinese people's great enemy is U.S. imperialism. This enemy is indeed most hateful and harmful to us; *but we must see that its existence also has a beneficial effect on us.* To have a ferocious enemy like U.S. imperialism glowering at us and threatening us day and night will make us Chinese people always bear in mind the danger of war while living in peace and raise our vigilance a hundred fold; will keep us always on the alert and enable our enthusiasm to burst forth; can help the Chinese people to always maintain preparedness and sharpen our fighting spirit. Wanton U.S. imperialist aggression and intimidation can further raise our political consciousness, strengthen our unity and enhance our combat readiness.[10]

It is within this twisted logic, born of Mao's fear of a flagging of the will to change at home, and a sense of threat to domestic political discipline in more moderate "revisionist" and "imperialist" policies abroad, that Mao-Lin seem to be pressing for the continuation of a "people's war" in Vietnam and unremitting hostility toward the Soviet Union: for in making an enemy of the Russians they seek to render invalid the appeal of more moderate foreign Communist policies to would-be Chinese "revisionists"; and in the continued conflict in Vietnam they see a confirmation of their view of "U.S. imperialism" and a context within which to renew the validity of Maoist policies to doubters at home.[11] "Enemies" abroad help to counter more fearful threats within. Or as *Chieh-fang-chün pao* (Liberation Army Daily) phrased it not too long ago:

> Historical experience proves that any enemy, however ferocious and whatever his tricks, is not to be feared. What is fearful is that we ourselves may lack vigilance and let our minds be disarmed.[12]

[10] Kuan-ch'a-chia, "Po Pang-ti" [A Retort to Bundy], *Jen-min jih-pao* [People's Daily], February 20, 1966, p. 4 (italics added).

[11] Indeed, the present United States posture in Vietnam would seem to be ideal from Mao-Lin's perspective, for in our continued bombing of the North and the introduction of ever greater numbers of troops into the South, reality is given to their image of "U.S. imperialism"; yet our self-imposed limitation of the conflict means that China bears no major or direct military cost herself.

[12] *Chieh-fang-chün pao* [Liberation Army Daily], "Never Forget the Class Struggle" (editorial), May 4, 1966; trans. in *Peking Review*, May 13, 1966, p. 42.

Foreign relations now seem to be playing a significant role in Mao's efforts to consolidate his leadership position within the party. During the latter half of 1966, the Cultural Revolution appears to have changed qualitatively from a dispute over issues and the implementation of policy to an unabashed struggle for organizational control, a conflict over basic power. This is now indicated openly in the domestic press, as in the anxious and insistent call of a *Jen-min jih-pao* editorial: "Proletarian Revolutionaries, Form a Great Alliance to Seize Power from Those in Authority Who Are Taking the Capitalist Road!"[13]

Central to an understanding of this breakdown in political authority is a perception of the basis upon which Mao has attempted to claim from his peers overriding control of party, state, and military policy. Prior to 1957 one would have said that Mao could have phrased his claim to full authority in the terms of strategic successes dating back as far as the days in the *Chingkang shan*. But beginning, I would say, with the failure of the Hundred Flowers strategy for winning the active support of China's intellectuals (and avoiding a "Hungary" in China), and through the near disaster of the Great Leap Forward, the high economic, military, and political costs of the dispute with the Russians, and the more recent failures to gain a following among the "revolutionary peoples of Asia, Africa, and Latin America," Mao's political judgment must have come under increasingly serious questioning within the party.

During the summer of 1966, when military clashes in north China are now reported to have been narrowly averted,[14] Lin Piao appealed for support of Mao's leadership in somber and blunt terms unheard of in China for several decades:

> Our country is a great land of seven hundred million people, and the entire country must have unified thinking. If we unite on the basis of the thought of Mao Tse-tung, then we can have united action. But if a nation of seven hundred million people does not have unified thinking then it will just be like a sheet of scattered sand.[15]

[13] Trans. in *Peking Review,* January 27, 1967, p. 7.

[14] A summary of Yugoslav and Japanese reports on these incidents was published in *Chung-yang jih-pao* [Central Daily News] (Taipei), December 29, 1966.

[15] *Hung-ch'i* editorial, "Victoriously Advance on the Road of Mao Tse-tung's Thought," no. 11, 1966, p. 21; and *Jen-min jih-pao,* August 22, 1966, p. 2.

That Lin felt compelled to invoke Sun Yat-sen's sad image, born of the turmoil of the warlord era, of China as a "sheet of scattered sand," is perhaps an indication of just how serious the threat of domestic political fragmentation was even during the summer of 1966.

If Mao's past successes, and even the threat of a return to domestic political chaos, have been insufficient to insure the continued legitimacy of "the thought of Mao Tse-tung" as China's unifying social ideology, how have Mao-Lin attempted to maintain and consolidate their position in the current struggle? There is no simple answer to this question, but a partial explanation again takes us to China's dealings with foreign nations, communist parties, and revolutionary groups—and back to some distinctly Chinese forms of political legitimation.

Most simply stated, the proposition advanced here is that, as the stability of Mao's domestic political position has *decreased,* the claims made for the universal acceptance and validity of his doctrines have concurrently *increased.* There are several ways in which this proposition might be illustrated, but perhaps the most convincing are those which indicate a relationship between domestic press accounts of foreign opinion and events, and internal Chinese political processes. Current research indicates that "isolation" forms of sanctions are both potent and dominant within the Chinese political culture;[16] isolation either in the sense of being made to "stick out" from one's proper place in society—as we see in the way Mao's political enemies are now paraded through the streets of Peking decked out in dunce caps and self-effacing signs—or isolation in the sense of being "cut off" from a base of support. As Mao's policies have increasingly envenomed relations with the outside world, and with the Soviet Union in particular, Chinese fears of becoming isolated internationally have undoubtedly been stimulated. We see indirect evidence of this in such domestic press materials as recent appeals to emulate the revolutionary writer Lu Hsün:

> Enemy encirclement and persecution made [Lu Hsün] all the more resolute. The enemy encirclement and persecution brought out and tempered [his] fighting spirit. *Lu Hsün did not feel alone when dark clouds obscured the sky and he was isolated.* This was because he breathed the same air as the masses and threw in his lot with them, because he stood with Chairman Mao, the great

---

[16] Solomon, "The Chinese Revolution and the Politics of Dependency" (working draft), pp. 70–71, 299–307.

leader of the Chinese people. At the time, although on the surface he was isolated, truth was on his side. . . .[17]

In an apparent effort to counter Chinese fears of the isolating effects
of Mao's policy of provoking enemies abroad, the central press is filled
with accounts of support for China's righteous policies, and praise of
Mao as the most creative Marxist-Leninist of the age, by Albanian,
Australian, and a variety of other "Marxist-Leninist" Communist party
factions. While in numerical terms these small parties and splinter
groups are a political cipher within the world Communist movement,
through the amplifying voice of *Jen-min jih-pao* they become a reassuring chorus giving a semblance of reality to the oft-repeated and
reassuring slogan, "Our friends fill the world."

Foreign support for Mao and his policies, as reported in *Jen-min jih-
pao,* appears to have increased markedly during the latter half of 1966
—just as his domestic political position has apparently met increasingly
serious opposition. Almost daily there are full-page spreads of the
successful progress of "people's wars" in Laos and Vietnam, and of the
righteous revolutionary struggles of oppressed peoples in the Middle
East and Latin America. What is more, the fulsome praise of Chairman
Mao emanating from the mouths of *foreigners* had reached new ex-
tremes. An Australian "Marxist-Leninist" party paper proclaims, "the
thought of Mao Tse-tung is the highest development of Marxism-
Leninism, and as far as the oppressed peoples are concerned it is the
embodiment of life; whereas to the oppressors it signifies destruction."[18]
Friends from the Congo, Syria, and Argentina proclaim Mao as "the
savior of the world's oppressed peoples," and affirm that "Mao Tse-
tung's thought is the most powerful weapon for the liberation of mankind."[19] Mao's works are reported to be read widely in Burmese, French,
and English translations. And the *Jen-min jih-pao* "Observer" proclaims with some pretense: "All revolutionary people are eager to find
a path to their own liberation. The path the Chinese people have taken
is exactly the one they want to take. China's influence spreads far and
wide because China's experience and destiny are also theirs."[20]

Such panegyrics, oriented above all for *domestic* consumption, cannot but evoke the image of China's traditional style of foreign relations:

[17] *Hung-ch'i* editorial, "Commemorating Lu Hsun—Our Forerunner in the
Cultural Revolution," trans. in *Peking Review,* November 4, 1966, p. 9 (italics
added).

[18] *Jen-min jih-pao,* December 3, 1966, p. 1.

[19] *Ibid.,* December 5, 1966, p. 5.      [20] Kuan-ch'a-chia, "Po Pang-ti."

of emperors who sought to insure the prestige and preeminence of their rule at home through the tribute of "barbarians" who approached the cultural center in ritualistic awe; and where the willingness of foreigners to emulate the cultural style of the Central Kingdom strengthened the validity of that style within China itself. For with Albanian and Australian Communists praising Mao's "anti-revisionist" stance, who within the party is to question his policy of hostility toward the Soviet Union? With Vietnamese and Thais proclaiming the validity of "people's wars" for their own national liberation, who is to challenge the correctness of Lin's strategy for defeating imperialism? And with Syrians and Argentines proclaiming the relevance of the thought of Mao Tse-tung for solving their own domestic problems, who among the Chinese masses is to doubt that similar policies are not appropriate for China? In *Jen-min jih-pao*'s world of universal praise for Chairman Mao and the implacable hostility of China's enemies, all policy alternatives lose their validity—and to propose alternatives is to side with those enemies.

In sum, the apparently paradoxical policies of Lin-Mao have an inner coherency based on the particular difficulties confronting the Chinese revolution. They represent an attempt to find a solution to the problems of how to put China firmly on the road to social modernization: a combination of tradition (the reassuring praise of the *foreigner* for the emperor, and validation of his policies through their emulation abroad) and innovation (the calculated cultivation of "enemies" at home and abroad to provide "contradictions" and tension) to energize popular participation in the revolutionary tasks of building a new China. A continuation of support for the "people's war" in Vietnam and calculated cultivation of hostile relations with the Soviet Union[21] and other neighboring countries at present are the embodiment of the Lin-Mao approach to placing foreign relations in the service of China's domestic political process.

[21] The recent incident of Chinese students in Moscow provoking scuffles at Lenin's tomb, and the subsequent mass rallies in Peking and "struggles" against the Russian diplomatic community in the Chinese capital, seems just one more indication of a calculated policy of seeking to eliminate foreign influence in China, and bring about domestic unity through creating "enemies" abroad. Similar tactics have even been used against the French. See *New York Times,* February 2 and 4, 1967.

Francis L. K. Hsü

# 10

# Chinese Kinship and Chinese Behavior

Observers of China have often polarized their views: before the Communist Revolution the theme of the unchanging East predominated. Even when some changes were noted, the difficulties in effecting those changes were underlined. Since 1949 the Western view has tended to converge on the opposite pole. All traditional Chinese ways are supposed to have been swept away by the new regime in one stroke.

Neither of these views is in accord with what we know about human behavior. Over the centuries every culture has changed to a greater or lesser extent—the problem is that some cultures have changed much faster than others. Chinese culture as a whole has changed much more slowly than its Western counterpart as a whole. Thus, though Marco Polo (1254–1324?) was greatly astonished by the cultural achievements of China, by the first half of the 19th century the Middle Kingdom could neither match Western power of production nor find any answer to Western encroachment. Whether we think of science and technology, or of modern government and education, or even of art and literature, the West and not China holds world leadership since then.

The problem of why some cultures have undergone astonishing changes while others have not is by no means easy to solve. However, so long as we keep thinking in terms of complete change or no change, instead of beginning to scrutinize—on a comparative basis—how far each culture has changed and in what ways, we shall never even come close to solving that problem.

Similarly, if we concentrate all our attention on details and do not rise above them, we can perhaps see the immediate causes and the superficial meaning of a few events, but we can never discover the fuller pattern of change and continuity in culture.

In the following pages I shall analyze certain aspects of Chinese behavior under communism and relate them to each other as well as trace their genesis in the Chinese kinship system. In this I have been

579

stimulated by a number of papers presented at this Conference. In his analysis of the present Red Guard movement in China, Franz Schurmann concludes that its object of attack is the party elite, and not the army and the bureaucracy. He is correct as far as he goes, but he merely tells us that the Maoists have taken action X and not Y or Z. He does not ask the more important questions: What is the relationship between X and Y and Z, or between X, Y, and Z on the one hand and A, B, and C (which are prominent factors in the larger picture) on the other? It is important to gain some idea as to the immediate target of so spectacular a phenomenon as the Red Guard, but unless we also attempt to assess happenings in conjunction with the larger and relatively more permanent objective of the regime, our interpretations will remain unrelated to each other or to the central characteristics of Chinese society and culture.

Moreover, Schurmann dismisses the problem of kinship as a major concern of the Chinese leaders in Peking. He writes:

> Kinship is an organizing principle for the perpetuation of authority. If it should turn out that the "rich peasants" of a certain county are related and actively pursue the achievement of kinship ties (through intermarriage), and if it should be that the party functionaries of a province are similarly related, then familism, that most ancient of China's sociational principles, still remains a strong force and China has indeed not changed that much. We obviously do not know. Yet, to my knowledge, cliquism based on kinship has not been raised by the Communists as a target for revolutionary action, at least not since the early 1950's, nor has it been raised now during the cultural revolution.[1]

I cannot agree with the narrow conception of kinship which underlies these observations. I believe that the present attack on the party elite is itself a phenomenon which must be seen in a much wider context. That context has to do with the overwhelming importance of kinship in the fabric of Chinese society, and the Communist leaders are determined to change that society. The larger and therefore relatively more permanent objective of the Chinese mainland authorities is to reduce the power of kinship in order to build a modern nation through rapid organization and industrialization. The present attack on the party elite by the Red Guards is, therefore, but an immediate step in the same direction.

[1] Franz Schurmann, "The Attack of the Cultural Revolution on Ideology and Organization," p. 541, this volume.

Contrary to Schurmann, I believe that the problem of kinship is still very real in China today. The fact that "kinship has not been raised by the Communists as a target for revolutionary action, at least not since the early 1950's, nor has it been raised now during the Cultural Revolution" is no evidence that kinship is not part of the picture. Appearances are deceptive. The burden of this article will be that in spite of the facts mentioned by Schurmann, important ingredients of kinship origin *are* at work. Our task is to identify these ingredients and to demonstrate their role, so as to relate the more recent developments in mainland China to those which preceded them and, thus, to be in a better position to anticipate future developments. To do this, of course, is only to follow a basic axiom of science: to explain the unknown by way of the known.

### Structure and Content

My first point of departure is that major determinants in human affairs are to be found in human relationships. Whether in politics, economy, or even religion, the primary objective of human action is the initiating, building, maintenance, or destruction of human relationships. The basic human relationship is the dyad. Complex human relationships are multiplications and permutations of the basic dyad. Thus a biological family consisting of parents and unmarried children has a smaller and a different structure than a joint family with several married couples under the same roof, just as a factory with assembly lines has a larger and more complicated structure than a household workshop in which the managers and the workers are all members of the same family.

Structure is an organization of dyads. Every class of dyads has a pattern of interaction that is usually peculiar to itself. Thus the pattern of interaction in a husband-wife dyad is different in essential ways from that in a mother-son dyad. And both are different from that in an employer-employee dyad. These different patterns of interaction are called attributes. When more than one dyad is involved, their respective attributes affect each other through combination, co-ordination, modification or elimination so as to form an overall pattern which we term content.

Content is an organization of attributes. Every organization, be it a biological family, a factory, a university, a labor union, has a structure with many sets of dyads and a content with a variety of attributes. Contents can differ where the structure is the same. Structurally, the Japanese husband-wife dyad is the same as its American counterpart, especially if we take, for example, suburban Tokyo, where the household is likely to be composed of parents and unmarried children. But the content of the Japanese husband-wife dyad (whether we find it in a Tokyo suburb or a Nagano village, where parents-in-law are more likely to be present) is very different from its American counterpart. Structurally, a factory in India and in Japan could be the same, each with its board of directors, president and vice-president, manager, foremen, and workers. But the contents (ways in which the officers interact with each other and in which the foremen treat the workers) can be demonstrably different.[2] Conversely, content may be similar where structures are different.

Yet structure and content can also lead separate existences. China's two houses of parliament, at different points of time during the warlord period, were little more than rubber stamps of the warlords. This was an example of structure without content, or at least of a content vastly different from what the structure would have led us to expect. A married couple who live apart and do not see each other is another example of structure without corresponding content.

The possibility which concerns us most in the present exercise is a situation where content operates in the absence of the corresponding structure. This possibility can be illustrated in a variety of ways. For example, the dream of every wife is that her traveling husband behaves as if she were present at all times, just as the highest hope of most parents is that after they have passed away or their children become independent, the youngsters will still conduct themselves according to the philosophy of life which the elders had tried to instill. In both instances the content may continue when the structure is temporarily or permanently absent. This is the aim of all education. The hope of teachers is that their students will carry from the classroom not only what they have been taught—the three R's, for example—but also something of the "school spirit." On a more scientific level, the task is to attempt to pinpoint the interactions which took place before the parents passed away or while a student was still in school (when the family and the school structures were still existent) to see in what specific ways these interactions bear on the behavior of the products of the family and of the school after the structures have been eliminated.

My view is that the main objective of the Communist authorities has been to transform Chinese society from its kinship foundation to a political (non-kinship) one. To accomplish this, they have not only to

[2] Francis L. K. Hsü, "Structure, Function, Content, and Process," *American Anthropologist,* 61 (1959): 790–805.

propel a majority of the Chinese from their kinship base (structure) but also to disengage them from ways of thinking and. interacting rooted in kinship (content). The difficulty is that ways of thinking and interacting rooted in kinship content may not bear any obvious resemblance to such things as "the achievement of kinship ties (through intermarriage)" or "cliquism based on kinship," which are matters of structure. Consequently, an observer unfamiliar with the real difference between structure and content is likely to conclude that kinship has nothing to do with present-day events, since he does not see activities usually asssociated with kinship.

In three previous publications I have (1) detailed the differences between structure and content;[3] (2) explicated the relationship between content and attributes; (3) introduced the terms "dominant relationship (dyad)" and "dominant attributes"; and (4) laid out a basic scheme for viewing a number of kinship systems in the world.[4] The details of my hypothesis and how they may help us to deal with the relationship between kinship systems and sociocultural patterns and developments on a worldwide scale need not concern us here.[5] The most relevant part of my hypothesis for the problem at hand is how it can enable us to see the forces of kinship in the Chinese scene today even when conventional elements of kinship are absent. Although our immediate concern is with the Chinese case, we need to examine its American counterpart in order to reveal the role of kinship content in either one of them.

According to my hypothesis, the Chinese kinship system is dominated by the father-son dyad, the United States kinship system by the husband-wife dyad. The main attributes of the father-dominated Chinese kinship content are as follows:

1. Continuity        3. Authority
2. Inclusiveness     4. Asexuality

[3] *Ibid.*

[4] Francis L. K. Hsü, "The Effect of Dominant Kinship Relationships on Kin and Non-kin Behavior: A Hypothesis," *American Anthropologist,* 67 (1965): 638–61, and "Dominant Kin Relationships and Dominant Ideas," *American Anthropologist,* 68 (1966): 997–1004.

[5] An international symposium on this hypothesis was held August 20–29, 1966, at Burg Wartenstein, Austria. The nineteen participants (sixteen anthropologists and three sociologists) each contributed a paper criticizing, revising, or substantiating the hypothesis. The results will be published in the book *Kinship and Culture,* under my editorship.

In contrast, the main attributes of the husband-wife–dominated American kinship content are as follows:[6]

1. Discontinuity     3. Volition[7]
2. Exclusiveness     4. Sexuality

### The Characteristics of Chinese Kinship and Behavior

While every human being may be related to other human beings on the basis of a variety of principles—kinship, contract, hierarchy, ideology, etc.—the kinship principle comes first everywhere. In the course of growing up, an individual may discard the kinship principle for other bases of relating to others, but the Chinese individual is less likely to do so because one of the attributes of his kinship system is continuity. Furthermore, the Chinese individual tends not only to be reluctant to leave his first principle of human relationship—no matter how old he becomes—but he is also reluctant to replace it or sever connection with it even when he assumes relationships with other people on other principles. Thus, when he is married he will still tend to maintain close ties with his parents; and when he has to make career decisions his elders' wishes are likely to figure largely in these decisions. This pattern of behavior is also an intrinsic expression of the attribute of inclusiveness in the Chinese kinship system. According to this attribute, relationships tend to be additive rather than to supersede one another. There is a minimum tendency toward breaking relationships, and a maximum tendency toward blending them or blurring them.

Of course not all Chinese kinship ties are of equal intensity. There are closer ties and more remote ones. But the characteristic is that the closer ties tend to last for life and beyond, while the more remote kinship ties can always be readily called into service when circumstances permit or dictate.

The longer the vertical ties last, the more inclusive the horizontal ties become. If parents and unmarried children alone have to maintain their ties, a nuclear family will be the result. But if parents and their married sons and the sons' children maintain close ties, the pattern nat-

[6] The derivations and definitions of these attributes are given in "The Effect of Dominant Kinship Relationships on Kin and Non-kin Behavior."

[7] In the 1965 statement of the hypothesis I used the term "freedom" here. I have since decided that "volition" is preferable; it means substantially the same thing without, however, the popular, misleading connotations of the other term.

urally becomes more commensurate with a joint family. By the same token, if there are close ties between lineal ancestors of many generations past and their descendants of many generations to come, then the number of collateral relatives involved will be large and some kind of clan or other forms of kinship-related larger grouping must necessarily come into play. In other words, inclusiveness also tends to be a function of continuity *and is a form of continuity itself.*

The attributes of discontinuity and exclusiveness inherent in the American kinship system mean that human ties are likely to be less long-lasting among Americans than among Chinese, that their boundaries will be more clearly defined, and that they will tend to supersede each other rather than be additive. As soon as it is physically and socially possible, Americans are encouraged to replace their kinship ties with other ties.

Of course not all Americans discard their kinship ties with equal facility. But those who do are praised with such terms as "mature," while those who do not are described as "poor marital risks." Consequently the American parent-child relationship legally comes to an end when the youngsters reach 18 or 21. The American household is characteristically one where even the husband and wife maintain individual privacy which cannot be intruded upon except by invitation, and where the parents alone can discipline their children—efforts at discipline by grandparents and others are resented and likely to be regarded as interference. Finally, marriage for any American means drastic reduction (if not total elimination) of psychosocial involvement with one's own parents.

The attributes of continuity and inclusiveness tend to cause Chinese kinship relationships not only to perpetuate themselves but also to expand their influences even when no kinship ties can be traced. For example, Chinese employees often make themselves "dry sons" or "nephews" of their employers. On the other hand, discontinuity and exclusiveness not only cause American kinship relationships to terminate themselves relatively soon in an individual's life, but even when kinship ties are indubitably in operation the tendency is to transform such ties into non-kinship form. For example, American parents have to try to make a point of establishing and maintaining friendship even with their grade-school children.

The attribute of authority in the Chinese system makes it relatively easy for the father and mother to exercise their authority. In fact, the authority of any superior relative tends to be as readily exerted as that of the father. Conversely the problem of the authority of the American father in his family is legendary and is rooted in the fact that volition and not authority is an intrinsic attribute of the American kinship system. The American father has so much of a problem with it precisely because the attribute of volition leads sons and daughters to challenge authority—everyone is to think for himself.

Some sociologists have tried to differentiate between authority and power. In my opinion, power is only one of three bases of authority. First, authority may be enforced by brute power of the physical or economic kind, but this is the least reliable base, for the authority will immediately become untenable when the force is withdrawn or weakened for any reason. Second, authority may be exerted by "charisma." My use of the term "charisma" is not entirely confined to the political sense in which Max Weber uses it. To me, charisma simply means a kind of attraction to a multitude of people for any reason whatever—technical, sexual, oratorical, etc. In this sense Marilyn Monroe and Babe Ruth had charisma just as did Franklin D. Roosevelt and Abraham Lincoln. A person enjoying charisma has influence and can command the voluntary following of a very large number of people. Such authority is easier to maintain than brute force but it is also subject to change because charisma fluctuates and does not last forever. The third basis for authority is tradition. Here the most important consideration is whether one should obey another person's commands for no other reason than that it is one's place to do so. Thus, where a system of slavery is prevalent the master does not have to explain to the slave why he must obey. The fact that the master holds the place of master and that the slave is in the place of a slave is enough reason for the slave to obey the master's commands. In the same way, in a caste society the duties and obligations between members of the higher and lower castes also do not have to be explained on any rational basis.

The Chinese father's authority was based on tradition, since authority is a deeply embedded feature of the Chinese kinship system. The Chinese son had to obey the father by virtue of the positions respectively occupied by the father and by the son. Hence the Chinese dictum: "No parents are wrong (vis-à-vis their children)" (*tien-hsia wu pu-shih chih fu-mu*). Contrariwise, in the American system the father can command the son, or the son is more likely to obey the father, only if the father's command seems agreeable or reasonable to the son. Otherwise, the son can challenge the father's command—and will get much sympathy from others for standing up to his father's unreasonable authority. Volition but not authority is a deeply embedded feature of the American kinship system, hence the American emphasis on child development and understanding. In America, authority is chiefly based on charisma with brute force lurking somewhere in the background (for example, parents can threaten recalcitrant children with disinheritance), never on tradition. In China, authority is chiefly based on tradition with brute force lurking somewhere in the background (for example, fathers could report disobedient sons to the authorities and secure immediate arrest and punishment). Occasionally charisma might expedite authority in some Chinese circumstances, but it has never been the most important basis for authority in China.

If tradition is the basis, authority is less likely to be challengeable, discontinuous, or temporary than if authority is based upon charisma or brute force. Hence, the attributes of continuity and authority are commensurate with each other, just as are the attributes of discontinuity and volition.

The attribute of asexuality in the Chinese kinship system finds expression in the custom of assigning sex to a restricted place. A woman has no business demonstrating her sex appeal to any except her husband (unless she wants to be considered "bad"), and then only for continuation of the family line. The strictures were so narrow, for example, that a mother-in-law was not supposed to conceive again if her married son already had a child. This custom was more or less prevalent throughout China, but more strictly observed in some localities than in others. In West Town, a community in southwestern China where I did a series of field studies between 1941 and 1943, I collected cases in which the mothers died as a result of abortion attempts undertaken because their daughters-in-law had already given birth to children. When the primary function of the continuation of the family line is already being assumed by the younger woman, there is no reason for the older woman to engage in sex.

Conversely the attribute of sexuality in the American kinship system expresses itself in the generalization of sex into all sorts of relationships. The customary American aversion on the part of young men to going out with their sisters (and vice versa), and the exaggerated fear on the part of American males of any kind of physical intimacy with each other are just two indications of this generalized sexuality.

### Influence of Kinship Content on Non-Kinship Behavior

In the foregoing analysis we have already seen at some points how the Chinese kinship system affected Chinese behavior beyond the kinship organization. Now let us look for further evidence. The first and foremost is the scarcity of secondary and non-localized groupings in Chinese society as a whole. For example, as Jerome Cohen noted, the Chinese never developed an organized bar of lawyers, even though they always had many lawyers. There have, in fact, been few cause-oriented groupings on any voluntary basis. In their long history the Chinese have never been known for large-scale cause-promoting or cause-preventing organizations, the kind of organizations so common in the West. The Chinese have not been interested even in seeking the "truth," holding the "truth" to be either relative or self-evident.

There were, however, some non-kinship groupings in China. One of these was the "society for giving away free coffins." With the enormous Chinese emphasis on continuity, those who died without the care of heirs deserved much sympathy. Stories extolling filial piety such as that in which a daughter sells herself into slavery in order to bury her father are well known in China. Another non-kinship grouping was the "society for the preservation of papers bearing written characters." Viewing all written characters as having been handed down from ancient sages, and therefore respected objects, this society hired men to roam the streets collecting any and all pieces of paper bearing written characters. At the end of the day the man went to the local Confucian temple and burned his collection. He did not collect trash or litter, only pieces of paper that bore written characters—the object being to save the written characters from being trampled on.

However, even these organizations always remained localized affairs. The Chinese never had a *national* federation of the society of free coffin givers or of the society for the preservation of papers bearing written characters, or national conventions to discuss ways and means of improving the societies' work. In fact most of the local societies were not even organized; they were simply the pet projects of energetic and well-to-do individuals.

A very interesting Chinese non-kinship organization was the *hui-kuan,* which according to Ping-ti Ho is best translated into the German *Landsmannschaften.*[8] Professor Ho's use of the term *Landsmann-schaften* is indeed sound, for these organizations are based on the Chinese idea of *tung-hsiang,* or fellowmen of the same local area, and are truly illustrative of the Chinese pattern discussed here.

Each *Landsmann*'s group was an organization of local people in another area. In American terms, for example, there might be an organi-

---

8 Ping-ti Ho, "Salient Aspects of China's Heritage," p. 34, this volume. Extensive data can be found in Ping-ti Ho, *Chung-kuo hui-kuan shih-lüeh* [An Historical Survey of *Landsmannschaften* in China] (Taipei: Student Publishing Company, 1966).

zation of Chicago traders in New York called "Chicago Hui-kuan," or of North and South Dakota traders in Miami, Florida, called "Two-Dakotas Hui-kuan." A *hui-kuan* would usually have a house with some dormitory space and offices. A Chicago trader or office seeker arriving in New York would find in it a convenient place to live and some facilities for contacts for his own purposes. Throughout China, as Ho has demonstrated, there were many hundreds of such organizations. Some were organizations in the provincial capital for travelers from a district or several districts. Sometimes they were organizations in the national capital for travelers from different provinces or a section of a province. But their purpose was the twofold one of lodging and contacts, and no others. Furthermore, none of these organizations was consolidated on a national scale. The growth or decline of each was generally dependent upon the increase or decrease of the need of the local travelers. They were not cause-promoting organizations with a kind of ideal toward which they worked, and there were no all-China or even regional conventions of *Landsmannschaften* to discuss ways and means for better fulfilling their functions or enlarging their memberships.

In the light of the absence of cause-promoting or cause-preventing groupings, it becomes relatively clear why, in modern Chinese military history, commanders could be so easily and so often bought over by rival leaders, a phenomenon Martin Wilbur has so eloquently reported on.[9] Not being committed to any kind of abstract and non-kinship causes, those commanders tended to make their decision on the basis of what it would mean to their families and larger kinship groups. When the price was right they naturally saw nothing wrong with switching sides.

The second major correlate of the Chinese kinship system is the lack of centrifugal tendency on the part of the population in general. Being tied not only to his kinship structure but also to his kinship content, the Chinese individual was unwilling to leave his home community, or would return to it if he had to make his fame and fortune elsewhere. An old Chinese saying goes: "A man who has reached fame and fortune but does not return to his home village (town), is like one who wears the best of silk, but strolls on the street during a pitch-dark night."

Since the Communist assumption of power in China, there has been an eruption of talk and writing in the United States concerning the alleged threat of millions of Chinese outside of China, especially in Southeast Asia. It is, of course, true that there are sizeable Chinese communities in many Southeast Asian countries. Forty per cent of Malaya's

[9] Martin Wilbur, verbal comments in this Conference.

population is Chinese; about 10 per cent of the population of Thailand is Chinese. But had the Chinese been as inclined to leave China as were the Irish and the Swiss, or all Western Europeans, one should not find it difficult to perceive the possibility that a majority of Southeast Asia territories and many other parts of the world would have been dominated by the Chinese instead of by Westerners.

The objective fact is that, in spite of poverty, dynastic changes, and invasion by tribal peoples from the north, very few Chinese—in proportion to the total Chinese population—have ever left China. The Chinese population in Southeast Asia was drawn overwhelmingly from the coastal regions of two Chinese provinces: Fukien, the province directly opposite Formosa, and Kwangtung (including Hainan Island), the province of which Canton is the capital. Ninety per cent of the Chinese population in Hawaii (which forms less than 5 per cent of the total population of that state even today) came from one district in Kwangtung province which happens to be the birthplace of Dr. Sun Yat-sen. More than 80 per cent of the forebears of the Chinese in mainland United States came from four districts, which are located next to that one. Chinese in other areas simply did not have this tendency to emigrate from their ancestral land. Here and there on continental Europe are infinitesimal groups of Chinese merchants from Chekiang province who went to France and Germany as part of the labor force contributed by China to the Allies in World War I.

Historically a few Chinese explorers achieved great renown. In the Ming dynasty, a eunuch admiral commanded a large fleet, collected vassals Chinese-style in various parts of Southeast Asia and reached as far as the east coast of Africa. (At one point Admiral Cheng's forces captured the King of Kandy in the highlands of Ceylon and brought him back to China a captive, where he eventually passed away.) In this regard, the developmental trends of Chinese immigrant groups abroad and European immigrant groups abroad have presented a sharp historical contrast. It was people of European origin who set up the independent countries of the United States, Mexico, and all the Latin American republics as well as Australia and New Zealand. No Chinese colony ever decided to declare itself a new nation in some new territory independent from China except once briefly for a span of about 10 years in Borneo. The Chinese were too much oriented toward their "homes."

Finally, the contrast between Chinese centripetality and European centrifugality (of which the American case is an extreme version) is nowhere shown more clearly than in the history of proselytism. Practically all the missionaries of the world are European or American, not Chinese.[10] Once in the T'ang dynasty about 3,000 devout Chinese monks went separately over a period of several hundred years to India *in search of the true teachings of Buddha for the purpose of bringing them back to China.* To the best of my knowledge only one Chinese monk ever went to Japan for the purpose of proselytism. Even in this case he went at the repeated urging of some Japanese monks who were in China on a pilgrimage first.[11]

A third correlate of the Chinese kinship system is the desire to seek authority in all interpersonal relations outside of kin. In fact, Chinese scholars and officials and others always made use of actual kinship ties or teacher-pupil ties whenever these could be traced. In the absence of such actual ties, they would not hesitate to initiate pseudo-kinship or pseudo-teacher–pupil ties through which the seeker of influence always took the part of the inferior. Those who have read the Chinese novel, *The Golden Lotus,* can readily call to mind the case of Hsi Men Ch'ing, the main character, who enjoyed enormous powers because of his alliances with various officials.[12] In one instance Hsi Men Ch'ing scored a major advancement by getting himself accepted by the Imperial Tutor as a ritual son. His success was preceded by a great deal of help on the part of the Imperial Tutor's household manager and twenty loads of extraordinarily extravagant gifts as Hsi Men Ch'ing's offering in celebration of that high official's birthday. In fact, Hsi Men Ch'ing even referred to himself as "your pupil" in conversation with the Imperial Tutor's household manager. Hsi Men Ch'ing is an imaginary character, but his action patterns are normal for China.

Richard H. Solomon of the University of Michigan has gathered a very interesting piece of evidence which supports our analysis of the characteristic Chinese approach to authority. He points out that "the notion that people relate to authority in very different ways has not been well recognized in political science—primarily because of the lack, until recently, of cross-cultural and comparative studies."[13] Solomon's

[10] The Arabs had one big outburst of proselytism linked with their military conquests, accompanied by forcible attempts at conversion.

[11] Edwin O. Reischauer, *Ennin's Travels in T'ang China* (New York: Ronald Press, 1955).

[12] Clement Egerton, *The Golden Lotus,* 4 vols. (New York: Grove Press, 1954).

[13] Richard H. Solomon, "The Chinese Revolution and the Politics of Dependency: The Struggle for Change in a Traditional Political Culture" (Ph.D. diss., University of Michigan, 1966), p. 406.

findings, based on intensive interviews and the use of some specially constructed TAT pictures in Taiwan and Hong Kong, indicate that in the traditional Chinese educational process

> parents and teacher both tended to discourage a child's efforts at autonomy and self-expression in terms of what they saw as a higher goal of group solidarity. The discipline of a traditional male's childhood centered about restraining his own impulses for action and "holding in" emotional frustrations that came from confrontations with harsh and manipulative authority. [The traditional Chinese child] developed a sense of self-control primarily in matters of emotional discipline, rather than in discipline of his body and physical behavior. Guidance in his actions, he learned, was to come from authoritative adults.[14]

I think the latter part of Solomon's observation contains a misreading of the Chinese personality configuration. For in making a rather sharp contrast between emotional discipline and physical discipline he has given the impression that the Chinese have little physical discipline. The fact is that when Chinese college students are compared with their American counterparts they tend to be less spontaneous and less active— that is, in a certain sense, more physically disciplined. (This difference is at least in part responsible for the stereotype of Chinese inscrutability.) What really distinguishes the Chinese from the Americans—a comparison Solomon seems to be making even though not explicitly—is their lesser emphasis on individual autonomy and self-expression and greater expectations from and receptivity to authority.

Another correlate of the Chinese type of kinship system comes from the attribute of asexuality. Sex tends to be restricted to a corner of the Chinese social and cultural world and not generalized into diverse aspects of it as in the West. For the Chinese, sex is relegated to where it belongs—so to speak—that is, to marriage or to prostitution. It does not operate in other areas where it is not directly relevant. Therefore, even today the Western term "sex appeal" tends to have an undesirable connotation when translated into Chinese. On the other hand, in the American culture, sex is so ubiquitous that it tends to appear in the most unexpected quarters, whether it is a question of buying one kind of soap or another, or smoking one kind of cigarette or another.

The Chinese have never had the problem of sexuality disguised as art. There has simply been no attempt at injecting sexuality into the arts; consequently, there is no body of Chinese literature devoted to explain-

[14] *Ibid.* p. 389.

ing or defending sex-infiltrated products as art. (Thus there can never be Chinese counterparts to the case of Greek statues found unacceptable for museums in Texas.) At different times the Chinese have had a great deal of pornography circulated—now surreptitiously, now openly; but these have been works solely of pornographic intent, not artistic.

If my observations are correct, then the so-called "puritanism" observed by many non-Chinese visitors to mainland China today must be regarded as a result of Western projection into the Chinese scene of a point of view rooted in the Western kinship system where sexuality is a prominent attribute.

Chinese women of good families have never worried about their sex appeal to the general public, even when they appeared in public. Their clothing was designed to conceal rather than to reveal their forms. Consequently the kind of blue and formless uniforms which have struck non-Chinese observers in mainland China so forcibly was not due to any particular Chinese Communist attempt to promote "puritanism," but simply a continuation of something that has always been Chinese. The Communist administration has now induced or enabled a much larger number of Chinese women than ever before to participate in public activities, whether in government, commerce, industry, schools, or public demonstrations. The Communist administration may have accentuated an age-old pattern to a certain extent, but it did not create it. Formless blue work clothes or uniforms are perfectly in keeping with the Chinese attribute of asexuality.

With their kinship attribute of asexuality, Chinese females who achieve professional competence or political prominence tend to be treated in terms of their professional competence or political prominence, but not of their sex. On the other hand, no matter how much equality of the sexes is discussed and emphasized in the United States, the female professional will always be subjected—either covertly or overtly—to discrimination by males. American males tend to see female professionals as always posing a threat, because members of the fair sex are automatically regarded as being able to offer something other than their professional competence which—inevitably—puts the males at a disadvantage. Sexuality being generalized, it is impossible for most American males to see females entirely free from that attribute.

This does not mean that the Chinese like to have female leaders. Their tradition is very clear and emphatic on this point: males are superior to females; males should handle affairs outside of the home, females should handle those inside it. Only a few times in Chinese history have empress dowagers actually usurped the imperial power. One empress even ruled as "emperor," but the point is that when and if such women succeeded, Chinese males tended to accept them, more readily than most American males, in terms of their power or talent. Even when Chinese eunuchs became powerful—as they did during parts of the Ming dynasty—they were accepted and obeyed by members of the bureaucracy in much the same way as were emperors or powerful ministers. The question of their being "sexless" did not seem to influence their functioning as administrators or authority figures. The only limitation was that, since female rule was not part of the Chinese tradition, Chinese female rulers were prevented by their countrymen's unwillingness to part with tradition—an expression of the kinship attribute of continuity—from making their rule permanent. Any such usurpation could not, therefore, be legitimatized and was always temporary.

A fifth correlate of the Chinese kinship system is to be found in the peculiar nature of Chinese bureaucracy. Bureaucracy everywhere has certain universal characteristics, but in addition to these, Chinese bureaucracy has had characteristics of its own. The members of the lower echelons of the Chinese bureaucracy have always looked up through a particular line of affiliation to the members of the higher echelons—either along kinship, pseudo-kinship, or teacher-pupil lines. Therefore, the programs for "self-strengthening" initiated in the late Ch'ing period by the four outstanding men—Tseng Kuo-fan, Tso Tsung-t'ang, Li Hung-chang, and Chang Chih-tung—were not coordinated with each other. Instead, they tended to undercut each other's strength because—since the groupings were organized on specific affiliations, and not on more abstract causes—it was not possible for them to join forces on any permanent basis. The primary lines of affiliation could not be disregarded, and such dividing lines always prevented generation of overall strength for overall causes necessary to do the job. The lines of human affiliation always stood in the way of the issues.

This analysis adds a new dimension to the fact noted by S. N. Eisenstadt at this Conference that Chinese society in the late Ch'ing period possessed no secondary elite to serve as an effective force for modernization and as an effective link between the general population and the power center. The infrastructure of the society could not deal with the conditions created by the impact of the West. In terms of my analysis, the kinship content of the Chinese made the kind of divided affiliation under able men like Tseng, Tso, Li, and Chang inevitable, and in turn such divided affiliation made the absence of an effective link between the general population and the new power center inevitable. The "self-strengthening" activities under these leaders could not spread into the

general population in any overall way. Old people were always in command in China because the lower echelons always looked up to their
own particular elders for guidance. The old people in each grouping
were in command because the younger men, being products of a kinship
system in which the attribute of authority was dominant, gave them
that command.

The last distinguishing feature of Chinese bureaucracy is that it
pigeonholed the individual even more than bureaucracies in the West
would have done in the normal course of events. Bureaucracy means
pigeonholing, and all bureaucrats anywhere are interested in "holding
the line" and "doing the right thing" and therefore are somewhat more
negative than positive in approach. But Chinese bureaucracy has ex-
celled in this regard. For example, the Chinese idea of *te jen* mentioned
by Philip Kuhn in this Conference is an essential expression of this
tendency,[15] and reminds us of what Solomon found in his interviews
among Chinese refugees in Taiwan and Hong Kong. In the West the
prevalent emphasis is on the development of the individual and on improving the society so that it provides additional opportunities for the
individual. The Chinese concept of *te jen* is not aimed primarily at individual development but, rather, stresses the need to find the right individual for the right pigeonhole so that affairs of the state (or of the
village) can be run smoothly in terms of the needs of the larger organization.

Corresponding to the concept of *te jen* in the case of bureaucracy, a
common Chinese concept in the kinship sphere is *hsing chia*. *Te jen*
means that you find the right man for the public office; *hsing chia*
means that you find the right member to prosper the kinship group.

In the light of the foregoing analysis we can also understand why the
Chinese have always shown a lack of concern for organized religion.
The history of religion in the West has been marked by great turmoil,
population movements, persecution, and wars. The history of religion
in China is singularly uneventful—at least, so far as the extent to which
religion has made any difference in Chinese history. The fact is, in the
first place, the Chinese never had the idea of a congregation, that one
"belonged" to a particular established religious faith and temple. The
Chinese approach to temples is essentially like their approach to stores.
Whichever store gave them the most satisfaction they would return to.

---

[15] Philip Kuhn, Comments . . . [on Kwang-Ching Liu's "Nineteenth-Century
China: The Disintegration of the Old Order and the Impact of the West"],
pp. 194–99, this volume.

And they would not hesitate to switch their patronage or to deal with several stores at the same time.

The lack of specific affiliation to particular faiths and temples is indicative of the absence of deep commitment on the part of the Chinese to such causes and organizations. It is not hard to see how this Chinese approach to various religions would supply little impetus for persecution. The usual analysis of persecution concentrates on those who persecuted, or were bent on doing so, neglecting the role of the persecuted. In my view, intensive and extensive persecution requires not only persecutors but also people who invite persecution because of their commitment. The Chinese lack of commitment to religion has made religious persecution unnecessary.

Some scholars may regard the persecution of Buddhists in the T'ang dynasty as contrary to the last observation.[16] But this is a misreading or exaggeration of the Chinese facts. A few T'ang emperors persecuted Buddhists, but not because they dsliked the new faith; rather, primarily because of their suspicion that treasonable elements were using monasteries and monkhood as a cover or temporary refuge. Consequently the persecution by the emperors took three forms. First, the monasteries and temples, as well as monks and nuns, were to be registered and regulated to make sure that no dangerous elements were disguising their rebellious activities. Second, in the so-called Great Persecution of 845–846, the Emperor Wu-tsung decreed that "only two temples with thirty monks each were permitted to stand in each of the two capitals, Changan and Loyang. Of the 228 prefectures in the Empire, only the capital cities of the 'first grade' prefectures were permitted to retain one temple each with ten monks."[17]

Compared with their European counterparts, such forms of persecution can only be described as perfunctory. If the Chinese authorities were really interested in the elimination of Buddhism as a religious faith, they would never have given Buddhist monks and temples regulated recognition and existence. They would have aimed at extermination, as did European kings and popes, even to the extent of detecting by inquisition or witch-hunting traces of the undesirable faith in persons who otherwise had already professed some form of government-accepted religion.

[16] C. K. Yang, *Religion in Chinese Society* (Berkeley: University of California Press, 1961), pp. 122–23.

[17] Hu Shih, "Ch'an (Zen) Buddhism in China: Its History and Method," *Philosophy East and West*, vol. 3, no. 1, April 1953.

The third form of Chinese persecution of Buddhists was to require monks and nuns in excess of the authorized number to return to civilian life. The interesting thing is that none of the hundreds of thousands of monks and nuns forced to return to civilian life seemed to have resisted the order; the persecuting T'ang Emperor got his wish without having to resort to execution or imprisonment. It is hard to find better and more direct proof of the Chinese lack of desire to invite persecution.

It is small wonder then that the Chinese persecution of Buddhism was short-lived, limited to four occurrences up to A.D. 955 and completely absent since. C. K. Yang, who, I think, has not perceived the significant difference between the Chinese and Western patterns of religious persecution, comments on the above facts as follows:

> After 955, there were no further major persecutions of the Buddhists, but Buddhism as a nationally organized force intimately linked to political issues also came to an end. From this period on, Buddhism became acculturated to the Chinese social milieu both in its theology and its organizational relationship with the secular authority.[18]

In view of the continuous history of religious persecution and strife in the West, one finds it difficult to accept such an observation. How did Buddhism in China become so *easily* "acculturated to the Chinese social milieu both in its theology and its organizational relationship with the secular authority" while Judaism, Protestantism, and Catholicism continue even today to be sources of trouble and to divide Westerners? The Chinese lack of commitment to particular faiths and, hence, their custom of having no firm memberships in particular congregations are the obvious answer.

Even the Chinese emperors, each of whom always had the absolute power of life and death, could not (or found it impractical to) force the people to worship them in separate public temples. According to Professor Ho, the founder of the Han dynasty had his ancestral temples erected in every province of the empire.

> From his death in 195 B.C. to 40 B.C., every deceased Emperor had his temples in the capital city and provinces. From the third Emperor to the eighth, each erected his temples during his lifetime. By about the middle of the first century B.C., there were 176 imperial temples and 30 temples for empresses and crown princes

[18] C. K. Yang, *Religion in Chinese Society*, pp. 122–23.

throughout the empire, which required 24,455 victuals and sacrifices annually, 45,129 temple guards, and a government staff of 12,147 in charge of sacrificial ceremonies and music.[19]

In spite of such obvious desire on the part of the rulers to deify themselves, and the tendency for them to proliferate their own temples, the custom of individual temples for individual emperors was shortly abolished, and the trend turned into consolidation of these separate temples into a single clan temple for each dynasty. "As a result of the debate of 40 B.C., imperial temples in the provinces were abolished. From eastern Han (A.D. 25–220) onward there was usually only one temple erected for the dynasty founder after his death to which all later emperors of the same dynasty were posthumously attached."

Professor Ho gives a functional explanation of this trend, from greater proliferation of individual temples to the consolidation of all the temples into one for the entire dynasty: "Since western Han time, the emperor's charisma had been generally taken for granted and an elaborate system of imperial temples was no longer needed."[20] I disagree with this interpretation. The tendency of autocratic or despotic rulers everywhere is the glorification of the ruler's person. There is simply no evidence that the emperor's charisma in China had at any time been so generally taken for granted. In fact, more symbols (such as prostration in audience) were added to the court rules to sanctify the Emperor's augustness as Chinese history unfolded. The clear trend was from a relatively more equalitarian approach to the emperor to a more hierarchical one. No Chinese emperor was ever known voluntarily to reduce external signs of his augustness.

My interpretation is that the consolidation of the individual emperors' temples into one dynastic temple was an expression of the strength of Chinese kinship in two ways. On the one hand, the people could not be induced to take the many temples as seriously as the emperors had wished. On the other hand, even for the august person of the emperor the kinship solidarity of his clan overruled his need for individual expression of his own power and prestige. The precedence of collectivity over individual prominence was the Chinese rule among commoners, and this rule obviously was strong enough even to overcome the desire and necessity on the part of the emperors to make themselves each a separate and final symbol of authority.

All Chinese prominent families used to eulogize their particular an-

[19] Ping-ti Ho, "Salient Aspects of China's Heritage," p. 17, this volume.
[20] *Ibid.*

cestors by the expression *tsu-te tsung-kung* ("ancestors' merits and efforts of the lineage") by which was meant "our prominence today is a result of the cumulative merits and efforts of our ancestors and clan members." How could the extreme power, prestige, and wealth enjoyed by any single emperor be due to his own merits and efforts only? It is from this angle that we can also understand why, as pointed out by Herrlee G. Creel, even though King Wu was really the de facto founder of the ancient Chou dynasty (*ca.* 1500 b.c.) because he conquered or subdued rival feudal lords, the official inscriptions always gave his father King Wen the greater place of honor.[21] All subsequent founders of Chinese dynasties, including that of the Manchu, pursued the same course of *chui feng* to their forebears; that is, posthumously conferring upon them greater places of honor.[22] This is the true way of the ancestors' shadow.

In a similar light we can now understand why, since later Han times, the ancestral temple of the ruling dynasty was the sole concern of the imperial descendants and not of the people. The emperor's ancestors were the concern of the emperor and his kinsmen alone, just as among the common people the ancestors of each clan were the concern of the members of that clan alone. There was no common worship of a common ancestor between members of different clans among the commoners, and there could not be any common worship of the same between the emperor's kinsmen and the ordinary people.[23] The kinship principle was so strong in China that it even separated the ruler and the ruled.

The unimportance of religious affiliation also explains why Chinese dynastic rulers seemed also to be very generous toward the ancestral

[21] H. G. Creel, Comments . . . [on Ping-ti Ho's "Salient Aspects of China's Heritage"], pp. 59–78, this volume.

[22] In Western usage, an honor awarded posthumously is a reward for merit or achievement on the part of some one who did not live to receive it. According to Chinese custom, *chui feng* means either a posthumous award in the Western sense, or a posthumous award for merit or achievement not on the part of the deceased recipient but for merit or achievement on the part of his descendant. When the founder of a dynasty conferred this honor on his deceased father (usually also on his deceased mother) the underlying assumption was that he owed all he had accomplished to his parents. The latter was the most essential element of *hsiao* ("filial piety").

[23] This is in sharp contrast to the Japanese custom, according to which the emperor's ancestor—especially the first ancestor—was regarded as being the progenitor of all Japanese and hence the imperial ancestral temple at Ise was, and is, a place of worship for all Japanese.

temples of the previous dynastic rulers. For example, instead of having them destroyed in order to eliminate symbols of previous power, most Chinese dynasties preserved them even to the extent of allowing regular offerings and sacrifices, though naturally on a reduced scale compared to those made to their own temples. When the Emperor K'ang-hsi of the Ch'ing dynasty visited Nanking, the original seat of the Ming dynasty where the tomb of the founder of the Ming dynasty was located, he did an unusual thing. He prostrated himself and kowtowed before the shrine of the founder of the Ming dynasty.[24]

To sum up the analysis so far, Chinese kinship content bred a kind of centripetal orientation in the individual, so that he tended not to leave or forsake his kinship base as he went through life. He could co-operate best among non-kins by creating pseudo-kinship ties, but he would find it extremely difficult to commit himself to groups or causes outside of his kinship base, especially if such commitments conflicted with it or required severance from it. Furthermore, and this is particularly important in our present connection, if and when he left his kinship base entirely, his ways of relating to his fellow human beings retained their roots in what we designate as Chinese kinship content and its component attributes.

The concrete expressions of these attributes are often so different from the usual kinship and pseudo-kinship ties that they tend to obscure the vision of even acute scholars. As early as the 1920's and 1930's, Chinese and Western observers spoke about the changing Chinese family when they saw some educated Chinese young men and women dating each other or choosing their own mates, living in nuclear households, or talking about independence from their parents. What they did not see, and what most observers still fail to see, is that such structural changes in Chinese kinship, even if they became more widespread than they actually have been, did not automatically alter the true influences of the Chinese kinship content in the Chinese society at large; these influences have been over two thousand years in their entrenchment and proliferation.

A number of participants in this Conference have also observed that the Chinese have the longest continuous civilization of the world. In fact, both Creel and C. P. FitzGerald feel that the Chinese civilization is unique. While I do not necessarily consider Chinese civilization unique, I do believe that it is because of the nature of the Chinese kinship structure and content that the system has lasted so long and developed in

[24] I am indebted to Professor Ping-ti Ho for this information.

essentially the same terms for more than two thousand years. The stable and resilient cornerstone is the Chinese kinship system which, on the one hand, has kept a majority of Chinese busy with their relatives and their local groups, and, on the other hand, has kept them away from strong or absolute involvement with larger organizations and causes which might alter or seriously challenge their kinship roots. The authority of the ruling dynasty was not challenged except when natural forces such as famine or population growth, or human forces such as external invasion or excessive bureaucratic corruption so tipped the scale as to threaten the bare existence of large segments of the people. Then, relatively temporary chaos ensued until some enterprising new man, aided by a decrease in population pressure through civil disorder and natural disorder, was able to restore balance by setting up a new dynasty. In so doing, he was bringing about no successful revolution but only a successful rebellion. He and his heirs would rule the country according to the same institutional framework and in the same spirit as before. So long as the larger factors were undisturbed, even an idiotic heir could run the country, for the emperors ruled by the negative acquiescence of the people rather than from their positive support. The people tolerated the emperors as long as the emperors knew how to play their part by not interfering actively, or too much with the private activities of their subjects.

This was a negative stability, based on a live-and-let-live policy, but not a positive stability with a high degree of active political integration and national solidarity, such as is found in either the democratic or the authoritarian West. At any given point in time, the number of Chinese who actively participated in governmental affairs, or who were even interested in governmental affairs, was very small. The primary concern of a majority of Chinese was how to protect and enhance their private kinship interests. They could do this by becoming the most favored bureaucrats or subjects of the rulers. If that did not prove possible, they would not greatly resist retirement to their primary kinship spheres where they would at least receive the adulation of their descendants.

Once this sophisticated and well-developed society and civilization (as Creel put it) was toppled, it fell with great force. It fell with such great force precisely because it was sophisticated and well-developed in its particular pattern of mutual adjustment between the rulers, the bureaucracy, the local gentry, and the common people, each with their own particular kinship sphere for psycho-social needs such as sociability, security, and status. Had it not been so sophisticated and well-developed, it would have been more open to large changes. It was not open to such changes because the Chinese were too tied to their kinship structure and content, finding too many satisfactions in them to be easily disengaged from them and assume absolute commitments to groups and causes unrelated or contrary to them.

This gave the Chinese society no suitable infra-structure for drastic breaks with the past. There was simply no across-the-board secondary elite which could serve as a link between the common people (with no reference to kinship affiliation) and any possible new centers of innovative power. Having developed so sophisticated a civilization, and having been reared in their kinship attributes of continuity, inclusiveness, and authority, the Chinese simply had too many answers from the past which they thought could deal with the new problems. When some answers were not effective in dealing with the new problems the Chinese could either retreat to their kinship sphere, or—too immersed in their kinship content to see its inadequacy—easily find other answers from the wealth of their sophisticated and well-developed past.

When the Chinese repeatedly failed in their attempts to deal with the impact of the West, they finally went into a number of convulsions beginning with the Taiping Rebellion, through the Boxer Uprising of 1900, the Revolution of 1911, the Northern Expedition of 1926–28, and finally the Communist Revolution which culminated in the establishment of the Peking regime in 1949. Throughout the century of turmoil, there were intellectuals and leaders who thought the correct answer was complete Westernization, or a revitalization of Chinese traditional values, or a compromise between the two. But the real problem was how to entice a majority of the people away from not only their traditional kinship structure but also its content.

## The Objectives Underlying the Cultural Revolution

Now we are in a position to return to Schurmann's analysis of the aim of the present Red Guard movement. The twin goals of any modern Chinese government—Nationalist or Communist—are national greatness and industrialization. The second goal will, of course, raise the general level of living, but it especially will serve as the sinew of national greatness. But so long as the Chinese are embedded physically in their traditional kinship structure and psychologically immersed in its kinship content, they are not likely to move very far in the desired direction.

As noted previously, the attack on Chinese traditional kinship structure began long before the Communist Revolution and lasted all the way down to the early 1950's, as Schurmann correctly observed. The inciting of some children to denounce their parents, recruitment of youngsters for youth corps and political activities, the assignment of college graduates to work in rural or border areas, the relocation of ancestral tombs and the discouragement of the continuation of the age-old custom of family and clan graveyards—these and others were means of getting the people out of their kinship structure. But the attack on Chinese traditional kinship content was much less obvious before, and only intensified since the early 1950's. The reason is that the stumbling block posed by Chinese kinship structure was much more obvious than that posed by Chinese kinship content. The latter is more difficult to identify than the former. Once this is understood, we can easily see that the Red Guards are simply one of the instruments for attacking the many underlying psychological legacies of Chinese kinship content characterized by, according to our analysis, the attributes of continuity, inclusiveness, authority, and asexuality. The unleashing of the Red Guards seems bizarre only to those who do not understand this.

However, not all attributes of the Chinese traditional kinship content are equally dysfunctional to the desired changes. The attribute of continuity was related to the fact that the Chinese were resistant to breaking with the past, so that there were only rebellions and no revolutions. What the Chinese Communists want, as did the Nationalists before them to a lesser extent, is a revolutionary break with the past and not merely a replacement of leadership personnel. This was why they have had public confessions, compulsory autobiography-writing, work-study programs, and extensive rectification campaigns (*san-fan, wu-fan,* etc.) even before the current upheaval.

Similarly, inclusiveness, another attribute of the Chinese kinship system, is also dysfunctional. This attribute was characteristically expressed in such Chinese behavior patterns as never allowing politics or religion or other non-kinship matters to divide human beings. For example, Chinese have never allowed religion to be a bar to marriage, or politics to separate children and parents. What the Communist leaders wish to bring about is a condition in which *only* those who share the same correct political views come and work together. Hence, divergence in political views has recently become, unlike former times, a bar to marriage, to association, and to friendship. The aim is to replace the age-old tendency of inclusiveness rooted in kinship with a tendency toward exclusiveness based on sharply drawn ideological lines.

The Communist leaders do not want to eliminate all attributes (or all aspects of them) of the Chinese kinship system. Some are being redeployed for achievement of new goals. Several times in this Conference it has been noted that in China, even under the Communists, old leaders keep command, regardless of how old they become. This seems highly consonant with the attributes of continuity, and especially with that of authority. In practical terms, this means that those who had authority tend to continue holding it, so long as they seem to be able to deal effectively with all or at least the most urgent problems. This was the substance of the age-old Chinese concept of Mandate of Heaven. It is difficult to imagine why the Chinese leaders would want to attack this aspect of the attribute of authority.

We have already noted how the alleged "puritanism" in mainland China today is a Western misreading of a traditional Chinese pattern, one rooted in their kinship attribute of asexuality. For Chinese girls to appear at work or in the streets wearing formless blue, or otherwise seemingly unmindful of their sex appeal, or for Chinese couples to converse unromantically about locomotives or commune production, these are in perfect keeping with Chinese custom. A popular Chinese love song in the 1930's depicted two lovers parting. The girl was seeing her sweetheart off by going a last extra mile with him. They were both enchanted by the beautiful scenery but saddened by the impending separation. And she went on: "For you I am willing to share the same pillow and mat." But he responded: "A gentleman must be moral in his conduct; how dare he follow his own private desires?" An American girl in similar circumstances would undoubtedly have found his response upsetting, to say the least, but the Chinese girl saw no cause for annoyance or worry.[25]

Since the revolutionary goals require that more Chinese become involved in non-kinship activities more intensively than ever before, any lowering of romantic fever in the interest of these larger goals is welcome.[26] In this we should remember that in essence early Christianity also tried to divert romantic energy to devotion to God. That was why St. Paul thought celibacy to be much better than the marital state. The

[25] The Chinese-American contrast between patterns of man-woman relationship is extensively analyzed in Francis L. K. Hsü, *American and Chinese: Two Ways of Life* (New York: Abelard-Schuman, 1953). (Revised and retitled edition: *Americans and Chinese: Passage to Understanding* [New York: Doubleday, in press]).

[26] Ezra F. Vogel has made an excellent analysis of this transition in terms of one from friendship to comradeship in his "From Friendship to Comradeship: The Change in Personal Relations in Communist China," *China Quarterly,* no. 21 (March, 1965), pp. 46–60.

difference is that the Chinese under Communism do not have to expend so much effort repressing their sexuality. The attribute of asexuality already characterized their pattern of husbanding their total energy so that sex did not have to be deposed; it never occupied a central place in their scheme of things as it did in the West.

Beside the measures which are relevant to specific Chinese kinship attributes, there is a whole series of others that aim at reducing kinship involvement and increasing social and political integration in general. But most of these have not been well understood by students of China.

Take the "Great Leap Forward," for example. There is no doubt that economically it was a failure. The backyard furnaces produced iron and steel that could not be economically and efficiently used. Agricultural production suffered terribly because of diversion of manpower and energy to non-agricultural objectives. Although the severe crop failure of 1959–61 could not entirely be laid at the door of the Great Leap, the latter had a great deal of bearing on the former. But the Great Leap was psychosocially a good thing and must be considered a success. For the first time in Chinese history, the common people were made to become aware of some relationship, some intrinsic and positive relationship, between what they did as individuals and the overall purposes of the state.

Another example is the commune. The Western press has often tried to feed the public's desire for cheap sensationalism by concentrating on the greatly exaggerated report of separation between husbands and wives or the breaking-up of the family. Several important aspects of the commune are particularly commensurate with our analysis, but only one of them will be dealt with here. This is its work-point system.

The system operates more or less as follows. Every member of the commune receives a number of work points in the total work accounts of that commune for one full day's work according to previously agreed upon criteria differentiating men, women, and adolescents. No one is paid daily, but everyone accumulates work points in the commune's accounts. The accounts are settled at fixed intervals and the total proceeds of each period are usually settled in the proportion of something like 40 per cent for the commune as a whole (to go to group benefits and improvements) and 60 per cent for the individual. The details of the accounting of work points vary from place to place, as does also the period of settlement.

There is no question as to what the work point does in terms of its possible effect on interpersonal relationships. For example, some women prefer to earn work-points instead of having more children who tend to tie them down, in spite of crèches and nurseries. Even more important, for the first time, women have come to appreciate their own labors in terms of some standards other than as wife, mother, or daughter-in-law, so that the importance of their contribution is economically, and therefore more objectively, measurable. This to me is a most important device for individualization, for loosening of kinship bonds, with corresponding possibility for increase in involvement in larger groups on non-kinship bases.

Curiously the mechanism indicated here is revealed in a letter to Ann Landers by an American lady. This lady said that in all of her married years she had "felt like a nobody because I was only a 'housewife.'" Her husband made her feel that she should be grateful to him for putting food in her mouth and clothes on her back. However, she now felt better because the home economics department of her state college had published a leaflet in chart form which showed "what a housewife is worth in dollars and cents per week on today's labor market." According to this chart's very moderate wage scale, her work came to something like $7800 a year. So she says,

> Believe it or not, this leaflet gave me dignity. I am no longer feeling like a parasite. Tonight when Mr. Greatheart comes home I am going to greet him like a woman who earns about $8000 a year, because that's what I am.[27]

In my view, this American lady's grievance and her way of redressing it explain very eloquently one of the most basic possible effects of the work-point system in Chinese communes. In both cases the question is the change of the woman from being an appendage of her husband or of a kinship group into an independent, valuable unit of production in the larger frame of reference. The difference is that the American lady, living in a civilization that is already individual-centered, has taken the matter in her own hands to make her man see the light, while her Chinese sister, living in a society which has always subordinated the individual to a place in a kinship network of privileges, duties, and obligations, is being ushered by way of the work-point system into a new view of her place in the national scheme of things.

The present Red Guard movement must be seen in the same light. I have no quarrel at all with the thesis that this movement is primarily

---

[27] *Chicago Sun-Times*, February 9, 1966.

aimed at the party functionaries. But it is unmistakable that this attack on the party functionaries came *after many different movements attacking bureaucrats from the previous regime, intellectuals, landlords, industrial and commercial leaders.*

The party people, since the revolution of 1949, have constituted a new elite. They have enjoyed seventeen years of special privileges and power. These people are not a single entity, any more than is the army. A multifarious party elite have to be, from time to time, made more uniform according to the overall ideology, just as a multifarious army has to undergo the same process. Furthermore, what is achieved in one generation needs not only to be enlarged in the next generation, but even the gains that have already been made need also to be maintained through a constant process of re-examination and reintegration. Under Chiang Kai-shek, a nationally publicized slogan consisted of two lines from Dr. Sun Yat-sen's last will:

> The revolution is not yet a complete success,
> Comrades must persevere still more.

Can we not see Mao's Red Guards as an attempt to encourage comrades to persevere still more?

But Mao's China is much better organized than that of his predecessor; Mao and his oligarchy also have much greater power and they have taken more drastic steps than their predecessors. Chiang's New Life Movement organization sent Boy Scouts and other New Life Movement workers to separate pedestrians on the sidewalks of Nanking, so that all should proceed forward on the left, according to Chinese traffic rules. In terms of Chinese history, that kind of "missionary" effort was already a departure from tradition. Mao's Red Guards are much more zealous and violent. Depending upon one's point of view, Mao's Red Guards are comparable to American White Citizens Councilors, the Ku Klux Klansmen, or frontier vigilantes; or they may be likened to prison reformers, protestant evangelists and revivalists, or Women's Christian Temperance Union members led by Carrie Nation, who, with hatchet in hand, busted up many saloons. In any case, they are even more drastic departures from China's past. But in the Chinese leaders' view what the country needs most is a sharp break with the past, a reduction of the attribute of continuity, a modified use of the attribute of authority, a greatly modified version of the attribute of inclusiveness, and an accentuation, at least for the time being, of the attribute of asexuality.

## Conclusion

The hypothesis presented here does not attempt to negate the importance of other factors such as (1) Western invasion of China (for example, what would have happened in China if the West had not actively knocked down her doors and kept up its intrusion?); (2) population pressure (for example, would the Communist leaders have chosen other courses if man-land ratio were more favorable?); (3) the condition of the Chinese economy (for example, did the economic difficulties of 1959–61 determine the subsequent policies?); (4) the wisdom, or the lack of it, of unleashing the Red Guards at this time; (5) the wisdom, or the lack of it, of the present near break with Russia.

Ths is a working hypothesis, to be further refined and tested. In presenting my thoughts, I hope to see if we may acquire new insights by looking at some of the facts presented by others from a different point of view. At the same time, I am inviting criticism so that the formulation of this hypothesis and its implications may be improved. Many problems pertaining to the hypothesis have not been worked out. Some of these will be treated in a forthcoming book, already referred to, and need not detain us here.[28]

It is not my intention to try to explain everything with this hypothesis. What I do emphasize is that there are certain discernible forces in the Chinese kinship system which may be linked, by means of this hypothesis, with certain regular patterns of activities and developments in the larger Chinese society. I maintain, therefore, that we can achieve a more complete and better understanding of what is going on in China today with this hypothesis than without it.

[28] In my *Kinship and Culture,* in preparation.

Ta-Chung Liu

# 11

# Economic Development of the Chinese Mainland, 1949–1965

Since 1949, changes in political and social conditions and institutions on the Chinese mainland have been so intensive and extensive that they perhaps overshadowed changes in the economy. Yet, in a basic sense, the performance of the economy has been, and will continue to be, a constraint on the ambitions and plans of the Communist regime in the political and social spheres. A study of the development of the economy is thus a necessary part in any attempt to gain an understanding of the Communist political system.[1]

This paper deals mainly with the quantitative features of economic development during the last seventeen years. Only a brief sketch of the institutional setting is presented in section I as a background. In section II, the periods of rehabilitation (1949–52) and steady growth (1952–57) are discussed, with emphasis on the latter period for which relatively abundant and reliable economic statistics are available. After the Great Leap Forward in 1958, systematic information about the economy can no longer be obtained, and only some exploratory estimates of the main

[1] This paper draws heavily on two previous contributions by the present author: (1) with K. C. Yeh, *The Economy of the Chinese Mainland: National Income and Economic Development, 1933–1959* (Princeton, N.J.: Princeton University Press, 1965); and (2) "Quantitative Trends in the Economy of the Chinese Mainland, 1952–1965," to appear in *Economic Trends in Communist China,* ed. Walter Galenson, Alexander Eckstein, and Ta-Chung Liu (Chicago: Aldine Publishing Co., 1967). The sponsorship of these two studies respectively by the RAND Corporation and the Committee on the Economy of China of the Social Science Research Council is gratefully acknowledged. For more detailed data, computation and analysis, the reader is referred to these two publications.

609

trends of development are given in section III. A summary analysis is presented in the concluding section of the paper.[2]

## I. Institutional Setting

The "Common Program" proclaimed by the Communists in October, 1949, to be carried out by Communists and non-Communists alike, was relatively mild in its effects on the economy except agriculture. Private enterprise was supposed to be allowed to exist side by side with state and joint state-and-private enterprises for a long time, and the Communists went so far as to permit "national capitalists" to play an important role in the Common Program. A major effort was made to arrest the inflation then rampant in the economy after twelve years of war and internal conflict. When the price stabilization measures became effective and the halt in the rise of the price level brought a mild recession in private industry, the Communist regime even came forward with contracts and other kinds of help for private enterprise. To be sure, government contracts were one of the effective means through which private enterprise was gradually being supervised and regulated. Other forms of indirect control included channeling through the government both the supply of raw materials to private enterprises and the distribution of their products. Moreover, in December, 1950, "Provisional Regulations Concerning Private Enterprises" were put into effect to govern the scope of operations, production, profit distribution, and labor relations of private business. Nevertheless, there was no outright hostility toward private businessmen who cooperated with the regime.

In the meantime, however, a centrally planned economy was first practiced in Manchuria and gradually put into effect in the rest of the mainland. State trading corporations were organized to engage in buying and selling operations so that for consumers in urban areas the government became the major supplier of the following essential commodities: food crops, cotton and textiles, "miscellaneous daily necessities," salt, coal, construction materials, and "miscellaneous local products." In addition, all foreign-trade products were handled by government companies. Salt had always been a government monopoly in China and government marketing of food grains, cotton textiles, and coal had begun during the war, but this was the first time in the history of China that the government actually engaged in the marketing of "miscellaneous daily necessities."

[2] Those readers who are impatient with the technical discussion of economic statistics in secs. II and III may immediately proceed to the summary discussion in sec. IV, referring back to secs. II and III for details as required.

While the reorganization of the urban economy was mild and gradual during 1949–51, land redistribution was carried out immediately after the regime came to power. Farms became even smaller in size than before the redistribution. From an economic point of view, it was difficult to achieve an efficient division of labor. Discussion of more efficient land utilization frequently turned up in the various publications and undoubtedly paved the way for the collectivization movement soon to come. Agricultural taxes were collected in kind, and compulsory sales of agricultural products to the government were soon effected at prices determined by the government. Relative to the prices of non-agricultural products, these prices were lower than before the war.

With the gradual completion of the rehabilitation of the economy in 1951, the regime had gained some experience in large-scale planning in Manchuria and in the operation of industrial and trading enterprises throughout the mainland. The Communists were now ready to push forward the socialization of the urban economy. Two groups of urban population, heretofore treated rather mildly and courteously, were put under firm discipline in 1951: the rank and file government workers, and the owners of private enterprises. A "Three-anti movement"[3] was initiated to single out and punish some of the distrusted civil servants. Early in 1952, a "Five-anti movement"[4] evolved which, in effect, amounted to a large-scale nationalization of private business and the liquidation of undesired businessmen.

Although the First Five Year Plan was not announced until 1955, the year 1953 was considered to be the beginning of the five-year period. Several important changes in economic policies did, in fact, start in 1953, among them a new policy toward the peasants. The peasants were urged to render "mutual aid" during busy seasons as early as in 1951, and "mutual aid" teams were formally organized in the spring of 1953. By the end of 1953, however, the decision had been made to organize agricultural producers' co-operatives. The ownership of land, livestock, and implements remained in the hands of the peasants, though these properties were to be used jointly by members of the cooperatives.

With the promulgation of the 1954 Constitution, a new phase of socialization began, emphasizing "voluntary cooperation" of peasants, the elimination of "rich peasants" and the "transformation" of "na-

[3] Ostensibly directed against (1) corruption, (2) waste, and (3) bureaucratism among government workers and employees of public enterprises.

[4] Outwardly to eliminate: (1) bribery of public officials, (2) tax evasion, (3) theft of public assets, (4) fraud in fulfilling government contracts, and (5) theft of government economic secrets.

tional capitalists." From the end of 1953 to July, 1955, however, only 630,000 co-operatives were organized, with a total membership of 17 million farm households. This was a very small percentage of the agricultural population. In July, 1955, Mao Tse-tung severely criticized Chinese Communist Party (CCP) members for the lack of progress in the co-operative movement. In November, 1955, the decision was made to organize first the "preliminary" and then the "advanced" types of co-operatives. In the preliminary type, the ownership of the land was transferred from the members to the co-operatives; however, the share a member was entitled to have in the total income of the cooperatives was partly determined by the land he had contributed. In addition, the peasants were allowed to own minor livestock and implements and to have a small private plot for their own use. In June, 1956, the advanced co-operative was introduced. The feature that distinguished this type from its predecessor was that the amount of land a peasant had contributed to the cooperative no longer determined his share in the cooperative's income. By the end of 1956, about 88 per cent of the peasants were organized into advanced cooperatives; approximately 8 per cent remained in the preliminary type.

Along with the collectivization of the farmers, a program of comprehensive control and rationing of food began to evolve. Starting in November, 1953, a system of "planned purchases and supply" of food crops was put into effect. The government became the sole supplier of food to urban areas, either directly, or indirectly through food merchants. No city dwellers, food stores, or manufacturers of food products were allowed to buy food supplies directly from the peasants, even though the latter could still engage in small food transactions in the countryside.

The control was further tightened in 1955. A new system of the so-called unified purchase and supply of food grains was introduced throughout the country. In the rural areas the so-called three-fix policy was put into effect—fixing the normal yields, the amount of compulsory sales to government, and (in the case of food-deficient farming areas) the amount of food purchased from the government. This policy was designed to wipe out whatever free market was left in rural areas. In the meantime, the urban population was subject to strict food rationing according to age and occupation.

During the same period, the socialization of private industry and business continued at a rapid pace. One regulation after another was introduced to organize the small business units into co-operatives in which the individual members gradually lost identity, and to transform the larger business concerns into joint or state enterprises. By 1956, the share of private enterprise in industrial production and trade practically vanished. This transformation to a socialist economy was accompanied by a significant and systematic attempt at comprehensive planning on a national scale, modeled to a large extent on the Soviet experience. It is recalled that the First Five Year Plan governing the period 1953–57 was actually announced in 1955. By the latter year, a serious effort to balance inter-industrial and inter-sectorial requirements and supply was more or less in actual operation. Rather detailed plans for industry, transport, trade, agriculture, capital construction, and cost and manpower controls were being fairly effectively implemented. The aims of the effort were clearly rapid industrialization and a high degree of self-sufficiency; and the effort was centered upon the approximately two hundred large-scale projects being constructed with Soviet assistance.

A change in policy toward a limited degree of economic liberalization, however, occurred in late 1956, accompanying the famous Hundred Flowers Campaign. "Free markets" for certain agricultural produce were again permitted and private plots once more became a source of income to the peasantry. A measure of decentralization of decision-making in industrial enterprises also began to evolve at about the same time. The Hundred Flowers Campaign, however, came to an abrupt end in July, 1957; and soon afterwards, the unprecedented Great Leap Forward was taken.

Before 1958, the emphasis of the development plan was on modern, large-scale, capital-intensive industrial projects. The Communists took much pride in the development of electric power and in the up-to-date machinery and techniques of production that had been introduced in an increasing number of factories and mines. In 1958, however, there was a sudden drive for the large-scale utilization of labor-intensive techniques to increase agricultural product and to produce industrial goods with the use of crude equipment. The importance of modern factories was never played down; the massive effort to employ crude equipment and methods was merely to be superimposed on the development of modern, capital-intensive plants. The most famous of these attempts was the backyard blast furnaces, made of crude clay and bricks. These furnaces used as raw materials all kinds of ore, coal, and scraps, including still-usable cooking pots and pans. The purpose was to double steel output from about five million tons in 1957 to ten million tons in 1958. In agriculture, such techniques as deep plowing and close planting were used, with the purpose of doubling agricultural output in one year. An immense effort was used to construct large-scale irrigation and flood-control systems in a hurry—without careful engineering designs. Free markets and private plots were abolished by September, 1958.

The Great Leap Forward apparently brought havoc upon the economy. Mass mobilization for one purpose or another made it impossible to pursue normal economic activities; leakages from the poorly designed irrigation and flood-control systems changed soil conditions and rendered large areas of arable land alkaline; transportation and communication systems were badly interrupted; and regular planning and statistical reporting systems were cast aside. The ill-conceived Great Leap Forward alone would have been sufficient to result in a severe setback in farm output; an agricultural disaster became unavoidable when, in addition, bad weather conditions hit the mainland. Output of light industries declined on account of the lack of agricultural raw materials. On top of this, Soviet technical experts were suddenly withdrawn in 1960, and this must have adversely affected the continued development of heavy industries and capital construction. As the agricultural and industrial crises deepened during 1960–61, sharp changes occurred in Communist economic policies. For the first time since 1949, the development of agriculture was given top priority. In an effort to arrest the falling standard of living, consumer goods were accorded more consideration and capital construction was sharply curtailed. The Great Leap Forward was all but abandoned by 1961. Due to the confusion brought about by the Leap, a formal Second Five-Year Plan (1958–62) has never been published to succeed the fairly elaborate First Plan. The few scattered target figures announced for the Second Plan period became obsolete soon after they were released. In fact, economic statistics have ceased to appear since 1961.

Policy pronouncements during 1961–64 indicated that the Communist regime entered a period of retrenchment, moderation, and adjustment. While heavy imports of food grain continued, by 1965 the economy appeared to have recovered from the setback suffered after the Great Leap Forward. It was announced that the Third Five Year Plan was to commence in 1966, with no details given—the Second Five Year Plan apparently covered eight years (1958–65). While economists everywhere were anxiously awaiting the release of more concrete information on past performance and future course of economic development, the advent of the Great Proletarian Cultural Revolution early in 1967 greatly dimmed the prospect of getting any systematic data to improve our scanty knowledge of the working of the economy during 1958–65.

## II. Rehabilitation (1949–52) and
### Steady Growth (1952–57)

### The Period of Rehabilitation (1949–52)

The initial effort of the regime to rehabilitate the economy was fairly successful for three main reasons. First, by the end of 1949, large-scale military operations had practically ended. For the first time in twelve years there was no fighting on the Chinese mainland. This alone was a boon to the whole country for it made possible the resumption of normal economic activities. Second, the successful Communist price stabilization program in 1950 curtailed the inflation which had run uninterrupted from the last years of the Sino-Japanese War, and greatly assisted in rehabilitating the economy. Victory bonds were issued and, quite understandably, private businesses and individuals had to come forward to subscribe to them. Vigorous efforts were made to increase government revenue (for example, to impose taxes in real terms so that tax revenue would increase with the price level). Except for a small surtax on agriculture, taxes were now collected entirely by the central government, and stringent controls were re-established over the receipts and expenditure of all government organs and state enterprises. These measures were undoubtedly effective in controlling and reducing inflationary pressure. Probably most important to the price stabilization program, however, was the regime's success in ending the flight from cash into commodities. Such transactions were limited, and people did not engage in them because they were afraid of the newly established revolutionary regime. Third, and very important, the mildness of the 1949 Common Program succeeded in relieving the urban population's feelings of anxiety and uncertainty toward the Communist regime.

There is no question that, as the economy recovered from the devastation of twelve years of war, production in all fields increased greatly from 1949 to 1952. The statistics during the period of rehabilitation, however, are very unreliable for the simple reason that the Communists did not have an effective national statistical reporting system of their own until the establishment of the State Statistical Bureau on August 8, 1952. The rate of growth of national income and the gross value of output of industry and agriculture given in table 1 are the official Communist data. It is impossible to say how much of the 70 per cent increase in national income from 1949 to 1952 represented genuine recovery and how much was merely a reflection of the gradual improvement in statistical coverage during this period. It is, however, possible to compare the economy in 1952 with the relatively normal pre-war year of 1933. As the data in table 2 show, the total and per capita products in 1952 exceeded those in 1933, indicating that by 1952 the economy had completed the phase of rehabilitation.

## The Period of Steady Growth (1952–59)

For the period 1952–57, relatively good economic statistics became available in increasing volume. This period roughly coincides with the First Five Year Plan period 1953–57. Since recovery from war damage had been completed by 1952, it becomes possible to evaluate a large portion of the Communist data for this period on the basis of what

TABLE 1

COMMUNIST DATA ON NATIONAL INCOME
AND PRODUCTION DURING THE PERIOD
OF REHABILITATION, 1949–52

| Year | National Income | Combined Gross Output Value of Industry and Agriculture (Billions of 1952 Yüan) |
|------|-----------------|-------------------------------------------------------------------------------|
| 1949 | 100.0 | 46.6 |
| 1950 | 118.6 | 57.5 |
| 1951 | 138.8 | 68.3 |
| 1952 | 169.7 | 82.7 |

SOURCE: The State Statistical Bureau, *Ten Great Years* (Peking: Foreign Language Press, 1960), pp. 16 and 20.

TABLE 2

TOTAL AND PER CAPITA PRODUCT, 1933 AND 1952

| YEAR | NET DOMESTIC PRODUCT (BILLIONS OF 1952 YÜAN) | | PER CAPITA PRODUCT (1952 YÜAN) | |
|------|-----------------------------------------------|------------------|--------------------------------|------------------|
| | Reconstructed Communist Estimate (1) | Liu-Yeh Estimate (2) | Reconstructed Communist Estimate (3) | Liu-Yeh Estimate (4) |
| 1933 | . . . . . . . . . . . | 59.5 | . . . . . . . . . . . | 119 |
| 1952 | 68.6 | 71.4 | 121 | 126 |

SOURCE: Net domestic product from Liu and Yeh, *The Economy of the Chinese Mainland*, pp. 66 and 221; per capita product computed from population data given *ibid.*, pp. 102 and 171.

little is known about the normal productivity of agriculture in China. Taking advantage of the relatively abundant Communist data, several scholars in the United States have made independent estimates of national product for this period.

*Available Estimates of National Product.* The different estimates of national product for 1952 and 1957, expressed in constant 1952 yüan, are presented in table 3, together with the estimated average annual rates of growth.

TABLE 3

NATIONAL PRODUCT ESTIMATES OF THE CHINESE MAINLAND, 1952–57

(Billions of 1952 Yüan)

| | | | | | LIU-YEH | | |
|---|---|---|---|---|---|---|---|
| YEAR | COMMU- NIST (NET MATERIAL PRODUCT)* | ECKSTEIN (GROSS NATIONAL PRODUCT) | HOL- LISTER (GROSS NATIONAL PRODUCT) | LI (NET NATIONAL PRODUCT, RECON- STRUCTED COMMU- NIST ESTI- MATE) | Net Do- mestic Product, Recon- structed Commu- nist Estimate | Authors' Estimate | WU (NET NATIONAL PRODUCT) |
| | (1) | (2) | (3) | (4) | (5) | (6) | (7) |
| 1952 | 61.1 | 71.3 | 67.9 | 72.9 | 68.6 | 71.4 | 72.4 |
| 1957 | 93.5 | ........ | 102.4 | 111.8 | 104.2 | 95.3 | 94.8 |
| Average An- nual Growth Rate | 9.0 | ........ | 8.6 | 8.8 | 8.8 | 6.0 | 5.6 |

* SOURCES: Col. 1: Liu and Yeh, *The Economy of the Chinese Mainland*, p. 220; col. 2: Alexander Eckstein, *The National Income of Communist China* (Glencoe, Ill.: The Free Press, 1961), p. 56; col. 3: W. W., Hollister, *China's Gross National Product and Social Accounts, 1950–57* (Glencoe, Ill.: The Free Press, 1958), p. 2; col. 4: C. M. Li, *Economic Development of Communist China* (Berkeley and Los Angeles: University of California Press, 1959), p. 106; col. 5: Liu and Yeh, *The Economy of the Chinese Mainland*, p. 213 (this estimate was reconstructed from basic Communist data without correc- tions for reliability, but was computed on the standard Western concept of net domestic product); col. 6: *ibid.*, p. 66; col. 7: Y. L. Wu, F. P. Hoeber, and M. M. Rockwell, *The Economic Potential of Communist China* (Menlo Park, Calif., 1964), p. 241.

While discrepancies exist among the different estimates for 1952, the reasons for the differences are now fairly clear.[5] The main differ- ence between the Communist estimate of the net *material* product, 61.1 billion yüan, and the Liu-Yeh reconstructed estimate of net domestic product, 68.6 billion yüan, lies mainly in the omission, from the former, of the contribution of the service sectors, following the well-known

[5] For a detailed analysis of the differences between the estimates, see Liu, "Quantitative Trends in the Economy of the Chinese Mainland, 1952–65," sec. II.

Communist convention of estimating national income. Eckstein's estimate of the gross national product, 71.3 billion yüan, and the Liu-Yeh estimate of the net domestic product, 71.4 billion yüan, can be almost completely reconciled. Hollister's and Li's estimates will be discussed presently in connection with the discussion of the rate of growth below. Wu's estimate is essentially the same as the Liu-Yeh estimate. One may put the net domestic product for 1952 at around 71 billion yüan without running a serious risk of misrepresenting the actual level of total product.

Of more importance than the absolute magnitude of the national product in 1952 are the differences in the growth rates implied in the different estimates during 1952–57. According to the Communist estimate (column 1, table 3) and in terms of the constant 1952 yüan, the average annual rate of growth of the net material product during 1952–57 is 9 per cent per year. In all likelihood this is an overestimate of the overall growth rate of the economy for several reasons.

First and most important, there is general agreement among scholars in this country that the Communist data on agricultural production during the early years in this period underestimated the actual output so that the rate of growth of this sector was overstated for the period as a whole.[6]

The second source of upward bias in the growth rate lies in the way the value of industrial production was computed by the Communists. The 1952 (third-quarter) prices were used as weights in computing the official gross values of production for years prior to 1957. Consumer goods prices were depressed in the fall of 1952 due to the "Five-Anti" campaign against private enterprises, but prices of producer goods were little affected. Thus, producer goods were "overvalued" relative to consumer goods. Since producer goods increased faster than consumer goods after 1952, the official rates of growth of industrial production were therefore upward biased. The valuation of new products at trial-manufacturing expenses, the so-called "new-product effect," also exaggerated the increasing trend. In addition, as will be shown later, there are indications of exaggeration in the reported increase in consumer goods production.

Another important source of upward bias is the omission from the estimate of employment of workers in many traditional, small, and scattered producing units in the handicraft, trade, and transportation

[6] See the following pages in the sources cited in table 3: Eckstein, p. 32; Hollister, pp. 19 and 29; Li, p. 63; Liu and Yeh, pp. 43–46; Wu, p. 185.

sectors.[7] Since the output of these workers hardly increased, if it did not actually decline, during 1952–57, the omission would result in an exaggerated overall rate of growth.

Fourth, there are admissions by the Communists themselves that local units deliberately falsified reports and overstated output in order to fulfill and overfulfill quotas.[8] It is reasonable to assume that the pressure to expand output intensified during 1952–57, and hence attempts to falsify reports may also have increased.

Finally, the concept of "net material product" excludes many so-called "non-productive sectors" which expanded apparently less rapidly than those included in it. This is reflected in the difference between the Communist estimate of a 9 per cent rate of growth and the 8.8 per cent computed from the estimate (column 5, table 3) reconstructed by Liu and Yeh on Communist data without correction for reliability but on the standard Western concept of domestic product which includes incomes originating in the non-productive sectors.

The reconstructed Communist estimates by Li (column 4, table 3) and Liu and Yeh (column 5) naturally yield a rate of growth, 8.8 per cent per year, almost as high as the Communist estimate. The Hollister estimate (column 3), 8.6 per cent per year, is not free from the sources of the upward bias in the Communist estimate discussed above, except the last one.

Attempts to correct the apparent defects in the Communist statistics on food crops and consumer goods and to supplement the deficient Communist data on the traditional and small enterprises were made in deriving the Liu-Yeh estimate given in column 6 of table 3.

That the Communist figures on the production of food crops for the early years during 1952–57 are underestimates of the actual output is no longer a question.[9] The difficult problem is to correct this bias. The procedure followed by Liu and Yeh is briefly outlined here.

First, the Communist figure of the per capita consumption of food crops in 1957 was accepted as roughly correct. It is unlikely that the Communist figure for 1957 is a clear-cut underestimate of the actual output, because the per capita consumption figure implied for that year is as much as 14 per cent higher than the estimated average ration allowed by the Communist regime. It is reasonable to assume that the

[7] See J. P. Emerson, *Nonagricultural Employment in Mainland China: 1949–1958* (Washington, D.C.: Bureau of the Census, 1965), p. 69.

[8] See, for instance, *Jen-min jih-pao* [People's Daily], September 12, 1953.

[9] See note 6.

Communists, knowing that rationing and control regulations could not be completely enforced, would fix the ration at a lower level than the actual amount of consumption. But the Communist rationing and control systems were probably effective enough for actual consumption not to have been more than 10 to 15 per cent higher than the ration amounts allowed.[10] On the other hand, it is also unlikely that the 1957 per capita figure overestimates the actual output. For the calorie intake implied in the 1957 per capita figure is 5 or 6 per cent lower than the estimated 1933 level, and there is no evidence that the per capita food consumption level in 1957 was much smaller than in 1933.

Second, the per capita consumption of food crops during 1952–56 must be estimated. This is an exceedingly difficult task; at the very best, we can give no more than an educated guess. There is no reason to assume that per capita consumption of food crops had been increasing during 1952–57. In fact, the control of food consumption had been gradually tightened throughout the period, and this would have been unlikely had there been increases in per capita supply of food crops. On the other hand, there is no evidence that per capita consumption was reduced during this period. It seems that the only reasonable assumption one can make is that it was more or less constant throughout 1952–57.

This assumption enabled us to estimate the production of food crops for all the years 1952–57. Crops were increasingly used for food, and Communist data are available on the annual percentage used for food in total food crop production, including quantities exported. If we assume that the importation of food crops during this period had been negligible and that there had been no change in the amount in storage, the output can be easily computed for 1952–57 on the basis of the population data. The increase in total production therefore reflects mainly the growth of population, modified only by the increasing percentage of crops used for food.[11]

[10] See Liu and Yeh, *The Economy of the Chinese Mainland,* pp. 47–51.

[11] A number of possible criticisms of this procedure have been discussed and answered (*ibid.,* pp. 43–54). They include such questions as whether the recovery from war damages could have been largely completed by 1952; whether the effects of increasing use of fertilizers and mechanized implements and of the completion of certain irrigation and flood-control projects have been taken into consideration; and whether the rationing controls were not imposed to prevent higher consumption of food crops in response to higher income, implying that per capita consumption of food crops may have been increasing during 1952–57.

Another adjustment was made in the Communist figure of hog production in 1957. It was reported by the Communists that the number of hogs increased by as much as 47 per cent during 1957, a claim which is not only improbable, but was contradicted by a number of events.[12] First, there is no evidence of increases in either exports or domestic consumption of pork subsequent to 1957. Second, animal feeds actually reduced from 1956 to 1957. For the lack of a better alternative, it seems reasonable to assume a percentage increase in the number of hogs equal to the rate of growth of population in 1957.

While it is clear that the particular price weights used, the "new-product effect," and the tendency to exaggerate performance all point to an upward bias in the Communist data on the output of producer goods, no adjustments were made in the Liu-Yeh estimate because of a lack of a reasonable procedure to do so. There is, however, a reported increase of 200 per cent in the production of a group of unidentified consumer goods from 1952 to 1957, much higher than the 45 per cent increase of the output of identified and essential consumer goods during the same period.[13] The latter increase is already fast, reflecting, as it did, not only the increase in actual consumption but also, to an unknown extent, a shift from handicraft output and consumption goods processed at home to modern factory production. Such a fast rate of increase (200 per cent over five years) of consumer goods of unknown identity, at a time when the rate of investment was not only high but also increasing rapidly, cannot be accepted at face value without further scrutiny. An effort must be made to examine what commodities they could have been.

From 1952 to 1956 the Communists published some aggregate data on daily consumption items including china and earthware; consumers' metal products; leather and fur products; glass products; furniture; soaps and cosmetic products; cultural, educational, and "technical" products; and an unnamed "others" category which varied in size from one-fifth to one-third of the total. The gross value of output of this aggregate group of consumers' goods increased 44 per cent from 3.7 billion yüan in 1952 to 5.3 billion yüan in 1956. This is about equal to the rate of increase of the identified portion of the total value of consumer goods, but is a great deal less than the 200 per cent increase reported for the unidentified portion from 1952 to 1956. This information fails to support the claim made for the rate of increase of the global total of the output of consumer goods. At the risk of duplicating some

[12] *Ibid.*, pp. 54–55.     [13] *Ibid.*, p. 60.

of the items already covered in the daily consumption items mentioned above, we have put together some fragmentary data on such "luxuries" as fountain pens, radios, clocks, hot water bottles, pencils, bicycles, and antibiotics. The total value of these goods (in 1952 yüan) cannot exceed about 1.1 billion in 1957, but there was a total value of 9.6 billion yüan worth of unidentified consumer goods (again in 1952 yüan). However fast the rate of increase of these "luxury" items may have been, their increased production could not possibly explain a 200 per cent increase from 1952 to 1957 of the unidentified portion of the gross value of consumer goods to a total of 9.6 billion (1952) yüan.

The 200 per cent increase in the unidentified portion of consumer goods from 1952 to 1957 is therefore inexplicable. Actually, even an increase of 45 per cent in the identified portion of consumer goods from 1952 to 1957 is probably too high in view of the fact that resources are increasingly channeled to investment. The nature of the identified consumer goods is largely known, and we have no reasonable basis on which to make an adjustment in the data; but there can be no doubt that the rapid rate of increase reported for the unidentified portion is exaggerated. To use the Communist data on the value of production of consumer goods without adjustment would result in an overestimate of the rate of growth of the national product. We have re-computed the total annual value of consumer goods production from 1953 to 1957 by assuming that the unidentified portion increased at a rate equal to that of the identified portion. If that assumption is wrong, it overstates the increase in unidentified goods and our estimate errs in the upward direction.

The Liu-Yeh estimate given in column 6 of table 3 was derived after adjustments were made in Communist data on agricultural output and consumer goods production, together with the consequent modification in the other sectors of the economy.[14] The average annual rate of growth according to this estimate is 6 per cent per year. While substantially lower than the Communist estimate of 9 per cent, it is by no means a low overall rate of growth compared to many other nations.[15]

All the adjustments described above can be criticized as more or less arbitrary. But, given the weaknesses in the Communist statistical system, the tendency of local producing units to exaggerate achievements, the known underreporting of crop production in the early fifties, the

[14] A smaller amount of production of agricultural products and consumer goods would reduce the incomes of the trading, transportation, and finance sectors, and would reduce the flow of raw materials to the handicraft sector.

[15] See sec. III of this paper.

inexplicable 200 per cent increase of unidentifiable consumer goods over a short period of five years, it would be even more arbitrary to accept the Communist statistics without adjustment. The question is whether the adjustments made are reasonable and plausible.

There are, of course, weaknesses also in the adjustments made by Liu and Yeh. In particular, the year to year change in the Liu-Yeh estimate of the value added by agriculture is unlikely to be as reliable as the average rate of change during the six years as a whole. For one thing, weather conditions have not been taken into consideration—it is indeed very difficult to calculate the effects of floods and drought on crop production. The adjustments made, however, are based on a detailed evaluation of the basic Communist statistics; and in all likelihood, they have reduced the margins of error in these data. A better knowledge of the economy of the Chinese mainland can be obtained only by improving the adjustments in the Communist statistics; it cannot be achieved by accepting the Communist data without correcting the known defects.[16]

*Key Indicators of Economic Development for a Comparative Appraisal.* There exist sufficiently detailed estimates of the components of the national product[17] which, together with estimates of the labor force and

[16] In a review in the *Journal of Political Economy* vol. 73, no. 4, August, 1965, pp. 419–21, Robert Dernberger criticized Liu and Yeh's *The Economy of the Chinese Mainland* as having an "antidevelopment bias." He wrote that "Among the many assumptions made are that increases in output are proportional to increase in population, that value added is a constant proportion of the gross value of output, that the ratio between the outputs of two industries are constant, and even that output is constant [p. 420]." Dernberger seems to have overlooked the following findings of the Liu-Yeh analysis: (1) The per capita product increased by 19 per cent from 1952 to 1957 (*The Economy of the Chinese Mainland,* Table 16, p. 84). (2) The proportions of value added in the gross value of output of both producer and consumer goods, as estimated by Liu and Yeh, are extremely close to the Communist data themselves, which are also fairly constant over the six years 1952–57 (*ibid.,* Table F-18, p. 496). (3) The ratios between the outputs of different sectors changed significantly from 1952 to 1957 (*ibid.,* Table 21, p. 89). The assumption that "output is constant" was made only for a negligible part of the total product—for instance, the services of domestic servants (*ibid.,* p. 206).

The assumption criticized by Dernberger were made by Liu and Yeh only for specific sectors and after a full consideration of the underlying conditions. Dernberger said that "the authors place great weight on the reasonableness of these crucial assumptions (p. 420)." Indeed, a reasonable criticism of these assumptions should be based only on an examination of the reasonableness of these assumptions; in his review, Dernberger did not do this.

[17] Because of the limitation of the basic data, the gross and net domestic product, instead of the national product, is used in the analysis. The *domestic*

some other data, make it possible to examine the pattern of economic growth in Communist China during 1952–57.[18] The analysis will be made on the format used by Simon Kuznets for his appraisal of the U.S.S.R. in comparison with other countries.[19] This will enable us to compare the performance of the Communist Chinese economy during 1952–57 with those of many other nations during more or less the same period of time.

The national income estimates in table 3 readily fall into two groups distinguished by the rate of growth. One group (the Communist estimate, Hollister's estimate, the reconstructed Communist estimate by Li, and that reconstructed by Liu and Yeh) has average annual rates of growth of 8.6 to 9 per cent during 1952–57. The growth rate of the other group (Liu-Yeh and Wu) is about 6 per cent. The analysis below will be made on the basis of both the reconstructed Communist estimate by Liu-Yeh and the Liu-Yeh estimate itself. These two estimates are selected because they have both the gross and the net versions of the domestic product, together with the required employment data by sector. The different growth rates implied in the two estimates would probably satisfy readers with different degrees of belief in the reliability of the Communist data.

The tentative, preliminary, and incomplete nature of the comparative analysis presented here cannot be overemphasized. Kuznets, however, is correct in saying that, if it is desirable to have quantitative evaluations of the economic development of a given country, "there is surely more justification for comparing them with those for other countries."[20] Not much can be learned from the statistical measurements of the development of one country in one short period taken in isolation. In looking at the record of one nation for one period, people would be making international and inter-temporal comparisons implicitly in their mind in any case. Comparative appraisal should be revised as better data became available; the poor quality of the existing informa-

---

product is also referred to as the total product (rather than per capita product) in this paper.

[18] For a more detailed analysis, see Liu, "Quantitative Trends in the Economy of the Chinese Mainland, 1952–65," sec. 3, and Liu and Yeh, The Economy of the Chinese Mainland, chap. 3.

[19] Simon Kuznets, "A Comparative Appraisal," in Abram Bergson and Simon Kuznets (eds.), Economic Trends in the Soviets (Cambridge, Mass.: Harvard University Press, 1963).

[20] Ibid., pp. 333–34.

tion is not a valid objection to getting some knowledge from preliminary comparisons, especially when estimates covering a range of possibilities (as indicated by the reconstructed Communist estimate and the Liu-Yeh estimate) are analyzed. In fact, international comparisons would also throw some light on the relative plausibility of the different estimates and point out directions for possible revision. Finally, for those who are not interested in tentative international comparisons, attention may be focused on the analysis of the data for the Chinese mainland alone.

For making the comparative appraisal, certain key indicators of the pattern of economic development in Communist China during 1952–57 are presented in table 4.

## Growth in Total, Per Capita, and Per Worker Product

According to the Communist estimate, the rate of growth of the domestic product, 9 per cent per year gross or 8.8 per cent per year net (table 4.A), is higher than those of all the 44 non-Communist countries studied in Kuznets,[21] except Israel and Jamaica, during early postwar years; and it greatly exceeds the long-term growth rates of 12 industrialized nations given in the same source.[22] It is also higher than the estimated overall rates of growth for the U.S.S.R. during any period, except those computed in the 1928 (pre-industrialization) prices for 1928–37 or 1928–40.[23] On the other hand, the Liu-Yeh estimates (6.2 per cent gross and 6 per cent net) are exceeded by 12 of the 44 nations compared in Kuznets' study.[24] On the basis of the Liu-Yeh estimates, however, the performance of the Chinese Communist economy still ranked far above the average of the 44 nations.

The two estimates of the rate of growth of per capita product (table 4.A) differ in about the same way as those of the overall rates. The reconstructed Communist estimate outstripped those of 40 out of the 44 nations compared,[25] and is also higher than those of the U.S.S.R. for all periods.[26] The Liu-Yeh estimate, however, ranks the Chinese mainland above 32 but much below 11 non-Communist countries, and is somewhat higher than that for the U.S.S.R. during 1928–40.

The reconstructed Communist and the Liu-Yeh estimates of the rate of growth of the per worker product are close (4.6–4.9 per cent, table 4.A), the higher Communist estimate of the rate of growth of the total product being more or less compensated for by the higher growth rate

---

[21] *Ibid.*, table VIII.4.    [23] *Ibid.*, table VIII.1.    [25] *Ibid.*, table VIII.4.

[22] *Ibid.*, table VIII.3.    [24] *Ibid.*, table VIII.4.    [26] *Ibid.*, table VIII.2.

TABLE 4

INDICATORS OF ECONOMIC DEVELOPMENT OF THE
CHINESE MAINLAND, 1952–57

| | Reconstructed Communist Estimate | Liu-Yeh Estimate |
|---|---|---|
| A. Rates of Growth of Product, Population, and Employment Per Year, % | | |
| Gross Domestic Product (1952 Prices) | | |
|     Total | 9.0 | 6.2 |
|     Per capita | 6.6 | 3.9 |
|     Per worker | 4.9 | 4.6 |
| Net Domestic Product (1952 Prices) | | |
|     Total | 8.8 | 6.0 |
|     Per capita | 6.5 | 3.6 |
|     Per worker | 4.7 | 4.4 |
| Population | 2.3 | |
| Employment | 4.0 | 1.5 |
| B. Average Proportion of Capital Formation in Domestic Product (1952 Prices), % | | |
|     Gross | 24.4 | 23.8 |
|     Net | 20.6 | 19.8 |
| C. Incremental Capital-Output Ratios, Computed in 1952 Prices, % | | |
| Total | | |
|     Gross | 2.7 | 3.9 |
|     Net | 2.3 | 3.3 |
| Fixed | | |
|     Gross | 2.0 | 2.8 |
|     Net | 1.6 | 2.2 |
| D. Rate of Growth of Inputs and Productivity, % | | |
|     Labor (L) | 4.0 | 1.5 |
|     Net Fixed Capital (K) | 6.8 | 6.5 |
|     Combined Inputs (L at 7 K at 3) | 4.8 | 3.0 |
|     "Productivity" of Combined Inputs | 3.9 | 2.9 |
| E. Total and Per Capita Consumption in 1952 Prices: 1952 and 1957 (Index Numbers, 1933 = 100) | | |
| 1952 | | |
|     Total | 95.2 | 99.4 |
|     Per capita | 83.7 | 87.3 |
| 1957 | | |
|     Total | 137.8 | 123.4 |
|     Per capita | 108.2 | 96.9 |
| F. Rates of Growth of Household Consumption (1952 prices), % | 5.2 | 1.9 |
| G. Share of Total Consumption in Gross Expenditure, % | | |
| 1952 | 72.8 | 73.9 |
| 1957 | 71.8 | 70.3 |
| Share of Increase in Consumption Per Capita in Increase in Gross Expenditure Per Capita 1952–57, % | 68.4 | 48.5 |

TABLE 4—*Continued*

|  | Reconstructed Communist Estimate | Liu-Yeh Estimate |
|---|---|---|
| H. Shares of Major Sectors in Net Product,* % | | |
| 1952 | | |
| A sector | 46.1 | 47.9 |
| M+ sector | 29.0 | 20.2 |
| S− sector | 24.9 | 23.9 |
| 1957 | | |
| A sector | 38.6 | 39.0 |
| M+ sector | 37.9 | 38.7 |
| S− sector | 23.5 | 22.3 |
| I. Shares of Major Sectors in Labor Force, % | | |
| 1952 | | |
| A Sector | 69.9 | 72.9 |
| M+ sector | 17.1 | 15.5 |
| S− sector | 13.0 | 11.6 |
| 1957 | | |
| A sector | 73.1 | 72.9 |
| M+ sector | 16.4 | 16.6 |
| S− sector | 10.5 | 10.5 |

* For meaning of A, M+ and S− sectors, see text note 32.
Source: Liu, "Quantitative Trends in the Economy of the Chinese Mainland," tables 5–17.

of employment. The implication of the two sets of estimates of per capita and per worker estimates, however, are very different. According to the reconstructed Communist data, there was an accelerated use of labor relative to population so that the per worker rate of growth is lower than the per capita rate. The Liu-Yeh estimate, on the other hand, shows that employment expanded more slowly than population, resulting in greater per worker than per capita growth.

## Capital Formation and Capital Output Ratios

The rather substantial increase in the per worker product may be ascribed to a large extent to the significant Communist drive toward industrialization during this period. The effort the Communist regime has made in this direction is best indicated by the very high proportion of capital formation in the total product achieved during 1952–57 (table 4.B). The reconstructed Communist estimate and the Liu-Yeh estimate of the proportion of capital formation in total product are very close (about 24 per cent gross and 20 per cent net), the more rapid increase in the reconstructed Communist estimate of capital formation being more or less compensated for by the greater rate of growth of total product.

These proportions of capital formation in total product, while high, are equaled or exceeded by the long-period records of many industrialized nations,[27] but are substantially greater than those of the less-developed countries during the same postwar period. It is clear that Communist China was making a much greater effort toward investment than most of the underdeveloped countries. These high rates of capital formation were made possible by an effective control of consumption through rationing, the more subtle means of taxation and forced saving, and by the importation of Russian technology and capital equipment.

While the reconstructed Communist and the Liu-Yeh estimates of the proportions of capital formation in total product are roughly the same, the reconstructed Communist estimate of the rate of growth of total product, as we have seen, is significantly higher than the Liu-Yeh estimate. The incremental capital-output ratios derived from the Communist data are therefore correspondingly lower than those derived from the Liu-Yeh estimate[28] (table 4.C). Take the gross total (in contrast to fixed) capital-output ratio as an example: the Liu-Yeh estimate is 3.9, whereas the reconstructed Communist estimate is only 2.7.

On the basis of Bergson's data on national income and Powell's and Moorstein's data on capital formation, Kuznets has found that the capital output ratios for the U.S.S.R. were about the same during the two periods 1928–40 and 1950–58. The ratios are about 3.5 to 3.7 on a gross total basis, 2.6 to 2.8 on a net total basis. For fixed capital, the ratios are 3.1 to 3.2 for gross and 2.3 and 2.1 for net.[29] The Liu-Yeh estimates do not differ greatly from these estimates for the U.S.S.R., whereas the reconstructed Communist ratios are substantially lower than the latter. Since during the First Five Year Plan period, Communist China pursued a development program modeled on the U.S.S.R., and in fact used Russian designs for her major plants, the lower reconstructed Communist estimates of the ratios seem less plausible.

## Growth in "Productivity"

In spite of its popularity, the capital-output ratio, as a measure of the input-output relationship underlying growth, leaves much to be desired. The role of labor is not explicitly brought out, and it gives no indica-

[27] *Ibid.*, tables VIII.13 and VIII.14.

[28] The incremental capital-output ratio can be derived by dividing the capital formation proportion by the rate of growth of product.

[29] Kuznets, "A Comparative Appraisal," table VIII.12.

tion of the contributions of improvements in knowledge, technology, and organization, or of the scale effect. The combined capital and labor-input approach, while far from ideal, throws some light on these other factors. The computation of inputs in this paper is limited to labor and reproducible fixed capital. Arbitrary weights of 7 and 3 are assigned to labor and capital, respectively, so that the result (table 4.D) can be readily compared with similar computations done by Kuznets for ten industrial nations.[30]

The reconstructed Communist estimate of the rate of growth of "productivity" (3.9 per cent per year)[31] would outrank all the other nations studied by Kuznets, coming ahead of West Germany (3.8 per cent), France (3.3 per cent), Japan (3.1 per cent), the Netherlands (2.6 per cent), the U.S.S.R. (2.5 per cent) and the other countries by increasingly large differences. One could seriously doubt the plausibility of this outcome. On the Liu-Yeh estimate (2.9 per cent per year), the Chinese mainland occupies the fourth place after West Germany, France, and Japan, but is still slightly ahead of the U.S.S.R. Since all the nations studied by Kuznets are developed countries, Communist China did rather well in terms of increase of productivity.

## Consumption

The reconstructed Communist estimate and the Liu-Yeh estimate differ most sharply with respect to the impact of the industrialization drive on personal consumption (table 4.E, F and G).

Both the reconstructed Communist estimate for the postwar years and the Liu-Yeh estimate for both the prewar and postwar periods indicate that per capita consumption was lower in 1952 than in 1933. The rates of growth of household consumption during 1952–57 are, respectively, 5.2 per cent and 1.9 per cent according to the two estimates. The Liu-Yeh estimate indicates that the 1933 per capita consumption level had not been regained as late as in 1957, whereas the reconstructed Communist estimate shows an increase of 8 per cent in 1957 over 1933. That the Communist data on consumption are subject to severe reservation can be seen from the data given in table 4.G. According to the Communist estimate, the marginal consumption–total expenditure ratio during 1952–57 (that is, the share of the increment in consumption per capita in the total increase in gross domestic expenditure per cap-

---

[30] *Ibid.*, table VIII.14.

[31] The growth rate of "productivity" may be roughly defined as that of the total product in excess of the growth rate of the combined labor and capital input.

ita) amounted to 68.4 per cent, not much below the reconstructed Communist estimate of the initial share of consumption in total expenditure in 1952 (72.8 per cent). This means that during this period of rapid industrialization, consumption shared about equally with the sum of the other categories of expenditure (including investment) in the total increase. This appears to be a rather unlikely situation. The Liu-Yeh estimate of the marginal increment ratio is 48.5 per cent, substantially lower than their estimate of the initial ratio of 73.9 per cent.

## Industrial Structure

The Communist industrialization drive has brought about a significant change in the industrial structure of the economy (table 4.H and I). The reconstructed Communist estimate and the Liu-Yeh estimate do not differ greatly in this respect. In 1952, on the eve of the First Five Year Plan, about half of the total product originated in agriculture (A), a little more than a quarter in the M+ sector, and slightly less than a quarter in the S– sector.[32] With respect to the labor force, roughly 70 per cent engaged in agriculture, 16 to 17 per cent in the M | sector and about 11 to 12 per cent in the S– sector.

Industrialization meant of course a reduction in the share of the total product originating in agriculture and an increase of the share of the M+ sector. These took place very rapidly from 1952 to 1957. A basically different pattern, however, emerged in the allocation of the labor force. The distribution of the labor force in Communist China was practically the same in 1957 as in 1952. This is so especially in the case of the Liu-Yeh estimate. The Communist estimate even reveals a slight increase and a small reduction in the shares of employment in agriculture and the M+ sector respectively. The change in the S– sector is very minor. The implication is clear. The increase in per worker product given in table 4.A was entirely due to the increase in output per worker in the different sectors; it was not at all the result of a shift of the labor force from a low-yield sector to a high-yield one. The increase in per worker product took place entirely in the M+ and the S– sectors, in both of which, however, there was a substantial shift from the traditional outfits to more modern establishments.

---

[32] The M+ sector includes manufacturing, mining, construction, transport, communications and certain components of utilities. The S– sector covers the rest of the economy other than A and M+.

## III. The Great Leap Forward and Its Aftermath, 1958–65

With the announcement of the Great Leap Forward in December, 1957, the central Communist regime exerted tremendous pressure on local party members, directors of communes, and managers of local enterprises to expand production at a pace practically impossible to achieve. The accomplishments of a few pilot projects using concentrated technical skill and scarce resources under the most favorable conditions and closest supervision were expected to be duplicated by producers all over the country. Soon enthusiastic reports were received from one locality after another claiming that the targets were being fulfilled and overfulfilled. When the *Communique on Economic Development in 1958* was issued in April, 1959, the regime announced that the output of such important products as food crops, cotton, iron and steel had more than doubled during 1958, and that the gross value of agriculture and industry had increased about 65 per cent.

It soon became apparent that these announced increases could not be true, as there was neither improvement in the food rations nor evidence of sufficient increases in the supply of industrial goods to sustain the claims. A drastic downward revision of the claims was announced in August, 1959, reducing the estimated production of food crops and cotton in 1958 by one-third. The claimed increase in iron and steel production was scaled down in a more subtle way. It was admitted that roughly 30 per cent of the iron and steel produced in 1958 was "native" and not really usable for modern industrial purposes. It is difficult to say what the native iron and steel were good for, but it is significant that the backyard blast furnaces were soon abandoned. As the output of iron and steel was not really reduced in the revised announcement, the total value of industrial production remained unchanged. The increase in agricultural production announced for 1959 was more restrained, but the increase claimed for steel and industrial production in general was high.

### Some Existing Estimates of the Post-Leap National Product

Because of the "statistical fiasco" brought about by the Great Leap Forward in 1958, it has become extremely difficult to estimate Communist China's national product and its components since that year with a reasonably high degree of confidence. Some of the existing estimates of the post-1957 total product are presented in table 5, together with the estimates for 1957.

The Communist estimate and the reconstructed Communist estimate by Liu-Yeh for 1958 and 1959 were based on the extravagant Communist claims of increase of agricultural and industrial output. An overall rate of growth as high as 34 per cent in a single year from 93.5 billion yüan in 1957 to 125.3 billion yüan in 1958 does not seem to belong in the realm of possibility. Hollister's estimate of an increase of 23 per cent (from 102.4 billion yüan in 1957 to 126.2 billion yüan in 1958), while lower than the Communist claim, appears to be quite unprecedented also.

TABLE 5

NATIONAL PRODUCT ESTIMATES OF THE CHINESE MAINLAND, 1957–62

(Billions of 1952 Yüan)

| YEAR | COMMUNIST (NET MATERIAL PRODUCT) (1) | HOLLISTER (GROSS NATIONAL PRODUCT) (2) | LIU-YEH (NET DOMESTIC PRODUCT) | | WU (NET DOMESTIC PRODUCT) (5) | WU (GROSS DOMESTIC PRODUCT) (6) |
|---|---|---|---|---|---|---|
| | | | Reconstructed Communist Estimate (3) | Authors' Estimate (4) | | |
| 1957 | 93.5 | 102.4 | 104.2 | 95.3 | 94.8 | . . . . . . . |
| 1958 | 125.3 | 126.2 | 145.0 | 108.0† | 104.8 | . . . . . . . |
| 1959 | 152.9 | 142.6 | 176.8 | 125.0† | 112.0 | . . . . . . . |
| 1960 | . . . . . . . | 158.1 | . . . . . . . . . . . . . . | . . . . . . . . . | 112.5 | . . . . . . . |
| 1961 | . . . . . . . | . . . . . . . | . . . . . . . . . . . . . . | . . . . . . . . . | 73.2 | 82.1 |
| 1962 | . . . . . . . | . . . . . . . | . . . . . . . . . . . . . . | . . . . . . . . . | . . . . . . . . . | 109.0‡ |

SOURCES: Communist, Liu and Yeh, *The Economy of the Chinese Mainland*, pp. 116 and 220; Hollister, *China's Gross National Product and Social Accounts, 1950–57*, p. 2; Liu-Yeh, "Reconstructed Communist Estimate," *The Economy of the Chinese Mainland*, pp. 218 and 660, "Authors' Estimate," *ibid.*, p. 66; Wu, *The Economic Potential of Communist China*, vol. 1, p. 241, and vol. 3, pp. 120–22.

† Conjectural estimate.

‡ Without taking into consideration possible "investment limitations and waste." Taking into consideration possible "investment limitations and waste": 101.4.

After the dusts of the Great Leap have settled, it is certain that all the estimates for 1959 (including the conjectural estimate by Liu-Yeh and Wu's estimate of a modest increase of 7 per cent, from 104.8 billion yüan in 1958 to 112.0 billion yüan in 1959) are overestimates. A basic reason for this conclusion is that agricultural production not only did not increase from 1958 to 1959 but, as will be shown later (see table 7), it actually declined substantially.

## A Reconstructed Communist Estimate of the Domestic Product, 1958–65

While it is admittedly difficult to derive a reliable estimate of the national product for the post-Leap years, the importance of having even a crude picture of the recent economic trends compels us to make such an attempt. Before doing so, it is desirable to reconstruct from scattered Communist information the Communists' own estimate of the domestic product for these years. The Liu-Yeh reconstructed estimates for 1958–59 are presented in column 3 of table 5. A very crude reconstruction for later years is possible on the basis of some Communist observations on food crops and on the total value of industrial production.

For the output of food crops, we have the report by Lord Montgomery after his visit to the mainland that the total output for 1960 was 150 million tons.[33] Since that time, it has been reported in Communist sources that the 1962 output was "better than 1961," that the 1963 output was "better than 1962,"[34] and that the 1964 output was "larger than 1957."[35] Finally, we have the Communist claim that the 1965 output was about 200 million tons.[36] By linear extrapolation on the 1960 and 1965 figures, the Communist "claims" for 1961, 1962, 1963, and 1964 may be put at 160, 170, 180, and 190 million tons.[37] On the assumption that the ratio of value added by agriculture to the output of food crops during 1960–65 is the same as in 1957,[38] agricultural net value added may be estimated at 32.6, 34.7, 36.9, 39.1, 41.2, and 43.4 billion 1952 yüan respectively for the six years 1960–65.

The net value added by manufacturing industries can be reconstructed in a similarly crude way. It has been reported by the Communists that the gross value of industrial output (manufacturing factories and handicrafts) increased by 18.4 per cent from 1949 to 1950.[39] Applying this percentage increase to the Liu-Yeh reconstructed Communist estimate of the net value added by manufacturing factories and handicraft for 1959,[40] the net value added in 1960 is estimated at 61.9 billion

[33] *The Sunday Times,* Magazine, Oct. 15, 1961.

[34] *Jen-min shou-tze* [Peoples' Handbook], 1964, p. 6.

[35] Report by Chou En-Lai, *Jen-min jih-pao,* December 31, 1964.

[36] *Chinese News Summary,* April 28, 1966, p. 1.

[37] The 1964 estimate, 190 million tons, is thus larger than that for 1957 (185 million tons). See the report by Chou En-Lai referred to in note 35.

[38] The 1957 ratio is computed from the data given in Liu and Yeh, *The Economy of the Chinese Mainland,* p. 223.

[39] This percentage is given by Edwin F. Jones from a published Communist source.

[40] See Liu and Yeh, *The Economy of the Chinese Mainland,* p. 660.

1952 yüan. In a forthcoming paper by Chao,[41] the Communist estimate of the gross value of output of manufacturing factories and handicrafts has been reconstructed at 79.8, 88.6, 101.9, and 113.1 billion yüan for the four years 1962 to 1965. The net value added for the same years may be estimated at 23.4, 26.0, 29.9, and 33.1 billion yüan on the 1957 ratio of net value added to the gross value of output.[42] All sources are in agreement that industrial production declined from 1960 to 1962. The 1961 net value added is therefore estimated at 42.6 billion yüan, the average of the 1960 and the 1962 figures (61.9 and 23.4 billion yüan respectively).

Applying the 1957 ratio of net domestic product to the sum of agricultural and industrial value added,[43] we derive the reconstructed Communist estimate of net domestic product for 1960–65 (presented in table 6) from the estimates of the net value added by agriculture and industry given above for these years.

It is desirable to have an approximate picture of the rough order of magnitudes of the per capita product during this period. The rates of growth of population during the post-Leap years, as given in various Communist sources, contradict one another. On the one hand, we have an estimate of 700 million, probably for 1965, given in a *Jen-min jih-pao* (People's Daily) editorial, June 8, 1966. The average rate of growth during 1959 to 1965, implied in this estimate, is only about 1 per cent per year. On the other hand, Chou En-Lai mentioned a 2 per cent rate of growth for 1960–62.[44] In reconstructing the per capita product, an average rate of growth of population of 1.5 per cent, the average of the two Communist estimates, is used. It should be noted that, if this percentage rate of growth of population is an underestimate, the reconstructed Communist estimate of the per capita product would be correspondingly overstated. The estimated per capita product during 1957–65 is given in table 6.

The plausibility of the reconstructed Communist estimate of the domestic product must be evaluated. While the Communists have assigned a high priority to the allocation of resources for exports, the level of exports attainable is basically constrained by domestic output.

---

[41] K. Chao, "Policies and Performance in Industry," in Walter Galenson, Alexander Eckstein, and Ta-Chung Liu (eds.), *Economic Trends in Communist China,* sec. 3b.

[42] The 1957 ratio is calculated from data given in Liu and Yeh, *The Economy of the Chinese Mainland,* p. 223.

[43] This ratio is calculated on the data given, *ibid.,* p. 223.

[44] *Jen-min jih-pao,* December 26, 1963.

To account for the time lag between domestic production and the arrival of exports at foreign ports, domestic product of a given year and exports of the following year are compared in table 6. The reconstructed Communist estimate of the domestic product increased very greatly from 1957 to 1959, but the percentage of exports in domestic product declined sharply from 4.5 per cent for 1957 to 2.7 per cent in 1959. Moreover, while the reconstructed Communist estimates of the domestic product for 1960 and 1961 (respectively 155.9 and 127.5 billion 1952 yüan) are a great deal higher than that for 1957 (104.2 billion

TABLE 6

RECONSTRUCTED COMMUNIST ESTIMATE OF NET DOMESTIC PRODUCT
(TOTAL AND PER CAPITA) COMPARED WITH EXPORTS
OF THE FOLLOWING YEAR, 1957–65

| YEAR | RECONSTRUCTED COMMUNIST ESTIMATE* | | EXPORTS OF THE FOLLOWING YEAR (IN BILLIONS OF 1952 YÜAN) (3) | PERCENTAGE OF EXPORTS IN DOMESTIC PRODUCT OF PRECEDING YEAR (4) |
|---|---|---|---|---|
| | Net Domestic Product (In Billions of 1952 Yüan) (1) | Per Capita Product (In 1952 Yüan) (2) | | |
| 1957 | 104.2 | 164 | 4.65 | 4.5 |
| 1958 | 145.0 | 222 | 5.31 | 3.7 |
| 1959 | 176.8 | 267 | 4.74 | 2.7 |
| 1960 | 155.9 | 232 | 3.59 | 2.3 |
| 1961 | 127.5 | 187 | 3.59 | 2.8 |
| 1962 | 99.5 | 144 | 3.67 | 3.7 |
| 1963 | 107.4 | 153 | 4.55 | 4.2 |
| 1964 | 117.3 | 165 | 4.91 | 4.2 |
| 1965 | 126.2 | 165 | .................... | .................... |

SOURCES: Cols. 1 and 2, for the 1957–59 figures of net domestic product, see Liu and Yeh, *The Economy of the Chinese Mainland*, pp. 213 and 660; for the 1960–65 estimates, see text. For the per capita estimates, the 1957–58 population figures used in the computation are the official Communist data (*ibid.*, p. 102); and for those for the later years, see text; col. 3: supplied by F. H. Mah.

* The figures given for 1958–65 are very crude reconstructed estimate.

yüan), the 1960 and 1961 percentages (respectively 2.3 per cent and 2.8 per cent) are substantially smaller than that for 1957 (4.5 per cent). This indicates that the reconstructed Communist estimates of the domestic product for 1958–61 are likely to be overestimates.[45] Since the

[45] Since the export data used are compiled from the import data of countries having trade relations with Communist China, they are fairly reliable data. While during the difficult years 1961–62 the percentage of exports in domestic product may be expected to be smaller than the more normal years 1957–58, the decline was too sharp to be plausible, especially since the reconstructed estimates of the domestic product for those years are substantially higher in absolute terms than that for 1957.

reconstructed Communist estimates of the domestic product for 1963–65 are based on claimed increases of agricultural and industrial production over the exaggerated estimates for the preceding years, they are also likely to be overestimates.

## An Exploratory Estimate of the Domestic Product, 1958–65

In spite of the practically total blackout of statistics on commodity output from Communist sources on the mainland since 1960, there has emerged a set of rough but educated estimates of the output of food

TABLE 7

ESTIMATES OF THE OUTPUT OF FOOD
CROPS AND COTTON, 1957–65

| Year | Food Crops (Million Metric Tons)* | Cotton (Million Bales) |
|------|-----------------------------------|------------------------|
| 1957 | 185 | 1.6 |
| 1958 | 194 | 1.9 |
| 1959 | 168 | 1.8 |
| 1960 | 160 | 1.4 |
| 1961 | 167 | 0.9 |
| 1962 | 178 | 0.9 |
| 1963 | 179 | 1.0 |
| 1964 | 183 | 1.2 |
| 1965 | 180 | 1.3 |

SOURCE: Reported in R. F. Emery, "Recent Economic Development in Communist China," *Asian Survey* (June, 1966), pp. 303–4. Estimates are those of the Agricultural Officer, U.S. Consulate-General, Hong Kong.

crops and cotton during 1959–65. These data, prepared by the U.S. Consulate-General in Hong Kong on the basis of piecemeal information on acreages and yields, are the most generally accepted estimates of the recent trend of output by qualified sources in Hong Kong and are given in table 7.

Agricultural output declined precipitantly from 1958 to 1960. Recovery in food crops production began in 1961. The output of cotton, the major commercial crop, lagged behind and did not start to recover until 1963. As late as 1965, neither food crops nor cotton had regained the 1957 level.

The movement in heavy industrial output may be typified by the output of steel. Estimates of steel output by sources in Hong Kong are given in table 8, together with the estimate made by the U.S. Bureau of Mines and some other data. The figures given for 1958–60 in columns 1–4 are Communist claims, and all non-Communist sources are in agreement that these data are highly inflated. Starting with 1962, the scattered data in columns 1–3 begin to converge to a fairly uniform pattern. The estimate made by the U.S. Bureau of Mines (column 4) differs rather sharply from those given in columns 1–3. It is explained

TABLE 8

SCATTERED DATA ON STEEL AND ELECTRIC POWER, 1957–65

| YEAR | STEEL (MILLION METRIC TONS) | | | | | | | ELECTRIC POWER, EMERY | |
|---|---|---|---|---|---|---|---|---|---|
| | Current Scene | Emery | Far Eastern Economic Review | U.S. Bureau of Mines | Liu-Yeh | Data Used in This Paper | | Quantity (Billions k.w.h.) | Index 1957 = 100 |
| | | | | | | Quantity | Index 1957 = 100 | | |
| | (1) | (2) | (3) | (4) | (5) | (6) | (7) | (8) | (9) |
| 1957 | 5.35 | 5.2 | 5.35 | . . . . . . . | 5.35 | 5.35 | . . . . . . . | 19.0 | . . . . . . . |
| 1958 | 8.00† | 8.0† | 11.08† | . . . . . . . | 6.3 | 6.3 | . . . . . . . | 27.5† | . . . . . . . |
| 1959 | 13.35† | 13.4† | 13.35† | 13.35† | 8.9 | 8.9 | . . . . . . . | 41.5† | . . . . . . . |
| 1960 | 18.45† | 18.5† | 18.45† | 18.45† | . . . . . . | 8.4 | . . . . . . . | 58.0† | . . . . . . . |
| 1961 | . . . . . . . | . . . . . . | 11–12 | 9.5 | . . . . . . | 7.9 | . . . . . . . | . . . . . . . | . . . . . . . |
| 1962 | 7–8 | . . . . . . | 7–8 | 10.0 | . . . . . . | 7.5 | . . . . . . . | . . . . . . . | . . . . . . . |
| 1963 | 7–9 | 7.0 | 8–9 | 12.0 | . . . . . . | 8.0 | 149.5 | 30.0 | 157.9 |
| 1964 | 8–10 | . . . . . . | 10 | 14.0 | . . . . . . | 9.0 | . . . . . . . | . . . . . . . | . . . . . . . |
| 1965 | . . . . . . . | 10.0 | 12 | . . . . . . . | . . . . . . | 10.0 | 186.9 | 33.0 | 173.7 |

SOURCES: Col. 1: April 15, 1965, p .9; col. 2: *Asian Survey* (June, 1966), p. 307; col. 3: March 31, 1966, p. 623; col. 4: mimeographed sheet obtained from the U.S. Bureau of Mines; col. 5: Liu and Yeh, *The Economy of the Chinese Mainland*, pp. 454 and 681–83. The 1958 and 1959 figures are obtained respectively by dividing the value figures of 3.8 and 5.36 billion yüan by the price of 600 yüan per ton; col. 6: for 1957–59, the data given in col. 5 are used. The 1962 figure is the midpoint of the range given in cols. 1 and 3. The figures for 1960–61 are obtained by linear extrapolation on the 1959 and 1962 data. The 1963 and 1964 data are the midpoints of the ranges given in col. 1. The 1965 figure is taken from col. 2. It is seen from cols. 7 and 9 that the steel figures for 1963 and 1965 bear relationships to that for 1957 similar to the data on electric power; col. 8: *Asian Survey* (June, 1966), p. 307.

† Communist claims.

by the Bureau of Mines, however, that these figures may be "grossly exaggerated by perhaps one-fifth or more."[46] No opinion is expressed on how much "more" than one-fifth. If the exaggeration were from one-fourth to one-third, the estimate by the Bureau of Mines for 1962–64

[46] This qualifying statement was originally given for the 1959–60 estimates in the *Minerals Yearbook, 1963*, table 2, pp. 1282 (Washington, D.C.: U.S. Government Printing Office, 1963); but in later mimeographed sheets distributed by the Bureau of Mines, it is given for the estimates for all the years 1959–64.

would be quite close to those in the first three columns. It is clear that steel production fell substantially from 1959 to 1962 and then recovered from 1962 to 1965.

A model of 16 structural relationships was developed in a previous paper[47] for estimating domestic product and investment for 1959–65, together with the value added by the two main branches of the economy (the traditional sectors and the relatively modern ones), on the basis of the data given in tables 7 and 8. The parameters in most of the structural relationships were estimated from the input-output relationships observed during the statistically more reliable years 1952–57. The derivation of these equations will not be discussed here;[48] the main feature of the model, however, can be outlined by explaining these relationships as follows. The value added by modern factories is determined by the agricultural and mining raw materials consumed. Agricultural raw materials consumed is assumed to be a function of the output of the agricultural sector of both the current and the preceding years. The total amount of mining raw materials consumed by modern factories is extrapolated on the quantities of coal and iron ore produced by modern mines. However, since the data on the latter two items are rather confused during recent years, a relationship is derived for estimating these quantities from the data on steel. The value added by all traditional sectors is related to the value added by agriculture; and that by the relatively modern sectors as a whole is determined by the value added by modern factories. The domestic product is obtained as the sum of the value added by the different sectors. The levels of employment in these sectors are then estimated on the basis of the value added by the respective sectors. Per capita consumption is then related to per capita productivity. Finally, domestic investment is derived by subtracting consumption from the total product.

With this system of equations obtained, the domestic product and investment for 1959–65 can be calculated in a straightforward manner on the basis of the estimates of food crops, cotton, steel and some other data. For the estimates on food crops and cotton, the figures presented in table 7 are accepted. The data on steel used in the computation are presented in column 6 of table 8. The estimates of net domestic product and investment are given in table 9.

[47] Liu, "Quantitative Trends in the Economy of the Chinese Mainland," sec. V.2.

[48] For a full explanation of the model, see Liu, "Quantitative Trends in the Economy of the Chinese Mainland."

The decline of the domestic product from 1958 to 1961 confirms the deepening difficulty encountered by the economy during these years. The domestic product in 1961, 92.2 billion 1952 yüan, was 15 per cent lower than the 1958 peak of 108 billion 1952 yüan. The economy began to recover in 1962. The annual rate of recovery, as measured by the percentage growth in domestic product, increased from 2 per cent in 1961–62 to 6.2 per cent in 1963–64. The speed, however, slackened to 3.7 per cent during 1964–65, mainly due to the drought in northern China.

TABLE 9

Estimate of Net Domestic Product
and Investment, 1957–65

(Billions of 1952 Yüan and Per Cent)

| Year | Net Domestic Product (Billions of 1952 Yüan) | Net Domestic Investment (Billions of 1952 Yüan) | Proportion of Net Domestic Investment in Net Domestic Product (In Per Cent) |
|---|---|---|---|
| 1957 | 95.3 | 18.2 | 19.1 |
| 1958 | 108.0 | 23.6 | 21.9 |
| 1959 | 104.4 | 20.0 | 19.2 |
| 1960 | 95.9 | 17.1 | 17.8 |
| 1961 | 92.2 | 15.6 | 16.9 |
| 1962 | 94.0 | 15.7 | 16.7 |
| 1963 | 98.1 | 16.7 | 17.0 |
| 1964 | 104.2 | 18.1 | 17.4 |
| 1965 | 108.1 | 19.5 | 18.0 |

Source: Liu, "Quantitative Trends in the Economy of the Chinese Mainland," Tables 24 and 25.

The 1957 level of domestic product was regained during 1962–63, and the 1965 product was about the same as in 1958. The economy in 1965 stood where it was in 1958, a "loss" of seven years without growth.

Net domestic investment decreased by 34 per cent, from 23.6 billion 1952 yüan in 1958 to 15.6 billion in 1961. The proportion of investment in total product declined fairly consistently, from 21.9 per cent in 1958 to 16.7 per cent in 1962. By 1965, however, investment exceeded the magnitude reached in 1957, but the proportion of investment in domestic product in 1957 had not yet been fully regained.

The plausibility of the post-1958 estimate must be investigated. The product estimate can be checked against the data on exports, and the investment estimate examined in the light of certain Communist policy pronouncements.

As shown in table 10, the ratio of exports to the domestic product of the preceding year rose fairly consistently from 1952 to 1959, within a range of 3.6 to 4.9 per cent. This proportion fell from 4.9 per cent in 1959 to 3.7 per cent in 1960, reflecting the increasing difficulty experienced by the economy.[49] It recovered thereafter quite consistently to 4.7 per cent in 1964. The post-1960 range of this proportion, 3.7 per cent to 4.7 per cent, is close to the one observed during 1952–57, but the ratios for the most difficult years, 1960–62 (3.7 per cent to 3.9 per cent), are lower than those in the best years before the Leap, 1956–57, and those attained in 1958–59 under the initial impetus of the Leap.

TABLE 10

NET DOMESTIC PRODUCT COMPARED WITH EXPORTS
OF THE FOLLOWING YEAR

| Year | Net Domestic Product (Billions of 1952 Yüan) | Exports of the Following Year (Billions of 1952 Yüan) | Percentage of Exports in Net Domestic Product of Preceding Year |
|---|---|---|---|
| 1952 | 71.4 | 2.59 | 3.6 |
| 1953 | 75.3 | 2.82 | 3.8 |
| 1954 | 79.3 | 3.36 | 4.2 |
| 1955 | 82.3 | 3.98 | 4.8 |
| 1956 | 92.1 | 3.89 | 4.2 |
| 1957 | 95.3 | 4.65 | 4.9 |
| 1958 | 108.0 | 5.31 | 4.9 |
| 1959 | 104.4 | 4.74 | 4.5 |
| 1960 | 95.9 | 3.59 | 3.7 |
| 1961 | 92.2 | 3.59 | 3.9 |
| 1962 | 94.1 | 3.67 | 3.9 |
| 1963 | 100.8 | 4.55 | 4.5 |
| 1964 | 104.2 | 4.91 | 4.7 |
| 1965 | 108.1 | ............... | ............... |

SOURCE: Liu, "Quantitative Trends in the Economy of the Chinese Mainland," table 26.

The picture reflected by these data appears plausible. While the foreign-trade data are also subject to a substantial margin of error, they are derived from the statistics of countries having trade relations with the Chinese mainland and are more reliable than our exploratory estimate of the domestic product. That a reasonable relationship exists between the data on exports and the product estimate would lend credibility to the latter.

Our estimate of net domestic investment (table 9) indicates a very substantial decline from 1958 to 1961–62. Investment in 1963–65 was

[49] The drop, however, is much less drastic than the implausible decline reflected in the reconstructed Communist estimate (see table 6).

still low in its ratio to the total product as compared to 1957 and the "Leaping Years," 1958–59. The magnitudes of investment during 1962–65 (15.7 billion to 19.5 billion 1952 yüan), however, remain substantial. This may seem to contradict certain policy pronouncements of the Communist regime.

When the agricultural crises continued into 1960, the Ninth Plenum of the Central Committee decided early in 1961 that "since there had been tremendous development in heavy industry in the last three years, its output of major products already far in excess of the planned level for 1961 and 1962, the scale of basic construction should therefore be appropriately reduced."[50] Moreover, it is known that in December, 1961, the Communist Party issued a secret document to cadres in the field directing that "all basic construction should be suspended, all those enterpirses that had been operating regularly at a loss be shut down, and the practice of recruiting labour from rural areas be abandoned for at least three years."[51] Then, on March 27, 1963, Chou En-Lai again reported the decision to reduce basic construction.[52]

In view of the apparently firm decision to cut down capital construction since 1961, it may be questioned whether investment in 1961–65 could have been as high as our estimate indicates. It is of course possible that the investment estimate presented in table 9 is unreliable. Yet there are grounds to believe that the actual investment may not have been significantly below our estimate.

According to our estimate, the average level of investment during 1961–63 (16 billion 1952 yüan) was lower than that during 1957–59 (20.6 billion 1952 yüan) by 4.6 billion yüan. In view of the large number of construction projects known to be underway at the end of 1959, the momentum might have been such that a more drastic curtailment was not possible to enforce—in spite of the announced policy of entrenchment. By 1964 the domestic product exceeded the 1957 level (table 9), and the policy of curtailing investment may have been relaxed. Moreover, while the 1965 product was virtually the same as in 1958, our estimated investment for 1965 is substantially smaller than that for 1958.

Also, while basic construction in general may have been reduced, it is known that the Communist regime increased investment in the petroleum and fertilizer industries and significantly expanded the produc-

[50] Chou-ming Li (ed.), *Industrial Development in Communist China* (New York: Praeger, 1964), p. 10.

[51] *Ibid.*, p. 11.          [52] *Ibid.*

tion of tractors and other farm equipment. Investment relating to the production of atomic weapons must have been very substantial. It is not possible, however, to make a quantitative estimate of the investment in these areas at the present moment.

Another possible explanation of the substantial amount of investment during 1961–65 is an excessive increase in the stock of inventory. Steel, machinery, and other producers goods were perhaps actually produced in quantities compatible with the investment estimate, but they were merely being piled up. They had not been installed and put to use. A degree of confusion in the management of economic affairs may have existed after the agricultural crises during 1959–61. Orders were issued to curtail basic construction—but there was no corresponding reduction in the production of those producers goods which did not rely upon agriculture as the major source of raw materials. In fact, the regime may have been more anxious to avoid the difficult problem of excessive unemployment, already serious due to the slowing down of activities in such industries as textiles and food processing, than concerned with the problem of excessive stockpiling.

### IV. Summary Analysis

The tempo of economic development on the Chinese mainland has been analyzed in this paper in terms of the national product[53] and related statistics. While the national output is the best available indicator of the total productivity of an economy, it must be emphasized immediately that it is quite inadequate as a measure of human welfare, especially in a totalitarian state where expansion in heavy industrial output is often achieved through rigid regimentation and coercive measures. Moreover, the productive capacity of the economy as a whole does not reveal the strength of the nation in carrying out a specific endeavor to which a large concentration of resources is devoted. Thus, the per capita product of the Chinese mainland is low by any estimate and on any standard, but a nuclear and missile program produced successful results in recent years when the economy as a whole was still experiencing difficulties. One must not be misled by the low per capita productivity on the Chinese mainland to a feeling of complacency regarding her technical capabilities in certain narrowly defined spheres. At the same time, it is equally erroneous to consider the achievement in a specialized field as an indicator of the degree of development of the economy as a whole. All these inadequacies notwithstanding, an analy-

---

[53] See note 17.

sis of the movement in its national product is a necessary and important part in any attempt to understand the working of the Communist economy on the Chinese mainland.

The performance of the Chinese Communist economy during the First Five Year Plan period has been described in terms of both an estimate of the national product reconstructed from the Communist statistics themselves without adjustment and an independent estimate by Liu and Yeh which incorporates some adjustments for the reliability of the Communist data. The relative plausibility of the two estimates has been discussed. For the years after the Great Leap Forward in 1958, an exploratory estimate by the present author has been presented, together with a crude reconstruction of the Communist estimate.

The "People's Political Consultative Conference," held in Peking in September, 1949, can be considered as the commencement of the Communist Regime on the mainland. The rehabilitation of the economy from the devastation of the Sino-Japanese War and the ensuing internal conflict was fairly rapid. By 1952, the reconstructed Communist estimate of the net domestic product reached 68.6 billion yüan,[54] 15 per cent higher than the 1933 level of 59.5 billion (1952) yüan; and the per capita product in 1952 (121 yüan) was slightly higher than in 1933 (119 yüan). On the basis of the Liu-Yeh estimate for 1952, the net domestic product (71.4 billion yüan) and the per capita output (126 yüan) were, respectively, 20 per cent and 6 per cent higher than in 1933 (see section II, "The Period of Rehabilitation"[55]).

The period from the completion of the rehabilitation of the economy in 1952 to the most recent year 1965 is of the greatest interest. For convenience of reference, the different estimates of the domestic product and per capita output are reproduced in table 11.

On either the reconstructed Communist data or the Liu-Yeh estimate, there was steady growth in both the total and the per capita product during 1952–57. (See section II, "Growth in Total, Per Capita, and Per Worker Product.")

According to the reconstructed Communist estimate, the rate of growth of the domestic product during 1952–57 was higher in Com-

[54] For well-known reasons, the use of the 1952 exchange rate of 1 U.S. dollar = 2.343 yüan to obtain estimates of total and per capita product in U.S. dollars will give misleading results.

[55] The reconstructed Communist estimate of the domestic product for 1952 is likely to be an underestimate. On account of this underestimation, the rate of growth during 1952–57 is overstated by the reconstructed Communist estimate. (See sec. II, "Available Estimates of National Product.")

munist China (9 per cent gross or 8.8 per cent net)[56] than in practically all of the more than 40 nations analyzed in a study by Kuznets[57] for more or less the same period of time. Relevant data for a few countries are given in table 12 as an illustration. The per capita product also grew at a faster rate (6.6 per cent gross or 6.5 per cent net) than all the

TABLE 11

NET DOMESTIC PRODUCT OF THE CHINESE MAINLAND,
TOTAL AND PER CAPITA, 1952–65

(Total Product: Billions of 1952 Yüan;† Per Capita Product: 1952 Yüan)

| YEAR | RECON-STRUCTED TOTAL† (1) | COMMUNIST ESTIMATE PER CAPITA‡ (2) | LIU-YEH ESTIMATE | | EXPLORATORY ESTIMATE | |
|---|---|---|---|---|---|---|
| | | | Total (3) | Per Capita (4) | Total (5) | Per Capita‡ (6) |
| 1952 | 68.6 | 121 | 71.4 | 126 | . . . . . . . . . . | . . . . . . . . . . |
| 1953 | 73.3 | 126 | 75.3 | 130 | . . . . . . . . . . | . . . . . . . . . . |
| 1954 | 77.8 | 131 | 79.3 | 133 | . . . . . . . . . . | . . . . . . . . . . |
| 1955 | 83.3 | 137 | 82.3 | 135 | . . . . . . . . . . | . . . . . . . . . . |
| 1956 | 96.4 | 155 | 92.1 | 148 | . . . . . . . . . . | . . . . . . . . . . |
| 1957 | 101.2 | 164 | 95.3 | 150 | . . . . . . . . . . | . . . . . . . . . . |
| 1958 | 145.0 | 222 | . . . . . . . . . . | . . . . . . . . . . | 108.0 | 166 |
| 1959 | 176.8 | 267 | . . . . . . . . . . | . . . . . . . . . . | 104.4 | 158 |
| 1960 | 155.9 | 232 | . . . . . . . . . . | . . . . . . . . . . | 95.9 | 143 |
| 1961 | 127.5 | 187 | . . . . . . . . . . | . . . . . . . . . . | 92.2 | 135 |
| 1962 | 99.5 | 144 | . . . . . . . . . . | . . . . . . . . . . | 94.0 | 136 |
| 1963 | 107.4 | 153 | . . . . . . . . . . | . . . . . . . . . . | 98.1 | 140 |
| 1964 | 117.3 | 165 | . . . . . . . . . . | . . . . . . . . . . | 104.2 | 146 |
| 1965 | 126.2 | 165 | . . . . . . . . . . | . . . . . . . . . . | 108.1 | 150 |

SOURCES: Cols. 1 and 3, figures for 1952–57, Liu and Yeh, *The Economy of the Chinese Mainland*, pp. 213, 660, and 66; for 1958–65 estimates, see Table 6; cols. 2, 4, and 6, population data used in obtaining per capita estimates for 1952–58 are Communist official data given, *ibid.*, p. 102; for population data used for years after 1958, see sec. III of this paper, "A Reconstructed Communist Estimate of the Domestic Product, 1958–65," and Table 6; col. 5, Liu, "Quantitative Trends in the Economy of the Chinese Mainland, 1952–65," Table 24.

† For well-known reasons, the use of the 1952 exchange rate of 1 U.S. dollar = 2.343 yüan to obtain estimates of total and per capita product in U.S. dollars will give misleading results.

‡ The figures given for 1958–65 are very crude estimates.

nations examined in Kuznets' study, except West Germany. Employment expanded at a much faster rate (4 per cent) than population (2.3 per cent), but because of the large number of unemployed in existence (including disguised),[58] this relative change would have been a pure blessing for quite some time to come. The growth rate of per worker product (4.9 per cent gross or 4.7 per cent net) was also exceed-

[56] All the statistical information quoted in this and the following three paragraphs can be found in table 4.

[57] Kuznets, "A Comparative Appraisal."

[58] See Liu and Yeh, *The Economy of the Chinese Mainland*, pp. 101–5.

ingly high. The proportion of total product invested (24.4 per cent), while equaled or bettered by many industrial nations both in long periods and in roughly comparable postwar years, was considerably higher than countries with equally low per capita product or with similar underdeveloped industrial structure. Yet, in spite of the high rate of savings, consumption expanded at 5.2 per cent per year on a per capita basis and shared almost equally with other expenditures in the increase in total expenditure. The various incremental capital-output ratios are low, substantially smaller than those of the U.S.S.R. and most other nations, industrialized or not. On the basis of the 1952 yüan, an incremental capital-output of 2.7, coupled with a capital formation proportion of 24.4 per cent, resulted in an overall rate of growth of the gross product of 9 per cent per year.[59] The rates of increase of labor and capital inputs, separate or combined, were high; but so was the growth rate of "productivity," 3.9 per cent per year.[60] As shown in table 12, the growth rate of productivity is higher than any other nation during roughly comparable post-war years.

The performance of the Communist economy during 1952–57, as represented by the reconstructed Communist data, must be considered a most outstanding success, exceeding those of West Germany and Japan. It approaches a miracle if one considers the very limited technical knowledge and personnel the Communist regime had to start with, the practical non-existence of uncultivated land, the gradual disappearance of private incentives to the peasants, the severe tightening of control of economic activities by cadres lacking training in such spheres, and the rather short period of time in which to condition the people and the economy to the rather unfamiliar modern industrial organization and operation.

But strong reservations must be made as to the credibility of such a picture. Indeed, one would seriously question why the Communist leadership, however ambitious they may have been, would have been so anxious to institute as radical a change in their economic policies as the Great Leap Forward in 1958 if everything was indeed making such great progress, unprecedented not only in China but also in the entire world.

The growth history represented by the Liu-Yeh estimate seems more in accordance with reality. The over-all growth rate (6.2 per cent gross

[59] The rate of growth of the product can be computed by dividing the capital formation proportion by the incremental capital-output ratio.

[60] The growth rate of "productivity" may be roughly defined as that of the total product in excess of the growth rate of the combined labor and capital input.

or 6.0 per cent net) is by no means low; in fact, it was higher than roughly two-thirds of the nations compared in the study by Kuznets. But population was expanding much faster (2.3 per cent) than employment (1.5 per cent). The rate of investment (23.8 per cent at 1952 prices), while high, was not sufficient to absorb the fast-growing population into employment. Per capita consumption was rising at a much

TABLE 12

AVERAGE ANNUAL RATES OF GROWTH IN TOTAL AND PER CAPITA
PRODUCT AND IN "PRODUCTIVITY" FOR SELECTED NATIONS:
COMMUNIST CHINA, 1952–57; OTHER NATIONS, 1950–58

| Nation | Total Product* | Per Capita Product | "Productivity"† |
|---|---|---|---|
| Communist China, 1952–57, Reconstructed Communist Estimate | 9.0–8.8% | 5.6–6.5% | 3.9% |
| Liu-Yeh Estimate | 6.2–6.0 | 3.9–3.6 | 2.9 |
| Burma | 6.3 | 5.1 | .......... |
| France | 4.3 | 3.4 | 3.3 |
| Italy | 5.6 | 5.0 | ..... .. |
| Japan | 8.0 | 6.6 | 3.1 |
| Philippines | 5.7 | 3.3 | .......... |
| Republic of China (Taiwan) | 8.8 | 5.4 | .......... |
| South Korea | 2.5 | 1.3 | .......... |
| Thailand | 0.7 | −1.2 | .......... |
| Turkey | 6.9 | 4.0 | .......... |
| U.K. | 2.2 | 1.9 | 0.7 |
| U.S. | 2.9 | 1.1 | 1.0 |
| U.S.S.R. | 7.2 | 5.4 | 2.5 |
| West Germany | 8.0 | 6.8 | 3.8 |

SOURCES: Communist China: Table 6; all other nations: Kuznets, "A Comparative Appraisal," tables VIII.2, VIII.4, and VIII.14. (For the U.S.S.R., the data on total and per capita product are those for GNP computed on 1937 factor cost, given in table VIII.2, *ibid.*)

* For the various versions of the total product (gross or net, national or domestic) presented in this table for the different nations, see Kuznets, "A Comparative Appraisal."

† For the meaning of "productivity," see note 31. The weights of labor and capital in the combined factor input are, respectively, 7 and 3. See Kuznets, "A Comparative Appraisal," table VIII.14.

more modest rate (1.9 per cent, excluding communal services) than that indicated by the reconstructed Communist estimate (5.2 per cent); but the pre-war 1933 level had not been regained even at the end of this period (1957). The capital output ratios were reasonably low. But an incremental capital output ratio of 3.9, coupled with an investment proportion of 23.8 per cent, yielded a growth rate of the gross product of 6.2 per cent per year which, while quite high, failed to bring about an increase in employment and consumption satisfactory to the regime.

Even the picture represented by the Liu-Yeh estimate for 1952–57 was very good; but to a leadership having extraordinary ambitions, both domestic and international, and an unusual confidence in their ability to put through radical reorganizations of the economy, a prospect of growth on the pattern during 1952–57 might have been considered unsatisfactory. A radically different program, which hopefully would utilize the increasingly underemployed human resources to the fullest extent without having to divert capital resources from large-scale modern projects, would have appeared attractive to the Communist leadership. In the light of the Liu-Yeh estimate, the motivation underlying the Great Leap Forward (1958–59) seems more understandable.

The Great Leap Forward was based on a sound diagnosis of the basic weakness of the mainland economy but a serious misconception of the proper way to deal with it. There was a tremendous amount of surplus labor and a serious shortage of capital and of highly trained manpower as late as 1957, in spite of the significant degree of industrialization achieved during 1952–57. Communes were organized in 1958. Life in the villages was almost completely regimented. Peasants were marched to the field to work impossibly long hours, and terrific pressure was imposed on industrial enterprises to expand production at unprecedented paces. The output of almost everything was to double in a single year from 1957 to 1958.

Since the reconstructed Communist estimate of the domestic product for 1958–65 is very unreliable (see section III, "Some Existing Estimates of the Post-Leap National Product" and "A Reconstructed Communist Estimate of the Domestic Product, 1958–65." The exploratory estimate in table 11 will be the basis of the summary discussion. Under the initial stimulus of the Leap, there was perhaps a 13 per cent increase in the total product from 95.3 billion (1952) yüan in 1957 to 108 billion in 1958. But the excessive regimentation in the communes, the denial of work incentives through the abolition of private plots and the change to equalitarian distribution systems for the peasants, the total miscalculation of technical possibilities in introducing the backyard furnaces and unworkable agricultural techniques (for example, deep ploughing, close planting, and the .poorly designed irrigation and flood control systems), and the exhausting pace imposed on the population, together with bad weather conditions, brought disaster to agriculture. Farm output declined sharply from 1958 to 1960. The supply of agricultural raw materials to the industrial sectors diminished severely. The whole economy suffered a serious leap backward from 1958 to 1961. The domestic product in 1961 (92.2 billion 1952 yüan) was 15 per cent lower than the 1958 peak (108 billion). The per capita product dropped perhaps 19 per cent from 1958 to 1961, roughly back to the 1955 level.[61]

As the agricultural crises deepened and industrial production slackened, the Communist regime relaxed the worst features of the Leap (for example, it abolished such unworkable schemes as the commune mess halls and the "miracle techniques of cultivation," and made a limited restoration of private plots and incentive payment schemes) and sharply cut back the investment program. The economy began to recover in 1962. The total product in 1965 probably regained the 1958 amount, with the per capita product perhaps back to the 1957 level. A total of seven years, however, has been lost without any growth during a period (1958–65) when practically all other nations experienced a significant measure of growth and development.

For the period 1952–65 as a whole, the relatively impressive record of development during the earlier years 1952–57 was marred by the poor performance during 1958–65 following the Great Leap Forward. The average annual rates of growth of total and per capita product during 1952–65 amounted to 3.3 and 1.4 per cent, respectively. Following the considerable achievement during roughly the First Five Year Plan period 1952–57, the Communist regime pursued a "big push" policy which resulted in a cycle of peak and trough, with practically no growth from 1958 to 1965.

With regard to the potential of economic development, the unrest which began in December, 1966, on the mainland makes it practically impossible to make any meaningful analysis. It is idle to say that the disturbances so far have been mainly in the political and social spheres. The Great Proletarian Cultural Revolution is bound to have serious impacts and repercussions on the economy. The Red Guard has already interrupted the transportation systems. Managers of enterprises and local cadres will hesitate to take any significant initiative until the party line again becomes clear and firm. At the present time, it is only possible for us to present a sketch of some of the factors, both favorable and unfavorable, that will have an important bearing on the economy.

In spite of the announced policies in favor of agricultural development in the last few years, independent observers in Hong Kong were unable to report significant increase of farm output over the 1957 level. The agricultural base, relative to the total product, is in fact smaller in 1965 than in 1957. It is possible that the investment made in agriculture

[61] The estimate of per capita product for 1958–65 is crude, and can indicate only the rough order of magnitude.

(including farm implements, electrification projects and fertilizer plants) in recent years requires more time to yield effects. If this view is correct, one should expect to see significant expansion of farm output during the next two or three years. On the other hand, the hard line pursued by the Great Proletarian Cultural Revolution will most likely exert restrictive effects on the incentives of the peasants for quite some time to come. As the experience of a number of Asian countries indicates, fertilizers and other agricultural inputs will yield the desired results only when the peasants are provided with the incentives for using them and when their applications are accompanied by proper irrigation systems and other complementary measures.

The farm sector has been, and will continue to be, of the most crucial importance. It furnishes the basic consumption requirements of the rural as well as most of the urban population; it supplies a major share of the raw materials for the light manufacturing industries; it provides the principal source of exports; and it generates a large portion of the savings required for capital investment. There is not yet evidence that the Communist regime has succeeded in developing a program for promoting rapid growth of agricultural output. The magnitude of this difficult task can be clearly seen in the fact that the Communists still have to regain first the 1957 per capita farm output before agriculture can be a source of strength, instead of a handicap, to the economy as a whole.

If we were merely to cumulate the net investment made after 1958 (table 9), add the sum to whatever estimate of capital stock one has for 1958, and then compare the various capital-output ratios in 1965 with those in 1958, we would see very substantial increases in these ratios from 1958 to 1965. This would be a very favorable consideration for a more rapid growth in the immediate future. As is well known, however, much of the investment made during and after the Great Leap Forward was of uncertain quality. We do not know how many of the smaller projects built for using indigenous techniques were really workable and how much of the additions to inventory were actually usable. After the Russian technical experts were withdrawn in 1960, we cannot be sure that all the unfinished large projects were in fact completed, nor how the uncompleted plants were modified and re-adapted to non-Russian techniques. For quite some time to come it may be very misleading to apply the standard analysis based on capital-output ratios to the Communist Chinese economy.

Another important unknown element is the likelihood of the recurrence of excessive acceleration of production targets as a consequence of the Great Proletarian Cultural Revolution. Will the regime be able to avoid exerting unreasonable pressure on the producing units to achieve unrealistic aims? Can the technicians and experts be bold enough to resist ideological approach to economic planning and management? Can normal incentive schemes be made somewhat consistent with the basic spirit and the atmosphere of the Great Proletarian Cultural Revolution? There is as yet no substantial basis for us to attempt an answer to these important questions.

## Comments by Robert Dernberger

A quantitative analysis of the mainland economy over the past seventeen years is indeed a necessary and important part in an attempt to understand economic developments in that country. In his paper for this conference, Professor Liu presents a concise yet comprehensive summary of his two highly significant and original contributions to this field[1]—the fruitful results of several years of intensive research. The value of these contributions is increased by his willingness to make readily available to his readers the sources of the raw data, his assumptions, and his methodology.

The Chinese Communists themselves, of course, have provided a good deal of quantitative information for the period 1952–57 and much of this information has been utilized by Professor Liu in forming his estimates. Using estimates of the value added for individual sectors of the economy, however, Professor Liu estimates that the official annual

---

[1] Ta-chung Liu with Kung-chia Yeh, *The Economy of the Chinese Mainland: National Income and Economic Development, 1933–1959* (Princeton, N.J.: Princeton University Press, 1965); and Ta-chung Liu, "Quantitative Trends in the Economy of the Chinese Mainland, 1952–1965," in *Economic Trends in Communist China,* ed. Walter Galenson, Alexander Eckstein, and Ta-Chung Liu (Chicago: Aldine Publishing Co., 1968). In this comment, estimates from these studies will be referred to as the *Liu-Yeh* and the *Liu* estimates, respectively.

rate of growth has an upward bias of approximately three percentage points. In other words, the Liu-Yeh estimates indicate that the actual annual rate of growth in 1952–57 was 6 per cent.

The upward bias in the official annual rate of growth is due to the following factors, all of which are discussed by Professor Liu in his paper: (1) the use of prices of commodities and services in the initial year of the development effort to value output during the ensuing years or, in other words, the use of prices that place a relatively high value on those commodities with the most rapid increases in production; (2) the exclusion of services judged "non-productive" by the Chinese Communists or the exclusion of those services with a relatively low rate of increase; (3) the exclusion of the output of some workers in the traditional sector of the economy, workers whose output probably did not increase significantly; (4) the increase in the propensity to exaggerate in statistical reports at the local level over the period; (5) the under-reporting of agricultural output in 1952–56; and (6) the exaggeration of industrial output of consumer's goods in 1953–57. It is very difficult to determine whether or not the extent of lying in statistical reports to higher levels increased or decreased over the period, inasmuch as the penalties for doing so increased along with the incentive to do so and the State Statistical Bureau increased its control over statistical reporting between 1953 and 1957. Nonetheless, the under-reporting of agricultural output in the early years and the over-reporting of industrial output in the later years would lead to the same result. With this one possible exception, I believe all students of China's contemporary economy would agree with the above reasons for and the existence of an upward bias in the official statistics for Communist China's economic growth in 1952–57. The important question is the extent to which the official statistics exaggerate the actual rate of growth.

Without constructing several sets of price indices linking successive two-year periods with changes in the weights to reflect the changes in the output mix as development progresses, it is impossible to accurately estimate the amount of upward bias introduced by the use of 1952 prices for the period as a whole. To compute these two-year price indices would be both difficult and time-consuming, even if all the necessary information were available. We can, of course, compute a rate of growth using the initial year (1952) prices and one using the final year (1957) prices—the former exaggerating and the latter underestimating the actual rate of growth—to determine an upper and lower limit. The Liu-Yeh study estimates that the annual rate of increase in net domestic product between 1952 and 1957 was 6 per cent when measured in 1952 prices and 5.7 per cent when measured in 1957 prices.[2] This relative difference would imply that the actual rate of growth in 1952–57 was between 9 per cent and 8.5 per cent, *if the index number problem was the only source of upward bias in the official statistics.*

To estimate the upward bias due to the exclusion of the "non-productive" services and the output of some labor in the traditional sectors of the economy, I have again borrowed from the Liu-Yeh study and Phillip Emerson's estimates of non-agricultural employment. When the official rate of growth is adjusted by including these services and outputs, the official rate of growth is reduced from 9 per cent to 8.7 per cent.[3] Thus, the official statistics for Communist China's annual rate of growth in 1952–57 may overestimate the actual rate by as much as one percentage point due to the use of initial year prices and the exclusion of "non-productive" services and output of some labor in the traditional sectors of the economy.

Thus, based on the Liu-Yeh estimate of the annual rate of growth, the upward bias in the official annual rate of growth due to the under-reporting of agricultural output in the years before 1957, the over-reporting of the industrial output of consumer's goods in the years after 1952, and the increase in statistical exaggeration at lower level, throughout the period, can be estimated at approximately two percentage points a year.

I have already argued elsewhere why I believe the Liu-Yeh estimate of the annual rate of growth is downward biased and will merely summarize those arguments here.[4] First, the attempt to derive an inde-

[2] Liu and Yeh, *The Economy of the Chinese Mainland,* p. 84.

[3] For the purposes of estimating the upward bias due to the exclusion of non-productive services, I have used the Liu-Yeh estimate of the value added in government, finance, services, and work brigades sectors (*ibid.,* pp. 221–24). For the upward bias due to the exclusion of the output of some of the labor force in the traditional sector, I have used the Liu-Yeh estimate of the value added in the traditional transportation sector (*ibid.*) and Emerson's estimate of the amount of non-agricultural labor excluded from the Chinese Communists' employment statistics, i.e., approximately 7 per cent of the reported employment (John Philip Emerson, *Non-agricultural Employment in Mainland China* [Washington, D.C.: U.S. Bureau of the Census, 1965], p. 70). I assumed the value added contributed by those workers excluded in the employment statistics was equal to the Liu-Yeh estimate for the value added of peddlers, i.e., 286 yüan in 1952 prices (Liu and Yeh, *The Economy of the Chinese Mainland,* pp. 167 and 200). I also assumed that the value added of these excluded workers remained constant throughout the period, 1952–57.

[4] *Journal of Political Economy,* vol. 78, no. 4, August, 1966, pp. 419–21.

pendent estimate of Communist China's net national product on the basis of the value added in individual sectors of the economy required a great many assumptions in the absence of detailed statistical information. While not quarreling with the particular assumptions made or the need to make them, many of the assumptions made in the Liu-Yeh study, such as those that assume increases in output were proportional to increases in population, that the value added was a constant proportion of the gross value of output, and that output remained constant, introduce an "anti-development bias" in the results. Each of these assumptions was adopted for individual sectors and it would be necessary to estimate the sensitivity of the estimate of total net domestic product to each of these individual assumptions in order to evaluate their importance, a task that would involve a good deal of time and effort. Nonetheless, even if the net effect of these individual assumptions on the estimated rate of growth were small, they would still introduce some downward bias in that estimate.

There are two particular assumptions, however, that do have a large impact on the estimated totals and do involve what I believe to be an anti-development bias: output of food crops is determined in the Liu-Yeh study by assuming per capita consumption of food crops in 1952–56 was equal to the officially reported per capita consumption of food crops in 1957, and the industrial production of consumer's goods in 1952–57 is determined in the Liu-Yeh study by assuming the output of those commodities for which individual data are not available increased at the same rate as the output of those commodities for which individual data are available.[5]

The official reported daily per capita consumption of food crops in 1957 was approximately 1,900 calories and the official statistics for food crop production in 1952–56 imply a lower daily per capita calorie intake from food crops. Professor Liu rejects this possibility for two reasons. On the one hand, the absolute level of per capita production of food crops could not have fallen below the 1957 level, inasmuch as the levels implied in the 1949–55 official statistics imply "a diet far below the starvation level" and, on the other hand, the absolute level of per capita production of food crops could not have increased significantly over this period because the increased control of food consumption through rationing would have been unlikely had increases actually occurred.[6] The Chinese are not physiologically identical with other peoples, but the available budget studies for several underdeveloped

---

[5] Liu and Yeh, *The Economy of the Chinese Mainland*, pp. 52–53 and 63.
[6] *Ibid.*, pp. 43–54.

countries, especially India, indicate that a substantial proportion of the population in these countries exist with a daily per capita consumption of foodstuffs less than 1,750 calories a day. Furthermore, one of the reasons for the introduction of rationing in the urban areas of China was to redistribute the available foodstuffs in favor of those doing the hardest work. The introduction of rationing also coincides with the introduction of planning and is compatible with increases in total output if the planners desire to divert a larger share of the available production of foodstuffs from domestic consumption to export and inputs in light industry.[7] The official data for agricultural production in 1952–56 may well under-report the actual levels of production, but Professor Liu's assumption is an extreme one and does introduce a downward bias in the Liu-Yeh estimate of the annual rate of growth.

Inasmuch as the official statistics for total industrial production of consumer's goods and for individual commodities within the category of consumer's goods imply that the output of the "unreported" commodities increased much faster than the "reported" commodities, Professor Liu rejects the official statistics for total output in this sector. He does present convincing arguments for making the assumption of fixed proportions between the "identified" and "non-identified" output in this sector and his results are supported by the index of industrial production estimated by Professor Kang Chao.[8] But this is not surprising, inasmuch as Kang Chao also assumed that the production of unreported commodities increased "more or less similar to that of the whole industry in question," and excluded military end products and products introduced in production after 1952 from his index.[9] Furthermore, the reported commodities for which data are available include those consumer goods industries that were well established before 1949 and those that rely heavily on the input of agricultural raw materials.[10] Therefore, while accepting the argument that the official statistics exaggerate the rate of growth of the industrial production of consumer goods, I believe the Liu-Yeh assumption concerning the rate of increase in the "unre-

[7] According to Chinese statistics, grain supplied as inputs in light industry increased by 12.2 per cent a year and the export of "consumer goods" increased by 8.4 per cent a year between 1952 and 1957 (Niu Chung-huang, *Relation Between Production and Consumption During the First Five-Year Plan Period in China* [Peking: Finance and Economics Press, 1959]).

[8] Kang Chao, *The Rate and Pattern of Industrial Growth in Communist China* (Ann Arbor, Mich.: University of Michigan Press, 1965), p. 89.

[9] *Ibid.*, pp. 47–48 and 82–83.

[10] Liu and Yeh, *The Economy of the Chinese Mainland*, p. 56.

ported" output introduces another source of downward bias in the estimated rate of growth for the economy as a whole.

Despite the above discussion about possible biases and the claim that the reconstructed Communist estimate represents an upper limit and the Liu-Yeh estimate represents a lower limit to the actual rate of growth in 1952–57, I see no reason for arguing that one must use one or the other for a quantitative description of economic developments in Communist China. In terms of meaningful economic analysis, it really doesn't make that much difference. Both estimates show a relatively high rate of growth in total output, a significant increase in output per capita, a high rate of capital accumulation, a relatively high rate of increase in productivity, and a rapid increase in the relative share of industry in total output. These developments all make sense in terms of the empirical evidence of economic development in other countries.

Due to the adoption of a capital-intensive technology in industry, both estimates indicate a relatively low rate of increase in the industrial labor force. Inasmuch as the reconstructed Communist estimates indicate that the total labor force increased faster and the Liu-Yeh estimates indicate it increased slower than total population, the reconstructed Communist estimates show that the relative share of the labor force in agriculture remained constant and the Liu-Yeh estimates indicate agriculture's relative share of the labor force actually increased over the period. From both estimates, one could conclude that the relatively high rate of capital accumulation in the capital-intensive industrial sectors was not sufficient to absorb an increasing proportion of the labor force in industry; a conclusion that would be an important factor in explaining the initiation of the Great Leap Forward at the end of the period.

The two sets of estimates agree on the average share of consumption in total output, but disagree as to the share of consumption in increments in total output. The reconstructed Communist estimates indicate that the increases in consumption per capita accounted for about two-thirds the increase in gross expenditures per capita, while the Liu-Yeh estimates indicate that the ratio was about one-half. Thus, even though both estimates indicate that the share of consumption in total output declined while per capita consumption increased between 1952 and 1957, the rate of increase indicated by the Liu-Yeh estimates is less than half that indicated in the reconstructed Communist estimate. On the basis of the available evidence, both quantitative and non-quantitative, one would certainly agree with the implications of the Liu-Yeh estimates, that is, that even though per capita consumption probably did increase in 1952–57, its rate of growth was not very high. Nonetheless, in light of the very high rate of capital accumulation, any increase in per capita consumption is a considerable achievement for an underdeveloped country in the initial stages of its development effort.

Finally, the incremental capital-output ratio estimated on the basis of the reconstructed Communist estimates is much lower than that implied by the Liu-Yeh estimates. Incremental capital-output ratios computed for the economy as a whole are, of course, subject to large errors, but they have extremely important implications for development. For example, according to the reconstructed Communist estimate, a given amount of investment would yield an increase in total output approximately 40 per cent larger than the increase indicated by the Liu-Yeh estimated incremental capital-output ratio. The Liu-Yeh estimated incremental capital-output ratio for China is similar to the ratio estimated by Kuznets for the Soviet Union in 1928–40 and 1950–58 and Professor Liu argues that this similarity makes sense inasmuch as Communist China "pursued a development program modeled on the U.S.S.R. and in fact used Russian designs for her major plants." On the other hand, the incremental capital output for particular plants or even industries in China may be similar to those in the Soviet Union for this reason, but the incremental capital-output ratio for the economy as a whole may be lower than that in the Soviet Union because the Chinese economy during the 1950's was much less developed than the Soviet economy of the late 1920's.[11]

The grossly inflated official statistics for 1958 and 1959 and the lack of any detailed statistics for individual sectors of the economy since 1959 have made it impossible for Professor Liu to extend his sectoral value added estimates beyond 1957. In a recently published study, however, Professor Liu has developed an econometric model of the Chinese economy that enables him to use the limited quantitative information available and estimate net domestic product and investment in 1958 through 1965 and he has included those estimates in his paper submitted to this Conference.[12] His "crude" estimates of the reconstructed

---

[11] According to Professor Simon Kuznets, "the incremental gross domestic capital-output ratios are distinctly lower in the low income, less developed countries" [Simon Kuznets, "Quantitative Aspects of The Economic Growth of Nations, V. Capital Formation Proportions: International Comparisons for Recent Years," *Economic Development and Cultural Change*, vol. 8, no. 4 (July, 1960), part 2, p. 54].

[12] T. C. Liu, "Quantitative Trends in the Economy of the Chinese Mainland, 1952–1965." I have not seen the revised version of Professor Liu's new study and, thus, will limit my comments to the results presented in the paper submitted to this Conference. In an earlier draft of the new study, a fixed co-

Communist estimate for the same period extend both series so that they cover the entire period 1949–65. The reconstructed Communist estimates for the absolute level of domestic output remain larger than the Liu estimates in the 1958–65 period, but they can no longer be referred to as the upper limit to the actual rate of growth.

The reconstructed Communist estimates indicate a decline in both net domestic product and per capita product in 1960 through 1962 and an increase in 1963 through 1965. The Liu estimates of net domestic product and per capita product indicate a decline in 1959 through 1961 and an increase in 1962 through 1965. More important, however, the reconstructed Communist estimates indicate that net domestic product declined in the depths of the crises in 1962 to more than 40 per cent below the pre-crises peak and by 1965 had recovered to a level higher than that in 1957, but below the 1958 level. The Liu estimates, on the other hand, indicate that net domestic product declined in the depths of the crises to 14 per cent below the pre-crises peak and by 1965 had recovered to the highest level during the past seventeen years. Based solely on the non-quantitative information available from the mainland, the decline in output in 1959 indicated by the Liu estimates, and the severity of the crises and slow pace of recovery in the reconstructed Communist estimates appear plausible. Inasmuch as the bulk of Communist China's exports are raw and processed agricultural products and the decline in agricultural output was the cause of the crises, the decline in the ratio of exports to domestic product during the crises would not appear as implausible as Professor Liu argues. In addition, the share of net domestic investment in net domestic product in the Liu estimates is rather high for the early 1960's and is not compatible with the Liu-Yeh net incremental capital-output ratios presented for an earlier period. On the other hand, the Liu estimates do show a 35 per cent decline in the absolute value of net investment between 1958 and 1961 and Professor Liu does present several convincing arguments for a relatively high share of domestic product being devoted to investment during the crises.

I have not referred to Professor Liu's estimate of the absolute level of output in any single year and the only way I know to judge the absolute level of economic activity in a country is to estimate it. Professor Liu is quite right in claiming that his estimate can be made consistent with

---

efficient inter-sectoral model with the coefficiencts estimated on the basis of the 1952–57 data was used to estimate the total net product in 1958–65. The use of a fixed coefficient model based on the 1952–57 data to estimate net product in 1958–65 requires the assumption of no changes in technology, efficiency, or product mix within sectors between the two periods.

other estimates for any particular year by examining the differences in assumptions, definitions, and commodities included in the estimates. For the purposes of most meaningful analyses of the development process on the mainland, however, it is not the absolute level of economic activity, but the rates of change in the level and structure of the economy that are most important. My purpose in the preceding sections of this comment has been to raise several questions concerning the possible biases in the Liu-Yeh (1952–57) and Liu (1958–65) estimates of these changes or rates of change.

Despite the questions I have raised, we are, of course, very fortunate to have the two sets of estimates provided by Professor Liu for a quantitative aspect of Communist China's economic development. Although a most important one, this quantitative analysis is but a first step in our understanding of that development effort. Against this background of available quantitative information, economists must ask what economic policies were adopted, why were they adopted, what alternative policies were available, and what were the results of these policies. In other words, there must be an analysis of the means selected to achieve given goals and the efficiency of these means in achieving these goals. Other important economic questions involve the relationship between the economic policies and concurrent political, social, and international developments. Finally, there are the difficult questions concerning the feasibility of the Chinese Communists' goals and their economic system itself. These are not easy questions, yet we must seek answers to them in order to gain a real understanding of Communist China's economic development effort during the past seventeen years and in the future. At the risk of sounding insincere, it is worth asking whether the choice of one set of quantitative estimates or the other will make a difference in our answers to these questions.

I do not want to appear dogmatic, for I am sure that if one were attempting to assess changes in the economic welfare of individuals in Communist China, the two sets of quantative estimates would lead to slightly different conclusions. The reconstructed Communist estimates of per capita net domestic product average about 12 per cent above Liu's estimates and the former estimates increase by 14 per cent, the latter estimates by 12 per cent, between 1952 and 1965. The Liu estimates, of course, would indicate a lower rate of increase in per capita consumption. Neither set of estimates, however, presents a very encouraging picture of the material benefits of the economic development effort to the welfare of the Chinese people.

Let me conclude with another example. Professor Liu argues that even though the Liu-Yeh estimate for the rate of growth was relatively high in 1952–57, it could have been considered unsatisfactory by a leadership with extraordinary ambitions and, confident of their ability to put through radical reorganizations, the Great Leap Forward may have been an attempt to increase an already substantial rate of growth. The Liu-Yeh estimated rate of growth, being lower, does support this explanation of the Great Leap Forward to a greater extent than the reconstructed Communist estimates. Nonetheless, the reasoning is consistent with either set of estimates, unless one were to define the "satisfactory" rate of growth as being between 7 and 8 per cent.

Another possible hypothesis concerning the introduction of the Great Leap Forward, and one that I have presented in another paper, is the following:[13] The relatively high annual growth rate in 1953–57 was the weighted average of a high rate of growth in the industrial sector and a low rate of growth in the agricultural sector, the capital-labor ratio and labor productivities increasing in the former sector and declining in the latter. The required repayments of Soviet loans and China's own foreign-aid program required an export surplus be maintained after 1955. The low rate of growth in agricultural production precluded sufficient increases in exports to finance both the necessary export surplus and imports of machinery and equipment to maintain continued high rates of growth in the industrial sector. To avoid a decline in the rate of growth of industrial output, the Chinese Communists attempted to change their industrial technology so that continued increases in industrial output need not rely on imported machinery and equipment.

There were, of course, many reasons for the introduction of the Great Leap Forward, and the brief summary of my own interpretation is not advanced here as the only reason, or even the correct reason. Rather, my purpose is to point out that, despite their differences, both sets of estimates—the reconstructed Communist estimate and the Liu-Yeh estimate—support my hypothesis.

This statistical support is essential in either the derivation or testing of hypothesis of Communist China's economic development and, therefore, Professor Liu's estimates of the quantitative changes in the Chinese economy, 1949–65, will be an essential component in any attempt to interpret the hows and whys of that development.

[13] Robert Dernberger, "On the Relationship Between Foreign Trade, Innovation, and Economic Growth in Communist China," pp. 739–52, this volume.

# Comments by Dwight H. Perkins

As Professor Liu states, China's economy places basic constraints on Chinese politics both at home and abroad. It is rather common for such constraints to be lost sight of, particularly in discussions of Peking's foreign policy. One reason it is so easy to ignore the economic side of political questions is because it is so difficult to determine just what China's economic performance has been during the past decade (1957–66). In my comments, therefore, I shall follow Ta-Chung Liu's lead in appraising the economic performance itself rather than discussing the effect of that performance on politics. For those interested, I have written about the latter aspect elsewhere.[1]

I should like to begin my comments by stating that Professor Liu's brief description of economic institutions (Section I) and of the economy's performance during the first five year plan (1953–57: Section II) are both very useful. The analysis in Section II, in particular, is balanced and clear. The assumptions underlying the Liu-Yeh national income formulation are brought out and the results compared with the official Communist figures. Those who may disagree with some of the Liu-Yeh assumptions can make their own adjustments with little effort.

Professor Liu has also performed a service by attempting to obtain at least a rough picture of economic growth since 1957 (Section III). All economists working on China will agree that any estimates for this period are tentative and subject to a wide margin of error. This great potential error has, I believe, discouraged many analysts from even bothering with estimates for this period. Most, in fact, have not even commented on or criticized those estimates that have been made such as those by the U.S. Consulate in Hong Kong. It is to Professor Liu's credit that he has looked with some care at the 1958–65 data.

The heart of any estimate of the growth rate of the Chinese economy

[1] See, for example, M. H. Halperin and D. H. Perkins, *Communist China and Arms Control* (New York: Praeger, 1965), chap. III.

since 1957 is made up of the production figures for grain and for a few selected industrial items. I should like to devote the remainder of my comments to these series and their implications.

## Agriculture, 1957–65

Professor Liu argues that for grain, the estimates of the U.S. Consulate in Hong Kong are preferable to figures derived from rather vague statements by Chinese Communist officials. I should like to suggest that the former figures for 1964 and 1965, although not completely out of the realm of possibility, are not really consistent with a number of things which we do know about the Chinese economy.

The issue can be approached from both the production and consumption side. Due to the constraints placed on any comment, I shall confine myself to the broad issues involved. On the production side, the principal determinants of grain output are acreage, weather, capital inputs such as fertilizer, and the incentives and skills of labor and management. I have no means at my disposal for estimating the effects of weather, but it seems reasonable to assume that at least one of the years 1963 through 1966, if not several, were as good or better than 1957, weather-wise. From the point of view of incentives and management, nothing can be said with confidence, but the facts we do have are that the basic unit controlling agricultural output in the 1963–65 period, the production team, was less than half the size of the 1957 agricultural producers' co-operative. Further, conditions in general were quite relaxed in the 1963–65 period. Grain purchase quotas, for example, may have been returned to roughly the levels of 1955–57.[2] Although almost any assumption about incentives and management could be defended, barring more hard evidence the only really reasonable position is to start from the proposition that conditions were no worse in this respect than in 1957.

A reading of the Hong Kong analyses makes it clear that acreage estimates are an important component of their construction.[3] This is proper, but one must be very careful in interpreting any decline in acreage if such is used. It is likely that a decline would result from such factors as the expansion of irrigation systems, taking marginal land out

[2] This statement is a very tentative one based on the assumption that grain imports together with policies designed to return urban people to the countryside have allowed the Chinese Communists to reduce quotas to roughly the 1957 level.

[3] See, for example, "Agriculture in China: 1963," *Current Scene*, 2, no. 27 (January 15, 1964).

of cultivation in order to concentrate resources on better land, and the like. Any acreage decline, therefore, should in the estimates be accompanied by an increase in yields which would at least offset the fall in acreage.[4]

From the above analysis, it seems reasonable to expect that grain output in one of the years 1963–65 reached 1957 levels. If one further adds the effect of fertilizers, then one reaches the conclusion that output in 1964 or 1965 must have reached a level of over 195 million tons.[5]

It is, of course, possible to argue that the increased use of fertilizer had little or no effect on grain output—presumably because of diminishing returns to one factor, in this case fertilizer, when other factors are held constant, such as water. But such a line of argument would only be valid if China's chemical fertilizer production were very large. Given the still comparatively small amounts she does produce, the necessary complementary factors can always be provided from the already existing supply. Thus if irrigation water is a problem, fertilizer can always be concentrated in areas where irrigation facilities are well developed, as in south China.

The more important basis for questioning the Hong Kong 1964–65 estimates, however, rests on the implications they contain for per capita consumption levels in China. The relevant data are presented in table 1. If one accepts the Hong Kong figures, one must be prepared to argue that per capita grain consumption first rose in 1962 and then slipped back by 1965 to the approximate levels of 1961. Most people will agree that 1961 was a year of great hardship due to grain shortages, a year when the government in Peking was in deep economic trouble. No one that I know of suggests today that consumption levels in 1964 or 1965 were anywhere near the figures for 1961 or that there was any *major* shortage in 1964 or 1965 at all.

The generally held impression that consumption levels in 1964 and 1965 were well above those in 1961 cannot be explained away by argu-

[4] If there were a shift in acreage away from grain to cash crops, there would be no compensating rise in grain yields, but the shift in this period was, if anything, in the opposite direction.

[5] This estimate of 195 million tons is a conservative one. Estimates of fertilizer output in 1965 plus imports range from 7 to 8.5 million tons. Studies by Kenneth Walker and Jung-chao Liu have shown that one kilogram of ammonium sulphate in China causes a grain yield increase of 3 kilograms or more. Hence, if two-thirds of the available fertilizer were applied to grain, output would increase by 14 million tons. I have conservatively used 10 million tons. Similar calculations for 1964 would lead to estimates of 10 million or a conservative 7 million tons.

ments that the age composition of China's population shifted to groups (the very young and the very old) whose consumption requirements were low. If one argues, as does Professor Liu, that the rate of increase in population fell off in the 1960's (presumably due to the very old dying sooner and some of the young not being born), then those in the 0–8 and over 60 age groups would make up an even smaller percentage of the population than in the 1950's. My own belief is that the rate of population increase fell off very little due to food shortages in the 1960's, but this belief is in no way necessary to the above argument. The basis for such a belief is that the worldwide post–World War II population boom has been primarily the result of a revolution in medicine

TABLE 1

CHINESE GRAIN USE

(Unhusked Grain)

| YEAR | RECONSTRUCTED OFFICIAL DATA | | | | | | |
|------|------|------|------|------|------|------|------|
| | Total Output − Exports + Imports = Total Use (Million Metric Tons) | | | Per Capita Use (Metric Tons) | | | |
| 1952 | 154 | | 154 | .271 | | | |
| 1953 | 157 | 1 | 156 | .269 | | | |
| 1954 | 161 | 1 | 160 | .270 | | | |
| 1955 | 175 | 1 | 174 | .286 | | | |
| 1956 | 183 | 1 | 182 | .293 | | | |
| 1957 | 185 | 1 | 184 | .284–.290 | | | |
| | | | | Assuming Population Growth of | | | |
| | | | | 1% | 1.5% | *% | 2% |
| 1960 | 150 | 1 | 151 | .227 | .223 | .220 | .220 |
| 1961 | 160 | 5 | 165 | .245 | .241 | .238 | .233 |
| 1962 | 170 | 5 | 175 | .258 | .251 | .250 | .245 |
| 1963 | 180 | 5 | 185 | .270 | .262 | .262 | .254 |
| 1964 | 190 | 5 | 195 | .281 | .272 | .270 | .262 |
| 1965 | 200 | 6 | 206 | .294 | .283 | .280 | .272 |
| | HONG KONG CONSULATE ESTIMATE | | | | | | |
| 1960 | 160 | 1 | 161 | .242 | .238 | .235 | .235 |
| 1961 | 167 | 5 | 172 | .256 | .251 | .248 | .246 |
| 1962 | 178 | 5 | 183 | .270 | .263 | .261 | .256 |
| 1963 | 179 | 5 | 184 | .268 | .261 | .260 | .253 |
| 1964 | 183 | 5 | 188 | .271 | .262 | .261 | .253 |
| 1965 | 180 | 6 | 186 | .266 | .256 | .253 | .246 |

* This series was constructed on the assumption that population grew 2 per cent per year through 1960, 1 per cent a year from 1961 through 1963, and 2 per cent thereafter.

and public health measures and has little to do with improved food consumption.

In any case, the rough grain output estimates obtained from statements by Communist officials seem much more in line with what we know of the performance of consumption than the 1964–65 figures of the Hong Kong consulate. It must be emphasized, however, that this "official" series does not lead one to conclude that the growth in grain output in China has been rapid. The rate of increase implied from 1957 through 1965 is only 1 per cent a year, or significantly below the rate of population growth. The figures do suggest that China has been able to raise agricultural output slightly but will have to invest an even larger share in agriculture if her program in that sector is to be successful.

### Industry, 1957–65

There is no single figure for industry that is as important for appraising the performance of the entire sector as grain is for agriculture. I should, however, like to raise two general questions concerning Professor Liu's analysis. The first is whether the reconstructed index for industry is really reconstructed from Chinese Communist statements or already includes major external revisions. The second is the more fundamental question of which index best approximates China's industrial performance.

A reconstruction of official Chinese statements can be transformed into gross figures for industrial output only by first assuming a figure for 1962 and a growth rate for 1962–63. The only official thing said about 1962 is that the output of light industry was above 1957. Professor Liu following Professor Chao apparently feels that heavy industry was also at the level of 1957. All external estimates of the output of individual heavy industry products, however, indicate that output of these items in 1962 was 50 per cent or more above 1957. This is the case for the two series in Professor Liu's Table 8 and for five of seven items in the study of R. M. Field (only cement and timber were the same as in 1957).[6] If one assumes that heavy industry was at least 30 per cent above 1957, then the reconstructed gross figure for 1962 becomes 90 billion yüan and the net figure 26.4 billion. The gross and net estimates for 1965 then become 127.8 and 37.5 billion yüan respectively.

The difference is not trivial. Liu's reconstructed Communist estimate

[6] R. M. Field, "Chinese Communist Industrial Production," Joint Economic Committee of the U.S. Congress. "An Economic Profile of Communist China," February 1967, pp. 269–98.

of net domestic product indicates a rise from 1957 to 1965 of 21 per cent; my interpretation of Chinese statements suggests a rise of 32 per cent to 40 per cent in agricultural and industrial product. How much of the difference is due to the inclusion by Liu in his figure of sectors for which no official statements are available is not clear from his paper.

The question remains whether either of these "reconstructed" estimates accurately reflects the true situation. Another attempt to estimate Chinese industrial products for the 1960's is that of R. M. Field. Field's figure is an independent, not a reconstructed, estimate. His estimates are in the form of indexes, but his implied net industrial product figure for 1965 is 30.8 billion yüan.

TABLE 2

GROWTH RATES, 1957–65

(Percentages)

| Source | Industry | Agriculture | Industry + Agriculture or Total Product |
|---|---|---|---|
| Reconstructed (Liu) | 4.6 | 1.0 | 2.4 |
| Reconstructed (this study) | 6.3 | 1–1.5 | 3.1–3.4 |
| R. M. Field | 3.8 | . . . . . . . . . . . . | . . . . . . . . . . . . |
| Hong Kong | . . . . . . . . . . . . | −.4 | . . . . . . . . . . . . |
| T. C. Liu | 2.0 (?) | −.4 | 1.6 |
| Field + Reconstructed Agriculture | 3.8 | 1–1.5 | 2.0–2.3 |

Adding Field's figure to an agricultural estimate that assumes farm output growth averaged 1 to 1½ per cent a year, one arrives at an increase in the two sectors combined of 17 per cent to 20 per cent between 1957 and 1966, or 2.0 per cent to 2.3 per cent per year on the average. This compares with my reconstructed official figure of 3.1 per cent to nearly 3.4 per cent a year and Liu's own estimate of 1.6 per cent a year. A summary of this information is presented in table 2.

The low estimate of Liu is partly the result of the use of Hong Kong agricultural data[7] and of a downward revision in his reconstructed industrial figure and perhaps also due to assumptions about such sectors as commerce, transport, etc. This downward revision appears to be based on an analysis of the relationship between exports and net domestic product. But Chinese exports are made up primarily of cash

[7] It is difficult to tell, but I believe Professor Liu also assumes that subsidiary output followed grain. This is a conservative assumption.

crops, processed or otherwise, and hence tell us little about the performance of heavy industry,[8] among other sectors. I agree with Professor Liu that the 1958–61 figures he presents as the reconstructed estimates are much too high, although I base that conclusion on different reasoning. But I do not feel that any evidence supports Liu's conclusion that "the reconstructed Communist estimates of the domestic product for 1963–65 are based on claimed increases of agricultural and industrial production over the exaggerated estimates for the preceding years." This is clearly not the case for the grain estimates and it is unlikely that it is the case for the industrial estimates.

Because of such considerations, I cannot accept Professor Liu's basis for revising downward the industrial estimates. I am also inclined to believe that Field's calculations result in a slight underestimate of the rate of industrial growth. Although this comment is not the place to go into detail, the formula Field uses to move from individual products to overall industrial output may well give excessive weight to certain slow-growing sectors. Given these considerations, I suspect that the rate of growth in national product between 1957 and 1965 was about 3 per cent per year on the average.

### Implications of the 1957–66 Performance

A more interesting question for this conference is what does a 3 per cent rate of growth imply for the future? To answer this question, one must approach the two sectors, industry and agriculture, separately.

In agriculture, as already stated, it would appear that large investment in chemical fertilizers and other modern inputs, if combined with severe constraints on the amount of collectivism, will lead to increases in farm output. It would also appear, however, that investment levels comparable to those in the 1962–66 period will not be adequate. The key figure is not the rate of growth from 1961 through 1965 or 1966, because much of this growth only represents recovery from bad weather and bad management. The relevant statistic is the long-term trend in farm output and this appears to have been only 1 or 1½ per cent per year, if the 1957–65 average can be said to reflect a long-term trend. If China is to experience a rise in the standard of living, this trend rate will have to be at least doubled. Grain output, for example, will have to rise by 4 or 5 million tons a year, on the average.

The implications of the 1957–65 performance of industry are some-

---

[8] Imports tell us far more about the performance of heavy industry than exports, but in the 1960's even imports are not a good guide, because China was not expanding capacity but trying to more fully utilize existing capacity.

what different. The average annual rate of industrial growth during this period was 4 or 5 per cent. This compares with a rate of 14 per cent to 16 per cent per year during the First Five Year Plan. The 1952–57 figure, however, can hardly be considered an indicator of long-term potential. Such a large rate was possible because of the small share of industry in total national product at the beginning of this period, the excessive allocation of investment funds to industry, and the existence of under-utilized industrial capacity at the beginning of the period.

A more reasonable guess as to what China could have achieved in the 1957 to 1965 period, if she had pursued proper economic policies, would probably be an annual industrial growth rate in the neighborhood of 8 per cent to 10 per cent. Thus the boom-and-bust policies of the years 1958–62 reduced the industry rate of increase by at least half. It is reasonable to assume that any return to "great leap" policies would have a similar effect in the future. Realization of this fact would seem to be a major element in the present disaffection of many Chinese Communist officials from the leadership of Mao Tse-tung.

# Comments by Anthony M. Tang

## I. Professor Liu's Contributions to Chinese Economic Study

The paper presented by Professor T. C. Liu constitutes an excellent summary of the principal findings of his two earlier contributions. Because of the great body of information which he found necessary to compress into the paper in order to adequately portray the general configuration of mainland China's economic development during 1949–65, it is perhaps inevitable that the central concern of the Conference has been given a less thorough treatment. For the economists, the theme of the Conference, I take it, entails an examination of how China's socioeconomic heritage may have influenced the course of economic development under the Communist regime and how the attendant growth problems might explain policy shifts by the Communist party, both past and current.

My comment, therefore, bears only in part on the substance of Professor Liu's paper. At the risk of being presumptuous, I would like to devote a substantial part of the comment to those aspects which I feel are relevant to the theme of this gathering. As a commentator before a conference attended mainly by non-economist scholars, I would be remiss if I did not first of all make a brief introduction of Professor Liu's two earlier pathbreaking contributions. The first of these contributions represents a truly monumental study which Professor Liu undertook jointly with Dr. K. C. Yeh of the Rand Corporation.[1] Embodied in this study is several years of painstaking, and no doubt frequently frustrating, work. The result is a volume whose quantitative documentation of mainland China's economy is and will remain unexcelled for many years to come. Unlike some quantitative studies of national economies, Professor Liu's work is unfailing in providing the reader with such crucial details as exact source references, the accounting concepts employed, and specific assumptions made to fill enormous information gaps or to adjust official series for over- or under-reporting. With the work thus documented, the reader is free to form his opinion about what constitutes a reasonable assumption and with little effort, to modify Professor Liu's adjusted figures to suit his own taste. It is, therefore, a reference volume as valuable to the critics as it is to the supporters of Professor Liu's assumptions and the conclusions about economic performance and prospects for mainland China.

It is perhaps surprising, then, that the author's estimates should have turned out to be as controversial as they have been. That this has been so is a testimony to the high regard in which Professor Liu is held professionally. Under similar circumstances, estimates made by a lesser economist would have been quietly dismissed by the critics. It should be emphasized that where great information gaps exist as they do in the case of Communist China, such gaps can only be filled by more or less arbitrary assumptions. Also, in situations where hard facts are difficult to come by, the reader's own judgment and assumptions about facts tend to be colored by his preconceptions of and taste for the system under investigation. This leaves Professor Liu or any other writer in a similar position with the unenviable prospect of not being able to satisfy all readers of varied persuasions, no matter what assumptions he may choose to adopt.

[1] T. C. Liu and K. C. Yeh, *The Economy of the Chinese Mainland: National Income and Economic Development, 1933–1959* (Princeton, N.J.: Princeton University Press, 1965).

For the purposes of this Conference, there was perhaps an implicit hope that the economists present might be able to come up with substantial areas of agreement on those economic magnitudes which are crucial to a *perspective* understanding of mainland China's economic achievements, potential and policy. I shall in this comment make a modest attempt to minimize some of the areas of contention.

Before turning to this, let me say a few words about the second of Professor Liu's significant contributions, a major paper prepared for a 1965 conference on economic trends in Communist China.[2] This work constitutes a bold attempt to employ econometric procedures in estimating China's output for the "information blackout" period, 1959–65. The system of equations portrays the structural economic relationships in the Chinese economy. These relationships were established from the data available for 1952–57. The scattered bits of information assembled for the 1959–65 period were then entered into the equations in order to estimate the other unknown magnitudes. In this manner, Professor Liu was able to put together conjectural estimates of the domestic product for the later period. That such estimates are exceedingly tentative is clear for a number of reasons: (1) the relationships were established from a very short period; (2) the relationships established from the more or less "normal" first Five Year Plan period may not be applicable to the Leap and post-Leap years; (3) in terms of any kind of reasonable standards, the scattered series which give rise to the 1959–65 estimates are in themselves unusable for the most part. Nevertheless, the exercise is of value for two reasons. First, it represents a significant methodological advancement in the speculative field of Chinese economic study. Second, it substitutes an objective and explicit procedure for estimation by judgment. Against this background, it would seem to be anticlimactic to take issue with any of the particulars of Professor Liu's procedure. The procedure is best accepted or rejected as a package. Professor Robert Solow once aptly remarked, on the occasion of his introducing an equally "vulnerable" estimation procedure, that "either this kind of . . . economics appeals or it doesn't."[3] I believe that this is the spirit in which Professor Liu's contribution should be received. He is to be commended for the seminal effort.

[2] T. C. Liu, "Quantitative Trends in the Economy of the Chinese Mainland, 1952–65," in *Economic Trends in Communist China* (ed. by Walter Galenson, Alexander Eckstein and T. C. Liu) (Chicago: Aldine Publishing Co., 1968).

[3] Robert M. Solow, "Technical Change and the Aggregate Production Function," *Review of Economics and Statistics*, vol. 39, no. 3 (August, 1957), p. 312.

## II. *Professor Liu and His Critics*

In this section, I shall attempt to show that the import of what appear to be sharp differences in view regarding Professor Liu's estimates for 1952–58 may not be as great as it might seem. It will be recalled that his estimated average annual rate of growth comes to 6 per cent, while his reconstructed figures show a rate of 8.8 per cent (which turns out to be virtually indistinguishable from the official rate of 9 per cent). The reconstructed data are simply the result of re-structuring the unadjusted official statistics in accordance with standard national income accounting concepts and procedures. The significant difference between the two growth rates is wholly due to the adjustments (that is, corrections) that Professor Liu applied to the agricultural output and the consumer goods output series. It is in connection with these two adjustments (in particular, the agricultural correction) that Professor Liu's estimates have been challenged. The reasonableness of the assumptions which underlie the adjustment procedures was checked and given a passing mark by Professor Liu. It is clear, however, that what appears to be reasonable to one may not appear so to someone else.

In trying to reduce the long-standing differences, let me offer the following thoughts. First of all, it is wrong to believe that all studies require "reliable" independent estimates. The statement stands even if the official releases are known beyond doubt to be faulty. This follows because in testing behavioral propositions useful to our understanding of why certain policy decisions are made, often it is precisely the official statistics that one should use. As long as Peking does not keep two sets of books (and this is generally granted), the Communist policy-making machinery must be guided by the same information subsequently released for public consumption. To try to understand policy-making in the light of the "reliable" estimates can only lead to faulty conclusions. And, as is well-known to economists interested in changes, the accuracy of the absolute magnitudes is often irrelevant. What is important is the change. Furthermore, much research can be done meaningfully by relying upon changes measured in qualitative rather than quantitative terms.

In my own work on Communist China,[4] for instance, I have found it possible to reach significant conclusions by using largely official statistics and statistical methods which require accuracy only in a qualitative sense. It is sufficient to know, for instance, whether the growth rate of

---

[4] Anthony M. Tang, "Policy and Performance in Agriculture," in *Economic Trends in Communist China*.

a particular year is higher or lower than that of the preceding and the following years. It is well to bear in mind that further quantitative refinements are subject to increasingly severe diminishing returns and that it might be more profitable to try to undertake more analysis with the data now available, official or otherwise, than to invest additional time and energy in re-working the data or, worse still, to immobilize ourselves in research on grounds of insufficient data. One may well wonder whether economists have not been at times unduly coerced by Professor Oskar Morgenstern's forceful demand that the data be accurate or that the errors be accurately measured.[5] To demand accurate data for sound decision-making is one thing; to do so in ex post facto analysis of decisions already taken is quite another.

Second, turning to Professor Liu's most frequently challenged estimation of agricultural output, the disagreement fundamentally rests on whether the low reported output in the early 1950's was due to under-reporting, as Professor Liu has argued, or to under-recovery in the agricultural sector. The under-recovery thesis implies that the early output, while low, was nevertheless more or less accurately reported. Professor Liu, as is well known now, argued that the reported output (and the implied per capita food consumption) is simply inconsistent with the caloric requirements needed to sustain the population without subjecting it to mass starvation. Noting the absence of mass starvation in the early 1950's, he thus revised upward the production figures for those years. This gives rise to a substantially lower rate of agricultural growth.

If Professor Colin Clark is to be believed, the science of physiology when it comes to the caloric domain is an art rather than a science. On the contemporary Chinese scene, the matter is further complicated by probable changes after the Communist take-over in income distribution and the food distribution system. This suggests the inadequacy of gauging the reasonableness of Communist food output claims on the basis of the pre-war per capita consumption standard in mainland China. Professor Liu's procedure also begs the question as to the quality of the population estimates, both pre- and post-war. Without entering into the complexities of the total argument, it is sufficient to observe that it is not surprising that Professor Liu's estimates of the food production should have been widely questioned. The critics, however, have no firmer basis for adjustment. A meaningful position for them to take would be that the reported figures for those years are essentially accurate

[5] See his *On the Accuracy of Economic Observations* (Princton, N.J.: Princeton University Press, 1963).

and that these low figures reflect under-recovery—an aftermath of thirteen years of sustained warfare. Viewing the difference between Professor Liu and his critics in this manner, I should like to suggest that for all practical purposes the difference is not a substantive one. Taking the reported figures for the earlier years as correct on grounds of under-recovery, the resulting growth rate would then contain two components, the "recovery" component and the "hard growth" component. From the calculations I have made, it would seem that the extent of under-recovery, as gauged by comparing the reported output with the expected level under pre-war yields, is comparable to the percentage adjustment which Professor Liu applied.[6] That being the case, the "hard growth" is not different from the growth rate estimated by Professor Liu. Since in evaluating the worth of a government's development policy it is the "hard growth" that counts, the apparent substantive difference between Professor Liu and his critics would simply disappear.

Professor Liu's adjustment of the official consumer goods output, while based upon arbitrary assumptions, is in my judgment less vulnerable. It is less vulnerable for two reasons. First, his acceptance of the official claim of output growth of 45 per cent for the identified consumer goods sector during 1952–57 appears to me to be rather generous. Second, although his arbitrary assumption that the growth of the unidentified consumer goods sector has been the same as that of the identified sector (instead of a 200 per cent increase as officially reported) is clearly open to challenge, it is obvious that any alternative assumption made by a challenger would be just as arbitrary. This is true so long as we known nothing about the composition of the unidentified portion. In brief, then, I for one believe that the estimated overall growth rate of 6 per cent per year by Professor Liu probably indicates the right kind of magnitude. And it seems to me that the conclusion would stand whether or not one prefers to view the reported agricultural output for the early years as reflecting either under-reporting or under-recovery. This is true so long as our concern is with a perspective appraisal of growth performance and future prospects.

### III. Understanding Policy Shifts— A Methodological Note

Elsewhere in his paper, Professor Liu suggests that the great policy shift toward the Great Leap was attributable to the party's dissatisfaction with the realized rate of growth during the first plan period. He places this rate at 6 per cent. It may be of interest to note that this rate would

[6] See Tang, "Policy and Performance in Agriculture," pp. 74–78.

double the national product approximately every eleven and a half years. The party might well have wished for a higher growth rate. But to suggest that the realized rate was deemed so low as to impel the leaders to take a plunge into the unknown world of the Great Leap is clearly conjectural. What must be obvious to the China analysts is the unsettling fact that every significant twist and turn in policy of the Chinese Communist Party (CCP) has given rise to a bewildering rash of seemingly plausible explanations in the outside world. The explanations tend to be of an ad hoc variety without recourse to a systematic frame of reference with which events are best viewed. Not infrequently, attempts are made to lend credence to such ad hoc speculative exercises by citing supporting passages from Mao's writings or by singling out isolated past events for assertion of historical continuity. The game is an exciting one to play. In a setting where few hard facts are known to the outside world, even "wild" speculations can be made to sound plausible. Without wishing to imply that the ad hoc game is useless, it is nevertheless tempting to suggest that it is hardly in accord with the spirit of economy in thinking—the essence of the scientific method of analysis.

The first analytical element of a unified framework to deal with Chinese Communist policy-making is the explicit recognition of the long-term goals of a party which regards itself as the sole repository of truth. In the spirit of Occam's razor, it can be asserted without violence to reality that the overwhelming goal of the CCP is economic growth. This implies austerity. Socialization of the economy is in general taken as an accommodating agent of growth, and rightly so when its instrumentality in amassing social savings for investment is considered. Socialism is, to be sure, also a cardinal principle of great value in itself whose sanctity must not be compromised lightly. So is nationalism, magnified as it is in China by a nostalgic vision of past grandeur and xenophobia. Yet, it is clear that both principles have been and are still being bent virtually beyond recognition in several notable instances. Cases in point are the continued tolerance of Western colonies on Chinese territory, the payment of rentier income to a large number of former capitalists in Shanghai and other industrial centers, and the granting of exclusive buying privileges to recipients of overseas remittances. In all such instances, the "higher" (as they are often supposed to be) principles are being compromised to unbelievable degrees for the sake of economic growth. There are, I suppose, limits beyond which the CCP will not go, but these limits are clearly very broad and elastic. Where else can one find a self-respecting independent nation taking a permissive policy for the sake of economic gains similar to that of the CCP toward Hong Kong and Macao?

If economic growth is the dominant goal, it is a selective growth that is sought in Communist China. Industrial growth—more strictly, that of the modern, heavy sector—is the object to be maximized. With the growth of the modern, heavy industrial sector—whose absolute size determines above all else the political-military power base of a country—holding sway over the CCP value complex, the usual measuring standards of economic progress lose their relevance. In these terms, it is not Professor Liu's overall growth rate (be it 6 per cent or some other figure) but the selective growth rate that the CCP would consider in appraising its handiwork. The latter rate, if taken to be approximated by the growth rate of the producer goods sector, was some 30 per cent per year (in value-added terms) during the first plan period!

In such a setting, agricultural production, consumer goods output, and even population size are properly thought of as policy instruments. The maximization of industrial growth, as defined earlier, is subject to limits posed by various potential bottlenecks. To understand policy shifts, it is essential to identify the effective bottleneck actually limiting the desired growth and to understand what is happening to that bottleneck.

By means of such an analytical framework, I found it possible to deduce empirically testable consequences. The tests, which admit the use of official rates of growth, show that agriculture (despite steady output growth) has been the effective constraint limiting industrial growth during 1952–57.[7] More important, my study yields persuasive evidence that by 1957 the sources of agricultural growth exploited by Peking were fast drying up. The economy stood at a critical crossroads. A fundamental policy switch was necessary not because the CCP leadership considered the industrial growth realized during 1952–57 as unexciting, but because that growth was threatened with serious cutbacks by agricultural problems.

China's socioeconomic heritage left Peking's leaders with significant slacks in rural-resource use which can be readily exploited by a growth-conscious government endowed with sufficient coercive and organiza-

[7] A similar test applied to the U.S.S.R. in its comparable first plan period leads to the opposite conclusion, despite great output declines in agriculture in 1928–32. The Chinese agricultural instrument having failed to discharge its assigned role in full, the policy toward it cannot be said to have been successful. In contrast, the Soviet policy was a success. This serves to point up the danger in assessing policy and performance of an "instrumental" sector such as agriculture by looking at output statistics.

tional power. These slacks and their output-raising potentials were recognized by J. L. Buck more than thirty years ago.[8] Land fragmentation, small holdings, "wasteful" land use represented by excessive division strips and burial sites, and a lack of cooperative development and use of irrigation facilities are some of the factors giving rise to slacks in resource use. Buck saw in them the potential of a 10 per cent increase in output. Peking tapped these sources of growth with vigor. Not to be overlooked are traditional grain losses attributable to such pests as rats and birds. With such losses variously put at 15 per cent or higher for countries similar to China, the extermination of them through massive Communist campaigns probably constituted another source of growth of food supply during 1952–57. The agrarian programs were articulated by a coercive labor-mobilization policy. Abundant though labor was in rural China, the traditional use of it nevertheless contained slacks largely of a seasonal character. As a potential source of growth, they were little expoited earlier for lack of competent social decision-making bodies—a void effectively filled by the CCP with its implementation of mass-labor projects.

What is noteworthy is that all such efforts constitute activities within the confines of traditional production possibilities. As such, they are either of the "once-and-for-all" type of improvement or subject to increasingly severe diminishing returns. Land-use improvement fits the first category, although the completion of the program may take several years. Labor mobilization belongs to the second category. In this light, it is clear that generation of agricultural growth on a sustained basis is beyond the reach of these programs—programs which constituted the mainstay of Peking's agrarian policy in the first plan period.[9]

Sustained agricultural growth is possible over the long haul only if new production possibilities are continually infused into the agricultural setting. Peking's "modernization" attempts during 1952–57 can be summarily characterized as hasty, ill-conceived moves. It is not surprising that my calculations should have revealed declines in agricultural productivity per unit of all resources employed in that period. Further estimations, which probably err on the high side, also show that the *average* rate of net returns to the bundle of "traditional" programs used by the CCP came to an unexciting 3–4 per cent during the

[8] J. L. Buck, *Land Utilization in China* (Chicago: University of Chicago Press, 1937), pp. 181–85.

[9] For a discussion, see Tang, "Policy and Performance in Agriculture," secs. III and IV.

first plan period. Bearing in mind diminishing returns, it is clear that the returns that can be had from *incremental activities at the 1957 margins* must be even lower than 3–4 per cent, possibly very close to zero.[10] Underlying all this is the further fact that agriculture remained the effective constraint on industrialization throughout the first plan period and that, because of this, the Chinese extraction policy for agriculture amounted in fact to an equivalent tax policy with confiscatory marginal rates on income above the minimum standard level. That such a tax gives rise to severe dis-incentive effect needs no elaboration. The dilemma facing Peking can now be clearly seen.

The supremacy of its industrialization goal required the imposition of an extractive policy on agriculture. Because agriculture effectively limited industrialization, agriculture needed to be developed. A policy that is at once developmental and extractive contains built-in contradictions. And this is aggravated by a concurrent need for an extraction procedure with severe dis-incentive or anti-developmental effect. In contrast, Stalin's agricultural policy needed only to be extractive—a task effectively carried out by collectivization and the institution of Machine Tractor Stations. At the same time, because Soviet industrialization was not restrained by agriculture there was no necessity for Stalin to employ a highly dis-incentive policy of extraction. In fact, Soviet extraction can be said (with some exaggeration) to be more akin to an agricultural tax of a "slump sum" nature (that is, with neutral effect on incentives).[11]

## IV. Present and Future Prospects

Within the confines of dispassionate economic analysis, the Leap suggested neither a re-shuffling in the Communist value hierarchy nor an outright ideological shift toward radicalism for its own sake. To meet the deepening agricultural crisis, the CCP had the option to launch a genuine modernization program requiring the co-operation of industrial and other scarce resources, or to attempt a self-contained bootstrap operation in the rural sector through further labor mobilization (via socialization of household activities) to create rural industries and to man mass-labor agricultural capital projects on an unprecedented scale. The party opted for the latter on the basis of superior *anticipated* economic results.

[10] *Ibid.*, pp. 52–56 and 61.

[11] For an elaboration of these points, see *ibid.*, sec. II, and especially pp. 63–64.

The fiasco that resulted is now a matter of record. This is not the place to analyze the reasons for it. It is sufficient to note that even a skillful implementation of the Leap could not have turned what was then a "traditional agriculture" in the Schultzian sense into a growth agriculture.[12] The crisis would not have been solved in a fundamental sense but merely given an additional grace period. And this gain would have been had at the cost of postponing the building of a sound institutional (experiment stations and extension service) and industrial (for example, chemical fertilizer) base that is essential to the generating of new production possibilities to support a "growth agriculture."

A few straws have been in the wind to suggest a belated recognition of this singular fact by the CCP. Among them, the most telling and the best documented is the large increases in resources devoted to fertilizer imports and to the production facilities in the post-Leap years. The modernization trend is likely to continue with probable extension to the all-important field of technical research, development, and information dissemination, unless the romantic Maoist view, in which revolutionary fervor is seen to be all-prevailing, should reassert itself.

The present seemingly deadly struggle in the name of the Great Proletarian Cultural Revolution does not appear to be an ideological confrontation as such. A true ideological dispute would not have been bound by stringent rules of the game of a purely economic character. It would have shown signs of a holy war long before now. Mao as a revolutionary par excellence is also by definition a romanticist in the more mundane arena of nation-building. As advancing age quickens his sense of urgency, impatience impels him to seek shortcuts in attaining the ultimate goal, that is, a Communist China whose power would be second to none. This goal is not under dispute. What is under dispute is the method to be employed. Mao's method is predicated on the mystic power of revolutionary fervor and sheer determination. His opponents —the administrators and professional party officials—see successful nation-building as a non-revolutionary (even unexciting) process whose essential ingredients for success are good administration, technical competence, and a healthy respect for the laws of nature and economics. Having taken to heart the costly lesson from the Great Leap Forward,

[12] Professor T. W. Schultz's insightful distinction between "traditional agriculture" and what I prefer to label as "growth agriculture" (see my book review in *Southern Economic Journal*, vol. 31, no. 3 [January, 1965]), together with his cogent analysis of what it takes to make the transformation, may be found in his *Transforming Traditional Agriculture* (New Haven, Conn.: Yale University Press, 1964).

they are loath to follow Mao on another journey to the unreal world of the Maoist visionaries. As the mounting economic cost of the struggle becomes too real for the latter to ignore, it appears that moderation is now beginning to re-assert itself. At the time of this writing in March, 1967, this seems to be very much in the wind.

# Further Observations by Ta-Chung Liu

The six sources of upward biases in the Chinese Communist estimate of the average rate of growth during 1952–57 mentioned by Professor Dernberger are a good summary of the nature of Communist data for that period. Dernberger agrees that the Communist estimate of the growth rate of 9 per cent per year during this period is upward biased. However, he believes that the Liu-Yeh estimate of 6 per cent per year has over-corrected this bias. On th basis of his own summary of the upward biases in the Communist data, it would be difficult for Dernberger to maintain that the average rate of growth during 1952–57 is higher than, say, 7 per cent per year. Thus, the difference between the Dernberger and the Liu-Yeh positions is no longer very important. It is nevertheless desirable to reply to Dernberger's opinion that the Liu-Yeh estimate is downward biased.

According to Dernberger, the important sources of the downward bias in the Liu-Yeh estimate are:

> Output of food crops is determined in the Liu-Yeh study by assuming that per capita consumption of food crops in 1952–56 was equal to the officially reported per capita consumption of food crops in 1957, and the industrial production of consumer's goods in 1952–1957 is determined in the Liu-Yeh study by assuming that the output of those commodities for which individual data are not available increased at the same rate as the output of those commodities for which individual data are available.

The reasons why these assumptions were made by Liu and Yeh have been explained in my paper. In addition, the assumption about the food crop output was based partly on the consideration that by 1952 agricultural production on the Chinese mainland had regained the prewar level.[1] Grain output in 1933 was about 173 million tons.[2] The Communist figure for grain production in 1952 is 154 million tons,[3] whereas the Liu-Yeh estimate is 177 million tons.[4] The Liu-Yeh position that the 1952 level of production was about the same as the prewar level is shared by both Dawson[5] and Larson.[6] It is reasonable to assume that the recovery from the effects of war took no more than three years from 1949 to 1952.[7] A corroborating evidence is that, according to the Communists' own data, livestock and poultry utilization in 1952 (including the important category of hogs) had more than regained the 1933 rate.[8] This also means that animal manure production (especially hog manure) had also regained the pre-war level, and animal manure was the chief source of fertilizer during both 1933 and 1952. While the assumption of a constant per capita grain consumption in the Liu-Yeh

[1] T. C. Liu and K. C. Yeh, *The Economy of the Chinese Mainland: National Income and Economic Development, 1933–1959* (Princeton, N.J.: Princeton University Press, 1965), p. 53.

[2] Computed from data in piculs given *ibid.*, p. 135. Potatoes are included at one-fourth of their natural weight.

[3] Computed from data *ibid.*, p. 361.

[4] Computed from data *ibid.*, p. 132.

[5] E. F. Jones, "The Emerging Pattern of China's Economic Revolution," *An Economic Profile of Mainland China* (Washington, D.C.: U.S. Government Printing Office, Joint Economic Committee of Congress, 1967), p. 43. Dawson estimates both the 1952 and the prewar peak output at 170 million tons.

[6] M. R. Larson, "China's Agriculture Under Communism," *An Economic Profile of Mainland China*, 1967, p. 257.

[7] By the spring of 1949, fighting had ended on the Chinese mainland. The effects of World War II and the ensuing internal conflict on agriculture were quite different from the abuses inflicted on land resources during the Great Leap Forward. The damage of war on agriculture occurred mainly through neglect by a relatively small proportion of peasants during the war. The area affected shifted with the fortune of war, and was in fact quite limited at any moment of time. The mutilation of land resources during the Great Leap Forward, through the harmful practice of deep ploughing and the construction of improper irrigation systems and leaking canals, covers most of the arable area, and the salinization had long-lasting effects.

[8] Liu and Yeh, *The Economy of the Chinese Mainland*, p. 398. There is no reason to believe that 1952 was a year of abnormally high utilization of livestock. Livestock and poultry were private property in 1952.

study is admittedly crude, the estimated *average* annual rate of growth of the value added by agriculture during the period 1952–57 as a whole is unlikely to be an understimate of the true magnitude.

With regard to the assumption about consumer goods output, Dernberger has overlooked the effort Liu and Yeh have made to check the Communist data on such items as consumers' metal products, leather and fur products, glass products, soap and cosmetic products, and certain "luxury products," a subject discussed in detail in my paper (see section I, "Available Estimates of National Product").

In addition, Dernberger repeats the following criticism he made in his review of the book by Liu and Yeh in the *Journal of Political Economy:*

> . . . many of the assumptions made in the Liu-Yeh study, such as those that assume increases in output were proportional to increases in population, that the value added was a constant proportion of the gross value of output, and that output remained constant, introduced an "anti-development bias" in the results.

He overlooks the reply I have made to this criticism in my paper (section I, "Available Estimates of National Product").

The most important remaining difference between Professor Dernberger and myself lies in the following comment by him:

> Despite the above discussion about possible biases and the claim that the reconstructed Communist estimate represents an upper limit and the Liu-Yeh estimate represents a lower limit to the actual rate of growth in 1952–57, I see no reason for arguing that one must use one or the other for a quantitative description of economic developments in Communist China. In terms of meaningful economic analysis, it really doesn't make that much difference. Both estimates show a relatively high rate of growth in total output, a significant increase in output per capita, a high rate of capital accumulation, a relatively high rate of increase in productivity, and a rapid increase in the relative share of industry in total output.

While both the Communist claim of an average annual growth rate of 9 per cent and the Liu-Yeh estimate of 6 per cent during 1952–57 are high rates of growth, the difference between the two is certainly not trivial. The difference is mainly reflected in the very substantially divergent estimates of the rate of increase of private consumption. If one were to believe in the Communist claim of a 9 per cent rate of growth of the total product, one would also have to agree that the rate of increase of *per capita* consumption was as high as 5.2 per cent per year during a period of rapid population growth and forced industrialization drive. There was no corroborating evidence that such a rapid increase in per capita consumption had occurred on the Chinese mainland. The fact is that per capita consumption in China had not even regained the prewar level as late as in 1957 (see my paper, table 4.E, p. 626).

TABLE 1

ESTIMATES OF PRODUCTION AND PER CAPITA CONSUMPTION OF GRAIN, 1957 AND 1960–1965

| Year | Population* (In Millions) | Dawson's Estimate of Output† (Millions of Tons) | Per Capita Consumption Implied in Dawson's Estimate of Output‡ (Kilograms) | Estimate of Output by the Agricultural Officer. U.S. Consulate-General, Hong Kong§ (Millions of Tons) | Per Capita Consumption Implied in Hong Kong Estimate‡ (Kilograms) |
|---|---|---|---|---|---|
| 1956 | ........ | 175–180 | ................ | | ................ |
| 1957 | 645 | 185 | 0.278–0.281 | 185 | 0.278–0281 |
| 1960 | 676 | 160 | 0.246 | 160 | 0.244 |
| 1961 | 680 | 170 | 0.247 | 167 | 0.246 |
| 1962 | 687 | 180 | 0.262 | 178 | 0.259 |
| 1963 | 697 | 185 | 0.270 | 179 | 0.264 |
| 1964 | 712 | 195 | 0.274 | 183 | 0.261 |
| 1965 | 728 | 193–200 | 0.275–0.279 | 180 | 0.257 |

* Jones, E. F., "The Emerging Pattern of China's Economic Revolution," *An Economic Profile of Mainland China*, p. 93.

† Quoted *ibid.*, p. 93.

‡ To account for the lag in time from production to consumption, total grain available for consumption in a given year is estimated at the average of the output of the current year (plus imports and minus exports) and that of the preceding year (again adjusted for exports and imports). The 1957 range is taken from the third column.

§ Quoted in my paper, this volume, table 7, p. 636.

Professor Perkins' comments contain two main points. First, analyzing from the points of view of both production possibilities and per capita consumption, Perkins believes that the data on food-crop production, as estimated by the U.S. Consulate-General in Hong Kong (which estimate I used in my paper), understated the recovery of agricultural production in 1964–65. Perkins feels that the reconstructed Communist data are more reasonable for these years. Second, Perkins believes that Field's estimate of the post-1957 industrial production is more plausible than my estimate.

With regard to the point on agriculture, a detailed analysis is called for. The estimate by O. L. Dawson for 1964–65 (see Table 1) is close to the reconstructed Communist estimate. The following analysis is made on the basis of a comparison of the Dawson and the Hong Kong estimates.

Dawson's estimate is significantly higher than the Hong Kong estimate, especially for 1963–65. A rough estimate of the level of per capita grain consumption implied in the two estimates is presented in table 1. Both estimates show that total production and per capita consumption fell sharply from 1957 to 1960–61. The 1960–61 per capita consumption, according to both estimates, was about 12 per cent lower than that in 1957. This decline, however, does not reflect fully the actual deterioration in food supply from 1957 to 1960–61, as supplementary foods obtained from "subsidiary farm production" must have fallen even more than grain production. In 1957, the value added by subsidiary farm production was as large as 32 per cent of the value added by agriculture proper.[9] As peasants were more highly regimented during 1960–61 than in 1957, with less time at their own disposal, this ratio must have been much smaller during 1960–61 than in 1957. However, we have no information on this ratio for 1960–61.

Both the Dawson and the Hong Kong estimates of total production and per capita consumption increased from 1960–61 to 1964–65. According to Dawson's estimate, per capita grain consumption in 1965 reached the 1957 level, whereas the Hong Kong estimate puts the 1964 and 1965 per capita consumption at about 7 per cent lower than that in 1957.[10] Controls over the peasants were loosened from 1960–61 to 1964–65. The Communists have claimed that subsidiary farm production again contributed one third of total farm output.[11] Hence, the total food supply during 1964–65, including sources from subsidiary farm production, was better than that during 1960–61 by a margin greater than the Hong Kong estimate of grain production alone reflects.

One would have serious doubt about the validity of the Dawson estimate. On the basis of all four models of population projection developed by Aird, the proportion of the Chinese population in the age bracket 0 to 14 years increased slightly from 1957 to 1965.[12] Children in this age bracket consume less food per head than older people. Accord-

---

[9] Liu and Yeh, *The Economy of the Chinese Mainland*, p. 223.

[10] Because of the severe drought in north China, the 1965 figure is lower than the 1964 one. Dawson's estimate for 1965 does not seem to reflect the drought in north China sufficiently.

[11] *Jen-min jih-pao* [People's Daily], February 12, 1966.

[12] J. S. Aird, "Population Growth and Distribution in Mainland China," in *An Economic Profile of Mainland China*, pp. 264–65; additional computations for 1957 supplied by Dr. Aird.

ing to Dawson's estimate, per capita grain consumption in 1965 had regained the 1957 level. After adjustment for the difference in age composition, the Dawson estimate would suggest that per capita grain consumption was somewhat better in 1965 than in 1957. If this was actually the case, it would be very hard to explain why the Communist regime was willing to spend roughly 30 per cent of their entire foreign exchange earning from exports on food imports during 1964–1965.[13] If a saving as large as 30 per cent of the entire foreign exchange earnings could have been made merely by reducing per capita food consumption by less than 2 to 3 per cent from the 1957 level (total grain imports being about 2 to 3 per cent of Dawson's estimate of grain output in 1964–1965),[14] it is rather surprising that the Communist regime would not have done so.

Moreover, Jones has given a vivid account of the "permanent damage to farm resources during the Great Leap."[15] The two important causes, quoted by Jones from the Communist press, were "salinization of land in the North through improper irrigation schemes and excessive removal of land in ill-planned and grandiose irrigation schemes" during the Great Leap years.[16] There were, of course, a number of additional unfavorable factors which led to a drop of the draft animal population by more than half from 1957 to 1961; and Jones reported that the draft animal population in 1965 was only a little over 60 per cent of the 1957 level.[17] Recovery from the ill effects of the alkalization of land would not be much faster than the recovery of the draft animal population. The reported increase in farm labor[18] could not have effectively substituted for large draft animals. It would be unreasonable to assume that all these unfavorable considerations had not resulted in a loss of grain output in 1964–65 at least equal to 10 per cent of the 1957 amount. The only really favorable factor in the agricultural picture in 1965 was the increase in the use of chemical fertilizers. Estimates of the increase in chemical fertilizer supply from 1957 to 1965 by government economists contradict each other. According to Jones, it was at least 7 million tons,[19] but it was only 5.2 million tons as estimated by Larson

---

[13] Robert L. Price, "International Trade of Communist China, 1950–1965," in *An Economic Profile of Mainland China*, p. 586.

[14] The reduction in per capita consumption would be less than 2 to 3 per cent because of the change in the age composition of the population.

[15] Jones, "The Emerging Pattern of China's Economic Revolution," p. 82.

[16] *Ibid.*, pp. 82–83.                    [18] *Ibid.*, p. 83.

[17] *Ibid.*, p. 82.                         [19] *Ibid.*

on the basis of sources in the U.S. Department of Agriculture.[20] It takes time, however, for the peasants to acquire the knowledge to use chemical fertilizers properly.[21] Moreover, chemical fertilizers can be effectively applied only in well-irrigated regions where natural fertilizers are relatively abundant; and the yields of chemical fertilizers would be subject to diminishing returns. At the most,[22] it can only be assumed that the beneficial effects of the increased application of chemical fertilizers[23] may have more or less compensated for the loss of draft animals and the deteriorated quality of land in 1964–65,[24] with the level of output roughly restored to the 1957 level. This is roughly the picture presented in the Hong Kong estimate. To say that grain output in 1965 was 15 million tons larger than in 1957 (as Dawson did), one has to assume that all the unfavorable factors mentioned by Jones had disappeared by 1965. This is an untenable assumption.

Concerning Perkins' comments on industrial production, it is necessary to examine Field's estimate in some detail. The inflated Communist claims of agricultural production during the Great Leap Forward years are now generally realized. But even trained economists are still not sufficiently careful in using the exaggerated Communist data on industrial output during these years. This situation is illustrated by the data on steel production presented in table 2.

The output of steel was first announced as 11.1 million tons for 1958. The Communists later admitted that of this total 3.1 million tons were "native steel," probably produced from the famous backyard furnaces. Presumably, therefore, only 8 million tons were really steel. But even the 8 million tons of so-called modern steel amounted to a 50 per cent increase over the amount produced in 1957. In 1959, modern steel production was reported to be 13.35 million tons, a 67 per cent increase over 1958. A further increase to 18.45 million tons was reported by the

20 Larson, "China's Agriculture under Communism," p. 246.

21 Larson gives "application by suspicious farmers who are slow to attempt new and progressive methods of crop cultivation" as one of the reasons for the lack of evidence of an increase in overall agricultural production (*ibid.*, p. 246).

22 At a return of 2 to 3 tons of grain to 1 ton of chemical fertilizers applied, a very high rate to assume for the Chinese mainland, where the use of chemical fertilizers is a new experience and where the supply of complementary factors (e.g., water) could hardly have kept pace with the reported rate of increase of the supply of chemical fertilizers.

23 Additional yields of grain in the range of perhaps 10 to 20 million tons.

24 A loss of output at least equal to 10 per cent (18.5 million tons) of the 1957 output.

Communists for 1960. Relative to the probably reliable figure of 5.35 million tons for 1957, the 1960 claim is 3.4 times as large.

In view of the fact that 1958 was the beginning of the Great Leap Forward, when cadres were under severe pressure to exaggerate achievements and when statistical reporting was admittedly confused, a serious research worker must raise the question whether a 50 per cent increase of output from 1957 to 1958 was possible and plausible. This is admittedly an exceedingly difficult question. But, to accept such a figure merely because it was official Communist information—without a careful study of all pertinent considerations—would be rather unsatisfactory.

TABLE 2

ESTIMATES OF STEEL PRODUCTION IN COMMUNIST
CHINA, 1957–65

| Year | Communist Claims* | Field† | Yeh‡ | Liu* |
|------|-------------------|--------|------|------|
| 1957 | 5.35 | 5.35 | 5.35 | 5.35 |
| 1958 | 8.00 | 8.00 | 6.89 | 6.3 |
| 1959 | 13.35 | 10.99 | 8.63 | 8.9 |
| 1960 | 18.45 | 15.22 | ......... | 8.4 |
| 1961 | ............ | 12.00 | ......... | 7.9 |
| 1962 | ............ | 8.00 | ......... | 7.5 |
| 1963 | ............ | 9.00 | ......... | 8.0 |
| 1964 | ............ | 10.00 | ......... | 9.0 |
| 1965 | ............ | 11.00 | ......... | 10.0 |

* Given in my paper, this volume, table 8.

† R. M. Field, "Chinese Communist Industrial Production," in *An Economic Profile of Mainland China*, Joint Economic Committee of Congress, 1967, p. 293.

‡ K. C. Yeh, "Capital Formation in Communist China," in *Economic Trends in Communist China*, Walter Galenson, Alexander Eckstein, and Ta-Chung Liu, eds. (Chicago: Aldine Publishing Co., 1967).

Field accepts the 8 million tons figure for 1958. There are, however, two ways to examine the plausibility of this figure. One is to check it against the capacity figures and the planned figure of production. K. C. Yeh did this, and estimated steel output in 1958 at 6.89 million tons.[25] Second, steel production and machinery output had a very good relationship during 1952–57. Extrapolated on the basis of this relationship and the 1958 figure for machinery output, the steel output in 1958 would be about 6.3 million tons.[26] These two estimates are rather close, and they

[25] Yeh, "Capital Formation in Communist China," in *Economic Trends in Communist China*, ed. Walter Galenson, Alexander Eckstein, and Ta-Chung Liu (Chicago: Aldine Publishing Co., 1967).

[26] See Liu and Yeh, *The Economy of the Chinese Mainland*, p. 118.

throw very serious doubt on the 8 million ton figure accepted by Field for 1958.

The Communist figure for 1959, 13.35 million tons (67 per cent higher than in 1958), is even more suspect. Field could no longer accept this figure; he adjusted it downward to 10.99 million tons without any explanation. The Communists themselves, however, have reported that of the 13.35 million tons, 4.72 million tons were obtained from "small and medium furnaces." During the confusion of the Great Leap Forward, when steel was being produced in every city and village, it would not have been possible to differentiate the output from the backyard furnaces and those from the "small and medium furnaces." K. C. Yeh estimates the 1959 output at 8.63 million tons (that is, the difference between 13.35 and 4.72 million tons).[27] This is roughly the same as the Liu-Yeh estimate, 8.9 million tons.[28]

Even on the basis of the Yeh and the Liu-Yeh estimates, the rates of increase of steel from 1957 to 1959 are very rapid, respectively 61 per cent and 66 per cent in two years. The basic capacity for steel production may have increased substantially during 1958–59, as a number of large plants were completed during that period. It is, however, doubtful whether during the confusion accompanying the Great Leap, skilled labor, raw materials and the transportation and distribution facilities required for such large increases of steel production could all have been available even if they had been carefully planned for. The 100 per cent increase implied in Field's estimate of steel production during 1957–59 seems impossible to achieve. The same criticism is applicable to Field's estimates of other industrial commodities for these years.

The upward bias in Field's estimate of industrial production in 1960 seems even greater than those in his estimates for 1958 and 1959. The Great Leap collapsed in 1960. The transportation system was badly out of order. The supply of raw materials required by the light industries was severely reduced. Yet Field's estimate of industrial production in 1960 was 3.8 per cent higher than that in 1959. The reasons for this upward bias seem obvious. First, Field does not include in his post-1959 sample the important food processing industries (except sugar)[29] which suffered severe cutbacks in 1960. Second, steel production in 1960 is given at 15.22 million tons, an increase of 38 per cent over 1959 on the

[27] Yeh, "Capital Formation in Communist China," pp. 46–47.

[28] Liu, "Quantitative Trends in the Economy of the Chinese Mainland," in *Economic Trends in Communist China,* Table 10, p. 71; and Liu and Yeh, *The Economy of the Chinese Mainland,* pp. 681–83.

[29] Field, R. M., "Chinese Communist Industrial Production," in *An Economic Profile of Mainland China,* pp. 293–94.

heels of his estimated 50 per cent and 37 per cent increases during 1957–59 and 1958–59 respectively. There are many reasons for doubting the validity of this estimate. First, the sudden withdrawal of Soviet technical personnel in the summer of 1960 must have exerted an immediate, serious effect on industries in Communist China. Not only would it have been difficult to maintain a large percentage increase of steel production for the third consecutive year since 1957, the demand for steel itself must have reduced very considerably during the second half of 1960 on account of the Soviet withdrawal. Second, such a large amount of steel could not have been absorbed by domestic uses in 1960.

TABLE 3

INDUSTRIAL PRODUCTION AND VALUE ADDED
BY RELATIVE MODERN SECTORS, 1957–65
(Index numbers, 1957 = 100)

| Year | Field's Estimate of Industrial Production* | Liu's Estimate of the Value Added by Relative Modern Sectors† |
|------|------|------|
| 1957 | 100.0 | 100.0 |
| 1958 | 131.4 | 116.2 |
| 1959 | 166.0 | 129.5 |
| 1960 | 172.3 | 115.0 |
| 1961 | 113.8 | 105.7 |
| 1962 | 110.2 | 104.7 |
| 1963 | 110.3 | 113.4 |
| 1964 | 123.3 | 124.8 |
| 1965 | 134.9 | 135.1 |

* Computed from data in Field, "Chinese Communist Industrial Production," p. 273.

† Computed from data in T. C. Liu, "Quantitative Trends in the Economy of the Chinese Mainland, 1952–1965," in *Economic Trends in Communist China*, ed. Walter Galenson, Alexander Eckstein, and Ta-Chung Liu (Chicago: Aldine Publishing Co., 1967).

Yet, there were no comparable increases in the export of steel[30] from Communist China during the near-famine years of 1961–62 when foreign exchange was sorely needed. Third, this estimate of 15.22 million tons for 1960 significantly exceeds the sum of the estimated capacities of all the large plants in existence five years later in 1965.[31]

While not exactly the same in scope, Field's estimate of industrial production is compared with my estimate of the value added by the relative modern sectors of the economy in Table 3. According to my

[30] A standard commodity for which there is a world market.

[31] The capacity estimates are those by K. P. Wang in his article on "The Mineral Resource Base of Communist China," in *An Economic Profile of Mainland China*, pp. 177–79.

estimate, the peak level of output during the Great Leap was reached in 1959, rather than in 1960 as indicated in Feld's estimate. Relative to 1957 as 100, Field's estimate of the 1960 peak industrial output (172.3) far exceeds my own estimated peak of 129.5 in 1959. The two estimates converge during 1964–65.

A careful reading of my paper would indicate that Perkins is incorrect in saying that I have revised downward the reconstructed Communist industrial figures "on an analysis of the relationship between exports and net domestic product." The relationship between exports and domestic product is used in my paper only to examine the plausibility of the various product estimates derived independently of data on exports.

Perkins has given no convincing reason for revising any of the estimates presented in my paper.

# Further Observations by Robert Dernberger

Inasmuch as Professor Liu presented an excellent summary of the Liu-Yeh study in his paper to the conference, I included the general gist of my review of that study in my comments on his paper.[1] I did not "overlook" Professor Liu's reply to my review contained in the footnote to his paper. I did presume the participants to this Conference would be more concerned with the issues presented in our papers submitted to the Conference than with any of our disagreements published in other sources. Nonetheless, in his reply to my comments on his paper, Professor Liu has again raised the question of what I did or did not say or may have overlooked in my review and, in this manner, implies my comments presented to this Conference are without merit inasmuch as they

[1] As used in this short note, "the Liu-Yeh study" refers to T. C. Liu and K. C. Yeh, *The Economy of the Chinese Mainland;* "my review" refers to the review of that study published in the *Journal of Political Economy*, vol. 73, no. 4 (August, 1965), pp. 419–21.

are based on errors contained in my review published elsewhere. There-fore, for the benefit of those who did not read my review and in defense of my comments made at this Conference, I find it necessary to present evidence to show that Professor Liu has either misunderstood or over-looked my review.

First, I did not "overlook" the findings in the Liu-Yeh study con-cerning *total* per capita product, the *total* proportion of gross value added in the output of both producer and consumer goods, and the ratio of *total* output of different sectors. I did argue, however, that the many assumptions made concerning the per capita output of *individual products*, the proportion of gross value added for *individual products*, and the ratio of output of *two industries* were such that they biased the resulting estimates of the growth of total output for the economy as a whole. The following quotation from my review should indicate my argument clearly.

> Individually, each assumption is not of great importance, but they are made so frequently that it becomes difficult to evaluate their role in determining the conclusions reached in *The Economy* [*of the Chinese Mainland*] concerning Chinese economic develop-ment. The most troublesome aspect of these assumptions, how-ever, is that they negate the most fundamental characteristics of economic development: the change in per capita output and the structure of output [my review, p. 420].

Second, as one of America's leading econometricians, Professor Liu is well aware of the meaning of my use of the term "anti-development bias." The word "bias" refers to a deviation from the true value and carries with it no indication of the magnitude of this deviation. When correctly used by the social scientist, the word "bias" should not be interpreted as an attack on the prejudices or political preferences of the person making the estimates, and I apologize to Professor Liu if any reader of my review misinterpreted my arguments in this manner. The purpose of my review was to assess the probable biases in the Liu-Yeh estimates, and I concluded that the biases were in a downward, that is, anti-development, direction. From his reply to my review and comments made at this Conference, I am still not certain whether Professor Liu believes that his estimates have no bias—are the accurate estimates of actual economic development in Communist China; are upward biased —overestimate the actual rate of growth; or are downward biased, but not for the reasons I give in my review or comment.

Third, Professor Liu also takes umbrage at my use of the word "reasonable," claiming I was not reasonable in my examination of his assumptions. My use of the word "reasonable" as quoted by Professor Liu in the footnote to his paper was not in connection with the assumptions also quoted in that footnote, but with the specific assumption that the per capita consumption of food grains remained constant in 1952–57. Food grains, of course, are not "a negligible part of the total product." Furthermore, I made a serious attempt to define my use of the word "reasonable" in my review. "The Liu-Yeh study asks the question, 'What was the actual or real rate of growth during the 1950's?' This question is 'of such importance that any information available must be utilized in an attempt to find tentative answers.' If this is the authors' implicit argument, then a criticism of the need to make so many assumptions is no longer justified [my review, p. 420]." I admitted the official statistics were exaggerations, and I did not claim to have any better assumptions. Nonetheless, I still believe it to be unreasonable to assume that the per capita consumption (output) of the largest single product in an economy remains constant when one is making an estimate of the actual or real rate of growth in that economy. In other words, while the per capita output of grain probably did not increase rapidly, why assume it remained constant?

Finally, in reply to my comments presented to this Conference, Professor Liu claims that my argument that in terms of meaningful economic analyses, it really doesn't make much difference whether one uses the Liu-Yeh estimates or the reconstructed Communist statistics "overlooks" the substantially divergent estimates of the rate of increase of private consumption. Alas, Professor Liu has overlooked the qualification included in my comment. Allow me to repeat:

> I do not want to appear dogmatic, for I am sure that if one were attempting to assess changes in the economic welfare of individuals in Communist China, the two sets of quantitative estimates would lead to slightly different conclusions. . . . The Liu estimates, of course, would indicate a lower rate of increase in per capita consumption. Neither set of estimates, however, presents a very encouraging picture of the material benefits of the economic development effort to the welfare of the Chinese people.

Alexander Eckstein

# 12

# Economic Fluctuations in Communist China's Domestic Development

## Definition of the Issues

Business cycles and endogenously generated economic fluctuations have generally been considered as peculiar characteristics of market-oriented free enterprise economies.[1] In effect, they have been considered as a hallmark of the capitalist order and of economic development under capitalism. This view has been commonly held by virtually all of the various schools of Marxism and the different wings of the socialist movement have been united in this belief. Recurring crises and alternating movements of expansion and contraction with their dire social consequences in the nineteenth century constituted one of the principal elements of Marx's indictment of the capitalist order. By the same token, implicitly and explicitly socialist systems of economic organization were assumed to be free of these economic fluctuations.

This view is also widely, if not uniformly, held by many professional economists. However, postwar developments in the socialist economies of Europe and Asia suggest a need for a re-examination of this assumption. It is perhaps an interesting paradox that just at the time when questions are being raised as to whether the business cycle is obsolete in so-called capitalist economies, economic fluctuations seem to appear with a certain degree of regularity in socialist economies. The possible presence of fluctuations in the economies of Eastern Europe and the Soviet Union was first noted by the present writer in 1958.[2] Since then

[1] I wish to express my thanks to Doak Barnett, Abram Bergson, Morris Bornstein, Walter Galenson, Gregory Grossman, Saul Hymans, Edwin Jones, Simon Kuznets, T. C. Liu, B. M. Oza, Dwight Perkins, Peter Schran, Warren Smith, and Ezra Vogel for their most helpful comments on an earlier draft.

[2] Alexander Eckstein, "Comment on Professor Reinhart Bendix's Paper Entitled 'The Cultural and Political Setting of Economic Rationality in Western

a growing interest in this problem has developed among economists and an international conference on business cycles and economic fluctuations held in the spring of 1967 had a special session set aside for an analysis and discussion of this phenomenon in socialist economies.[3]

Assuming that further empirical research validates the hypothesis that economic fluctuations can be endemic to socialist as well as to capitalist economies, one may presuppose a priori that no single theory could be equally applicable to all these different types of economies. Thus a theory of economic fluctuations for socialist economies may need to incorporate a different set of variables than those that would be considered relevant for a private business economy. Given the much larger role of central management and planning, a theory of economic fluctuations applicable to socialist economies would have to give much greater weight, or would have to pay much more attention, to the economic behavior of the central planners and policy makers than would need to be the case for the business economy. It is also doubtful that a single theory can serve as an adequate explanation for economic fluctuations even in various types of socialist economies. Thus one would imagine that a rather different type of theory would be required for a preponderantly foreign-trade–oriented socialist economy as compared to a much more inward-oriented system. Similarly one would expect a rather different pattern of cyclical behavior in a preponderantly industrialized, commercialized, and monetized system as compared to a predominantly agricultural economy.

Bearing these general considerations in mind I will attempt to develop a tentative theory of economic fluctuations applicable to China. I will then attempt to subject this theory to some empirical tests by analyzing the actual course of economic policy behavior in China and the behavior of a number of important economic indicators. All refer-

---

and Eastern Europe,' " *Value and Plan,* ed. Gregory Grossman (Berkeley: University of California Press, 1960), pp. 262–66.

[3] Josef Goldmann, "Fluctuations and Trends in the Rate of Economic Growth in Some Socialist Countries," *Economics of Planning,* 4, no. 2 (1964): 88–89. Goldmann, who is a Czechoslovak economist, has written several other articles in Czechoslovak economic journals. For different approaches to economic fluctuations in socialist economies see: Julio H. G. Olivera: "Cyclical Economic Growth under Collectivism," *Kyklos,* 13, fasc. 2 (1960): 229–55; L. M. Faltenbuchl: "Investment Policy for Economic Development: Some Lessons of the Communist Experience," *Canadian Journal of Economics and Political Science,* 29, no. 1 (February 1953): 26–39; Alfred E. Oxenfeldt and Ernest van den Haag, "Unemployment in Planned and Capitalist Economies," *Quarterly Journal of Economics,* 68, no. 1 (February, 1954).

ences to economic fluctuations in this paper will be to changes in the rates of growth rather than changes in the absolute levels of economic activity. In a sense, one might view level cycles merely as special cases of growth cycles. Generally, in this paper economic fluctuations, unless otherwise specified, will not refer to business cycles in the conventional sense of that term. Obviously, by definition, we could not identify *business* cycles in socialist economies such as that of China, since we are not dealing with a business system; we are not dealing with private enterprises and private businessmen as important actors in the system, as independent actors that affect levels of economic activity and patterns of resource allocation.[4]

In most general terms, fluctuations in rates of economic growth in Communist China can be viewed as resulting from a confrontation between Mao's vision of development possibilities in the Chinese economy and society and the country's economic backwardness—particularly as evidenced by a high degree of population pressure, rapid population growth, a technically backward agriculture, and a low per capita food supply resulting therefrom. The essence of the theory to be developed further below is that the constant interplay between these two sets of forces creates a perpetual conflict between the goal structure of the policy makers and the economic capabilities of the system. This conflict and attempts to resolve it leads to a dialectic process which provides both the basic engine of growth and the sources of cyclical fluctuation in Communist China.

## Some Key Concepts

Before proceeding with an outline of the theoretical framework on which this analysis is based, it is necessary to define a few standard concepts in the theory of economic fluctuations. First of all I am using the term *economic fluctuations* rather than *business cycles* advisedly, since the former is a more comprehensive concept while, obviously, the latter is more restrictive; the former can be applied both to economies based

---

[4] Fluctuations in rates of change in economic activity are often referred to in the business-cycle literature as *Kuznets cycles* because of the latter's pioneering work in this field. See W. A. Lewis and J. O'Leary, "Secular Swings in Production and Trade, 1870–1913," *The Manchester School*, 23 (May, 1955): 113–52, and Simon Kuznets, *Capital in the American Economy, Its Formation and Financing* (Princeton, N.J.: Princeton University Press, 1961); also Simon Kuznets, *Secular Movements in Production and Prices* (Boston and New York: Houghton Mifflin Co., 1930). *Kuznets cycles*, however, usually refer to long swings for periods up to 20 years, while our references to economic fluctuations in rates of growth refer to much shorter periods.

on private business organization as well as on other forms of economic organization.[5] Second, for our purpose, fluctuations may best be defined as recurring alternations of expansion and contraction in rates of growth in economic activity.[6]

These economic fluctuations bear certain definite characteristics. They tend to be cumulative and self-reinforcing so that a change in a given direction generates further change in the same direction. Thus, in a sense, movement in one direction tends to feed on itself; once begun it persists until endogenous forces accumulate to reverse the direction. Moreover these fluctuations tend to be pervasive in their effects. They affect virtually all sectors of the economy but not necessarily simultaneously, that is, not necessarily at the same time, or in the same way and at the same rate. There is no evidence that these fluctuations recur over and over again in precisely the same form, that they are precisely of the same duration, or that the amplitude of movement is the same in each case. Analyses of business cycles in capitalist economies suggest that the duration of a cycle may vary anywhere from two to ten years. Business cycle history for the United States suggests a range of duration from 28 to 99 months.

For purposes of analysis, we can distinguish four phases in these movements: the upper turning point, the downswing or contraction, the lower turning point, and the upswing or expansion. In measuring duration, we usually consider the lapse of time between two consecutive upper or lower turning points. A theory of economic fluctuations must meet certain minimum requirements in order to have adequate explanatory value. First, it must distinguish between endogenous and exogenous variables, that is, variables which are endemic to the economic system and to the character of economic activity as compared to variables which lie outside the economic system or outside the explanatory model. Second, the theory must incorporate an explanation and a set of hypotheses about the turning points and a set of hypotheses about the character of the downswing and the upswing. Moreover it must indicate and explain how the ingredients and characteristics of one phase endogenously generate the next phase.

In proposing a theory of economic fluctuations, there is no presumption that all changes in levels and/or rates of growth in economic activ-

[5] Therefore, whenever the term *cycle* or *cyclical fluctuations* appears in this paper it is intended to refer to economic fluctuation as defined in this and the preceding section.

[6] These definitions of cyclical concepts are largely based on R. A. Gordon, *Business Fluctuations*, 2nd ed. (New York: Harper, 1961), chaps. 8, 9, and 10, with some slight modifications.

ity, or all disturbances in these, are endogenously generated or necessarily take the form of cyclical fluctuations. Any economic system may be, and is in fact, subject to random disturbances which necessarily interact with the cycle and may affect the particular characteristics of a single cycle or, in some cases, even several cycles. Another factor to be considered is that fluctuations are closely intertwined with long-term secular changes and secular movements in the economy. These secular changes and movements revolve around the operation of such variables as population growth, labor force participation rates, changes in technology and labor productivity, changes in the quality of the labor force, changes in tastes, and long-term changes in economic organization and institutions. In a sense, economic change, economic growth and decline, and the whole economic process represent a continuous interaction between cycles and trends, both of which mutually interact and mutually shape each other. In the Chinese Communist case, the period we are dealing with is really too short to permit too many generalizations about trends and secular movements, although as we will try to show below there are definite indications that these have affected fluctuations in certain ways. However, the period does not seem to be too short—18 years since 1949—to reveal the presence of several successive cycles.

Finally, the predictive value of the model developed in some detail below is necessarily more limited than its explanatory value. The theoretical framework on which the model is based rests on certain givens, namely the character of Mao's cosmology, the prevailing system of economic organization, a low per capita agricultural product, and a critical dependence of the non-farm sectors on agricultural output changes. The first of these characteristics may perhaps be the most ephemeral of the four and to the extent that Maoism should not survive Mao, the model may need to be modified accordingly. However, unless Mao's death leads to sudden and drastic alterations in official ideology and in economic institutions, the behavioral characteristics of the system may be expected to change rather slowly and gradually. In time, as these changes lead to significant departures from presently prevailing features of the system, both the explanatory and the predictive value of the model is bound to be reduced.

## The Theoretical Framework

As indicated, mainland China's economic history since 1949 could be viewed as a perpetual confrontation between Mao's cosmology, Mao's vision, the vision of the Chinese Communist Party (CCP), on the one hand, and the realities of the country's economic and technical backwardness, on the other. It is the conflict between these two sets of forces and continuous attempts to resolve and reconcile this conflict that ultimately produces cyclical behavior in patterns of economic growth. The core of the hypothesis to be further developed below is that these fluctuations are generated by the interactions of a harvest cycle and a policy cycle. The harvest cycle is in part weather-induced and in part policy-induced. On the other hand the policy cycle revolves around a *vision*-induced pursuit of industrialization which leads to resource mobilization measures with attendant input augmentation effects, but at the cost of disincentives and inefficiencies in the utilization of these added inputs. Therefore, before proceeding further, it will be necessary to define the elements of the *vision* and the elements of Chinese economic backwardness.

## Mao's Vision

An analysis of Mao's writings, speeches, articles, editorials, as well as those of his close associates, reveals his ideal of a Communist man and of the possibilities open for development and transformation of society and economy made possible by the particular characteristics of Communist man. Similarly they reveal Mao's *vision* of a future industrialized socialist society.

Possibly one of the most interesting characteristics of Maoism is its overwhelming stress on man. Man is the most precious thing. "Of all the things in the world, *people are the most precious*. As long as there are people, every kind of miracle can be performed under the leadership of the Communist Party."[7] Actually what Mao means is that man is *potentially* most precious or, more specifically, that man being malleable, he can be energized and committed and his potential mobilized provided that he is properly organized and indoctrinated by the CCP.[8] Coupled with this stress on man is an almost messianic quality, a conviction that almost all men may be saved, although salvation is enormously difficult and backsliding is an ever-present danger. This danger can only be countered by vigilance, continuous indoctrination, and periodic "rectification" movements.

[7] Mao Tse-tung, *Selected Works*, Vol. 4 (Peking: Foreign Languages Press, 1961), p. 454; this is an extract from an editorial dated September 16, 1949; emphasis added. For more detailed references, see Stuart R. Schram (ed.), *The Political Thought of Mao Tse-tung* (New York: Praeger, 1963), p. 251.

[8] See Benjamin Schwartz, "Modernization and the Maoist Vision—Some Reflections on Chinese Communist Goals," *China Quarterly*, no. 21 (January–March, 1965): 3–19.

This Communist man, once properly imbued, indoctrinated, and committed, can become a fountain of tremendous energy and consciousness which can conquer nature and overcome virtually all obstacles. "The more it is possible for men to carry out a conscious revolution in their own social relationships, the more they increase their power in the combat with nature, the more they can really command as by magic the latent productive forces, making them appear everywhere and develop rapidly."[9] The same theme was reiterated by Mao in 1955 when he said, ". . . people consider impossible things which could be done if they exerted themselves."[10]

Another outstanding characteristic of Communist man, or perhaps one should say of model Communist man, is his capacity for total self-denial. For instance A. S. Chen in an analysis of 48 stories published in mainland China during the first half of 1960 found in them two preoccupations about work: first, the sacrifice of sleep for the sake of work, particularly for carrying out scientific experiments and pursuing inventions, and second, a complete imperviousness to weather conditions. Thus these stories in effect tended to glorify man's dedication to work and his ability and willingness to overcome natural limitations and to subordinate his bodily needs and personal comforts to the tasks of socialist construction.[11] The same theme of self-denial is stressed much

[9] Wu Chiang, "Pu-tuan ko-ming lun-che pi-hsü shih ch'e-ti pien-cheng wei-wu lun-che" [Theorists of Uninterrupted Revolution Must Be Thorough Theorists of Dialectical Materialism] *Che-hsüeh yen-chiu*, no. 8, 1958, p. 25, as quoted by Schram, in *The Political Thought of Mao Tse-tung*, p. 54. It is very interesting to note that this transformist view of man, society, and nature assumed growing importance in Stalin's mind after World War II. This was evidenced in the so-called "Stalin Plan for the Transformation of Nature" formulated in 1949, and in Stalin's approach to biology, linguistics, and psychology. As Robert Tucker puts it in his most thoughtful essay on "Stalin and the Uses of Psychology" in *The Soviet Political Mind* (New York: Praeger, 1963), "People were not responding in the expected way to the technique of political education and indoctrination. This led the Stalinist mind to seek a formula for making people respond properly. If Russians were failing to respond to the goals set before them, then something was the matter with the Russians and with the means employed to elicit their response. *Their minds had to be remolded to the point where inner acceptance of the Soviet ideology and all the behavior patterns it imposed would come as a matter of course* [emphasis added]."

[10] "Preface by Mao Tse-tung to the book *Socialist Upsurge in China's Countryside*, Dec. 27, 1955." The English text is reprinted as Document no. 4, pp. 117–19 in Robert R. Bowie and John K. Fairbank, *Communist China 1955–1959: Policy Documents with Analysis* (Cambridge, Mass.: Harvard University Press, 1962).

[11] A. S. Chen, "The Ideal Local Party Secretary and the 'Model' Man," *China Quarterly*, no. 17 (January–March, 1964): 229–40.

more explicitly and repeatedly in one of the basic party documents drafted by Liu Shao-ch'i "On the Training of a Communist Party Member." In it Liu stresses that "the individual interests of the Party member are subordinate to the interests of the Party, which means subordinate to the interests of class and national liberation, of Communism and of social progress. The test of a Communist Party member's loyalty to the Party and to the task of the revolution and Communism is his ability, regardless of the situation, to subordinate his individual interests unconditionally and absolutely to those of the Party." This is given added emphasis in Ch'en Yün's directive on "How to Be a Communist Party Member." He points out that "every Communist Party member should not only have an unwavering faith in the realization of Communism, but also be resolved to fight to the very end, undaunted by either sacrifices or hardships, for the liberation of the working class, the Chinese nation, and the Chinese people." At the same time "Communist Party members are fighters for a Communist *mission* under a leadership of the Party. Thus the interests of a Party member are identical with those of the nation, the people, and the Party. Every party member should give his unlimited devotion to the nation, to the revolution, to our class, and to the Party, *subordinating individual interests* to those of the nation, the revolution, our class, and the Party."[12]

Another essential ingredient of Communist man is his initiative and inventiveness, his willingness to experiment, to innovate, to try out new things. This is another one of the very important themes found by Mrs. Chen in her studies of the Chinese stories published in 1960. These stories convey the impression that an ordinary factory worker or young technician without research training and sometimes even without much formal scientific education can, by sheer determination and long hours of persistent work and study, come up with inventions which can make an immediate contribution to production. Similarly in agriculture, innovative efforts can overcome limitations imposed by weather, soil conditions, water supply, etc.

Very significant operational and policy consequences follow from this vision of Communist man possessed with these particular attributes of self-denial, total commitment, energy, struggle, initiative, and inventiveness. The stress on "men over machines" or "men over weapons" or

[12] For the quote from Liu, see Conrad Brandt, Benjamin Schwartz, and John K. Fairbank, *A Documentary History of Chinese Communism* (Cambridge, Mass.: Harvard University Press, 1952) p. 336. For the quote from Ch'en Yün, see the same source, pp. 330–31; emphasis added.

"better red than expert" logically follows from the above vision of Communist man. This does not mean that Mao necessarily believes that man in Chinese Communist society actually conforms to this ideal. It merely means that he is convinced that, given certain conditions, man *can* approximate the ideal and the model spelled out above. Furthermore a careful analysis of the writings and directives of the fifties and sixties will show that at least as far as the top leadership is concerned, "red" and "expert," "men" and "machines," and "men" and "weapons' are not as sharp dichotomies and dualities as they are at times interpreted to be in different writings on Chinese Communist ideology, polity, society, and economy. In the short run, these are viewed by the leadership as possible substitutes. Under certain conditions, and most pronouncedly during the Great Leap, ideological commitment, mass mobilization, and organization were viewed as possible substitutes for expertness, professionalism, and the availability of capital equipment.

However, it was all along recognized that in the longer run professionalism, technological progress, advanced weapons, and complex machinery were necessary for continuing economic growth. In this longer run, expertness was, and probably still is, viewed as an integral part of redness; that is, part of being "red" is to be inventive and innovative, and to seek scientific training and education sufficient to enable one to carry out innovations either of a simple or of a more complex character, depending on one's role in the economy. Conversely, even a scientist or an expert who has all the necessary qualifications will not be innovative and inventive unless he is imbued with a spirit of boldness, zeal, and ideological commitment.

In Mao's and the Chinese Communist's view all of these qualities combined are necessary to realize the vision of a powerful industrialized China which is beginning to catch up in terms of ecanomic progress and in terms of growing national power with the Soviet Union and with the countries of the West.

The accent on man, on consciousness, on the human will, on the role of policy and organization, and the primacy of politics represent Leninist elements in Maoism. However, these elements have been given much greater emphasis by Mao and seem to play a much more central role in his cosmology as compared to Lenin's. This strong streak of voluntarism can be viewed as an outgrowth of China's backwardness and lack of the classical Marxist-type preconditions for revolution. It reflects a recognition that revolutions must be willed and organized rather than expected to arise more or less spontaneously out of conditions of economic and social disintegration or crisis.

In this cosmology, industrialization plays a double role and is derived from two different wellsprings: Marxism and nationalism. On the one hand, the revolution re-creates the Marxist evolutionary path through rapid industrialization. Thus, through rapid industrialization a proletariat is developed and strengthened so that the end result of the process conforms to the Marxist schema of a proletarian dictatorship. On the other hand, industrialization serves as a prime means and as a necessary condition for attaining military and economic power. It provides the only road to great-power status in the modern world.

## The Realities of China's Backwardness

The salient elements of China's economic backwardness are relatively well known and need not detain us too long. It may be sufficient just to sketch them out briefly.[13] For our purposes, the most essential fact about the Chinese mainland economy is its preponderantly agricultural character. While population and labor force data are unsatisfactory, and the same applies to agricultural production statistics, there is a wide degree of consensus that 70-80 per cent of the country's labor force is tied down in agriculture and about 40–50 per cent of the national product is generated in the farming sector. This is a preponderantly pre-modern agriculture based on highly labor-intensive methods of cultivation within a framework of traditional and pre-modern technology. Given the high degree of population pressure on the land, labor productivity is low, per capita product is low, and total food supply availabilities per person are consequently quite low as well. Given the prevailing pattern of land use combined with agricultural backwardness, production has traditionally been subject to more or less marked harvest fluctuations. With a low average per capita agricultural product, the farmer and his family necessarily live close to the subsistence margin, agricultural surpluses have tended to be relatively small, and the bulk of the agricultural product has been generally consumed within the farming sector itself. In such a preponderantly agricultural economy, aggregate levels of economic activity are necessarily closely dependent upon the fates of the farming sector. The production of goods and services in the non-agricultural industries is directly or indirectly dependent to a greater or lesser degree upon agriculture.

[13] For a more detailed analysis of China's economic backwardness see Alexander Eckstein, *Communist China's Economic Growth and Foreign Trade* (New York: McGraw-Hill, 1966), and *Economic Trends in Communist China,* ed. Alexander Eckstein, Walter Galenson, and Ta-Chung Liu (Chicago: Aldine Publishing Co., 1968).

What is the character of this interdependence? First of all agriculture serves as a potential source of labor supply for the non-farm sector. Given a high degree of population pressure on arable land resources, rapid rates of population growth, and no opportunities—or at best only limited opportunities—for new land settlement, labor surpluses are likely to be generated in agriculture. Second, it is the principal supplier of wage goods to the non-agricultural labor force. Thus, fluctuations in farm output will not only affect the availability of food supplies, but of clothing as well, with the latter largely dependent upon the production of cotton and wool. In turn, the state of wage good supplies not only conditions the consumption levels of the non-agricultural labor force, but also affects industrial labor productivity both through its effect on incentives and on nutritional standards. Third, as indicated above, agriculture is a major supplier of raw materials to the consumer goods industries, most particularly to the various branches of food processing and textiles.

Fourth, levels of investment activity are also closely intertwined with levels of agricultural activity. However, these investment linkages are mostly indirect. As noted before, fluctuations in farm output and changes in raw materials supplies resulting therefrom tend to have a marked effect on the output of consumer goods industries. This, in turn, will necessarily have an effect on the investment good demand of the consumer goods industries. In socialist systems, fluctuations in investment goods demand by the consumer goods industries could—at least theoretically—be made up by counterbalancing movements in investment goods demand by the investment goods industries themselves and by industries producing the inputs for these branches of manufacture.

Let us examine this proposition. Suppose that agricultural output declines and that as a result consumer goods industries are faced with raw materials shortages. ("Declines" as used here is intended to refer to declines both in rates of growth and in levels. The inter-relationships traced here would hold under *ceteris paribus* assumptions for both, although one would expect the effects to be milder for rate declines than for level declines.) A decline in agricultural output will necessarily lead to a decline in the output of manufactured consumer goods, which then will affect investment goods demand by these industries. Why should this affect total investment in a centrally planned and managed economy? As noted above, a decline in agricultural production will lead to a decline in the supply of wage goods. This, in turn, may be expected to produce strong dis-incentive effects with a negative impact on industrial labor productivity. Should real stringencies in wage good supplies develop, these might affect the physical health and strength of the workers, thus leading to very sharp declines in labor productivity. Such effects would not be confined to consumer goods industries but may be expected to encompass all branches of mining and manufacturing, leading to a possible decline in output or at least to sharply rising real costs per unit.

Quite apart from these effects, investment goods output is likely to be curtailed amidst declining farm production due to the large import component in China's capital goods output. At this stage of development, China's exports must necessarily be largely agricultural. More specifically, the bulk of these exports consist of foodstuffs, raw materials of agricultural origin, and processed products and manufactures dependent upon agricultural raw materials such as cotton textiles. Therefore a decline in farm production will necessarily depress exports and, thus, the capacity to finance imports. To the extent that China's investment goods industries have been critically dependent on imported components, a curtailment in capital goods imports can in and of itself produce serious bottlenecks in the investment goods industries. Moreover, the more serious the downturn in farm production, the more acute will be the effect on capital goods imports, and thus on capital goods output.

It is apparent therefore that the international sector constitutes a fifth link between agriculture and the non-farm branches of the economy. Theoretically, the constraints imposed by agriculture on food supply, raw materials for consumer goods industries, and the supply of wage goods could be relieved through imports. The only problem is that these same constraints affect exports, and thus the capacity to import. As a result, just when the constraints are most severe it is also most difficult to relieve all of them simultaneously via the import route. That is, one set of supply bottlenecks can be relieved either at the expense of leaving another set untouched or possibly even aggravating it.

One might presuppose that in a centrally managed economy with far-reaching political controls the link between fluctuations in farm production and urban food supplies could be broken. This indeed was the case in the Soviet Union when grain exports were rising while farm production was markedly shrinking under the impact of collectivization in the early thirties. However, in China it was apparently not possible to duplicate this Stalinist "feat." It is not entirely clear to what extent this was due to the fact that the Chinese peasantry lives much closer to the subsistence margin than its Russian counterparts, or to the reluctance of the mainland regime to apply brute force in the same or in greater measure as that used by Stalin. As a result, the constraints imposed by agriculture on the economy as a whole are necessarily more severe in Communist China than they were in Russia during the period of the First Soviet Five Year Plan.

## The Policy Cycle

The central economic objective of the Chinese Communist regime, as stated on many occasions, is rapid industrialization. This in turn requires large-scale mobilization of resources—most particularly capital, labor, and technical, scientific, and managerial manpower—and its allocation to desired ends. For these reasons—as well as for a host of noneconomic reasons—soon upon attaining power the regime embarked on a process of collectivization in agriculture and socialization in other sectors of the economy.

Given the pattern of its implementation, socialization was not a cyclical but an irreversible and once-for-all phenomenon which, however, proceeded in an unstable and jerky, rapid advance-consolidation-rapid advance fashion. The jerkiness and instability of this socialization trend was occasioned by several factors. Major institutional changes—for example, collectivization, nationalization of industry—were carried out in the form of large-scale campaigns which taxed to the limit the organizational and bureaucratic capacities of the regime. At the same time, to the extent that they disrupted prevailing forms of economic organization, they contributed to disruptions in the production process, gave rise to disproportionalities, strains, and supply bottlenecks. These factors in combination forced slowdowns in the pace of the campaigns and a period of consolidation before embarking on another. This particular phenomenon is, of course, not unique to Communist China; it seems to be a significant feature of all command economies.

Of primary interest for purposes of this paper is what may be termed the *pure policy cycle*. The hypothesis to be developed is that cyclical fluctuations in economic policy have characterized the Chinese Communist system from its inception. However, during the period when the socialization process was being consummated, these fluctuations were closely intertwined with it. Beyond it, the policy cycle acquired, in a sense, a life of its own, independent of the socialization trend. The essence of the policy cycle revolves around the resource mobilization—production nexus on the one hand, and the dichotomy between model Communist Man and Economic Man on the other. Consequently, the dilemma facing the regime is that precisely the kind of measures imposed to mobilize resources tend to (a) produce strong disincentive effects, and (b) lead to losses in productive efficiency.

Actually, these two effects are closely inter-related inasmuch as losses in productive efficiency are in part due to dis-incentive effects occasioned, for instance, by measures designed to keep consumption in check and raise the savings rate. However, certain mobilization measures may affect production more directly. Thus, agricultural changes such as periodic reductions in the size of private farm plots, or movements of labor from locality to locality or task to task, may have profoundly disruptive effects on production processes, most particularly if these measures are carried out with great speed. Similarly, sharp increases in investment and large-scale expansion of plants in many different locations simultaneously tends to produce acute imbalances, strains, disproportionalities, and serious supply bottlenecks.

In effect, then, resource mobilization measures enlarge the bundle of inputs placed at the disposal of the production process. In its early stages a mobilization phase may proceed without substantial losses in incentives or efficiency. However, beyond a certain point disincentive effects and inefficiencies are likely to cancel out some of the gains due to increased mobilization of inputs. This then leads to a decline in the rate of growth. If in spite of this slowdown, mobilization measures continue to be enforced, a point may be reached when the negative incentive and efficiency effects outweigh the positive input expansion effects with an attendant level decline in output. In a centrally managed economy such as the Chinese, one would expect the planners to step in and adjust mobilization policies so as to check the slowdowns—provided they are recognized—before they degenerate into an absolute level decline. This is one of the principal reasons then that economic fluctuations in an economy such as the Chinese usually take the form of movements in rates of growth rather than in absolute levels.

The disincentive effects accompanying mobilization measures may be viewed as due to a clash in the scales of preference, particularly time preference, of planners and households. The conflict could, of course, be resolved either if man could be remolded into the model Communist Man of Mao's vision, who would internalize the preference scales of planners and policy-makers, or by giving more or less free play to market incentives and the motivations of Economic Man. Unfortunately, remolding proved to be a most intractable task on a mass scale and surrendering to Economic Man was a most unpalatable alternative because of its undesired allocative and political control effects.

To sum up, the roots of the policy cycle are to be found in the regime's commitment to the Maoist vision. This commitment leads to the adoption of economic mobilization measures. Collectivization of agriculture and socialization of the non-farm sectors is carried out to augment the regime's mobilization capacity. Both the mobilization measures accompanying the collectivization and socialization process and those following its consummation tend to produce a pattern of economic fluctuation in rates of growth, even though the socialization process as such is a terminal, once-for-all trend phenomenon. The fluctuations arise from the fact that each new wave of mobilization tends to be carried to the point at which it (a) begins to tax the organizational and bureaucratic capacities of the regime; (b) leads to disruptions in the production process due to disruptions in economic organization; (c) leads to disproportionalities, strains, and supply bottlenecks in the production process; and (d) produces unfavorable incentive effects. Therefore the initial phase of a mobilization wave tends to be characterized by an acceleration in the rate of growth until the disincentive and inefficiency effects begin to cancel out the input augmentation effects. When the resulting slowdowns in rates of growth are recognized they lead to policy adjustments, dampening of the mobilization pace, or the suspension of mobilization measures altogether. This may then lead to a reversal in the rates of growth as incentive and efficiency effects are more fully taken into account. However, as these effects are given freer play and market incentive policies are pursued, a point may be reached beyond which another slowdown occurs due to the fact that savings rates may be reduced. Thus, while capital and other factors may be more efficiently utilized, the total inputs applied may be reduced so much that the incentive and/or efficiency gains are at least partially canceled out. Once this is recognized by the planners and policy-makers, another input mobilization phase tends to be instituted, and so the pattern repeats itself.

## The Cyclical Process

According to the theoretical framework developed here, economic fluctuations are generated by the interactions of this policy cycle and a harvest cycle. One might distinguish between a *pure harvest cycle* which is exclusively induced by periodic weather fluctuations of an exogenous character, and the harvest cycle of our model which is in part weather-induced but in part policy-induced. Correspondingly, the *pure policy cycle* outlined above is modified by the harvest cycle.

The character of this cyclical process will be outlined below in terms of four phases which are generally used in the theory of economic fluctuations, that is, the upswing, the upper turning point, the downswing, and the lower turning point. I will attempt to sketch the dynamics of each and the transition from one stage to the next. In the theoretical framework used here, the points of departure, the givens, or the independent variables are the elements of Mao's vision outlined above, on the one hand, and the elements of China's economic backwardness, on the other. Most specifically, as far as the latter is concerned, the crucial factors to be considered as givens are the low per capita agricultural product and the dependence of the non-farm sectors on agricultural output in the various ways indicated in the preceding section.

*The Upswing.* Given a low per capita product in agriculture and in the economy as a whole, a good harvest provides a much larger surplus potentially available either to the farm population and/or to the economy as a whole. A good harvest can mean either higher food consumption by the peasantry and/or larger marketings of agricultural products, and thus more availability of farm produce for the urban labor force, for stockpiling, and for export. In either case, it provides much greater room for maneuver, more policy choices, and the opportunity for new policy ventures or an intensification and renewal of old ventures. In the case of Communist China, favorable harvest prospects or a high realized harvest out-turn has invariably led to attempts to step up the rate of fixed capital investment, and the rate of growth in heavy industry in particular and in all non-agricultural sectors in general. In pursuit of this objective, the rate of resource mobilization in the economy tends to be stepped up. This may take a variety of forms, depending on what period in Communist China's economic history we are considering. This may be reflected in an acceleration of collectivization and communization policies in the countryside, in circumscribing the scope of the private plot, in narrowing the scope of the rural market, raising the tax pressure, raising the collection pressure, and in general pursuing policies which are designed to raise the level of extraction from the countryside. Similar policies are pursued in the non-agricultural sectors with curtailment of the scope of private industry and commerce, or whatever is left of it, a general lessening of the reliance on material incentives both in agriculture and industry, and placing greater reliance on normative, exhortative, ideological, and to some extent even coercive appeals for increasing effort and commitment by the peasantry and the non-agricultural labor force.

The upswing is generated and gains cumulative strength from two inter-related sources. On the one hand, the good harvest provides more agricultural raw materials for industry. It also provides more foodstuffs for the industrial labor force, and it supplies more produce for export. As a result, the rate of industrial growth can be, and in fact is, greatly accelerated: in consumer goods industries because of the much larger raw material supply, in all industries because of the possibility to supply an increased labor force with the necessities of life, that is, with wage goods. Investment goods industries expand due to both of the reasons just cited and also by virtue of the fact that with higher export levels it becomes possible to finance an increased volume of imports, particularly of capital goods, which constitute an important component of domestic investment goods production as well as a significant component of capital formation at home. However, these more or less automatic results of a good harvest are greatly reinforced by the policies which are initiated following improvements in agricultural production. These policies provide the second source for the cumulative impact of the upswing. The particular policies are of course the mobilization and accumulation measures referred to above, with a shift from remunerative to normative appeals designed to raise not only the level but the rate of capital accumulation.[14] To the extent that these policies succeed, they tend to reinforce the upswing—at least in the short run. However, these very policies tend to be self-destructive in the same sense that they contribute to the gradual negation of the upswing.

*The Upper Turning Point.* After a certain point these mobilization, capital accumulation, and high investment rate policies are necessarily brought to a halt by the simple fact that they cannot be pushed any further. After a certain point it becomes increasingly difficult, if not impossible, to increase state procurement of produce in the countryside and to raise the rate of extraction from the agricultural sector. Attempts to increase procurements beyond a certain point are bound to bump up against a minimum subsistence ceiling.

Moreover, tightening socialization and collection policies tend to have strong disincentive effects on the peasantry. This is aggravated by the fact that very frequently, if not invariably, these policies are accompanied by the introduction of some new institutional forms in agriculture such as the collectivization drive following the good 1955 harvest

[14] The terminology and use of these concepts (i.e., *remunerative* and *normative* appeals) were derived from an unpublished paper by William G. Skinner, "Leadership and Compliance in Communist China." In this paper, Skinner develops a cycle theory of policy behavior in sociological and organizational terms rather different from ours. Yet Skinner's and my analysis mutually complement rather than contradict each other.

and the communization drive and the Great Leap policies following the 1958 harvest. They not only produce disincentive effects, but are in and of themselves quite disruptive, with negative consequences for agricultural production flowing therefrom. The disincentive effects, of course, arise in large part from the fact that the Chinese peasantry and the realities of its motivations and behavior do not accord with the Maoist vision of ideal Communist man. As noted earlier the cosmology of Mao and the Chinese Communist leadership does not necessarily presuppose that the Chinese peasantry in fact behaves like the model Communist man. But it does presuppose that if properly led, properly indoctrinated, and properly organized and mobilized, it can be imbued with the kind of values that would yield a pattern of behavior more or less approximating that of the ideal vision. However, actual experience thus far would suggest that this does not seem to be generally the case even for the masses of the poorer peasants upon whom the regime places its principal reliance for attaining its objectives and for ideological remolding. Normative appeals based on Chinese Communist ideology, patriotic and nationalist appeals, and appeals to the self-interest of the poorer peasantry, can have an effect up to a point and on some occasions. However, appeals to self-interest can be repeated only if the earlier appeals did in fact lead to significant improvements in the lot of the poorer peasants. Normative appeals also lose in force as they are repeated again and again, even though the slogans might be slightly different, or the appeal might be couched in slightly different terms.

Therefore, the upswing is brought to a halt basically for two kinds of reasons. First, because mobilization and accumulation policies sooner or later are bound to bump up against some real subsistence and organizational ceilings. Second, because these same policies tend to produce strong disincentive effects, partly because of the organizational disruption that may result from them, partly because they usually increase the pressure on the peasant. This pressure may take the form of increased collections or manipulation of the terms of trade in ways which are adverse to agriculture, or through a series of other measures which are directly or indirectly designed to raise the extraction ratio from agriculture.

*The Downswing.* Sooner or later, the kind of policies just referred to will lead to a decline in agricultural production, that is, a slowing down in the rate of growth of agricultural ouput or, under some circumstances, even an absolute decline. This may come about not only because of disincentives and disruptions in the production process engendered by the policies outlined above, but may also result from certain resource allocative effects engendered by these same policies. For instance, during periods of "socialist upsurge," labor tends to be diverted from the private plot to the collective or to the commune, from agricultural production per se to mass labor projects, with negative consequences for livestock production in the first case, and with adverse effects on crop production in the second case. Similarly, these policies can lead to large-scale diversion of organic fertilizer, from the private plots where they are produced to the collective or to the commune, to the point that fruit and vegetable production on the private plot suffers. Moreover, this fertilizer production itself may be undercut by the declines in livestock production which may result from the re-allocation of labor from the private plot to the collective.[15] The effects of a harvest downturn (either absolute or relative) then tend to spread throughout the economy, generating a cumulative downswing or contraction. The factors operative in this cumulative downswing are very much the same as in the upswing except that they have the reverse effect and work in the reverse direction, that is, a poor harvest can and does force a contraction all along the line throughout the economy. A fall in agricultural output leads to shortages of industrial raw materials, to shortages of export supplies, and to food-supply shortages both for the rural sector and for the expanding industrial labor force.

The cumulative downswing forces the regime to shift its policy mix and to place primary emphasis on measures which are congruent with the peasantry's own scale of preferences. This means that for a relentless pursuit of the Maoist vision there must be substituted a more realistic recognition of peasant motivations and the incentive structure as it actually is, rather than as the regime would like it to be. Concretely, this means a shift from policies based preponderantly on normative and even coercive appeals to those relying much more heavily on remunerative appeals.

Such a shift in the policy mix would then be reflected in a general easing of the pressure on the peasantry, that is, more favorable prices, more favorable terms of trade, easing of the collection pressures, greater scope for the private plots, greater scope for the free rural markets, and less control over labor allocation and degree of labor mobilization.

*Lower Turning Point.* These policies then tend to lead to the development of what the Chinese Communists refer to as "capitalist tend-

---

[15] See Kenneth R. Walker, *Planning in Chinese Agriculture, Socialisation and the Private Sector, 1956–1962* (London: Cass, 1965).

encies" in the countryside. Increased reliance on material rewards and greater scope for the exercise of material and financial incentives will necessarily mean less control over the daily activities, the daily lives, and the day-to-day pattern of resource allocation in the villages, on the farms, and in the countryside at large. This type of a policy will also encourage most those peasants, those households, and those collectives that are most involved in the market nexus, that are most responsive to financial incentives, and that are most enterprising. Correspondingly, policies of this type will tend to encourage better effort, more careful husbandry, growth in livestock production, and growth in crop production, but at the same time they will also tend to encourage greater income inequalities within villages and between villages.

The new policy mix leads to at least three kinds of consequences: first, it tends to undermine the economic and political control system in the countryside; second, it interferes with the regime's economic and political power goals; and third, as already indicated, it does tend to have positive effects on agricultural production to the extent that the new policies do, in fact, lead to an improvement in agricultural production. They then provide once more new room for maneuver following a good harvest. At the same time, because of the negative economic and political-power effects emanating from these policies, strong inducements are built up for the suppression of the "capitalist tendencies" in the countryside and the re-imposition of controls.

The cumulative downswing then forces the regime to change its policies. This policy shift tends to encourage agricultural production. But it also has adverse power consequences as far as the regime is concerned. Therefore, to the extent that the new policies sooner or later contribute to a good harvest, following such a harvest strong inducements are generated for a new policy shift to suppress capitalist tendencies, to raise the rate of investment, and to increase the socialization and accumulation pressures all along the line. This policy shift is in turn made possible by the increased room for maneuver gained by the good harvest. This very harvest then enables the system to turn the corner and once more embark on a process of expansion reinforced by high rates of investment which are in part engendered by the new policies.

## Learning Effects

As indicated above, one of the crucial ingredients of these economic fluctuations is a policy cycle. The question may legitimately be posed as to why this cycle keeps recurring. Are there no learning effects? How is it that the experience and the lessons that could be drawn from one cycle are not utilized for preventing or obviating the next? Do not these lessons and experiences affect the behavior of policy-makers in ways which could lead to systematic attempts to pursue counter-cyclical policies—policies designed to reduce the amplitude of the fluctuations at the least? Actually, the evidence would suggest that there are some learning effects, although different segments of the leadership and the bureaucracy may be learning different and, at times, contradictory lessons. Thus the absence of apparent learning effects on Mao and some of his associates can probably be explained by the particular characteristics of their vision and image of the model Communist man. Needless to say, this vision or cosmology is not a fixed, static, or unchanging entity, but it travels in certain definite directions and is based on certain clearly crystallized biases and preferences.[16] To put it more precisely, it is not that no lessons are drawn from experience by Mao and some of his associates; rather, it is that the learning effects are likely to be of a character that might tend to aggravate instead of diminish the force of the cycle.

From a Maoist point of view, optimal policies are those designed to inculcate the masses with the values of Communist man. Ideally and hopefully, these values could and would be internalized by the peasantry, workers, and the intelligentsia. However, to achieve this aim, the CCP must be well organized and the cadres must be imbued with the right ideological posture, a proper ideological zeal and commitment, and strong leadership qualities. Therefore, if the pursuit of the Maoist vision—and policies based on it—leads to strong disincentive effects, on the one hand, and the rise of "capitalist tendencies," on the other, the fault is to be found in policy implementation, in cadre leadership, or in inadequate organization, rather than in the basic policy guidelines. This then does not call for major changes in policy direction but for measures designed to insure tighter organization and an ideologically purer posture by the cadres.

On the other hand, a host of indications would suggest that at least some elements of the leadership were quite conscious of the fluctuations in rates of economic growth.[17] It is, however, unclear whether they

[16] This point is well developed by Benjamin Schwartz in "Modernization and the Maoist Vision."

[17] For instance Liu Shao-Ch'i states in his "Report on the Work of the Central Committee of the Communist Party of China to the Second Session of the Eighth National Congress" that "The development is U-shaped, i.e., high at the beginning and the end, but low in the middle. Didn't we see very clear-

regarded this as a necessity or a virtue. Some students of Communist China's economic growth go as far as to suggest that this may even be based on a deliberate development strategy.[18] While this possibility can not be totally ruled out, it is very doubtful that the economic strains of 1956 or of 1959 for instance were allowed for or anticipated in advance. At the same time, one can be quite certain that the crisis of 1960–62 was not at all foreseen.

Nevertheless, it would seem that the leadership groups which were conscious of the reality of cyclical fluctuations also recognized the crucial role of agriculture in imposing severe constraints upon the economy. The rise of an "agriculture first" strategy after the onset of the economic crisis, and strenuous attempts to keep the Cultural Revolution contained, to prevent it from spilling over into the economy, may be considered as possible symptoms of such learning effects. This conclusion would also seem to be borne out by the fact that economic fluctuations have been milder since the Great Crisis of 1961.

On balance, the issue of learning effects and its impact on economic policy is unresolved and is likely to remain in this state as long as the current policy and power struggle remains unresolved. Should Maoist influences prevail, the learning effects may be such that they would not only continue to push the system into recurring policy cycles but also further away from the economic realities of the Chinese mainland. On the other hand, should the Maoist vision become less influential, one could begin to see a different set of learning effects at work, which might reduce the amplitude of the policy cycle.

## Qualifications

The first qualification to be noted refers to weather effects. In outlining the cyclical process, I have focused explicitly on the interplay of policy and harvest. However, the quality of the harvest is necessarily also affected by weather changes. In the absence of detailed data, it is really very difficult to determine the extent to which the quality of any one harvest is affected by weather, on the one hand, and by policy, on the other. One can very clearly test the quality of the harvests themselves

---

ly how things developed on the production front in 1956–1958 in the form of an upsurge, then an ebb, and then an even bigger upsurge or, in other words, a leap forward, then a conservative phase and then another big leap forward," in *Second Session of the Eighth National Congress of the Chinese Communist Party* (Peking: Foreign Languages Press, 1958).

[18] See, for instance, Walker, *Planning in Chinese Agriculture, Socialisation and the Private Sector, 1956–1962,* chap. 1.

and the ebb and flow of policy, but at this stage it is impossible to determine the extent to which harvest fluctuations are caused either by the policy cycle or the weather factor alone, or the two in some particular combinations. To put it differently, the empirical evidence will show that certain policies tend to follow certain types of harvests. They will also show that certain types of behavior by the actors in the system follow from these policies. Whether these policies and this behavior then produce the good or bad harvests in and of themselves is very difficult to state categorically. Relevant weather information is potentially available, but to collect and correlate these data would constitute a major undertaking well beyond the scope of this study.

There are other factors besides weather and policy that might affect harvest fluctuations, and economic fluctuations in general, in this type of an economic system. I am referring particularly to a phenomenon which could be labeled as a communications cycle, implementation cycle, or perhaps a bureaucratic-error cycle. This type of a cycle may be generated by the particular leadership structure and the particular character of the party and administrative bureaucracy permeating a system such as the one we are dealing with here.

This type of a cycle might arise from the particular way in which programs and new policies are enunciated, on the one hand, and the way in which they are communicated from the top to the lower level organs, and finally the way they are implemented at the various levels. Very frequently the specific goal structure articulated in a new campaign or new program tends to be ambiguous or very delicately balanced. For instance, its general spirit might be "collectivize but do not disrupt agricultural production" or "push ahead with measures to promote agricultural production without slowing down collectivization." This type of directive confronts the cadres with a number of problems and difficulties. First, they are not sure how to read it, since to some extent the directive is mutually contradictory. They know that collectivization cannot help but have a disruptive effect and a negative impact on agricultural production, at least in the short run. Similarly, they are conscious of the fact that if they are to promote improvements in agricultural production, collectivization may need to be slowed down. Therefore, they tend to read the first type of directive as meaning, "collectivize even if you do have to disrupt agricultural production," and interpret the second type of directive as meaning, "place major emphasis on improving farm output even if you have to slow down collectivization."

A second type of difficulty may arise from the fact that even if the directive, the message, is less ambiguously formulated, it may get more or less distorted in the process of communicating it from the top down; that is, the communications channels themselves may distort the message. For both of these reasons, ambiguity and distortion, there tends to be a considerable gap between the outcome of certain policies and the intent of the policy-makers at the time they formulated the new directive. To the extent that this happens and there is a bureaucratic deviation from the policy intent, and an implementation error in terms of the policy intent, to correct it a new directive will have to be issued. The new directive, however, may itself be in turn distorted in the process of transmission and may lead to an overcorrection of the errors resulting from the earlier directive. As a result, there may be a deviation in the opposite direction which now again needs to be corrected.

These problems may produce "secondary" waves around the "primary" waves outlined earlier in the section on "The Cyclical Process." Needless to say, none of these cyclical effects work themselves out simultaneously. Thus it takes time for the effects of the harvest cycle to permeate throughout the system. Similarly, changes in policies are implemented not instantaneously but over a period of time, so that the impact of new policies on the economy may also be more or less delayed. The same, of course, holds for the bureaucratic cycle. Therefore, these different cycles are likely to intersect and their effects may be expected to operate with lags.

In terms of the model presented in the preceding sections, the policy and harvest cycles reinforce each other. Whether the distortion-correction-distortion oscillations of the "secondary" waves would tend to reinforce or dampen the "primary" waves cannot be determined since the bureaucratic-error cycle does not constitute an integral part of our model. It was introduced here as an element which could modify the model, but one that could not be taken into account since it is not yet clearly enough understood.

### The Empirical Evidence

#### The Statistical Indicators

*The Character of the Statistical Series.* In the preceding sections I have advanced certain reasons as to why one might expect to find cyclical fluctuations in rates of economic progress and expansion in Communist China. In this section I will attempt to test this proposition in terms of certain statistical indicators of levels and rates of change in economic activity between 1949 and 1965.

A host of statistical complications stand in the way of testing these hypotheses thoroughly and rigorously. Communist China has been enshrouded in a virtual statistical blackout since 1960. Prior to 1960 many of the official data are poor and of limited reliability. Some of the statistical indicators are better than others and, similarly, the quality of the data is better for some periods than for others.[19] Furthermore, in order to test more accurately the presence of economic fluctuations and the relationships and behavior of different economic sectors and different economic components during the cycle, we would really need quarterly data. With two harvests in China, and the major one in the fall, quarterly data could give us a much more precise view of the timing of the fluctuations and their duration. Also, such data would enable us to pinpoint better the turning points and to measure the leads and lags in the relations between the different sectors and components. Most particularly, it would give us a better idea of the lag with which the quality of the harvest impacts on the various non-agricultural sectors of the economy. As it is, we have to be satisfied with annual data.

In spite of these statistical shortcomings, the data in table 1 are based on official series for several reasons. Many of the independent estimates —due to the assumptions used in their derivation and due to the methods on which they are based—do not lend themselves readily for short-run analysis. This applies particularly to the national income and agricultural output estimates of T. C. Liu and K. C. Yeh. They assume a stable per capita consumption of foodstuffs for 1952 to 1957 and this assumption is a critical building block in their agricultural product estimate. Therefore this estimate by definition cannot take account of year-to-year harvest fluctuations. For a number of series and components we do not have as yet independent estimates. Finally, the official data even with all of their shortcomings may serve our purposes reasonably well. To test short-run changes in rates of economic growth, the indicated absolute levels and absolute values are of less importance than the rates of change. The official data undoubtedly contain an upward bias due to statistical improvements over time and also due to changes in coverage over time. These problems are probably less serious for the period after 1955 than before that date. However this may be,

---

[19] For detailed discussions of China's statistical system, its strengths and weaknesses, see Choh-ming Li, *The Statistical System of Communist China* (Berkeley: University of California Press, 1963); T. C. Liu and K. C. Yeh, *The Economy of the Chinese Mainland* (Princeton, N.J.: Princeton University Press, 1965) and Alexander Eckstein, *Communist China's Economic Growth and Foreign Trade*, Appendix A.

TABLE 1

SELECTED ECONOMIC INDICATORS, YEAR-TO-YEAR PERCENTAGE CHANGES, 1949–59

| Year | Grain Production Tonnage (1) | Gross Value of Agricultural Production (2) | Gross Industrial Production Value (3) | Railroad Freight Turnover Tonnage (4) | Total Value of Retail Sales (5) | Economic Construction Outlays (6) | Total State Investment Outlays (7) | National Income (8) | Export Value (9) | Import Value (10) | Total Trade Values (11) |
|---|---|---|---|---|---|---|---|---|---|---|---|
| 1949–50 | 15.0 | 17.7 | 36.3 | 78.6 | n.a. | n.a. | n.a. | 18.6 | n.a. | n.a. | n.a. |
| 1950–51 | 8.0 | 9.3 | 37.8 | 11.0 | 37.3 | 101.1 | 108.0 | 17.0 | 25.0 | 89.8 | 56.6 |
| 1951–52 | 14.0 | 15.8 | 30.2 | 19.2 | 18.1 | 117.3 | 85.5 | 22.3 | 12.9 | −8.4 | −0.3 |
| 1952–53 | 1.6 | 3.0 | 30.2 | 22.0 | 25.5 | 13.3 | 83.4 | 14.0 | 19.2 | 24.3 | 21.7 |
| 1953–54 | 2.1 | 3.4 | 16.2 | 19.5 | 9.5 | 42.8 | 13.3 | 5.7 | 7.7 | 13.8 | 10.8 |
| 1954–55 | 9.0 | 7.5 | 5.6 | 0.4 | 2.9 | 11.3 | 2.5 | 6.5 | 20.1 | 4.8 | 12.0 |
| 1955–56 | 4.4 | 5.0 | 28.2 | 26.9 | 17.5 | 15.6 | 60.0 | 14.0 | 19.1 | 10.9 | 48.9 |
| 1956–57 | 1.3 | 3.4 | 11.4 | 11.4 | 2.8 | −6.3 | −6.7 | 4.6 | 0.1 | −5.1 | −2.4 |
| 1957–58 | 10.7 | 25.0 | 67.9 | 39.0 | 15.5 | 76.2 | 93.0 | 34.0 | 18.3 | 34.0 | 25.6 |
| 1958–59 | −16.7 | .... | 40.0 | .... | 16.4 | 22.4 | 18.7 | 22.0 | 16.2 | 7.9 | 12.0 |

SOURCES: Year-to-year percentage changes calculated by the author. Except for 1958 and 1959 grain production figures, all data in columns 1–10 are based on official series; they were obtained from: Dwight Perkins, *Market Control and Planning in Communist China* (Cambridge, Mass.: Harvard University Press, 1966); T. C. Liu and K. C. Yeh, *The Economy of the Chinese Mainland* (Princeton, N.J.: Princeton University Press, 1965); A. Eckstein, *Communist China's Economic Growth and Foreign Trade* (New York: McGraw-Hill, 1966); State Statistical Bureau, *Ten Great Years* (Peking: Foreign Languages Press, 1960). Foreign trade data are based on A. Eckstein, *Communist China's Economic Growth and Foreign Trade* and on *Communist China's Balance of Payments 1950–1965*, CIA/RR ER 66-17, August, 1967; 1958 and 1959 grain production figures obtained from E. F. Jones, "The Emerging Pattern of China's Economic Revolution," in *An Economic Profile of Mainland China* (Washington, D.C.: Joint Economic Committee of Congress, 1967) 1:93.

for purposes of a crude and preliminary statistical test, these data may serve reasonably well, inasmuch as they undoubtedly reflect the actual direction of change and reflect acceleration and deceleration in annual rates of change. This probably is the case even though the particular annual percentage changes may be overstated. None of these observations applies to the three trade series, since these are derived independently for the whole period, 1950–65, on the basis of trading partner statistics. Since publication of official statistical series virtually ceased

TABLE 2

SELECTED ECONOMIC INDICATORS, YEAR-TO-YEAR PERCENTAGE
CHANGES, 1959–65

| Year | Grain Production Tonnage (1) | Industrial Production Index (2) | Value Added by all Modern Sectors except Government (3) | Net Domestic Product (4) | Net Domestic Product Adjusted (5) | Export Value (6) | Import Value (7) | Total Trade Values (8) |
|---|---|---|---|---|---|---|---|---|
| 1959–60 | −5.9 | + 3.8 | −11.3 | −8.1 | −8.2 | − 9.5 | − 5.0 | − 7.3 |
| 1960–61 | +6.2 | −34.0 | − 8.2 | −3.9 | −1.2 | −21.9 | −26.1 | −23.9 |
| 1961–62 | +5.8 | −12.0 | − 7.6 | +2.0 | +2.6 | + 1.6 | −19.6 | − 8.4 |
| 1962–63 | +2.8 | +10.1 | + 8.2 | +4.3 | +5.0 | + 2.0 | + 4.9 | + 3.0 |
| 1963–64 | +5.4 | +11.7 | +10.2 | +6.2 | +6.5 | +11.2 | +22.1 | +15.9 |
| 1964–65 | 0.0 | + 9.4 | + 8.2 | +3.7 | +5.0 | +20.2 | +21.2 | +21.2 |

SOURCES: Calculated by the author based on the following: col. 1: E. F. Jones, "The Emerging Pattern of China's Economic Revolution," in *An Economic Profile of Mainland China* (Washington, D.C.: Joint Economic Committee of Congress, 1967) 1:93; col. 2: R. M. Field, "Chinese Communist Industrial Production," Table 1, in *An Economic Profile of Mainland China;* cols. 3 and 4: T. C. Liu, "Quantitative Trends in the Economy of the Chinese Mainland, 1952–65," Table 24, in *Economic Trends in Communist China;* col. 5: This is based on T. C. Liu's estimate as adjusted by the author. The difference revolves around the agricultural estimates. Liu's are based on a grain series presented by R. F. Emery in an article on "Recent Economic Development in Communist China," *Asian Survey* (June, 1966), p. 303. Mine are based on a series developed by O. L. Dowson and published by E. F. Jones in "The Emerging Pattern of China's Economic Revolution." Foreign trade data (cols. 6 and 7) from sources cited in table 1.

in 1959 and 1960, we had to rely on a different set of indicators for the 1960–65 period. These are given in table 2. They are necessarily very tentative and conjectural estimates based on fragmentary data. However, they probably reflect reasonably well the direction of change year by year, and they are consistent with a host of qualitative indicators culled from the Chinese press, official Chinese publications, and official statements.

*The Trend of Economic Activity, 1949–65.* The Chinese mainland economy was carried forward by an unusually strong momentum between 1949 and 1959. During the early part of the period, this momentum was reinforced by a strong recovery trend and by a number of once-for-all changes in the economy and the society. The reunification of China under a strong and highly centralized polity, the introduction of law and order, and the restoration of nationwide transport and distribution were factors which in and of themselves would have led to rapid expansion even without additional investment. Over and above this, however, a host of institutional changes made possible significant increases in the rate of capital accumulation and thus an acceleration in the rate of expansion for the period of the fifties as a whole. In effect, the decade between 1949 and 1959 was characterized by a continuous and strong upward trend which was broken by the acute and sharp economic crisis of 1960–62. This crisis not only slowed down the rate of economic growth, but resulted in an actual absolute decline in the levels of economic activity—and a sharp decline at that. As a result, this crisis had many of the attributes of a classical-type great depression, with considerable underutilization of plant capacity and large-scale industrial unemployment. Since 1962 we have witnessed a continuing and steady economic recovery, as a result of which by 1965 agricultural production may have more or less approximated 1958 (the previous peak) levels, while total national product probably exceeded the former peak levels of 1958–59. Therefore, in a sense the recovery may be considered to have been more or less completed by 1965.

*Evidence of Cyclical Fluctuations.* The data presented in tables 1 and 2 and figures 1, 2, 3, and 4, strongly suggest the presence of cyclical fluctuations in rates of growth and economic expansion since the Communists came to power in 1949. These data seem to indicate the presence of four to five short cycles.

The first three of these occurred before 1959 and were conditioned by three very good harvests, one in 1952, another in 1955, and a third in 1958. Each of these was then reflected in an accelerated rate of expansion in total retail sales, investment outlays and total budgetary outlays on the economy, rates of growth in industrial production, and national income. These cycles seem to have been of two to three years duration. However, several qualifications are in order. The first cycle, peaking in the early fifties, is quite blurred because it is still overwhelmed by the strong recovery trend from the very low levels of economic activity in 1949 and 1950. It is also blurred by the very marked institutional transformation of the economy resulting from socialization of the non-agricultural sectors and broadening of the scope of the government budget, both of which are clearly reflected in the very high

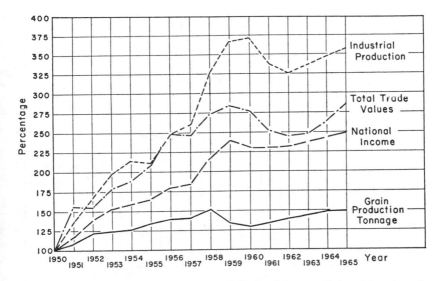

FIG. 1.—Cumulative Percentage Change of National Income, Industrial and Grain Production, and Total Trade Values

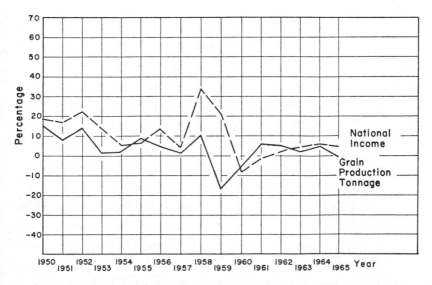

FIG. 2.—Yearly Percentage Change, National Income and Grain Production

FIG. 3.—Yearly Percentage Change, Industrial and Grain Production

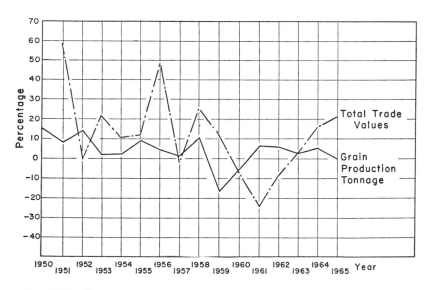

FIG. 4.—Yearly Percentage Change, Grain Production and Total Trade Values

rates of growth in economic construction and total state investment outlays for the early years. The recovery element similarly shows up in the very high rates of expansion in industrial production. This strong recovery trend probably also accounts for the fact that in 1952 acceleration in the rate of national income growth shows up in the same year as acceleration in the rate of growth in agricultural production.

On the other hand, following the good 1955 harvest, all of the non-agricultural indicators show a marked acceleration and peaking with a one year delay. However, in 1958 these same indicators show an acceleration at the same time as the harvest. The absence of a one year lag in this case can be explained by certain special factors. Mass labor mobilization and accumulation measures were beginning to be stepped up in late 1957 and early 1958. However, the pace of mobilization was quickened after the exceptionally favorable summer harvest of 1958. In this case, the autonomous force of the policy cycle was so strong that the harvest almost played a secondary role. Therefore, the evidence for the first decade seems to suggest the presence of cyclical fluctuations which in some cases show up in the non-agricultural sectors with a one year lag following a good or bad harvest, while in some other cases, due

---

NOTES FOR FIGURES 1, 2, 3, AND 4: The grain production and total trade series are continuous and comparable for the periods preceding and following the Great Leap. Therefore, the series as presented in tables 1 and 2 could be used for graphing. The same, however, cannot be said of industrial production and national income.

For the industrial production series Chao's and Field's indices were combined (Chao Kang, "Policies and Performance in Industry," in *Economic Trends in Communist China*, ed. Alexander Eckstein, Walter Galenson, and T. C. Liu [Chicago: Aldine Publishing Co., 1968], and R. M. Field, "Chinese Communist Industrial Production.") Both of these are partially value-added indices. Since they are not methodologically fully comparable, the relevant curve in fig. 1 is broken for the period since 1959, that is, the period for which the Field series were used.

For the national product series, Hollister's data were used for the period up to 1957 (W. W. Hollister, *China's Gross National Product and Social Account, 1950–57*, [Glencoe, Ill.: Free Press, 1958]), and Liu's estimates ("Quantitative Trends in the Economy of the Chinese Mainland, 1952–1965," in *Economic Trends in Communist China*, table 24) as adjusted by the author for the years beginning in 1958 (see col. 5, table 2). The two sets of estimates are not strictly comparable. Hollister's is for gross national product, while Liu's is for net domestic product. Otherwise, too, the two differ in their estimating methods and approach. We could not use the Liu series throughout, because for the 1952–57 period their derivation is crucially dependent on the assumption that food consumption per capita was stable year by year. Hollister's estimate suffers from other methodological flaws. Therefore, the linking of these series represents at best an unsatisfactory expedient. These flaws undoubtedly affect the amplitude of the annual rates of change. However, there is very little doubt that even if these methodological shortcomings were obviated, the shape and character of the national product curve in fig. 1 would not be markedly altered.

to special policy, trend, or random factors, they appear at the same time as the harvest.

In general terms then it would seem that, looked at from the standpoint of the agricultural sector, the first upswing took place between 1949 and 1952 with the upper turning point coming in 1952. The downswing phase then lasted until 1955 when there is a new upswing and an upper turning point, with the next downswing in 1956 and 1957 and the following upswing in 1958. Seen from the vantage point of national income the upper turning points came in 1952, 1956 and 1958. The latter two years were also upper turning points for all of the other sectors.

The harvest impact also affected quite clearly exports and imports, with a one year delay following the good 1952 harvest, but without any delay in 1958. In the case of the 1955 harvest the impact on exports seems to have occurred the same year, while imports were only affected the following year. Of course the relationship between exports and agricultural output is quite direct, while that between agricultural output and imports is only indirect. Given the character of China's export markets, exports may be considered largely a function of supply availabilities, while imports are a function of domestic demand. To the extent that a favorable harvest accelerates rates of growth in the rest of the economy, this expansion in the non-agricultural sectors then tends to lead to a rise in import demand, and this mechanism seems to have been operative in 1953, 1956, and 1958.

The rate of economic growth began to decline again after 1958, but in this case a downswing which started as a decline in the pace of development was converted into a sharp absolute level decline. The role of Mao's vision and its concrete policy concomitants in producing economic fluctuations came most clearly to the fore during this fourth cycle. It was at this time, during the Great Leap of 1958–59, that these policies were pushed to their extreme and achieved full crystallization. This did indeed lead to a marked acceleration in the rate of economic growth, but at the cost of being self-destructive. It was self-destructive in several senses, but most particularly in that the Great Leap policies played a very crucial role in sharply reducing the level of agricultural output beginning in 1959 and then again in 1960. This marked downturn in the agricultural sector spread throughout the rest of the economy with a one- to two-year lag. Thus, industrial production turned down sharply in 1961 and again in 1962. The output of all modern sectors (modern industry, trade, transport, and banking) was beginning to be markedly curtailed in 1960 and the same applies to total domestic product and to foreign trade. In effect, industrial production was slowed down one year following a poor harvest, but was still expanding to some extent, while all of the other non-agricultural sectors experienced a level decline within a year after the poor harvest and continued to do so for one or two more years.

The sharp decline in agricultural output, and in levels of economic activity in general, forced a major re-assessment in planning priorities and in general economic policies. As a result, beginning in 1961 agricultural policies were markedly revised. The communes were decentralized with the production team gradually re-acquiring its responsibilities as the basic accounting and resource allocation unit. Private plots were re-instituted and were given much greater scope. Free rural markets were re-instituted; price terms of trade for agriculture were improved, and this sector was accorded a significantly higher investment priority. This, in turn, made possible a gradual improvement in the agricultural situation, with the 1962 harvest initiating the recovery from the crisis. The agricultural improvement was then reflected in a one year lag in all of the other sectors of the economy as shown by the indicators in table 2.

The downswing phase of this fourth cycle was extended over a period of about three years, 1959 to 1962, thus lasting longer than any of the previous recessions. This was but another symptom of a deep depression, of an acute economic crisis, rather than just a slowdown in the rate of growth. The lower turning point of this crisis can be dated as about the last quarter of 1962, with the upswing getting under way in 1963. The upper turning point may possibly be placed in 1964, in which case the mainland Chinese economy might now be in the throes of a fifth cycle. On the other hand, it is possible that as of this writing (mid-1967) the economy is still in the upswing following the crisis and that the upper turning point is yet to come.

## The Policy Cycle

In the preceding section, I tried to test the presence of harvest fluctuations and to show how these were related to cyclical fluctuations in the rest of the economy. The presence of short-run fluctuations seems to be fairly clearly borne out by the data in the tables and in the figures. Prior to 1952, as noted earlier, the economic scene was dominated by a marked institutional transformation and by a rapid recovery trend. On the other hand, since 1962 the economy has once more been in the process of recovery from a deep-seated crisis.

Against this background, I would now like to trace briefly the ebb

and flow of economic policies and most particularly agricultural policies in Communist China. I will try to explore whether a distinct policy
cycle can be detected and then functionally related to the behavior of
the economic indicators presented in the preceding section. Given limitations of time and space in this paper, these policy fluctuations can be
presented only in an outline fashion and therefore only in a tentative
and preliminary way.

The annual rate of growth of investment outlays probably provides
us with a fairly sensitive index of the Chinese Communist regime's
short-run economic policy direction, ambitions, commitments, targets,
and expectations. The investment series in table 1 show a sharp percentage rise in 1953, 1956, and 1958. Correspondingly they indicate a
marked decline in 1954 and 1955, in 1957—when the decline was not
only relative but absolute as well—and then again in 1959. Unfortunately for the period since 1960, we have no reliable investment data
and therefore cannot use this index. In each case, the sharp upturn in
investment followed a good harvest, except in 1958 when it accompanied
or, in a sense, even anticipated such a harvest. In 1958 there was a
bumper summer crop; this was coupled with the expectation of a record
autumn harvest which then encouraged policy-makers to forge ahead
with increasing rates of investment even without waiting for the actual
production results. On the other hand, mediocre harvests were followed
by relative, and in the 1957 case by absolute, cutbacks in investment.
The year 1959 represents an exception to this rule, inasmuch as the
decline in the rate of growth of investment accompanied, rather than
followed, a mediocre crop. This was in part due to the record rise in
investment in the preceding year, which would have made an equal or
higher rise in the following year as well most difficult, if not impossible.

Good harvests tend to stimulate investment, of course, not only by
setting up strong inducements for accelerating the rate of economic
progress, of rising optimism and a more ambitious outlook, but also by
improving the capabilities of the economic system to support higher
levels of investment. Undoubtedly both of these elements were important in accounting for the prevailing pattern of investment behavior
in China.

Quite apart from the rhythm of harvest-induced investment cycles,
there is very little doubt that each good crop signaled the beginning of
a new economic policy phase, except for the initial land-reform phase
which was launched as soon as Chinese Communist authority was established in particular areas. Thus, after the good 1952 harvest, not only
is investment stepped up, but the first Five Year Plan is launched in

1953, and compulsory grain-purchase quotas are introduced late that year. After 1955 we witness a sharp acceleration in the collectivization drive, a similar acceleration in the socialization of trade and the remnants of private enterprise, the launching of a very ambitious twelve-year agricultural plan in January, 1956, a step-up in investment in 1956, and a very significant rise in the production targets for that year. Similarly, after the bumper summer harvest of 1958, communization is officially launched, and the full crystallization of Great Leap measures and policies unfolds.

The cyclical character of these economic policies is particularly pronounced since 1955 and will therefore be traced in somewhat greater detail. Under the impact of the collectivization and socialization campaigns of 1955–56, the private plots in agriculture began to be encroached upon. As a result, while official regulations provided that these private plots could occupy a maximum of 5 per cent of the arable land in a village, in fact on the average they encompassed a considerably smaller land area.[20] In some areas, private plots were abolished altogether during the collectivization campaign. At the same time trees, implements, and livestock (including poultry) were forcibly collectivized, in some cases without any compensation or at low prices. Moreover, the use of labor on private plots was restricted. The collectivization campaign also led to marked centralization in agricultural planning, with the assumption of resource allocative powers by the collective itself rather than by the production brigades or teams. This was coupled with the setting of very high agricultural production targets to be fulfilled in too little time with too few means. It was also accompanied by the closing of rural fairs and markets.

The combination of these measures naturally had negative consequences for agricultural production. They were reflected in large-scale slaughter of livestock (in part also due to fodder shortages), in a general decline in private plot production, a fall in the output and sales of subsidiary products, such as vegetables, fruit, and meat, and a concomitant decline in farm-household income, particularly cash income. The decline in livestock numbers then led to a fall in the production of organic fertilizer and to a reduction in draft animal numbers. Both of these developments had a negative effect on the collectivized sector of agriculture as well, with shortages of draft animals and organic fertilizer exercising a depressing effect on grain production.

These consequences were clearly visible by the time of the Eighth

[20] Walker, *Planning in Chinese Agriculture,* p. 62.

Chinese Communist Party Congress in September, 1956. They were, of course, accentuated by a mediocre 1956 harvest. It is not surprising, therefore, to see that the Eighth Congress marked the beginning of a relatively liberal phase in economic policy. In agriculture this involved improving the incentives for the collectivized sector, through gradual decentralization of allocative responsibilities within the collective, through better prices for pigs and industrial crops, and through a system of incomes and rewards which were more closely linked to production.[21] The collectives were also ordered to pay a fair price for the fertilizer produced on the private plot. Free markets were re-opened in September, 1956,[22] and cadres in the collectives were directed to implement faithfully the regulations permitting the operation of the private plots. These liberalizing tendencies in agriculture were strongly reinforced by the statement of Teng Tzu-hui (Director of the Central Committee's Rural Work Department) in May, 1957, confirming and elaborating on these policies, calling for the return of livestock to the private plots, and raising the permissible limit for them to 10 per cent of the arable land per capita in a village. This new limit was then given the sanction of an official directive by the standing committee of the National People's Congress in June, 1957.[23]

These policies did lead then to a gradual revival of subsidiary food production and particularly to a rapid increase in hog production in 1957. However, the possible benefits flowing from this revival were seriously marred from the regime's point of view for two reasons: on the one hand, lack of substantial progress in the collectivized sector as reflected in another mediocre grain harvest in 1957, and, on the other hand, the revival of "capitalist" forces and tendencies in the countryside. The latter was reflected in a fairly rapid erosion of certain distinguishing features of the collectives, such erosion being directly traceable to the liberalization policies. From the regime's point of view, the ad-

[21] See, for instance, the directive of September 12, 1956, "On Strengthening the Building of Organization and Control over Production in the Cooperatives," *Hsin Hua pan-yüeh-k'an* (hereafter cited as *HHPYK*) 93, no. 19 (1956): 53–59.

[22] See Chou En-lai's "Report on the Second Five Year Plan for the Development of the National Economy," *HHPYK*, 94, no. 20 (1956): 35–49.

[23] Teng Tzu-hui, "On Internal Contradictions of Cooperatives and Democratic Management," *HHPYK*, 109, no. 11 (1957): 94–100, and Standing Committee of the NPC, "Decision on Increasing Members' Retained Plot in Cooperatives," June 25, 1957, *HHPYK*, 112, no. 14 (1957): 153.

vantages of collectivization were considered to be economies of scale, collectivized ownership of land so that no rent had to be paid to members, collectivized ownership of draft animals, thus providing important control over one of the strategic inputs in agriculture, and the possibility of increasing the rate of investment.

In the face of these corrosive tendencies, the government closed the free market once more in August, 1957.[24] Thereafter, the private sector began to be gradually curtailed. Later in the year additional measures were adopted which signaled the radicalization of economic policies all along the line. They gradually fed into the Great Leap concepts and measures and most particularly the communes, which swallowed up the private plots altogether. This was followed by the collectivization of all livestock, a high degree of centralization of authority in communes, centralized labor allocation, and a further separation of work from reward as evidenced by the introduction of the part wage, part supply system. The high degree of centralization then led to numerous technical blunders in irrigation and reclamation projects and to a host of planning errors. One of the consequences of centralized labor allocation was marked labor shortages in crop and livestock production. These measures, aggravated by a whole host of other dysfunctional policies, then produced a disastrous effect on farm output in 1959, 1960, and 1961. However, the shape, proportions, and consequences of the Great Leap are too well known by now to detain us further here.[25]

Signs of serious food and raw material supply difficulties became increasingly visible in 1959 without yet leading to a full recognition of crisis by the regime. The information and statistical gap resulting from the virtual dismemberment of the State Statistical Bureau obscured the full dimensions of the crisis so that the response in terms of policy shifts came more slowly than was the case in earlier agricultural downturns. However, in response to growing food shortages, rural markets were re-opened in September, 1959. By the summer of 1960, the regime began to encourage the restoration of small private plots. By 1961, the

[24] State Council Decision "On Not Allowing Commodities Subject to State Planned Purchase and Planned Supply and Unified Purchase Along with Other Commodities to Enter the Free Market" issued August 9, 1957, *HHPYK*, 116, no. 18 (1957): 207–8.

[25] See Alexander Eckstein, *Communist China's Economic Growth and Foreign Trade,* chaps. 2 and 3. See also P. P. Jones and T. T. Poleman, "Communes and the Agricultural Crises in China," *Stanford Research Institute Studies,* 3, no 1 (February, 1962): 4.

decentralization process in the commune had gone a long way, with production brigades being designated as basic ownership units. By early 1962, this was carried a step further with the production team becoming the basic ownership and allocative unit. At the same time, hog raising was once more restored largely to the private plots. Gradually, all vestiges of the part wage, part supply system had disappeared to be replaced by the pre-commune system of rewards based on the quantity and quality of labor input.[26] Therefore, by 1962 the system of agricultural organization, resource allocation, and incentives prevailing in early 1957 was restored in fact, even if not in name.

In a sense, this whole process of policy reversal and retreat, which started in late 1959, was most clearly epitomized by the marked change in planning priorities, probably decided upon at the Ninth Plenum of the Central Committee in January, 1961, and made public at the May, 1961 session of the National People's Congress. In keeping with these decisions, agriculture seems to have been assigned highest priority. The combination of new policies and measures was then reflected in gradual recovery of agricultural production beginning in 1962, affecting both grain and the output of subsidiary products. However, the price of this recovery was the kind of erosion of the collectivized sector that had occurred before during periods of liberalization. Most particularly in a number of areas "individual farming" began to rear its ugly head. Not too infrequently communes, through the production teams, would subcontract specific production tasks to individual farm households. For instance, in some cases the cultivation of dry lands would be assigned to individual farm households with an obligation to deliver certain quotas to the production team. In other cases the early ripening crop may be assigned to the farm household.[27] To counteract and curb the spread of these "capitalist tendencies," the "socialist education campaign" was launched once more in the countryside, first on a more modest basis in 1963 and then, after the relatively good 1964 harvest,

[26] See *Jen-min jih-pao* editorial, "The Three Level Ownership System with the Production Brigade as the Basic Level Is the Basic System for People's Communes at the Present Stage," *Jen-min jih-pao*, December 21, 1960, and *Jen-min jih-pao*, editorial, "Conscientiously Implement Policies of Rural People's Communes," *Jen-min jih-pao*, April 2, 1961, and the New Year's editorial in *Jen-min jih-pao*, January 1, 1962.

[27] This is brought out in an as yet unpublished paper by Peter Chen based on an analysis of documents captured during a Nationalist raid on Lien Chiang *hsien* in Fukien Province.

pursued with much greater vigor and on a national scale. However, up to 1965 this had not yet resulted in a reversal of rural policies.

In terms of the theoretical framework outlined in this paper, we are dealing with two separate but closely inter-related movements—a policy cycle and a harvest cycle. However, if and when the forces propelling the policy cycle are particularly strong, they can overwhelm the influence of harvest fluctuations. This happened to some extent in late 1957 and early 1958, when radicalization in economic policy followed a mediocre and preceded a bumper harvest.

Correspondingly one would not expect a reversal of agricultural policies in the sixties until there is again a bumper harvest, that is, one that provides higher than 1957 levels of per capita grain output, unless the policy cycle moves again with such force as to swamp the effects flowing from changes in farm production. Thus the Cultural Revolution could, for instance, lead to a radicalization in economic policy without the benefit of a spectacular harvest.

## Concluding Comments

At the outset I suggested that the cyclical fluctuations in Communist China's economic policy and in the rates of economic expansion on the mainland could be viewed as a function of a deep-seated conflict between the Maoist vision and the realities of the country's economic and technical backwardness. The realities of this backwardness could not be changed very rapidly even under the most optimistic assumptions. Thus it will necessarily take China a long time to modernize its agriculture and to attain high levels of industrialization. But what about the Maoist vision? Will it survive Mao? Assuming no radical systemic change emanating from the Cultural Revolution, Mao may be expected to leave a fairly durable legacy in terms of world outlook, values, and attitudes. Nevertheless, if the successors should turn out to be in some sense "pragmatists," one would expect an alleviation in the cyclical character of economic policy. The successors might draw different lessons from the recent past than Mao did; they could conclude that the agricultural failures were not just failures in implementation by the cadres but also failures in policy formulation and conception. They might also be less optimistic concerning the possibilities of remolding Chinese man to approximate the ideal Communist model than Mao was. However, even under these presuppositions, it is not too likely that the policy cycles will disappear altogether since they are deeply rooted in the very structure of the Chinese Communist decision-making and value system.

# Comments by Peter Schran

I have enjoyed reading Alexander Eckstein's paper on "Economic Fluctuations in Communist China's Domestic Development," and I find it most challenging. To give you my conclusions in advance, I basically agree with Eckstein's premises and their generic implications. But I infer that his cycle theory requires a very limiting specification of these implications. Furthermore, the empirical evidence leads me to a less cyclical interpretation of Chinese Communist policies.

## Eckstein's Theory

Eckstein proceeds from the observation that whereas in Marxist as well as in non-Marxist theory socialist systems are free of economic fluctuations, they in fact have been afflicted with them. The apparent "contradiction" between theory and practice can be resolved on Marxist as well as on non-Marxist premises.

In non-Marxist terms, a centrally administered economy eliminates economic fluctuations by internalizing variables which are external to the administrative processes in a market economy. Eckstein emphasizes, and I concur, that the Chinese Communists have not been able to internalize in particular the motivation of the peasantry and the whims of nature. By definition, they also could not internalize foreign economic events. Their inability to control especially the former two variables accounts for fluctuations.

In Marxist terms, such a state of control of man over man and over nature is to be achieved under Communism, at the end of a process of development when man has mastered all laws of nature and society. It cannot be realized until then, and especially not in a backward economy where transition to socialism begins prematurely by classical Marxist standards for Leninist-Maoist reasons. Marxist doctrine, too, implies in particular the limited control of the Chinese Communists over the consciousness of the peasants and the fortunes of nature.

In addition, however, Marxism holds that man can and must progress toward the state of complete control. As an ideology, it engenders activism in pursuit of the objective, and it also entails the expectation of gradual progress in this direction. Such progress is to be induced not only by socialization and technical modernization but also by indoctrination and training. The presumptively consequent changes in the social and technical consciousness of the peasantry must manifest themselves also in diminishing fluctuation.

The inference of decreasing fluctuation conflicts with the observation of increasing fluctuation during the late fifties and the early sixties, and this conflict has to be resolved. The Chinese Communists at first explained it with references to variations in the magnitude of change in natural fortunes, and they still emphasize the occurrence of unprecedented natural disasters during the early sixties. In addition, they have attributed it to the uncomradely behavior of the Soviets, and they continue to blame them as well.

Subsequently, however, the Chinese Communists also recognized errors of their own. In identifying these errors, they admitted originally to unconscious deviations from doctrine, primarily by lower ranking cadres. It was their miscalculation of natural and social circumstances and their misapplication of Maoist doctrine which contributed to the disaster. The validity of Maoist doctrine did not become a public issue until recently, when a new leap appeared to be in the making. The Maoists are currently struggling to root out heresy.

A denial of the validity of Maoism is fundamental to Eckstein's cycle theory. He hypothesizes that the Chinese Communists cannot reconstruct the Chinese peasantry ideologically. He infers that this inability implies the failure of any Communist effort to continuously increase production and accumulation in agriculture and the transfer of surplus from agriculture merely by means of the gradual socialization of agriculture and by the continuous indoctrination of the peasantry. I can go along with this argument.

In addition, Eckstein asserts that improvements in the technical possibilities and in the technological abilities of the peasantry cannot have been great. I can accept this assertion, too. But I would welcome in its context an explicit assessment of the agricultural development program of 1956. This program promised substantial returns to behavior in accordance with Mao's vision of man. Such returns could offset the adverse incentive effects of social change, and the instrumental relationship of social change to the program is evident.

I find it interesting to note in this connection that most of the technical planks of the program and notably the agrotechnical ones are practically identical with the measures which John Lossing Buck recommended first in his *Chinese Farm Economy* and again in his *Land Utilization in China*.[1] Moreover, the returns which Buck expected are similarly great. However, Buck warned against collectivization and crash programs, and he also called for the extensive use of modern technical experts and scientific procedures.

In view of these similarities and differences, I find two elements of error which are really the two dimensions of bias in Maoist "humanism." Mao and his followers tend to overestimate the technological as well as the ideological adaptability and pliability of man. This bias causes them to manipulate unduly the social and technical environment of man. It also induces them to attribute, under conditions of uncertainty, unexpected success as well as unexpected failure to man, that is, to man's unexpectedly rapid or slow consciousness-formation.

The latter implication tends to strengthen Eckstein's cycle theory. But it also reduces it to a special case. Man may be credited with unexpected progress not only when the gains are greater but also when the losses are smaller than anticipated. Correspondingly, unexpectedly small gain as well as unexpectedly great loss may be related to man's unforeseen retardation. And the results may exceed or fail to meet uncertain expectations in any situation, that is, in favorable as well as in unfavorable natural circumstances.

The policy cycle which Eckstein hypothesizes thus requires in addition to a particular cycle of natural or man-made results, a particular cycle of Maoist conjectures. The latter must run counter to the former to the extent that expectations fall short of results during superior years and that they exceed them during inferior years. The policy cycle repeats itself so long as these conditions are met. And Maoist policies must vary differently in response to different relations between actual achievements and Maoist anticipations.

In Eckstein's case as well as in general, the fluctuations can be expected to subside *ceteris paribus* in response to increasing empirical certainty and to correspondingly decreasing Maoist ideological certainty on the part of the Chinese Communists. They can be expected to become more violent in response to the opposite developments. Maoist orthodoxy in agrarian policy thus appears in the same light as Maoist orthodoxy in other policy spheres.

---

[1] Cf. John Lossing Buck, *Chinese Farm Economy* (Chicago: University of Chicago Press, 1930), pp. 143–44; and *idem, Land Utilization in China* (New York: Council on Economic and Cultural Affairs, Inc., 1956), pp. 20–22.

## Empirical Evidence

I next turn to Eckstein's verification of his theory. As he sees it, agricultural development in China covers an initial recuperative phase (1949–51) which is statistical terra incognita, plus three three-year cycles (1952–54, 1955–57, 1958–60) which appear to become increasingly violent. The early sixties are clearly a new recuperative phase.

Table 1 shows that each of the three three-year cycles during the years 1952–60 began in a year of assertedly good natural fortunes. In each of these years, however, policy changes were also pronounced. The Five-anti Campaign raged in early 1952, and peasant membership in mutual aid teams as well as the scope of state trading increased notably during its course. The share of co-operator households in all peasant households pumped from 2 per cent during the 1954 season to 14.2 per cent during the 1955 season, and the share of socialist commerce grew substantially, too. Finally, the Great Leap Forward in agricultural production was initiated in 1958 long before the natural fortunes of the year could be ascertained. In each of these years, it was therefore possible to attribute success to policy as well as to nature.

Interestingly, table 1 suggests that the Chinese Communists recognized the impact of natural fortunes in 1952. Mutual-aid team membership stagnated from 1952 to 1953, and the share of state trading did not increase as greatly as before. The role of state trade was strengthened by the introduction of planned marketing of agricultural staples. But there is also the indication that the urban-rural terms of trade changed substantially in favor of the peasantry. It thus seems that the Chinese Communists attempted to increase sales of agricultural products relative to their production by more conventional methods in order to sustain the mounting industrialization drive. They assertedly achieved moderate increases in production, plus not so moderate increases in sales in the face of deteriorating natural fortunes.

In 1954, the Chinese communists revised these policies. They induced drastic increases in mutual-aid team membership and in the scope of state trading, while they kept the urban-rural terms of trade practically constant. By these measures, they allegedly achieved similar increases in production and in sales as in 1953, again under conditions of worsening natural fortunes. These positive results seemed to contain a lesson. Social change could be viewed as a practicable and less costly alternative to price change. And more gain from further social change could be anticipated, nature permitting.

The policy change in 1954 conflicts with Eckstein's hypotheses in

## TABLE 1

### Selected Agricultural Indicators, 1950–59

| Year | Natural Fortune (1) | Relative Share of Peasant Households Belonging to— | | | Relative Share of Retail Sales of— | | Urban-Rural Terms of Trade (7) | Relative Year-to-Year Increase in— | |
|---|---|---|---|---|---|---|---|---|---|
| | | Mutual Aid Teams (2) | Low-Level APC's (3) | High-Level APC's (4) | Socialist Commerce (5) | State-Capitalist + Cooperative Commerce (6) | | Agricultural Production (8) | Sales of Agricultural Products (9) |
| 1950 | ...... | 10.7 | ...... | ...... | 14.0 | 0.1 | 111.0 | 17.7 | ...... |
| 1951 | ...... | 19.2 | ...... | ...... | 24.4 | 0.1 | 102.1 | 9.4 | 9.7 |
| 1952 | good | 39.9 | 0.1 | ...... | 42.6 | 0.2 | 100.0 | 15.3 | 21.6 |
| 1953 | normal | 39.3 | 0.2 | ...... | 49.7 | 0.4 | 89.5 | 3.1 | 7.2 |
| 1954 | poor | 59.3 | 2.0 | ...... | 69.0 | 5.4 | 88.1 | 3.3 | 9.6 |
| 1955 | good | 50.7 | 14.2 | ...... | 67.6 | 14.6 | 89.6 | 7.7 | 3.1 |
| 1956 | poor | ...... | 8.5 | 87.8 | 68.3 | 27.5 | 86.1 | 4.9 | 0.4 |
| 1957 | poor | ...... | 2.0 | 96.0 | 65.7 | 31.6 | 83.0 | 3.5 | 5.0 |
| 1958 | good | ...... | ...... | (60) | ...... | ...... | 80.7 | 25.0 | 9.8 |
| 1959 | poor | ...... | ...... | ( 0) | ...... | ...... | 78.0 | 16.7 | 23.9 |

SOURCES: Col. 1, Various official statements; cols. 2, 3, and 4, *Ten Great Years* (Peking: Foreign Languages Press, 1960), p. 35, and *Report on the Fulfillment of the First Five-Year Plan* (Peking: T'ung-chi Press, 1959), p. 2; 1958 and 1959: personal estimates (100 minus commune member households); cols. 5 and 6, *Ten Great Years*, p. 40; col. 7, derived from *T'ung-chi kung-tso*, no. 17, 1957, pp. 4–5, *Ten Great Years*, p. 173, and Chao Kuo-chun, *Agrarian Policy of the Chinese Communist Party*, 1921–1959 (Asia Publishing House, 1960), p. 230; col. 8, gross value, 1949–57 at 1952 prices, 1957–59 at 1957 prices, *Ten Great Years*, p. 18, and *Chi-hua yü t'ung-chi*, no. 1, 1960, p. 1; col. 9, at 1952 prices, derived from *Ten Great Years*, p. 168, *Chi-hua yü t'ung-chi*, no. 1, 1960, p. 28, and col. 7, reference 1959, estimated on the assumption that the index of rural retail prices of industrial products remained constant from 1958 to 1959.

regard to cyclical behavior, and it therefore must be explained. Eckstein points to a one-year lag between changes in agricultural production and changes in industrial production plus disposal during the years 1952–57, and he notes that this lag disappears in 1958. I contrast in table 2, in addition, variations in industrial consumer goods production, in retail sales, and in exports of processed plus unprocessed agricultural products with variations in the supply of agricultural products

TABLE 2

YEAR-TO-YEAR PERCENTAGE CHANGES IN SELECTED
ECONOMIC INDICATORS, 1950–59

| YEAR | VALUE OF SALES OF AGRICULTURAL PRODUCTS (1) | GROSS VALUE OF INDUSTRIAL CONSUMER GOODS PRODUCTION (2) | VALUE OF TOTAL SOCIAL RETAIL SALES (3) | VALUE OF EXPORTS OF PRODUCTS OF AGRICULTURAL ORIGIN | | |
| | | | | Total (4) | Processed Products (5) | Unprocessed Products (6) |
|---|---|---|---|---|---|---|
| 1950 | .......... | 30.8 | .......... | .......... | | .......... |
| 1951 | 9.7 | 32.6 | 16.5 | 14.1 | 14.9 | 13.7 |
| 1952 | 21.6 | 23.8 | 18.2 | 6.7 | −19.5 | 21.8 |
| 1953 | 7.2 | 26.7 | 21.8 | 28.1 | 46.8 | 21.0 |
| 1954 | 9.6 | 14.2 | 7.1 | 7.0 | 23.1 | −0.05 |
| 1955 | 3.1 | −0.03 | 2.2 | 18.9 | 24.1 | 15.9 |
| 1956 | 0.4 | 19.8 | 17.5 | 12.6 | 25.2 | 4.9 |
| 1957 | 5.0 | 5.6 | 0.7 | −4.9 | −1.1 | −7.6 |
| 1958 | 9.8 | 33.7 | 15.9 | 26.9 | 47.1 | 11.0 |
| 1959 | 23.9 | 34.0 | 16.4 | .......... | | .......... |

SOURCES: Col. 1, at 1952 prices (cf. Table 1); col. 2, 1949–57 at 1952 prices, 1957–59 at 1957 prices, *Ten Great Years*, p. 89, and *Chi-hua yü t'ung-chi*, no. 1, 1960, p. 24; col. 3, at 1952 prices, derived from *Ten Great Years*, pp. 166, 172–73, and *Chi-hua yü t'ung-chi*, no. 1, 1960, p. 25; 1950: deflated by wholesale price index; 1959: undeflated; cols. 4, 5, and 6, at current prices, derived from *Asia Keizai Jumpo*, March 1, 1957, pp. 6–13, *Ten Great Years*, pp. 164, 175–76, and *Hsin Hua pan-yüeh k'an*, no. 16, 1957, pp. 90–94.

for such purposes. I find strong indications that the lag between supply and demand diminished rapidly from the beginning, and critically in 1954. Such indications suggest that the industrialization drive was hampered at once by input constraints. These could be reduced primarily by increases in agricultural production which the peasants would not consume. The experimentation with social and technical change in the unfavorable circumstances of 1954 is thus meaningful, and especially so in view of Chinese Communist predispositions.

Further changes were made from 1954 to 1955, and the development of production in 1955 could be interpreted as proof of the practicality of collectivization. On such a premise, there was cause for its acceleration. However, sales grew less than before as well as less than production did. And the proof was at issue among the Chinese Communists. Mao had to wage a campaign against "rightist conservatives" when he called in July, 1955, for a much more rapid collectivization of agriculture than the First Five Year Plan had envisaged. The propagation of the agricultural development program followed rather than preceded this event. But its contours are visible in previous experiments as well as in Mao's reasoning. By increasing and improving traditional peasant efforts and by realizing organizational economies of scale, great gains were to be made in production which not only would yield the increases in consumption to sustain these efforts but also would bring substantial increases in sales and in rural accumulation.

Table 1 shows that agriculture and trade were collectivized or socialized in 1956/57. And it indicates that in addition minor improvements in the urban-rural terms of trade were made. But it also reveals that these changes yielded results which must have been disappointing. Agricultural production allegedly continued to grow during 1956 and 1957 at rates which were comparable to those of 1953 and 1954. However, sales stagnated in 1956 during a year of *two steps forward,* and they increased very little relative to production in 1957 during the *one step back.*

As a consequence, table 2 suggests, and inventory data confirm, that during 1956 increases in industrial consumer goods production, in retail sales, and in exports of processed plus unprocessed agricultural products had to be sustained in large measure with reserves. The Chinese Communists must have decided to draw on reserves and thus to postpone a re-evaluation of the strategic situation in anticipation of commensurate gains in 1957. However, these gains failed to materialize. Part of the limited increase in the supply of agricultural products probably served to replenish reserves to some extent. As a result, retail sales stagnated while exports declined. The momentum of the industrialization drive was thus in greater danger than ever before.

The developments of 1955–57 tended to vindicate the position of the "rightist conservatives." But the Chinese Communists nevertheless decided to make the best of the situation. In the fall of 1957 the Central Committee concentrated on improving the co-operatives. It focused on peasant attitudes and cadre skills. To improve the former, it advocated indoctrination and the limitation of individual opportunities. To simplify cadre tasks, it called for a reduction of the size of co-operatives. And to improve their management, it publicized a much more detailed version of the agricultural development program. This revised program promised optimistic but not unprecedented returns. The 1958 plan, which was reported to the National People's Congress as late as February 3, 1958, exhibited the same progressive moderation and cautious optimism. The targets of both documents appeared to be in line with the 1956 draft of the Second Five Year Plan.

In order to call effectively for more than that, Mao and his followers had to argue first that the unexpected failure of the co-operatives was attributable to nature and to the cadres rather than to the peasants who allegedly were prepared to go ahead. They had to demonstrate in addition that these faults could be remedied immediately. Mao's solutions were the conquest of nature by a great leap forward and the conquest of cadres by the mass line. And he demonstrated the practicality of both by the unplanned origination first of the Leap and then of rural people's communes. In retrospect, it appears to be meaningful to compare these developments with the events which have led to Mao's proclamation of a Great Proletarian Cultural Revolution and to the formation of Red Guards.

Early indications and exaggerations of success seemed to prove Mao right and the planners wrong. There consequently appeared to be cause for the scrapping of all plans and for a continued leap forward in 1959. Then the magnitude of the exaggerations became evident. According to the revised official data, agricultural production increased greatly but much less than predicted in 1958, and it increased considerably once more in 1959. According to Western estimates, production increased less than claimed in 1958 and fell notably in 1959. Sales according to the Chinese Communists increased at the rate of 1954 in 1958 and at the rate of 1952 in 1959. If the latter claim and the Western production estimates were true, these two facts by themselves would account for much of the following debacle.

In response to such increases in supply, as well as due to the increasing dependence on inputs of non-agricultural origin, industrial consumer goods production assertedly increased greatly during both 1958 and 1959. Retail sales as well as exports increased less, and the difference between these changes and changes in production may be an indication of the degree of exaggeration rather than of stockpiling. As a result of undoubtedly substantial increases in industrial consumer goods production, however, the lag between supply and demand did not reappear.

The course of subsequent events is reasonably certain, but the magnitudes are still in question. Agricultural production declined in 1960, and it recuperated slowly during the years thereafter. Western estimates of the annual rates of change—which are very rough guesses—indicate that the fluctuations were comparatively weak. The Chinese Com-

munists have stated that the slow pace of recuperation and, by implication, the absence of major fluctuations in agricultural production were
attributable to continuously and at times "unprecedently" bad natural
fortunes. But they also have shown by their retrogressive actions that
they have related their problems as well to their policies of the late
fifties. And they have refrained from new visionary ventures until now,
probably for both reasons.

The effects of changes in agricultural production on the supply of
agricultural products, on industrial consumer goods production, and on
retail sales have to be guessed as well. The greater lag in the relation
between changes in agricultural production and changes in industrial
production during 1959–62 seems to be attributable to delayed adjustments in producer goods production. Industrial consumer goods production in all likelihood declined in 1960 and at least stagnated in 1962.
For lack of adequate stockpiles and carryovers, it must have continued
to fluctuate closely with the supply of agricultural products. The new
lag in the relation between industrial production and exports probably
reflects efforts to facilitate recuperation through increases in domestic
sales. The year 1964 thus tends to mark a new beginning, which is also
evident in the acceleration of the Socialist Education campaign.

## Conclusion

My summary of the coincidences of events suggests that the relation between natural change and policy change in agriculture was not as purely cyclical as Eckstein indicates. The three three-year periods 1952–54,
1955–57, and 1958–60 do not conform to one pattern. The intermediate
1955–57 cycle approximates most closely Eckstein's prototype. Social
progression was strongest in 1956, and retrogression set in in 1957. During the two other periods, policy change occurred prior to or simultaneously with the natural event rather than in response to it. Moreover, during the first cycle, social progression recurred during 1954. And
in the third period, retrogression began at the end of 1958 but accelerated very slowly.

In my view, these coincidences fall into a pattern of attempts to sustain and accelerate the process of China's industrialization. As such,
they add up to a unique and perhaps peculiar process of learning on the
part of the Chinese Communists. This process seems to be compatible
with Eckstein's basic theory, even though it transgresses the limits of
every short-term cycle and even though it extends through the new
recuperative phase. The Chinese Communists were predisposed toward

social change as a policy instrument. But not all of them were willing to follow Mao in his visionary venture in 1955, and apparently fewer were prepared to try it again on a more grandiose scale in 1958. The Great Proletarian Cultural Revolution appears to be the prelude to a third attempt. But the current events suggest that many more Chinese Communists have learned to beware of Mao's visions.

# Notes by Robert Dernberger:
# The Relationship between
# Foreign Trade, Innovation, and Economic
# Growth in Communist China

It would appear that foreign trade played a relatively minor role in Communist China's economic growth during the past seventeen years.[1] In 1953–57, the only period for which adequate statistics are available, total exports were only 6 per cent of national income, while budget receipts from foreign loans and credits were only 2 per cent of total budget receipts and only 12 per cent of total imports.[2] In view of the magnitude of the development effort on the mainland, and in comparison with other underdeveloped countries of comparable size (for instance, India), China's foreign trade and foreign loans and credits do appear rather small. On the other hand, as a percentage of national in-

[1] Professor Dernberger's contribution to this volume was not originally intended as a commentary on Professor Eckstein's paper. Since it deals with the impact of foreign trade on economic development, however, it supplements effectively Professor Eckstein's reference to the impact of economic fluctuations on foreign trade. It is, therefore, included in this chapter.—*Editor.*

[2] Data used in this paper, unless otherwise noted, are from Robert F. Dernberger, "Communist China's Foreign Trade and Capital Movements" (unpublished manuscript).

come, the total foreign trade of China was larger than that of the United States in 1952–58. In addition, the budget receipts from Soviet loans and credits in 1950–55 were sufficient to finance the entire Chinese import surplus in Sino-Soviet trade over the same period. During the First Five Year Plan period, total imports accounted for 49 per cent of total domestic basic construction investment. Obviously, these ratios do not tell us much about the quantitative effect of China's foreign trade or of foreign loans and credits on China's rate of economic growth. Rather than attempt to measure the impact of China's foreign trade on the rate of growth in quantitative terms as I have done elsewhere,[3] the importance of foreign trade and aid in Communist China's economic development effort may be indicated by investigating the general relationship of foreign trade, innovation, and economic growth.

The purpose of this paper is to show that the pattern of Communist China's economic development and development policy itself was determined, to a significant extent, by developments in Communist China's foreign-trade and capital movements. Specifically, I hope to show that the rather high rates of growth in the early 1950's were made possible, given the desire to create a capital-intensive heavy industry, by Soviet loans, supplies of machinery and equipment, and technicians; that the change in capital flows after 1955 made continued increases in heavy industrial capacity most difficult; that when Communist China's capacity to import machinery and equipment from abroad was restricted by the relatively low rate of growth of export earnings and the need to repay the Soviet loans, the Great Leap Forward movement was introduced, in part, to establish with native technology a labor-intensive industrial sector; that when the Great Leap Forward appeared successful, the Chinese Communists again used the increased export capacity to expand the capital-intensive industrial sector; that the agricultural crises created excess capacity in industry, and foreign trade was utilized to acquire foodstuffs and inputs for agricultural production to survive the crises; and that, finally, with the economy restored to the pre–Great

---

[3] Using a very simple model with fixed coefficients for the relationship between imports and domestic investment, domestic investment and output, and domestic costs of import replacements during the First Five Year Plan period, 1953–57, I have estimated that China's *official* annual rate of growth would have been reduced by 20 to 30 per cent if China had been unable to import machinery and equipment from abroad. Using a similar model, Alexander Eckstein has estimated that the inability to import machinery and equipment from abroad would have reduced China's *estimated* rate of growth by 20 to 50 per cent (Alexander Eckstein, *Communist China's Economic Growth and Foreign Trade* [New York: McGraw-Hill, 1966], pp. 123–24).

Leap Forward levels of production, future development of the heavy industrial sector will continue to depend upon Communist China's foreign-trade and capital movements and the import of foreign technology.

Before turning to a discussion of the particular relationship between foreign trade, innovation, and economic growth in Communist China during the past eighteen years, it may be worthwhile to briefly specify a more general frame of reference for the discussion. The rate of economic growth is determined by the interaction of the domestic accumulation of human and material capital through net domestic saving and investment, the accumulation of human and material capital through foreign aid and trade, domestic innovation and innovation introduced by imported capital, and increases in the economy's efficiency. The gains from trade enable a country to increase its rate of growth by allowing it to accumulate a larger amount of capital with a given amount of resources than would be possible in the absence of foreign trade. Depending upon a country's comparative advantage, foreign trade enables a country to import either producer's goods or consumer's goods cheaper than they could be produced domestically. Imports of producer's goods directly convert a given amount of resources into a larger amount of capital; imports of consumer's goods release a greater amount of domestic resources for the production of producer's goods.

Imported producer's goods also may increase the rate of growth by introducing innovations or changes in technology. Inasmuch as an innovation leads to a revaluation of the stock of capital, however, it is very difficult to distinguish those increases in production capabilities that are due to an increase in the quantity of capital and those due to innovations. Despite these conceptual difficulties, it is evident that the import of producer's goods increases the productive capacity of an economy not only by adding to that economy's stock of capital, but also by introducing new techniques of production. Indigenous innovation is also possible, but one of the major benefits or gains from foreign trade and aid to an underdeveloped country is the function of trade and aid as a transmission belt for innovation.

When the Chinese Communists took power on the mainland in October, 1949, they were faced with the immediate problems of a rampant inflation, a below-capacity level of production, and a chronic import surplus. The solution of these problems, however, did not involve a significant policy decision as to the role of foreign trade, the choice of technology, or the setting of a desired rate of growth. Rather, the restoration of the economy was largely concerned with the restoration of efficiency. The major economic innovation during the period of restoration was land reform, but the land-reform program changed the system of land ownership much more than it affected the method of production. By the end of 1952, the inflation had been stopped, domestic production had been restored, the balance of merchandise trade had been brought under control, and, in mid-1953, a cease-fire had been secured in Korea. While not entirely consistent with the facts, it is conceptually convenient to argue that production had been restored to its pre-war peak by the end of 1952 and to began an analysis of the interrelationship of foreign trade, innovation, and the rate of growth with Communist China's First Five Year Plan period, 1953–57.

The essential obstacle to the maintenance of a high rate of growth in Communist China was not the difficulty in achieving a high rate of saving, but the difficulty in converting these savings into the accumulation of both material and human capital: machines and technicians. In other words, as is true in all Communist economies, the Chinese Communists were able to secure a large share—between one-fourth and one-third—of gross domestic product for allocation to investment, defense, and government consumption. These domestic savings, however, represented a claim on domestic product, essentially agricultural products. Lacking a supply of native technicians or domestic production capabilities, it was necessary to convert these savings into investment by means of foreign trade. It is true, of course, that the available supply of technicians and domestic production capabilities could have been used to accumulate producer's goods for the agricultural or light industrial sectors. The Chinese Communists, however, desired to invest in heavy industry and between 30 and 45 per cent of total fixed capital investment in 1953–57 was in that sector.

It also might have been possible for the Chinese Communists to have introduced a labor-intensive technology in heavy industry and to have utilized domestically produced producer's goods in this sector. Their objective, however, was to maximize the rate of growth of heavy industrial output and not the level of employment. Furthermore, I find it difficult to envisage an efficient labor-intensive method of heavy industrial production, labor-intensive being defined as a capital-labor ratio similar to that found in the agricultural sector. Even if possible, one could argue that when social overhead capital was included in the calculation, the capital-output ratio would not be much higher in a capital-intensive heavy industry than in a labor-intensive heavy industry. This is not to imply, of course, that the Chinese Communists could not have increased the rate of growth by adopting a *relatively* more labor-intensive method of production in heavy industry than the method actually adopted.

Whatever alternatives were available to the Chinese Communists on the eve of the First Five Year Plan period, their actual choice was to import technicians and producer's goods for investment in heavy industry in exchange for exports of raw and processed agricultural products supplemented by Soviet loans.[4] The results of this policy were a high rate of capital accumulation and a high rate of growth of output in industry.[5] It is very difficult, of course, to divide the rate of growth of industrial output into its separate sources. Nonetheless, the available data are consistent with the argument that the rate of capital accumulation in this period was greatly facilitated by the Soviet loans and the gains from trade with the Soviet Union, that the imported producer's goods introduced a capital-intensive technology, and that efficiency also increased over the period.[6]

Despite the rapid rate of growth in fixed assets, the introduction of a capital-intensive technology resulted in an increase in total industrial employment between 1952 and 1957 of only 2.5 million and total non-agricultural employment increased by only 3.1 million.[7] The rural population increased by almost 50 million over the same period and some Western specialists estimate that the agricultural work force in-

[4] The following data are offered in support of the above statement. Raw and processed agricultural products accounted for over 70 per cent of Communist China's exports and imported machinery and equipment accounted for over 40 per cent of total investment in machinery and equipment in 1953–57. Over 11,000 Soviet technicians worked in China during the 1950's and Communist China received almost 1.7 billion U.S. dollars in Soviet loans in 1950–57.

[5] Between 1952 and 1957, annual net domestic investment increased over two-fold, the annual additions to new fixed assets in industry increased almost five-fold, and the gross value of industrial output increased by 18 per cent a year (*Ten Great Years* [Peking: Foreign Languages Press, 1960]). While the official data undoubtedly overstate the actual magnitude of these increases, the available estimates by Western specialists still depict a relatively high rate of growth of investment, fixed assets, and output in industry.

[6] In 1953–57, imports of machinery and equipment were equal to 40 per cent of total domestic investment in machinery and equipment, fixed assets per worker in industry increased by 50 per cent, power machinery and electricity per worker in industry increased by 80 per cent, productivity of labor in industry increased by 50 per cent, and there was a 29 per cent reduction in the cost of comparable industrial products.

[7] John Philip Emersen, *Nonagricultural Employment in Mainland China: 1949–1958* (Washington, D.C.: U.S. Department of Commerce, Bureau of the Census, 1965), p. 128.

creased by as much as 100 million.[8] Inasmuch as annual fixed investment in agriculture is estimated to have increased from about one billion yüan in 1953 to slightly more than two billion in 1957, it is doubtful that there was a significant increase in the ratio of fixed capital per
worker in the agricultural sector during the First Five Year Plan period.
Furthermore, what accumulation of capital did occur in agriculture was
not dependent upon imports from abroad and did not involve a significant change in agricultural technology.[9] The major source of innovation in agriculture came from the successive stages of institutional reorganizations—first, land reform, then the elementary producer's co-operatives, then the advanced producer's co-operatives—and from the introduction of better seeds, pest control, utilization of water, double crop-
ping, etc. The increase in sown area alone could explain almost one-
half of the officially reported 25 per cent increase in agricultural output
between 1952 and 1957. The remainder could easily be explained by
the very large increase in the number of agricultural workers.

Thus, the overall growth rate in 1953–57 was the weighted average of
a relatively high rate of growth in the industrial sector with an increase
in the capital-labor ratio and the productivity of labor and a relatively
low rate of growth in the agricultural sector with a decrease in the
capital-labor ratio and the productivity of labor. If this pattern of
development were to be projected into the future, it would have been
only a matter of time before the productivity of labor in agriculture
would have declined to such a level that the agricultural sector was no
longer able to supply exports or foodstuffs for the urban population.[10]

The failure of the repeated institutional re-organization of agriculture to obtain significant increases in labor productivity may have been
one of the reasons for launching the Great Leap Forward movement at
the end of 1957. It would be a mistake, however, to trace the origins of
the Great Leap Forward movement exclusively to developments in the
agricultural sector. Relatively high rates of growth in industrial output

[8] T. C. Liu and K. C. Yeh, *The Economy of the Chinese Mainland* (Princeton, N.J.: Princeton University Press, 1965), Table II, p. 69.

[9] Most of the imported agricultural machinery and equipment was allocated
to the newly created state farms in the northeast. By 1957, these state farms
accounted for only one per cent of the cultivated area.

[10] The official aggregate data depict a one per cent increase per annum in
per capita food grain production during the First Five Year Plan period. Some
Western specialists, however, estimate that per capita food grain production
actually declined during the period as a whole, although it may have increased
through 1955 and declined thereafter.

had been realized in 1953–57, but changes in Communist China's international economic relations in 1956 and 1957 made continued high rates of growth in industrial output with capital-intensive methods of production as difficult to achieve as increases in labor productivity in the labor-intensive agriculture sector.

Receipts from Soviet loans in 1956 and 1957 were only 117 and 23 million yüan, respectively, and Communist China received no additional Soviet loans after the First Five Year Plan period. The annual repayments of earlier loan receipts and outpayments for Communist China's own foreign-aid program resulted in a net capital outflow after 1955. The required export surplus to finance this capital outflow was obtained by a reduction in total imports. Despite the change in the direction of capital flows, investment in industry increased by more than 50 per cent and, although total imports declined, imports of machinery and equipment were increased by almost 45 per cent. Nonetheless, the ratio of imports of machinery and equipment to domestic investment in machinery and equipment declined and the attempt to maintain a high rate of growth in the capital-intensive industrial sector resulted in a budget deficit financed by a large expansion of currency in circulation, severe bottlenecks in the supply of complementary producer's goods, and inflationary pressures.

The Chinese Communists reacted to the imbalance between investment in industry and available imports of machinery and equipment by adopting a policy of retrenchment in 1957.[11] The reduction in the rate of increase in the accumulation for the capital-intensive industrial sector resulted in a relatively low rate of growth.[12] After 1955, therefore, when the Chinese Communists were required to maintain an export surplus and when the export capacity was limited by the rate of increase in agricultural production, continued increases in industrial output became dependent upon the rate of increase in agricultural pro-

[11] Investment in heavy industry increased by only 4 per cent in 1957 and total investment in capital construction was reduced by 7 per cent. Total imports were again reduced, but imports of machinery and equipment were maintained at the previous year's level and the ratio of imports of machinery and equipment to domestic investment in machinery and equipment increased to slightly above the average for the First Five Year Plan period.

[12] Industrial production increased by only 11 per cent and the rate of growth for the economy as a whole was only 8 per cent in 1957. These official rates of growth undoubtedly exaggerate the actual rates, but it is the relative rates of growth, not the absolute rates, that are important for the argument presented in this paper.

duction. By 1957, the relatively low rate of increase in agricultural production was leading to a reduction in the rate of increase in industrial production, not because increases in food grain output were unable to keep pace with the growth in population, but because increases in agricultural production were unable to keep pace with export requirements for imports of machinery and equipment and loan repayments.

Another development in Communist China's foreign trade in 1957 also worked to preclude relatively high rates of growth in industrial production in the future. During the First Five Year Plan period, the major contribution of imports to Communist China's development effort were the complete industrial and mining projects supplied by the Soviet Union and Communist countries in Eastern Europe. In terms of both the supply of producer's goods and the transfer of technology, the 205 industrial and mining projects worth over two billion U.S. dollars supplied by the Soviet Union are indeed the core of Communist China's heavy industrial sector.[13] It is difficult to think of a similar attempt to transfer industrial technology from one country to another on such a large scale in such a short period of time.

Actual deliveries of the complete plants, however, had reached a peak in 1956 and declined in both 1957 and 1958. Unlike other commodity imports purchased through negotiations between state trading companies either annually or at more frequent intervals, the import of complete plants was arranged for through high-level negotiations and

[13] The Soviet Union agreed to construct 51, 90, 15, and 55 industrial and mining projects in China in agreements signed in February, 1950, September, 1953, October, 1954, and April, 1956, respectively. These 205 individual projects were later incorporated into larger units, and reports issued after 1957 refer to 166 Soviet aid projects. The East European countries assisted Communist China in the construction of 68 industrial projects during the First Five Year Plan period. When completed, the Soviet projects were to account for the following per cent of the increases in output in the relevant industry: 92.1 per cent in iron, 82.8 per cent in steel, 90.4 per cent in rolled steel, 22.7 per cent in coal, 28.5 per cent in chemical fertilizer, 45 per cent in electrical generating equipment, 50.3 per cent in metallurgical equipment, and the total increase in the domestic production of trucks. Many of the 11,000 Soviet technicians who worked in China during the 1950's were involved in collecting the construction data, surveying, clearing the construction site, planning and designing the plant, arranging for the supply of all necessary equipment and materials, managing the construction and operation of the plant, training Chinese technicians to take their place, and providing the necessary technical data and plans for the daily operation of the project when it was transferred to the Chinese. In addition, 8,000 Chinese workers were trained in similar plants in the Soviet Union during the 1950's.

long-term agreements. According to one Soviet writer, the decline in Soviet exports of complete plants to China after 1956 was "a result of the fact that the Soviet Union had completed certain of its commitments in technical assistance with respect to the building of a considerable number of industrial units."[14] By the beginning of 1959, all but 31 of the Soviet-supplied complete industrial and mining projects were wholly or partially in production. Even if China's export capacity had increased rapidly enough to finance increased imports of machinery and equipment for capital-intensive industrial projects after 1955, there was still a problem of obtaining their supply. The large expansion of the Soviet Union's economic aid and trade in producer's goods with the other Communist countries in Asia and the non-Communist countries of Southeast Asia, Africa, and the Near East increased the opportunity costs of these exports to the Soviet Union abroad as well as domestically.[15]

From 1956 through 1958, Communist China was able to maintain a relatively high level of imports of machinery and equipment from the Soviet Union while total imports from that country were reduced to yield an export surplus in Sino-Soviet trade only by switching purchases of metals from the Soviet Union to Western Europe.[16] These increased purchases of metals were made possible by the successive reductions in the number and types of commodities on the embargo list for trade with Communist China by the countries of Western Europe. In the absence of long-term credit, however, these increased imports of metals from Western Europe also relied on increased export earnings and, therefore, were also limited by Communist China's ability to increase agricultural production.

It was argued earlier that the Great Leap Forward movement was not launched to increase agricultural production in the face of declining per capita food supplies. In the light of the discussion above, it would be possible to interpret the Great Leap Forward movement as an attempt by the Chinese Communists to increase agricultural production to avoid a decline in the rate of industrial production by increasing

[14] A. M. Smirnov, "Soviet Technical Assistance in the Construction of Plants Abroad," *Problems of Economics*, 2, no. 9 (January, 1960): 56.

[15] In 1955 through 1958, Communist China received more than two-thirds of the more than one billion U.S. dollars worth of complete sets of machinery and equipment exported by the Soviet Union to Communist countries (*ibid.*, p. 60).

[16] Communist China increased imports from Western Europe by 400 per cent between 1955 and 1958, and imports of metals increased from less than 2 per cent to more than 45 per cent of the total over the same period.

their export capacity to finance greater imports of producer's goods. Both explanations for the Great Leap Forward movement are plausible. Yet, I believe the developments of late 1957 and early 1958 can be interpreted as an attempt by the Chinese Communists to avoid a decline in the rate of growth of industrial output by changing their industrial technology, and were not specifically directed to increase labor productivity in agriculture.

The three important developments during this period were the decentralization of industry, the "walking-on-two-legs" campaign, and the commune movement. One of the major problems of a high rate of capital accumulation in industry and the exports required to facilitate that accumulation was the burden it placed on the budget of the central government.[17] Under the provisions of the regulation on industrial control of November, 1957, many industries were placed under the control of provincial or local administrators who, within four guidelines, were given control over the direction of investment and power to issue bonds, if necessary, to raise capital for investment.[18] In this manner, a large share of the financial burden for capital accumulation in industry was transferred from the central government to lower-level authorities who were to raise the investment funds in a non-inflationary manner.

Even so, in order to achieve high rates of capital accumulation in industry without relying on large-scale imports of machinery and equipment, the Chinese Communists also introduced a drive for greater technological innovation under the slogan, "walking-on-two-legs."[19] The creation of a great many medium-scale, or small-scale, native industries in the rural areas, however, greatly increased the demand for labor in industry. To meet this demand and to provide an organization of agricultural production into units with sufficient "disguised unemployment" to maintain several medium- or small-scale, labor-intensive

[17] Capital accumulation in industry and the export surplus required to finance Soviet loan repayments accounted for almost 30 per cent of total budget expenditures in 1956 and 1957.

[18] Eighty per cent of the enterprises formerly controlled by the industrial ministries of the central government had been turned over to the local authorities.

[19] This campaign does not refer to the backyard steel movement which preceded it, but to the change in emphasis from the rapid expansion of large-scale, modern, capital-intensive industrial projects imported from abroad to the rapid creation of medium-scale, native industries in the rural areas with domestically produced producer's goods.

industrial projects at the local level, the advanced producers' collectives, containing an average of less than 200 households, were merged into communes containing an average of 5,000 households. Although the commune movement also centralized agricultural decision-making, altered the system of wage payments, and eliminated the private plots, it did not alter significantly the method of production, nor the pattern of land use, with the exception of the elimination of the private plots.

Large increases in both industrial and agricultural output in 1958, due in part to good weather and a large increase in the labor effort through increases in the work day, temporarily vindicated the change in development policy. Moreover, in the first half of 1959, the Chinese Communist leadership apparently accepted the greatly exaggerated claims of the local cadres of continued large increases in output. Their fundamental desire to develop a capital-intensive heavy industry was revealed when, convinced of the increase in agricultural production and export capacity, they increased exports to the Soviet Union by 25 per cent and reduced their trade with the West. The increased exports to the Soviet Union were not used to repay the Soviet loans ahead of schedule, but to finance new shipments of capital-intensive heavy industrial projects. In agreements signed in August of 1958 and February of 1959, the Soviet Union agreed to supply China, in exchange for current Chinese exports, 125 complete plants worth about 2 billion U.S. dollars.[20]

These new agreements were short-lived, however, and not merely because of the Sino-Soviet split. The overestimate of the available disguised unemployment in agriculture, the excessive work day, the elimination of the private plot coupled with a system of payment that divorced individual wages from work performed, the increase in inefficiency, the deterioration in quality of output, the excessive centralization of decision-making in agriculture, and bad weather led to an agricultural crisis in 1959 and the failure of the Great Leap Forward. In the early 1960's, Communist China's greatly reduced export capacity was utilized to repay the Soviet loans, obtain imports of agricultural inputs, such as chemical fertilizers, from Western Europe and Japan, and imports of foodstuffs, such as wheat, from Canada, Australia, and

[20] Author's estimate, based on the value of the 78 complete plants (1.25 billion U.S. dollars) included in the agreement of February, 1959. As a result of these agreements, imports of complete sets of equipment increased by more than 225 million U.S. dollars in 1959 while total imports increased by only 150 million U.S. dollars.

Argentina.[21] Inasmuch as the decline in available agricultural inputs and demand for output produced excess capacity in industry, investment in industry was reduced and capital accumulation was concentrated in the agricultural sector in an effort to revive agricultural production.[22] The results of the extensive program of agricultural rehabilitation during the early 1960's must have been disappointing to the Chinese Communists. The available evidence, scarce indeed, indicates that it was not until the end of 1964 that the 1957 levels of production in agriculture had been achieved and, possibly, surpassed.

Although the production of several industrial products such as petroleum and chemical fertilizer continued to increase during the agricultural crises, Western experts believe that excess capacity in industry also had not been eliminated until the end of 1964. It would be erroneous, however, to depict the Chinese economy of 1965 as a mere restoration of the Chinese economy of 1957. In 1957, inefficiencies, poor quality of products, and a low level of technical competence had been serious problems and these problems were aggravated by the Great Leap Forward in 1958 and the withdrawal of Soviet technicians in 1960. During the period of economic revival in the early 1960's, the Chinese Communists made an effort to develop their own technical competence, improve the quality of output, and eliminate waste in industry. These problems still remain as constraints to the expansion of China's industrial capacity, but considerable progress has been made.[23] As to the problem of inefficiency and poor quality of output, the very wasteful labor-intensive, native industrial projects of the Great Leap Forward have been abandoned and it is most unlikely they will be revived.

[21] China's exports declined by over 35 per cent in 1960 and remained less than 75 per cent of their 1959 level in 1961–64. In 1960–64, Soviet loan repayments were 14 per cent of total exports and in 1961–64 imports of foodstuffs were more than 25 per cent of total exports.

[22] According to official statements and external estimates, the supply of chemical fertilizer and tractors was doubled between 1958 and 1963. By mid-1965, rural electrification had been extended to the point where 6.6 million hectares of farm land in 90 per cent of China's *hsien* were irrigated by mechanized pumps. To stimulate production, decision-making was restored to the lower-level production units, private plots were returned to the peasants, free markets were allowed for the products of these private plots, and a greater effort was made to relate wage payments (work points) to work performed by the individual peasant.

[23] The detonation of a nuclear device in October, 1964, was an impressive example of China's technological development and capabilities, but more important for future development potential was the construction of the first Chinese-designed and -equipped, modern industrial plant in June of 1965.

By the mid-1960's, therefore, the Chinese Communist economy had achieved its pre–Great Leap Forward levels of output, but with greater technical capabilities, a higher level of efficiency, and better quality products. At the end of 1964, the Chinese Communists announced a new Five Year Plan that was to be introduced in 1966. The details of the new plan have never been made public and, before their new development policy had been revealed, the Cultural Revolution erupted to obscure current economic developments.[24] The Chinese Communists are unlikely to repeat the costly mistakes made in 1958, but they have recently revived the slogans of the Great Leap Forward. Possible reasons for reviving the phraseology of the Great Leap Forward may include the desire to silence critics of the leadership, to eliminate those concessions made to the private sector during the period of recovery, and to re-introduce some of the functions of the commune in organizing the peasants for another effort to increase agricultural production.

In the future, however, even though agricultural production will remain labor-intensive for some time to come, greater efforts will be made to increase the supply of industrially produced agricultural inputs such as chemical fertilizer. The ability of the Chinese Communists to increase agricultural output at a sufficient rate to support their industrial development effort will depend upon their ability to increase the production of these agricultural inputs. With the exception of defense, the Chinese Communists probably will make the greatest effort to develop their own industrial technology in these industries. Their immediate goal appears to be the capability to design and produce complete sets of equipment for the chemical fertilizer and agricultural machinery industries.[25] In the meantime, however, much of the supply of these inputs as well as the plants that are to produce them must come from abroad.[26]

In the capital-intensive industrial sector itself, the Chinese Communists probably will build more medium-scale plants for which they can supply a greater proportion of the machinery and equipment than

[24] For example, it is most difficult to determine if the statements exonerating the Great Leap Forward and urging its acceptance as a model for economic development by the underdeveloped countries are mere rhetoric or introduce a new phase of mass mobilization of labor for development.

[25] The first Chinese-designed and -equipped, modern industrial plant produces high-pressure valves to be used in chemical fertilizer plants.

[26] Although China's first urea-making machinery went into production in March of 1965, complete plants for the production of urea, ammonia, and chemical fertilizers are being purchased from Western Europe and Japan.

they could during the First Five Year Plan period. Their ability to do so has been made possible by recent technological developments in the metallurgical and machine-building industries.[27] Nonetheless, according to their own admission, Communist China must still rely on imports for many types of machinery and equipment, including complete plants for the synthetic fiber, chemical, petroleum, metallurgical, and machine-building industries. In the future, as was true during the 1950's, the expansion of Communist China's heavy industrial production will depend upon the ability to convert saved agricultural exports into imports of producer's goods and technicians—i.e., it will be limited by the increase in export earnings and foreign loans and credits.[28]

Thus, until that date in the future when Communist China is indeed self-sufficient in industrial technology, the rate of Communist China's economic development will continue to depend upon developments in Communist China's foreign trade. One must never forget, however, that a minimum rate of growth in agriculture to keep pace with per capita food requirements, export requirements, and raw material requirements for light industry is a necessary condition for development. It is not a sufficient condition only because the Chinese Communists continue to define economic development as the creation of a self-sufficient, capital-intensive, heavy industrial sector.

[27] For example, Communist China is now able to produce many types of sheet steel, steel plates, rolled steel, steel tubes, automatic-precision machine tools, and even a 12,000-ton free forging press, one of the largest in the world.

[28] Unlike the First Five Year period, however, these imports and credits will come from Western Europe and Japan. The negotiations with a West German firm in 1966 for the purchase of a complete steel mill worth 150 million U.S. dollars financed by a five-year credit may be the first of several such purchases. The West German cabinet has issued an export credit guarantee of 87.5 million U.S. dollars which covers the share of the German firms in a consortium of West European firms who will supply the equipment for this plant.

S. N. Eisenstadt

# 13

# Tradition, Change, and Modernity: Reflections on the Chinese Experience

### Tradition and Modernity—Restatement of the Problem

In the following pages I would like to make some brief comments about the central topic of the Conference—namely, China's heritage and the Communist regime.[1] These comments will be made in the framework of the more general problem of the relations between China's heritage or tradition and the processes of its modernization, and of the nature of its response to the impact of modernization.

This approach necessitates already in the beginning some restatement of the problem of relations between tradition and modernity. As is well known, the dichotomy between "traditional" and "modern" societies has played a very important role both in "classical" writings and in more recent literature in sociology, history, political science, and anthropology. Without going into a detailed exposition of this dichotomy, we may briefly summarize it as it has, till recently, been rather generally accepted in social sciences literature. There, a "traditional" society has often been depicted as a static one with but little differentiation or specialization, together with a low level of urbanization, and of literacy, while a "modern" society has been viewed as one with a very high level of differentiation, of urbanization, literacy, and exposure to mass media of communication. In the political realm, traditional society has been depicted as based on a "traditional" elite ruling by some Mandate of Heaven, while modern society has been viewed as based on

[1] Parts of the research on which this paper is based have been supported by a grant from the Wenner Gren Foundation for Anthropological Research.

wide participation of masses which do not accept any traditional legitimation of the rulers and which hold these rulers accountable in terms of secular values and efficiency. Above all, traditional society was by definition bound by the cultural horizons set by its tradition, while a modern society is culturally dynamic and oriented to change and innovation.

This way of contrasting modern and traditional societies—which in its own limits is correct—has often led to another, more problematic view about the relations between modern and traditional elements for the development of a viable modern society. This view assumed that the conditions for continuous development and modernization in different institutional fields are dependent on, or tantamount to, the destruction of all traditional elements in modern life. According to this view the less traditional a society is, the more modern it would be—that is, by implication, the better it would be able to develop continuously, to deal continuously with new problems and with new social forces, and to develop a continuously expanding institutional structure.

But however plausible at first glimpse such an approach or view may seem, a somewhat more careful look at the available evidence will very quickly show some contrary evidence.

First, very often the more any single component in the traditional settings—be it family, community, or even sometimes political institutions—is disrupted, the more the disruption tends to lead to disorganization, delinquency, and chaos rather than to the setting up of a viable modern order. Second, there are many instances—Japan, Abyssinia, and, perhaps, even in a way England—in which modernization has been relatively successfully undertaken under the aegis of traditional symbols and even traditional elites, and the importance of these instances for our problem has been more and more recognized. Third, it has also been recognized that in many cases in which the initial impetus to modernization came from anti-traditional elites, very soon they tried, even if in a halting way, to revive the more traditional aspects or symbols of society. All these instances imply that however great in principle the contrast between a traditional and a modern society may be, successful modernization—the successful establishment of a viable modern society—may greatly benefit from some elements within the traditional setting from which modernity develops or which respond to the impact of modernity. They also suggest that the continuous functioning of a modern society may greatly depend on the extent to which such traditional forces may indeed be available, utilized in the process of modernization, and incorporated into the modern setting.

All these considerations necessitate some reformulation of the problems of the relations between tradition and modernity. First, they necessitate the re-examination of the relations of tradition to change, the analysis of those forces within a given tradition or traditional society which help or facilitate the process of change as against those which hinder it, and the scrutiny of the relations of such forces to various structural and cultural characteristics of so-called "traditional" societies. Second, they pose the problem of the differences between those changes which are contained within the framework of traditional societies, and those which may lead beyond them into modernization. Third, they point to the necessity of examining the characteristics of those processes of change which may help in the transition to modernity, as against those which may hinder it, and those which lead to the development and continuity of modern frameworks, as against those types which impede the viability of such frameworks once they are established.

In order to be able to approach these problems in a more concrete way, we may ask ourselves questions concerning, first, the nature of the general impact of modern forces of change on the traditional system; second, the extent to which the traditional order influenced the perception of these forces and of the problems which it had to face in the new situations; and, finally, the degree to which it could develop from within its own heritage the ability to deal with these problems—either by adapting itself to the new setting without greatly changing its central institutional and symbolic sphere or by transforming them. In the following sections, I shall attempt to apply these general considerations to a preliminary analysis of China's encounter with modernity.

### The Major Stages in China's Encounter with Modernity

China's encounter with modernity in the form of various impingements of the West has been studied at length and its course can be divided, according to various schemes, into different historical stages. For the purposes of our discussion here, we shall divide it into three major stages: first, the initial encounter of Imperial China with the West; second, the stage of the crumbling of the Imperial order and the attempts to establish, after the Revolution of 1911 and the period of warlords, a new national regime under the aegis of the Kuomintang; and last, the period of the Communist regime. These three periods are, of course, historically interconnected, but prima facie there exists a great continuity between the first and the second periods, and a seemingly great discontinuity between these first two and the last one. But each of these periods evinces several specific and distinct characteristics from the point of view of the central problem of our discussion, and the nature of both such continuities and discontinuities is rather complex and would bear a closer examination.

What, then, was the nature of the impact of modernization on China? What were the problems which China had to deal with under the impact of these forces? The impact of modernity on China took on continuously two forms, and accordingly posed two different but closely interconnected sets of problems before the Chinese social, political, and cultural order. The first such force and problem was the external one—the impingement of the West and Japan which posed the problem of China's ability to maintain its national integrity in the new international setting. The second problem was an internal one—how to overcome the potential breakdown of the existing Imperial order and, after this order broke down, how to overcome the divisive forces in the new situation of internal anarchy (such as the attempts of various warlords to establish separate regimes); and how to establish a new viable order in the wake of the old one.

As has often been stressed in discussion at the Conference, this period of division evinced many characteristics of such periods of division known in Chinese history up to at least the Sung. From this point of view, the attempts of the Imperial center, of the warlords, and, especially later, of the Kuomintang, to establish a new central order, could be seen as not entirely dissimilar from those of the other unifying dynasties. There were, however, several crucial differences between the historical, "traditional" periods of division and unification and the more modern one. The nature of these differences can perhaps be best seen in the nature of the convergence of the external and internal forces on the existing order. Not only was the external threat in the nineteenth and twentieth centuries probably greater than in any former period of Chinese history, but in addition this challenge was, with respect to its impact on the internal order, of a different nature. It not only undermined an existing dynasty, or the very possibility of maintaining a centralized regime—something which did, of course, also happen in the past—but it also undermined the very bases and premises of the traditional sociopolitical and cultural order. This undermining was effected by the development of expectations or demands for the creation of a new, modern type of social order—both in the ideological and in the institutional sense.

## China's Response to Modernity
### in the Imperial Period

Here there exist already important differences between the first two periods—the Imperial and the Kuomintang periods. During the Imperial period, the basic challenge of modernity was not perceived, especially by the central institutions (the Court and most of the bureaucracy and literati), in terms of the necessity to restructure the whole sociopolitical order. At most, the response to the challenge was conceived in terms of the necessity of the existing order to adapt itself to new technical, international, and to some extent ideological conditions. During the later, post-Imperial, period, the problem of the challenge was indeed already conceived in terms of the necessity to create a new, modern order.

And yet despite this basic difference, these first two periods of China's encounter with modernity have one very general characteristic in common—namely, that in both of them the Chinese social and political order evinced a very low level of adaptability to the new changing situations, to the impact of modern forces, and to the challenge of modernity. This low level of adaptability in the first period was evident in the failure of the existing Imperial center and of the traditional sociopolitical and cultural order to re-adapt themselves to the new setting, to change several aspects of Chinese institutions so as to be able to cope with the new "foreign" forces. The general reactions of the Imperial center to the impact of foreign forces and to the demands of the various reform movements were oriented to the promotion of a very limited and controlled modernization, limited to technical and some economic and administrative spheres. Along with this limited response, there was an unwillingness to foster any more far-reaching changes that would assure the participation of broader groups in the political order. The policies of the center were characterized by a strong emphasis on the maintenance of the prevailing social structure. The Court and the bureaucracy attempted to suppress any social movements and more independent public opinion, and employed toward them various repressive measures so as to minimize the possibilities of their developing into active and highly articulated political elements and organizations.

As against these very limited modernizing tendencies of the Imperial center, there developed the different modernizing groups, usually composed of traditional and modern intellectuals, which constituted the core of the various reform movements. These groups evinced, however, on the whole a very small degree of organizational or political effectiveness in changing the existing symbolic and institutional orders.

### The Response to Modernity in the
### Second Period

It was indeed these groups—the various reformist, revolutionary, and nationalist movements—especially the political group subsequently known as the Kuomintang—that constituted the major link between the first two periods of China's response to the West, and to a very large extent it is the basic characteristics of these groups that can explain also the broad similarity between the first two periods of China's response to the impact of modernity and of the West. This similarity can best be seen in the Kuomintang's ultimate neo-traditionalistic orientations and in its concomitant lack of capacity to adapt to new international, modern settings or to transform the existing Chinese social and political order.

This neo-traditionalism was manifest on several levels. On the most general symbolic level, the Kuomintang elite tended to define the central symbols of the social, political, and cultural order in a traditionalistic way which minimized the possibility of integrating within them those new symbols or orientations which were developed by the more innovative groups. In the organizational sphere, these traditionalistic tendencies of the Kuomintang elite were manifest in the major policies developed by them. These evinced some marked, or at least formal, similarity to those of the older Imperial center. In general, they tended to develop strong monolithic orientations, attempted to control other groups and elites and to confine them within their traditional limits, to segregate them from one another, to minimize and control the channels of mobility among them and from them to the center, and to limit their participation and access to the cultural and political centers. Whatever adaptations or innovations were adopted by them were usually largely segmented and segregated in what was often defined by them as technical or "external" fields.

On the macrosocietal level, these responses tended to develop in two closely related and overlapping general directions. One was a militant "traditionalism" on the central levels of the new social order, characterized mainly by the development of militant conservative ideologies and coercive orientations and policies, and by an active ideological or symbolic closure of the new centers. The other direction, which in China was closely related to the warlords tradition, was that of the development of a new type of patrimonialism, that is, the establishment or continuation of new political and administrative frameworks with but little symbolic (cultural, religious) orientations, with very weak and non-committing symbols of centrality, and concerned mostly with the maintenance of the existing regime and of its modus vivendi with the major—mostly traditional—groups in the society.

## The Neo-traditionalism of the Kuomintang

It is from the point of view of these basic attitudes and orientations—and the concomitant policies—that the similarities between the Imperial and the Kuomintang period stand out in terms of their response to the challenges of modernity. But the Kuomintang regime worked already, as we have seen above, in both external and internal circumstances which greatly differed from those of the Imperial system. It worked under the assumption of the necessity to establish a new modern order under greater internal pressures of various traditionalistic and more modern and alienated internal groups, as well as under greater international pressure. Hence the policies of the Kuomintang tended already to evince some specific characteristics of their own, leading to situations of internal and external breakdowns which precluded the possibility of development of a neo-traditional order viable in modern conditions.

The most important common denominator of these policies has been the continuous oscillation between attempts of the ruling elite at controlling all the major power positions and groups in the society and monopolizing the positions of effective control, and a continuous giving in to the demands of various groups. For instance, there took place a continuous expansion and swelling of the bureaucracy by new aspirants, and a continual giving in by the rulers to the growing demands of the holders of these positions for tenure of office and for increased (even if not fully adequate to catch up with the growing inflation) wages and emoluments. Similarly, in the field of education, the rulers oscillated between attempting to repress autonomous activities of the students and direct them in their educational activities, on the one hand, and giving in to their demands, on the other. In implementing these policies, the rulers of the Kuomintang not only succumbed to pressures from different groups, but very often themselves created and legitimized such pressures. They did it often for symbolic or ideological reasons, because of the search of the rulers for support and their attempts to attest in this way to their legitimation in such neo-traditional terms.

And yet these central symbols of the new order, the neo-traditional Confucian orientations composed of a mixture of traditional and more extremist modern or anti-Western symbols, could not provide adequate guidance to many of the concrete, instrumental organizational and institutional problems attendant on the creation and development of a viable modern polity. In general, these policies tended to encourage the attempts of broader groups and strata to re-structure their relations to the new settings, or both organizational and symbolic levels, according to traditional, relatively non-differentiated patterns of relation. This resulted in the perpetuation of previous "traditional" types of relationships—that is, paternalistic arrangements in industrial settings and relations in dealing with officials, politicians, or intellectuals, coupled with a lack of readiness to undertake responsibility or initiative in the new settings. What is even more important, this resulted in far-reaching attempts by such traditionalistic groups to control the major broader frameworks of the society, to take advantage of rapid change, in order to bolster their own power and positions and to minimize the development of more differentiated and effective intermediary and central institutions. The major result of these policies and tendencies was the squandering of vital resources and the undermining of the very bases of the sociopolitical order which the Kuomintang attempted to establish.

### The Frailty of the Neo-traditional Response —Comparison with Thailand

It is, of course, a moot question whether the lack of success of the Kuomintang regime in surviving and in withstanding the combined onslaught of the Japanese and internal dissension was due to its neo-traditionalism and various consequent policies and problems created by them, or whether this failure was due to the sheer strength and impact of the external and internal forces of disruption that converged on it. In other words, the question is whether it is possible to envisage some conditions under which a non-transformative, neo-traditionalistic and semi-partrimonial regime like the Kuomintang could have survived and established a new order which would have proven viable in modern conditions.

The question is, of course, almost entirely hypothetical, and yet some conjectural comparisons may be attempted. The case of the contemporary Taiwan regime may serve as a starting point of such comparison. First of all it shows—as to some extent does the case of Thailand—the possibility of coexistence of a neo-traditionalistic, semi-patrimonial regime with a relatively high level of economic development and with the development of internal policies which evince a higher level of adaptation to some of the exigencies of modern international economic and political forces. It does also show that partial institutional innovations can be contained within such a regime. This can be done because the relative acceptance of the neo-traditional premises, and consequent smaller pressure for wide participation in the institutional centers, prevented the policies developed by such an elite from escalating into a situation of breakdown. But there comes into the picture the second aspect of the Taiwan regime—again very similar to the case of Thailand —namely its almost total dependence on a certain very specific international situation—that is, its almost total insulation under the aegis of the United States from the pressures of international political and economic exigencies.

It is these conditions which point to some of the possible, even if perhaps somewhat tautological, answers to the hypothetical question which we have posed above. These considerations point out that in the international conditions under which the initial impact of modernity on China took place, there were but few possibilities of survival of a neo-traditional, semi-patrimonial regime, not only because of the force of the combined impact of the internal and external pressures, but also because of the very central position of China in its own perception and in the perception of the world. This central position raised both internal and external expectation and was perceived internally and externally both as a challenge and a threat to the existing and developing regimes in China. In other words, the possibilities of relative international marginality or isolation, which are open to Taiwan or were open to Thailand, were denied to mainland China, and it was, at least partially, because of this that a neo-traditional regime could not, in central China, forge out a new polity viable in the new international setting.

## A Brief Comparison with Japan's Neo-traditional Modernizing Elite

The preceding discussion indicates that it might be worthwhile to compare very briefly this neo-traditional pattern that developed in China with some other cases which seemingly were in comparable, even if not similar, situations. The best cases of such comparison would perhaps be Japan and, as a contrast, Thailand. Japan constitutes an illustration of the case in which a relatively independent international position was maintained and its importance even increased through a successful transformation of the traditional sociopolitical center in the direction of modernity. Japan evinced a very special characteristic from the point of view of our concern with relations between tradition and modernity. It constituted a case of modernization initiated by an autocratic oligarchy which was able to direct and control the course of modernization for a relatively long time, absorbing many new social forces within the frameworks it established. This particular characteristic may perhaps be explained by the fact that this oligarchy was, in itself, a revolutionary modernizing one, but at the same time basing itself on a revival of traditional Imperial symbols. This continuity of the Imperial tradition was not purely symbolic; rather, it served as the major focus and content of the new national identity.

While the Meiji oligarchs fostered these traditional symbols, they overthrew the older (Tokugawa) political system in which the Emperor was a mere figurehead; and they were successful in developing, within the new political system, more flexible central institutions and collective goals. Moreover, this elite, while strongly emphasizing innovation in the political field and most adept in political and administrative activity, was also very much oriented to the other social spheres, especially those of educational and economic activities. By virtue of these characteristics, and because of the fact that it could rely, to some extent, on support from the wider social groups (such as some of the urban and peasant groups), it could channel (albeit after rather strong initial coercive measures) some of the traditional (feudal and national) loyalties of the wide strata, and through bureaucratic means draw these strata into the new central framework without really granting them, at least at first, full effective political rights. It was only later, when many new groups and strata developed, that the system was faced with very difficult problems of adaptation and absorption.

Thailand constitutes, in a way, a contrary example. It constitutes perhaps the best illustration of a case of great adaptability of a traditional polity without changes in its basic central symbolic and institutional core, and without great changes in the ideological and effective institutional bases of social and political participation. This adaptation was effected through changing some of the internal aspects of these institutions—especially through rationalization of the bureaucracy and widening of the participation in the center and in the ruling cliques to more, but structurally not greatly different from old, groups. But this relatively high level of adaptability to changing modern conditions was greatly contingent on a relatively peripheral international position, as we noted before.

### Sources of Responses to Modernity— Characteristics of the Traditional Social and Cultural Order

While it would be out of place here to go into a very detailed analysis of all the major differences between China, on the one hand, and Japan and Thailand, on the other, some implicit explication of such differences will come out in the next step of our analysis which will deal with the search for some of the historical-sociological conditions which can explain the specific features of China's different responses to modernization. In the more general term of our discussion, we are looking here for those aspects of China's heritage which can indeed explain the nature of its response to modernity in the first two phases of China's encounter with it.

These conditions can be analyzed on several inter-connected levels. The first such level is that of some general characteristics of social and cultural order which have been found, in comparative research, to be most important in explaining its adaptability to change and the development from within it of internal transformative capacities. The second such level of conditions is focused around what may be called the tradition of change, innovation, and rebellion in a traditional society, which may also be very indicative of the nature of the adaptive and transformative potential existing in the heritage of any such society.

Among the most general aspects of the social order which are highly relevant from the point of view of the development of adaptive and transformative capacities is the relative mutual autonomy of the social, cultural, and political orders. Here we find in China, among the great historic imperial civilizations, the closest interweaving, almost identity, of cultural with political centers. Although in principle many universalistic ethical elements in the dominant Confucian ideology transcended any given territory or community, in actuality this ideology was very closely tied to the specific political framework of the Chinese empire. The empire was legitimized by the Confucian symbols, but the Confucian symbols and Confucian ethical orientation found their "natural" place and framework, their major "referent," within the empire. This, of course, was also related to the fact that no church or cultural organization in China existed independently of the state. The Confucian elite was a relatively cohesive group, sharing a cultural background which was enhanced by the examination system and by adherence to Confucian rituals and classical teachings. But its organization was almost identical with that of the state bureaucracy, and except for some schools and academies it had no organization of its own. Moreover, political activity within the Imperial-bureaucratic framework was a basic referent of the Confucian ethical orientation, which was strongly particularistic and confined to the existing cultural-political setting.

The relation between Chinese political and cultural orders is parallel to that between the political system and social stratification. The most interesting point here is that the total societal system of stratification was entirely focused on the political center. The imperial center, with its strong Confucian orientation and legitimation, was the sole distributor of prestige and honor. Various social groups or strata did not develop autonomous, independent status orientations, except on the purely local level; the major, almost the only wider orientations were bound to this monolithic political-religious center. Of crucial importance here is the structure of the major stratum linking the imperial center to the broader society—the literati. This stratum was a source of recruitment to the bureaucracy and also maintained close relations with the gentry. Their double status orientation enabled the literati to fulfill certain crucial integrative functions in the Imperial system. Their special position enabled them to influence the political activities of the rulers and of the leading strata of the population. But they exerted this influence by upholding the ideal of a hierarchical social-political-cultural order binding on the rulers and these strata. The very existence of the literati as an elite group was contingent on the persistence of the ideal of a unified empire.

These characteristics of the literati were among the most important stabilizing mechanisms in the Imperial system, helping it to regulate and absorb changes throughout its long history. But these same characteristics have also severely inhibited development of a reformative or transformative capacity in China's culturally and politically most articulate groups.

The extent of the capacity for reform or transformation in the broader groups of Chinese society is also related to the basis of their internal cohesion and self-identity: "familism." This familism has often been designated as one cause of China's relatively unsuccessful modernization. But as Marion Levy has shown in his later analysis, it is not the familism as such that was important, but rather the nature of internal cohesion in the family and its links with other institutional spheres. The family was a relatively autonomous, self-enclosed group, with but few autonomous broader orientations. Beyond the commitment to the bureaucracy of those who attained position within it, the primary duty of individuals was to increase family strength and resources, not to represent the worthiness of the family according to some external goals and commitments.

## Sources of Response to Modernity—Reform and Rebellion in Traditional Chinese Society

These characteristics of the Chinese social and cultural scene were very closely related to the pattern of change, innovation, and rebellions in Chinese history. The patterns of potential transformation from within the more central (primary or secondary) elites were greatly influenced both by the social characteristics of the major elite—the literati, which were analyzed above, as well as by the basic orientations of the Confucian and neo-Confucian ideology.

Perhaps the most important aspect of Confucian ideology, from the point of view of our discussion, is the strong emphasis on worldly duties and activities within the existing social frameworks—the family, kin groups, and Imperial service—and on a relatively strong identity between the proper performance of these duties and the ultimate criteria of individual responsibility. In a way, Confucianism has been the most "this worldly" of the great ideologies or religions, with a very strong emphasis on the crucial importance of the political dimensions as a basic dimension of human existence. True enough, these orientations were not devoid of strong emphasis on individual, even transcendental, responsibility; but this responsibility was couched largely in terms of the importance of the political and familial dimensions of human existence. Hence, most of the ideological innovations or transformative orientations that tended to develop within the fold of this ideology were mostly oriented inwardly toward the perfecting of the scope of individual responsibility within these social frameworks, or toward withdrawal from them, but contained only few orientations to change the concrete structure of these social relations and the basic facets of the sociopolitical order.

Structurally and ideologically parallel characteristics can be found in the principal marginal types of change that occurred in China, namely, rebellions, and the development of provincial governors into semi-autonomous warlords. From the point of view of political organization, these rebellions and military outbursts did not usually feature a markedly different or new level of political articulation. The rebellions were often sporadic or undertaken by various cults and secret societies which, while fashioning many symbols of social protest, developed relatively little active articulation of political issues and activities. Their specific symbols included strong apolitical, ahistorical, and semi-mythical or utopian elements. These were, as a rule, bound to the existing value structure and orientations. Thus these rebellions usually provided only secondary interpretations of the existing value structure and did not innovate any radically new orientations. Insofar as they had any sort of active political orientations and aims, these were, on the whole, set within the existing political framework. Usually, they aimed merely at seizing the government and the bureaucracy, and at establishing new governments on the same pattern.

The political orientations of the military governors and warlords were usually also set within the existing value and political frameworks. Although they strove for a greater extent of independence from, or the seizure of, the central government, they envisaged but rarely the establishment of a new type of political system. In certain periods, such developments and the activities of the military governors occasioned the extreme results of the dismemberment of the empire—the establishment of several different states, in which the force of the Confucian tradition and institutions was often weakened. However, even within these states many tendencies evolved toward the unification of the empire, which remained, in a way, the ultimate political ideal. These inclinations were greatly encouraged by the Confucian literati; they naturally implied the re-installment and the reinforcement of the traditional institutional structure.

### *Traditional Order, Rebellions and Reforms, and the Initial Tendency to Neo-traditional Response to Modernity*

These characteristics of the traditional Chinese social structure in general, and of the literati in particular, explain the trend toward dissociation between the different rebellions and reformist traditions analyzed above—that of warlordism and peasant rebellions, basing themselves on the closure of the broader groups and strata from the center, on the one hand, and the more centrally and ideologically oriented ideological "withdrawal" movements aiming at the "idealistic," "individualistic" reformation of the central order, on the other. While certainly some connections between these different reformist and rebellious trends can be found in many concrete cases—and especially in cases of the "secondary" religions, like Buddhism and Taoism—on the whole, the relations between them have been rather tenuous and did not exert any far-reaching transformative influences on the Chinese social and political order. This, in turn, explains the fact that two tendencies—that toward greater independence and status autonomy of the urban-merchant and professional groups, and that toward the development of activistic, universalistic religious-cultural orientations which could influence the transformation of the Chinese traditional structure in the direction of a more differentiated social and cultural order—did not develop beyond embryonic phases. The existing framework could accommodate them even if special places had to be found for them within this framework. The most important common denominator of these characteristics is the weakness of various inter-linking mechanisms between the center and the broader strata, the absence of relatively strong secondary elites which, while internally cohesive, were yet not dissociated from the center. All these factors tend to explain the stability of the Chinese imperial system—but they also explain the low level of its adaptability to the new, modern, conditions. It is the combination of these various characteristics that explain also some of the basic characteristics of those groups—the various reform groups, and the nationalist movement —which, as we have seen, constituted the major link between the first two periods of China's response to the West. From many points of view these movements were, of course, very similar to revolutionary, reformist, nationalist, and social movements which developed under the impact of modernity in many other Asian and non-Asian countries. But beyond these basic common characteristics, they were characterized by some features which are of special importance from the point of view of our discussion, and which were greatly influenced by some of the traditional Chinese social and cultural order analyzed above.

The identity between the cultural and political orders and the specific characteristics of the literati tended to maintain the dominance of a stagnant neo-traditionalism that continuously reinforced the non-transformative orientations of Chinese culture. Under the first impact of modernization, Chinese intellectuals and bureaucrats faced certain problems stemming from the fact that their basic cultural symbols were embedded in the existing political structure. Any political revolution or reformation necessarily entailed rejecting or destroying the cultural order. Similarly, the strong ideological emphasis on upholding the social-political status quo permitted few centers for the crystallization of new symbols to legitimatize new social institutions relatively independent of the preceding order.

This has greatly influenced the ideological orientations of these movements. First of all, they were characterized by a very ambivalent and totalistic attitude toward their tradition and its relation to modernity. They tended to oscillate between the rejection of this tradition totally and the concomitant acceptance of the Western values, on the one hand, and the rejection of the Western values and attempts to subordinate technical aspects to the traditional center and its basic orientations, on the other. Hence there were lacking the flexibility and potential transformative capacity which might otherwise have developed if the question of Westernization versus traditionalism constituted a continuous focus of discussion and did not give rise to mutually exclusive solutions.

But this weakness of initial reform and revolutionary movements in imperial and post-imperial China was only partly due to the ideological identity between the cultural and the political orders. No less important were the relations between political institutions and the system of social stratification. In the social sphere, as in the ideological or cultural sphere, there were few points of internal strength, cohesion, and self-identity for various groups on which new institutional frameworks could be founded or which could support institutional changes. Hence, the various reform and national movements were characterized by a certain "closeness," a ritual emphasis on certain specific and very limited types of local status. They were mostly composed of relatively noncohesive groups alienated from the existing elites and from the broader groups and strata of the society.

This weakness was reinforced by the limited reformative capacities of the Chinese family system. When the empire crumbled and processes of change swept over it, disorganizing and dislocating the traditional structure—especially the major links to the center, that is, the literati and the bureaucracy—family groups were largely dissociated from the center, but they lacked the strength to create new autonomous links. These family groups tended also to develop neo-traditional orientations, but because they were "closed" groups they could not regulate such demands effectively. This tended to sap the resources available for internal redistribution. In the more modern setting, family groups became highly politicized, making demands on the new, and for them not fully legitimate, center and thus further undermining the functioning of new institutional frameworks.

All these characteristics explain the great weaknesses of these movements in terms of institution-building and their difficulty in forging the new interlinking mechanisms, the secondary centers between the center and the broader social periphery. They also, partially at least, explain the ultimate leaning of these movements to neo-traditionalism with all its implications for policy and institution-building.

But we have advisedly said the "ultimate" victory of neo-traditionalisms. Whether such victory was "written in the stars," predicated on those characteristics of Chinese society that were analyzed above, or was the result of the specific interaction between the international situation and internal disintegration is one of those hypothetical questions that admit of no simple answer. But even within this framework of conjectural questions and answers there are some very important indications about possible other outcomes. One such indication, or insight, may be gained through a comparative view of other similar "weak" or neo-traditional and/or semi-modernistic movements with but little adaptive or transformative capacities and with but little ability to establish a new viable institutional order. One such basic difference between these movements and the Chinese one is the very strong predisposition, within the Chinese movements toward the re-establishment of a strong institutional and ideological central order. Paradoxically, it may well be true that if these predispositions and expectations had been weaker, they could have prevented the quick crystallization of an overall neo-traditional order, and it might have been possible for other types of movements to have their chance in attempting to establish a different type of new order. Be that as it may, it is this strong predisposition towards the re-establishment of a strong order that brings us closely to the third major stage of China's response to the impact of modernity—to the phase of the Communist regime and order.

### The New Phase of China's Response to Modernity—The Communist Regime and Its Sociocultural Roots

The specific characteristic of this phase of China's response to the impact of modernity does not lie, of course, in the mere existence of a Communist movement—which can be found in most Asian countries—but in the characteristics of this movement. Most important among these are, first, the ability of the Chinese Communist movement to forge out relatively cohesive leaderships and cadres, and, second, the ability of this leadership to seize power and to attempt (at least with degrees of success as yet very difficult to estimate) to forge a very strong center capable of re-establishing a new, revolutionary, yet seemingly viable (at least in its first phases) social order.

What are the main characteristics of this regime, from the point of view of the central focus of our discussion—its relation to China's heritage and its attitudes to this heritage, on the one hand, and the impact this heritage has on this regime, on the other? From both these points of view we find a very interesting mixture of discontinuity and continuity. The basic discontinuity between the Communist regime and the tradi-

tional and neo-traditional Chinese orders is clear from the attempts of
the Communist regime to destroy most of the concrete traditional symbols, strata, and organization, to forge new social and political goals and
new types of social organization. And yet, even here, some continuity
becomes evident—especially on certain levels of value and institutional
orientations, in the use of different traditional symbols and orientations, and in some attachment to them (although these seem, uncertain
as the evidence is, to vary greatly in different periods in the history of
Chinese Communism). But whatever these shifts, the Communist regime tends, as Ping-ti Ho has stressed, to evince a great continuity with
the more traditional regimes in what may be called some basic modes
of symbolic and institutional orientations.[2]

First of all, this regime tends to perceive some of the basic problems
of social and cultural order in broad terms (for example, emphasis on
power, and on the combination of power and ideology) which are not
very different from those of the traditional order, although both the
concrete constellations of these problems (for example, how to establish
a "strong" autocratic, absolutist society as against a "strong" industrial
society) and the answers to them necessarily differ greatly from those
of the traditional one, Imperial, Confucian, or Legalist. Because of this
we often find attempts to utilize many of these traditional orientations
—but shorn of a great deal of their concrete contents and of their identification or connection with the older order or parts thereof. This can be
seen, for instance, with regard to the incorporation of symbols of partial
groups or even some of the older central symbols (especially "patriotic"
ones) into the new central symbols of the regime. On the one hand, the
Communist regime tended to develop an almost total negation of these
symbols, especially the various symbols of partial groups such as families and regions. But, on the other hand, it tended also to develop parallel attempts to use or uphold such symbols, or general symbolic orientations, detached from their former context and denied almost any partial
autonomy of their own. In other words, we find here an attempt to unleash the basic motivational orientations inherent in the older systems
but, at the same time, to control it in a new way and to change its contents and basic identity.

Moreover, just as the Communist elite shares with its Confucian-
Legalist predecessors some of the basic ideological perception of the
basic problems of the social order, it may also evince a relatively high
degree of continuity with regard to the use of different institutional set-

[2] Ping-ti Ho, "Salient Aspects of China's Heritage," pp. 1–37, this volume.

tings and of their relative predominance—as, for instance, in the continuous predominance of state service and centralized bureaucracy. Here it may also develop a tendency to utilize the former personnel, know-how, and organizational settings, but again to tear them from their former context and to deny them any autonomous identity of their own.

### The Possible Impacts of Chinese Tradition on the Communist Regime's Response to Modernity

It seems, thus, that from many points of view the Communist regime's attitude toward tradition, and the concomitant policies developed by it, have not only been the reverse of those of the neo-traditional Kuomintang regime—as was only natural to assume—but that at the same time the CCP was also, in its own way, oriented toward this tradition and greatly influenced by it. In order to be able to analyze this influence in a somewhat fuller way, we have to ask ourselves, first, about the roots of the Communist regime in the Chinese sociohistorical background; second, about the nature of the problems it has faced by virtue of the persistence of traditional forces and of its own perception of these problems; and, finally, about the influence of this heritage on the CCP's attempted solutions of these problems. This may also perhaps enable us to see to what extent this regime has indeed been able to overcome the various weaknesses inherent in the Chinese traditional structure which were found to impede, in the first two stages of China's response to the West, the institutionalization of a viable modern social and political order.

Let us start by asking ourselves about the roots, in the traditional and modernizing Chinese social structure, of the development of such a relatively strong, cohesive, and militantly change-oriented elite. It seems that these roots can be found, as we have already implied, in the tradition of a strong political-ideological center. It was this tradition which probably created the continuous predisposition to and expectation of re-establishing such centers and tended to deny legitimation to any regime which was not successful in this respect.

The realization of this predisposition, however, was dependent on two sets of conditions. The first was the ability to forge out of some elements of the preceding social and cultural order a cohesive revolutionary elite, able to seize power and to maintain it. The second was the ability of such groups to select from within the impinging new international forces those ideological and social orientations, elements, and symbols which could serve as foci of their revolutionary transformative orientations and of the new sociopolitical and cultural order, the foci of the new political-ideological center.

It seems that the ability of the Chinese Communists to forge out such a relatively cohesive movement were facilitated by creating a very peculiar type of linkage between the different threads of Chinese "reformist" and "rebellious" tradition—a link between the more "idealistic" secondary tendencies of literati and gentry groups, on the one hand, and those of "secret societies" and peasant rebellions, on the other. It was probably this linkage, rather unusual in Chinese history, that enabled some gentry groups (sustained on traditions of secondary intellectual interpretations of Confucianism), some secret societies, some warlords, and some peasant rebels to go beyond their own restricted social orientations and to find a wider social basis and forge out new, broader orientations. Another factor which helped to forge the Chinese Communist movement (and in which already some of the important differences from the Russian Communist movement stand out) was that it was molded in a war of national liberation, so that from the very beginning there did not develop within it great incompatibilities between the transformation of the symbols of the national order and of the social order, and the two could (even if in fact this did not always take place) reinforce one another continuously. These factors have also greatly influenced the nature of the symbols and orientations which were selected by the Chinese Communist regime from within the impinging new international forces, and which served as foci of the new cohesive elite and of transformative orientations.

Here the answer about the nature and origin of these symbols seems to be simple. They were taken from the tradition of international Communism in general, of Marxism-Leninism in particular. But, as the growing literature about Maoism—and the discussion at this Conference —attest, the exact nature of the various symbolic elements and orientations which were taken up by Mao from this broad tradition and transferred to China is not simple and has probably not been constant throughout the last forty years. As has been pointed out by Benjamin Schwartz, at least two basic differing ingredients, or orientations, of Communist ideology were emphasized in different degrees in different periods—the "utopian" communal-totalistic one, and the more instrumental-institutional one oriented to economic and technological advance.[3]

It is here that the impact of Chinese tradition and heritage on the Chinese Communist regime can be seen in several, sometimes contradictory, ways. It may explain the high predilection to an emphasis on the communal-totalistic aspects of Communist thought—which was much more akin to some of the traditional modes of Confucian-Legalist thought—and of their perception of the social order (although, as has been stressed by Ping-ti Ho, in a greatly transformed way). Beyond this, it may also be that the specific combination of the alienated gentry-literati and peasant-rebellious orientations, out of which the solidarity of the Communist leadership was forged, gave rise to a continuous oscillation between these two aspects of Communist thought, and to greater difficulties than, for instance, in the Russian case, of merging them into a relatively differentiated symbolic system applicable to some continuous modern nation- and institution-building.

This had several important repercussions, not only on the attempts to undermine the older, traditional, social units and organization, but also on the ability of the regime to build up a new, viable modern organization and institution. True enough, it may well be, as Donald Munro has indeed pointed out, that many of the concrete activities of the Communist regime are rooted, not so much in the "communal-totalitarian aspects" of the Maoist creed, but in the more "rational" attempts to break down restricted traditional loyalties and to open up new motivations, motivations for new types of economic and organizational activities, and to inculcate loyalties to the new broader social order, loyalties unmediated by closed groups and organizations.[4] It is quite possible that these "traditional" forces and loyalties, whether of families, regions, or bureaucratic factions are very strong indeed and continue—as some of the more recent events appear to show—to exert their influence even in institutions and organizations built up by the Communist regime.

But it seems that the regime, as Tang Tsou and John W. Lewis have pointed out, faces not only the problem of the persistence of such traditional loyalties, but also of controlling the new "motivations" or orientations which are being released through its own attempts to break

[3] Benjamin Schwartz, "China and the West in the 'Thought of Mao Tse-tung,' " pp. 365–79, this volume.

[4] Donald Munro, Comments . . . [on Benjamin Schwartz's "China and the West in the 'Thought of Mao Tse-tung' "], pp. 389–96, this volume.

down these loyalties, and of channeling them not only into expressions of continuous revolutionary solidarity, but also into more secondary, "daily" routines of modern institution-building.[5] This difficulty seems to be rooted in the great distrust of both existing and emerging institutional patterns: the bureaucracy, the regional organizations, the new economic enterprises; in all these organizations and even in the CCP itself, distrust seems to characterize many parts of the Chinese Communist elite.

This distrust may indeed be related to both ideological and social structural factors. On the ideological level it can be seen in their oscillation between the two different modes of Communist thought, in the stronger emphasis on the communal-totalitarian mode which is, as we have seen, more akin to the traditional perception of the social order. In the structural-social field it may be rooted in the fact that the linkage effected by the Communist regime between the secondary literati and gentry and the peasant-rebellious traditions did not give rise to any new autonomous intermediate institutions or organizations; that is, they did not develop any new autonomous social group organizations and bases of social status—in this way also perpetuating some important aspects of traditional Chinese social structure.

It is, of course, impossible to predict at this moment to what extent the Communist regime will be able to overcome these weaknesses and problems, or whether, like the Nationalist regime, the problem will be too much for it to cope with. For the purpose of our discussion here it is sufficient to indicate only that in both cases the Chinese heritage was of great importance in shaping the destiny of its encounter with modernity. At the same time, however, the fact that there did develop such different types of response to the challenge of modernity shows us that any such heritage contains within itself different, often contrary—but not endless or structureless—possibilities.

[5] Tang Tsou, "Revolution, Reintegration and Crisis in Communist China," pp. 277–347, this volume. John W. Lewis, "Leader, Commissar, and Bureaucrat: The Chinese Political System in the Last Days of the Revolution," pp. 449–81, this volume.

# Contributors

*Derk Bodde,* professor of Chinese at the University of Pennsylvania, has written *China's First Unifier, Peking Diary,* and many other books, including *Law in Imperial China* (with Clarence Morris). He has translated from the Chinese the standard two-volume work, *A History of Chinese Philosophy,* by Fung Yu-lan. He is a member of the American Philosophical Society and the American Academy of Arts and Sciences.

*Jerome Alan Cohen,* professor of law at Harvard University, is the author of articles on Chinese law and *The Criminal Process in the People's Republic of China, 1949–1963: An Introduction.*

*Herrlee G. Creel,* the Martin A. Ryerson Distinguished Service Professor of Chinese History at the University of Chicago, is the author of *The Birth of China; Studies in Early Chinese Culture; Confucius, the Man and the Myth;* and *Chinese Thought from Confucius to Mao Tsetung.*

*Robert Dernberger,* assistant professor of economics and chairman of the Committee on Far Eastern Studies at the University of Chicago, is former editor of *Economic Development and Cultural Change* and has contributed articles on China's contemporary economy to *Three Essays on the International Economics of Communist China, Contemporary China,* and *Economic Nationalism in the New States.*

*Alexander Eckstein,* professor of economics and director of the Center for Chinese Studies at the University of Michigan, has written, among others, *The National Income of Communist China* and *Communist China's Economic Growth and Foreign Trade.*

*S. N. Eisenstadt,* the Rose Isaacs Professor of Sociology at the Eliezer Kaplan School of Economics and Social Sciences, the Hebrew University, is the author of *The Political Systems of Empires, Essays on Sociological Aspects of Political and Economic Development, Absorption of Immigrants, From Generation to Generation, Essays on Comparative Institutions, Modernization: Protest and Change, Israeli Society,* and (forthcoming) *The Protestant Ethic in Comparative and Analytical Perspective.*

*Albert Feuerwerker,* professor of history and, from 1961 to 1967, director of the Center for Chinese Studies at the University of Michigan, is the author of *China's Early Industrialization* and (with S. Cheng) *Chinese Communist Studies of Modern Chinese History* and the editor (with R. Murphy and M. C. Wright) of *Approaches to Modern Chinese History* and *History in Communist China.*

*C. P. FitzGerald,* professor of Far Eastern history at the Australian National University, has written *Son of Heaven, China: A Short Cultural History, Tower of Five Glories, Revolution in China, The Empress Wu, Floodtide in China, Barbarian Beds: The Origin of the Chair in China, The Third China, A Concise History of East Asia,* and (forthcoming) *Classical China.*

*Herbert Franke,* professor of Far Eastern studies at the University of Munich, is president of the German Oriental Society and author of *Beiträge zur Kulturgeschichte Chinas unter der Mongolenherrschaft* and (with Dr. Trauzettel) *Geschichte Chinas.*

*Ping-ti Ho* is the James Westfall Thompson Professor of History at the University of Chicago and a member of Academia Sinica. He is the author of *Studies on the Population of China, 1368–1953, The Ladder of Success in Imperial China: Aspects of Social Mobility, 1368–1911,* and *History of Landsmannschaften in China* and has contributed extensively both to sinological journals and to Western journals of history and social sciences. He is a fellow of the Center for Policy Study.

*Hsu Dau-lin,* professor of linguistics and Oriental and African languages at Michigan State University, is the author of *History of Chinese Law* and (forthcoming) *Chinese Local Administration under the Nationalist Government.*

*Francis L. K. Hsü,* professor and chairman of the Department of Anthropology at Northwestern University, is the author of *Under the An-*

cestors' Shadow, Americans and Chinese: Two Ways of Life, Clan, Caste and Club, and The Study of Literate Civilizations.

Chalmers Johnson, associate professor of political science and chairman of the Center for Chinese Studies at the University of California, Berkeley, is the author of Peasant Nationalism and Communist Power, An Instance of Treason, and Revolutionary Change.

Philip Kuhn, assistant professor of history at the University of Chicago, is the author of articles on modern Chinese history and (forthcoming) Local Militia and State Power in China, 1796–1864.

John W. Lewis, associate professor of government and director of the Cornell Committee, London-Cornell Project at Cornell University, has written Leadership in Communist China, Major Doctrines of Communist China, and (with George McT. Kahin) The United States in Vietnam.

James T. C. Liu, professor of oriental studies and of history at Princeton University, is the author of Reform in Sung China, Ou-yang Hsiu, and (forthcoming) Sung China, Innovation or Renovation?

Kwang-Ching Liu, professor of history at the University of California, Davis, and associate editor of The Journal of Asian Studies, is the author of Anglo-American Steamship Rivalry in China, 1862–1874 and Americans and Chinese: A Historical Essay and a Bibliography, and co–author of Modern China: A Bibliographical Guide to Chinese Works, 1898–1937.

Ta-Chung Liu, Goldwin Smith Professor of Economics and director of the Program on Comparative Economic Development at Cornell University, is the author of The Economy of the Chinese Mainland: National Income and Economic Development, 1933–1959 (with K. C. Yeh), Manufacturing Production Functions in the United States (with George H. Hildebrand), and Economic Trends in Communist China (with Walter Galenson and Alexander Eckstein).

Donald J. Munro, assistant professor of philosophy and associate of the Center for Chinese Studies at the University of Michigan, is the author of (forthcoming) The Concept of Man in Early China and The Concept of Man in Communist China.

*Michel Oksenberg,* assistant professor of political science at Stanford University, is the author of numerous articles on China and of a forthcoming case study of policy formulation in China concerning the mass irrigation campaign of 1957–58.

*Dwight H. Perkins,* associate professor of modern China studies and economics and associate of the East Asian Research Center at Harvard University, has written *Market Control and Planning in Communist China* and (with Morton H. Halperin) *Communist China and Arms Control.*

*Stuart R. Schram,* formerly director of the Chinese and Soviet Section of the Centre d'Étude des Relations Internationales of the Fondation Nationale des Sciences Politiques, is now reader in politics in the School of Oriental and African Studies, University of London. He has written *The Political Thought of Mao Tse-tung* and *Mao Tse-tung.* He has also translated and edited *Basic Tactics,* a manual on guerrilla warfare by Mao Tse-tung, and is coauthor (with Hélène Carrère d'Encausse) of *Le marxisme et l'Asie,* of which an English edition will be published in 1968.

*Peter Schran,* associate professor of economics in Asian studies at the University of Illinois, has written many articles on China.

*Franz Schurmann,* professor of sociology and history at the University of California, Berkeley, is the author of, among other publications, *Ideology and Organization in Communist China.* Professor Schurmann is the editor (with Orville Schell) of a three-volume reader on China and is one of the authors of *The Politics of Escalation in Vietnam.*

*Benjamin I. Schwartz,* professor of history and government and member of the executive committee of the East Asian Research Center at Harvard University, has written *Chinese Communism and the Rise of Mao* and *In Search of Wealth and Power: Yen Fu and the West,* and many articles on China.

*Richard H. Solomon* is assistant professor of political science and a research associate of the Center for Chinese Studies at the University of Michigan. Analyses drawn from a larger study of the Chinese political culture will be published under the title, *The Chinese Revolution and the Politics of Dependency.*

*Anthony M. Tang* is professor of economics at Vanderbilt University. He was visiting professor of economics at the Chinese University of Hong Kong, where he also served concurrently as director of the Economic Research Center and director of University Studies in Economics. His publications include "Policy and Performance in Mainland China's Agriculture," in *Economic Trends in Communist China.*

*S. Y. Teng,* University Professor at Indiana University and member of the Organizational Committee at the Ming Biographical History Project, has written *The Nien Army and Their Guerrilla Warfare 1851–1868* and *New Light on the Taiping Rebellion.*

*Tang Tsou,* professor of political science at the University of Chicago, is the author of *America's Failure in China, 1941–50* and *The Embroilment over Quemoy: Mao, Chiang and Dulles.* He is a fellow of the University of Chicago Center for Policy Study.

*Ezra F. Vogel,* professor in the Social Relations Department and associate director of the East Asian Research Center at Harvard University, is the author of *Japan's New Middle Class* and numerous articles on China, and (forthcoming) *Canton under Communism.*

*Wang Gungwu,* professor of history at the University of Malaya and president of the International Association for the Historians of Asia, has written *The Structure of Power in North China During the Five Dynasties, The Nanhai Trade: A Study of the Early History of Chinese Trade in the South China Sea,* and *A Short History of the Nanyang Chinese.*

*C. Martin Wilbur,* the George Sansom Professor of History in the School of International Affairs, the department of Chinese and Japanese, and the department of history, and the co-director of the Chinese Oral History Project, East Asian Institute at Columbia University, is the author of numerous publications and the editor (with Julie Lien-ying How) of *Documents on Communism, Nationalism, and Soviet Advisers in China, 1918–1927: Papers Seized in the 1927 Peking Raid.*

*Arthur Frederick Wright,* Charles Seymour Professor of History at Yale University, has written *Buddhism in Chinese History* and was editor of *Studies in Chinese Thought, The Confucian Persuasion, Confucianism in Action* (with David S. Nivison), and *Confucian Personalities* (with Denis Twitchett).

*C. K. Yang*, professor of sociology at the University of Pittsburgh, has written *Chinese Communist Society: The Family and the Village* and *Religion in Chinese Society: A Study of Contemporary Social Functions of Religion and Some of Their Historical Factors.*

# Index

## A

Absolutism: doctrine of imperial, 18–19
Abyssinia, 754
Africa: Communist China's setback in, 565; mentioned, 575
Agricultural producers' cooperatives, 307, 321
Agriculture: Chinese Communist failure in, 278; Great Leap Forward and crisis in, 312; and wartime mass line, 418–21; free rural markets, 504. *See also* Chinese Communist Party; Economy of Communist China; Economic fluctuations; Land reform
"Ah Q spirit": defined, 392
Albania, 577
All Chinese Federation of Literary and Art Circles: rectification movement within, 331
Allen, Young J., 140, 147, 151, 154
An Lu-shan, 266
*Analects*, 32
Ankuochün, 254, 256
Anti-bureaucratism, 288
Anti-rightist campaign (1957–58), 466, 541
Argentina: trade with Communist China, 749; mentioned, 577
Associations: in traditional China, 533
"August First School," 522
Australia: trade with Communist China, 749; mentioned, 577
Authoritarianism. *See* Autocracy
Authority: distinguished from coercion and persuasion, 399, 399–400n; defined, 528, 529n; in traditional China, 534–35; and power differentiated, 586
Autocracy: growth and intensification of, in imperial China, 22–25, 53–54, 56, 57–58, 59–60; during Ch'ing, 95, 123, 124, 177
Autumn Harvest Uprising, 404

## B

Babeuf, François-Noël, 369, 371, 372
Bakunin, Mikhail A., 491
Bandung Conference: Peking and Second, 341
Banner forces, 112
"Big character posters," 352, 493
Blücher, General Vasilii K.: also known as Galin, Galen, or Galents. *See* Galin
Borodin, Mikhail: influence in KMT, 235; mentioned, 225, 233, 236, 238, 248, 252
Bourgeois: elements and Cultural Revolution, 338–39; and mass line, 409
Bourgeoisie: non-development of, in China, 57, 84; urban, 535; mentioned, 302–8 *passim,* 536
Boxer Uprising, 219
Brainwashing. *See* Thought reform
Brezhnev, Leonid Ilyich, 531
Britain: and Northern Expedition, 246; mentioned, 124, 212, 215, 235, 248, 249, 251, 262
Buck, John Lossing: warns against collectivization and crash programs, 732
Buddhism: persecution of, during T'ang, 596, 597; mentioned, 13, 38, 44, 144, 145, 188, 266, 268, 349, 534
Buonarroti, Philippe M., 369, 371
Bureaucracy: in imperial China, 184, 533–34, 763, 768; of Communist China, 289, 538, 545, 546; PLA in state, 546; state administration and Cultural Revolution, 552; as correlate of kinship, 594–95; mentioned, 56, 57, 569, 758, 771
Bureaucratic organizations: and control of communication, 332, 333, 334
Bureaucratic politics: decision-maker and factional polarization in, 557
"Bureaucratism," 306
Bureaucratization: and routinization, 322–24, 332, 333; defined, 528; as index of stabilization, 558

tioned, 3–9, 14, 19, 27, 34–40, 46, 56, 58, 218, 256, 267, 268 *passim*
Chou Dynasty: nature of government of, 62–64; and kinship concepts, 599; mentioned, 65, 84, 266, 267
Chou En-lai: on new bourgeois elements, 308; on revisionism, 321–22; on alliance of workers, peasants, and intellectuals, 464; conducts self-criticism for State Council, 504; restricts Red Guard activities, 511; admits CCP internal dissensions, 568; mentioned, 193, 357, 411, 431, 494, 641
Chou Feng-chi, General, 244
Chou Ku-ch'eng: attacked by Maoists, 332
Chou Yang: on intellectuals, 330–31; as secretary of League of Left-Wing Writers of China, 332; as deputy director of Propaganda Department, 332; views and activities of, 332, 333, 333n, 334; denounced for revisionism, 471, 504–5, 507, 513, 514, 518; restricts publication of Mao's writings, 510; opposes primacy of politics in art and literature, 516, 519; promotes traditional culture, 520; "literature for the whole people" slogan, 521; accused of hostility to Lu Hsün, 548; organizes "National Defence Literature," 548, 548n; mistakes of, 549; mentioned, 322, 494
Christian missionaries: as innovators, 125–26, 191
Christianity, 42, 101–2, 220, 246, 349
Chu Hsi, 14
"Chu-ke liang Meetings": in PLA, 407
Chu P'ei-te, General, 230
Chu Teh: explains Long March, 410; accused of stressing expertise in army, 517; mentioned 412
Chu Yüan-chang. *See* T'ai-tsu (Ming)
*Chü-jen* degree, 116, 147
Chuang people, 43
Chuang Ts'un-yü, 96
Ch'un-ch'iu chan-kuo (Warring States), 266
Civil Service examination: during T'ang, 27; abolished, 27, 192, 197; influence on social mobility, 67–68; mentioned, 95, 123, 128, 141, 143, 147, 153, 162, 163, 183, 185
Clan organizations, 32, 37, 55, 208, 533
Class analysis: of Mao, 461–63; in Yenan period, 461–62; by Liu Shao-ch'i, 463; change in, 463–64; summed up in Elev-

enth Plenum directive, 470; Chinese Communist, 540
Class struggle: theory of, 303
*Classic of Filial Piety*, 58, 70
Collectivization: and rich peasants, 541; mentioned, 48, 421, 464, 489, 537, 566. *See also* Economy of Communist China; Economic Fluctuations
Comintern: theory of "two camps," 296; Seventh Congress of, 443
Commissars: in guerrilla communism, 450–51, 453; Liu Shao-ch'i as political commissar of New Fourth Army, 455; given wide powers during war, 457; Cultural Revolution and Yenan, 470, 472, 474; and traditional "meritorious" officials, 484; and their underlings relative to industrialization, 494–96; mentioned, 482, 488, 569. *See also* Liu Shao-ch'i; Mao Tse-tung
Communes: and Nanniwan ideal, 424–25; uncertain nature of, 511n; local character of, 543; and impact of work-point system on interpersonal relations, 605–6; mentioned, 48, 292, 306, 312, 313, 314, 321, 467, 471, 749. *See also* Economy of Communist China; Economic fluctuations; Mao Tse-tung
*Communique on Economic Development in 1958*, 631
Communism: and "Hundred Schools," 268
Communist China: strategic geographical location of, 2; reestablishes effective control of outlying regions, 4; policy toward national minorities, 5–7, 41, 42, 43; educational system and social mobility, 28–29; social tensions in, 171; intellectual outlook of, compared with late Ch'ing modernizers, 174–75, 176–77, 178; as society characterized, 539–41; kinship in, 541; class war in, 541–42; low level of interest in foreign affairs in, 565; its continuity and discontinuity with tradition, 769–71, 771–74. *See also* Chinese Communist Party; Cultural Revolution; Economy of Communist China; Political integration
Communist Youth League, 552
Condorcet, Marquis de, 368
Confucian self-cultivation: and Communist self-criticism, 288–89
Confucianism: as state ideology during Han, 9–10, 11–13; political functions of, 11; in socioeconomic matters, 12;

682; food crop production, 620, 633, 636, 652, 653, 671, 679, 681; consumer goods output, 621–22, 652, 653, 654, 672, 680; annual growth rate of, 622–24, 666–67, 680; growth rate of, compared with industrialized nations, 625, 628, 645; per capita product, 625, 646, 648, 657; growth rate per worker product, 626, 627, 644; indicators of development of, 626–27; and capital formation in total product of, 627–28, consumption in relation to industrialization, 629–30; industrialization and agriculture, 630; and industrial production, 633–34, 637, 664–65, 684–88; and population growth, 634, 646, 682–83; and international trade, 634–35, 640, 657, 702, 739–40, 741, 742, 745–47, 749–50; cotton output, 636; and investment, 639, 641–42, 645, 646, 648, 657; and fertilizers, 641, 662, 665, 666, 683–84; analysis of development of, since 1949, 642–50; employment expansion in, 644, 646; and communes, 647, 725, 749; post-Leap recovery, 648, 676–67; and Cultural Revolution, 648–49, 650; agricultural character of, 649, 700; and labor force, 655; and industrial technology, 655, 742–44; per capita consumption, 655–56, 662–64; acreage estimates, 661–62; agricultural developments (1957–65), 661–64, 674–76; production teams, 661; agriculture and weather conditions and, 661, 666; and grain use, 663; and industrial growth rate, 665, 666, 667; and agricultural growth rate, 665–66; statistics on, 670–71; and agricultural output, 671; policy-making and development of, 673; economic fluctuations in, 692–93; interdependence between agricultural and non-agricultural sectors of, 701–2; socialization of, 703, 705, 725; forms of resource mobilization in, 706; Soviet aid and the growth of, 740, 743, 745, 746–47; "walking-on-two-legs" campaign, 748; and industrial decentralization, 748; future trends of, 751–52. *See also* Agriculture; Chinese Communist Party; Cultural Revolution; Economic Fluctuations; Great Leap Forward; Liu Shao-ch'i; Mao Tse-tung

Economy of Imperial China: state control and private enterprise, 35–36, 44

Economy of twentieth-century China,

pre-1949: expanding state-controlled sector under KMT, 36–37; common views of, challenged, 200–201; per capita grain output, 200; industrial growth, 200; per capita income, 200; tenancy, 200–201; communications, 201

Education: and Confucian social ideology, 26–27, 55; clan charitable schools, 27; private academies, 27; community schools, 27; in Communist China, 28–29, 55; in traditional China, 592; mentioned, 758

Egoroff: Soviet military attaché at Peking, 235

Eighth Route Army: and Nanniwan land reclamation, 423–24; mentioned, 313

Elder Brother Society (*Ko-lao hui*), 118–19, 120, 169

Elite: self-interest and idealism of Confucian, 40; political stability and traditional local, 195; militia and local, 196; *pao-chia* and local, 196; changing nature of twentieth century, 197; twentieth century sub-county administration and local, 197; emergence of new urban, 198; structural effect of modernization on Chinese, 198–99; concept of, 283–84; elite system in China and concept of, 283–84; integration, 284; in China, traditional and Communist, 289; elite and the masses, 302–15; unity and conflict in elite, 315–16; defined, 530, 530n; local, in traditional China, 534–35; in Republican China, 535; CCP as, 538, 770, 774; discreditation of, 551; ruling, 758; Mao warns of formation of authoritarian, 558–59, 563; lack of secondary, in China, 594, 602, 767; Japan's neo-traditional, modernizing, 761–62; Confucian, 763; mentioned, 94, 188, 278, 286, 344, 481, 758, 771

Emperor Chia-ch'ing (Ch'ing), 24, 97

Emperor Ch'ien-lung (Ch'ing), 96

Emperor Hsien-feng (Ch'ing), 108

Emperor Hsüan (Han): on character of Han state, 12–13; mentioned, 11, 39, 76, 79

Emperor K'ang-hsi (Ch'ing), 23, 600

Emperor Kuang-hsü (Ch'ing): Hundred Days' Reform, 77, 161–68; transvaluation of values during reign of, 139; shows interest in reform, 160; launches Reform, 161–65; supports "people's rights" and constitution, 165; failure